1-22-75

STOCK & INTERNATIONAL
COMMODITY
EXCHANGE
DIRECTORY

STOCK & INTERNATIONAL COMMODITY EXCHANGE DIRECTORY

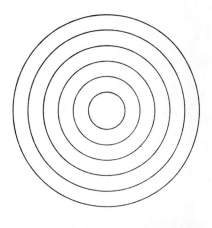

1974-75 EDITION

PETER WYCKOFF
Editor-in-Chief

ADRIAN A. PARADIS
Editor

GRACE D. PARADIS
Assistant Editor

Barbara Gyra
Editorial Assistant

PHOENIX PUBLISHING Canaan, New Hampshire, USA

Printed in the United States of America
by Courier Printing Company
Binding by New Hampshire Bindery
Design by A. L. Morris

Library of Congress Catalog Card Number 74-78118
ISBN 0-914016-09-1

1859506

CONTENTS

New York has its Wall Street, Paris its Rue Notre Dame des Victoires, Tokyo its Kabutosho. Every important city has a certain area—a financial district—which much of the public regards with awe and disbelief. It might be uptown; it might be downtown. It could be large or small; compact or sprawling. Size and location are irrelevant; they are never detractable from the real significance of this area to the city in which it dwells.

There certainly is nothing very new or unusual about the concept of free international capital markets. Improved technological and communications facilities have made it possible for any investor, anywhere in the world, to contact any stock exchange and trade in any security listed there. However convenient and easy this may seem, and notwithstanding the aspirations of most brokers, bankers and securities dealers, the present outlook for the international operations of securities firms is unfortunately rather murky.

Aside from obvious language and currency barriers, the majority of the world's markets are organized differently. In the United States banks may not trade in equity securities; in certain other countries banks do most of the trading. As Charles N. Stabler of the *Wall Street Journal* summed up the situation: "Internationalism is easy when it's a generality. But when it comes down to specifics . . . things get more complex."

U.S. securities firms operate more than 250 foreign branches, which reportedly account for $250 to $300 million annually in commissions, about 10% of the total, on the New York Stock Exchange. Considering that 27 foreign brokerage firms in New York are owned by foreign banks, that purchases of American securities from abroad amounted to $2.8 billion net in 1973, against $197 million in 1963, the need for developing overseas pipelines and for keeping them open and free of red tape seems imperative.

Some nations tend to restrict the flow of capital outside their borders and to prohibit or limit domestic share purchases by foreigners, just as other nations are more lenient in such matters. For example, six foreign companies—the first ever in Japan—were listed for trading on the Tokyo Stock Exchange in December, 1973. In Spain, mutual funds are now permitted for the first time to invest in foreign stocks. In Mexico, the attitude toward investment by outsiders recently experienced a complete change. Whereas earlier in this decade Mexican government officials were concerned that domestic business might become foreign-dominated, businessmen from abroad now are being told that new investment proposals will be viewed in a brighter light.

Conversely, at a press conference held in New York late in 1973, Dr. Friedrich

Priess of the Hamburg Stock Exchange observed: "Until recently any German was free to buy foreign shares and any foreigner was free to buy German shares. Now there are some restrictions. Foreigners cannot buy German shares. We hope that very soon this situation will change again."

Periodic monetary crises in the past several years appear to have encouraged a certain spirit of internationalism. The Arab oil embargo drew nations closer too. Moreover, the dilemmas of inflation and food and other shortages are worldwide. Like strangers, who automatically become friends during a period of mutual crisis or danger, so now have some fears and suspicions which formerly hindered closer trade relationships been eased somewhat.

Delegations from the New York and Pacific Stock Exchanges have traveled separately to London and Paris, seeking the advice of financial leaders about amalgamating the American stock exchanges. Britain accomplished this after eight years of study, when the London Stock Exchange and the provincial exchanges of England, Scotland, and Ireland merged to become The Stock Exchange.

James J. Needham, New York Stock Exchange Chairman and a vice-president of the International Federation of Stock Exchanges, hosted a gathering of world exchange officials in October, 1973. Various common problems were debated and future opportunities for cooperation were explored. Six of the officials, acting as spokesmen for the group after the meetings were concluded, expressed their view that the major deterrents to free and open markets—available to anyone, anywhere in the world—were disclosure and listing standards, different accounting systems and principles, and different taxation methods. They recommended that currency restrictions be removed and suggested it would be helpful if governments realized that stock exchanges are much more beneficial than they are detrimental. However, when queried by the *New York Times* about how long it might take to realize these ambitions, the consensus was gloomy — at least ten years.

The Securities and Exchange Commission has been studying the question of free access to American markets. It has established an Office of International Corporate Finance to supervise international securities transactions. University of Chicago Professor James H. Lorie has urged the United States to "take the lead in generating a freer climate for the international operations of securities firms," but the wheels of change grind slowly. The problems of different regulations on the various exchanges and the manner of achieving a competitive balance that would be fair and satisfactory to all continue to defy a solution.

While the bankers and brokers have been discussing and arguing these matters, most individual investors and certainly all speculators have not just been holding their breath. Speculation has always been a part of life; the human appetite for it has often seemed insatiable.

Jacob Little, inventor of the short sale as it applies to convertible securities, was reported able "to gorge and digest more stocks in one day than the weight of his whole body in the certificates." The modern counterparts of Mr. Little now feed principally on gold. When the Paris Bourse was shuttered by a strike in April 1974, the hungry gold traders transferred operations out-of-doors to a lively market nicknamed "the market of wet feet." The business they transacted there was nearly as large as it had been on the regular exchange before the strike.

Meanwhile trading has been frantic on the Chicago Board Option Exchange. Another speculative outlet has been the fledgling American Real Estate Exchange, which began operating on an experimental basis late in 1973. At each of the first five trading sessions about $50 million of real estate was offered in lots. In Panama City, mainly as a result of currency controls imposed by Latin American countries, there is a flourishing market in Latin dollars. Growing nationalism in many Caribbean islands and recurrent jitters in the money centers of Asia and Europe have naturally nourished the boom. Most of the dollars belong to Latin Americans; interest rates on loans and deposits are generally set at ½ to ¾ of one percent above daily Eurodollar rates.

Meanwhile, the trading volume in securities around the world has dwindled sharply. The average individual seems disenchanted with most of the traditional investment media. The average daily turnover in Tokyo dropped to around 150 million shares recently, a pittance compared with the all-time high of 635 million registered in January, 1973, and uncomfortably below the 200 million share break-even point estimated for Tokyo's member firms. On the New York Stock Exchange, where volume for a day has limped along in the area of 10-15 million shares, the break-even level is about 16-18 million.

Contracted volume, coupled with rising costs and the downward price action of many stocks since the Dow Jones Industrial Average attained a record closing peak of 1,051.70 on January 11, 1973, have prompted budget cuts and layoffs at the American exchanges. The markets are now undergoing major surgery in an effort to alleviate their difficulties and restore investor confidence. A composite stock tape will soon be introduced; fixed commissions are scheduled to end by April 30, 1975; a national securities-clearing system is not far distant. These and other innovations, already scheduled or on the drawing boards, presage a single, central market for the United States, although the exact timing of its debut remains indefinite.

Britain has already established such a market. The exchanges of Japan all observe the same commission rates, regulatory laws and trading methods. In Italy, Spain, India, Mexico, The Federal Republic of Germany and certain other countries the situation is similar.

Securities traded on the exchanges of Brazil enjoy interlisted privileges. Venezuela's two stock exchanges—situated only four miles apart—are virtually identical. From Italy's largest stock exchange in Milan to the tiny exchange in Mauritius; from New York's giant Merrill Lynch to a firm in Australia titled "Two in the Bush," the need to establish and maintain free markets is immediate and urgent. A mutually acceptable way to integrate their different capital market methods and structures must be devised.

The benefits of free capital flows are numerous and important; not only for expanding trade and investments, but for generating and encouraging new enterprise. Unless some of the major restraints are at least relaxed and an atmosphere of conciliation and reciprocation is allowed to develop and mature, the brave new world of the future that so many try to envision may be a lonely place indeed for the securities industry.

If the information contained in this volume assists in any way toward bridging certain gaps, or helps to penetrate various barriers that stand between the securities or commodities exchanges of the world, then the efforts made in gathering and editing such data will assuredly be rewarded.

June, 1974   Peter Wyckoff

PREFACE

Information Sources

Most of the data contained in this Directory was supplied by the commodity and stock exchanges in response to questionnaires. In those cases where repeated follow-up mailings failed to bring response, information was obtained through foreign commercial attachés or consular offices of the U.S. Department of State, chambers of commerce, trade associations, and helpful individuals within the financial community who felt the need for this reference work.

Compilation of this data involved extensive correspondence, requiring in many cases at least three letters before first contact was made with an exchange. The unreliability of the mails, especially in Latin America precluded reaching a number of exchanges, though in some instances cablegrams proved effective. We believe that exchanges with small staffs found it difficult and in some cases impossible to respond.

Accuracy and Completeness of Information

Every effort has been made to ensure accuracy and completeness of information. In all instances exchanges were sent drafts of the text for their review, revision, and approval and the majority returned the drafts corrected and updated where appropriate. It is recognized that some listings are incomplete. In a few cases we could not reach the exchange. In others the responding official indicated he did not have the data compiled and available, and in still others the management chose not to release certain information. Undoubtedly this was the first time the officers of some exchanges had received a request to make public data which heretofore had been considered confidential. Understandably they were reluctant to comply or found it difficult to change policy in time to meet our publishing deadline.

It was our hope to present all information in a standardized manner for ease of use and reference. This was not feasible throughout the book because the ability of many exchanges to follow a standard format was contingent upon the availability of data within their own records. As a result, the form of presentation varies greatly in organization, content, and completeness reflecting the fact that no two exchanges are alike. The very fact that they differ radically in operational policies and procedures emphasizes the need for compiling and publishing this comprehensive reference work.

We extend our apologies to all those officers and other individuals listed whose names were stripped of titles, educational degrees, and other marks of distinction. Inasmuch as many respondents did not include these symbols, we felt it was fairer to all if we printed names only, even though we perhaps defied convention in some countries.

If some important organization has been omitted, it was due primarily to the fact that we were unable to open productive channels of contact. Two such exchanges were the Bolsa de Comercio de Quito in Ecuador and the Bolsa de Comercio de Bogota in Colombia and it is hoped that any such discrepancies will be corrected in future editions.

Acknowledgments

During the almost two years of editorial preparation of this volume we encountered unfailing courtesy and cooperation on the part of all whom we contacted. Those who helped are too numerous to list here, but we do want to make special mention of individual exchange officials; members of American consulate offices; officials of the Association of Commodity Exchanges, the International Federation of Stock Exchanges and the Canadian Association of Stock Exchanges; and government officials of foreign countries located both in the United States and their native lands who provided immeasurable assistance.

Finally, we should like to thank those members of the financial fraternity and librarians who encouraged us to undertake this task. Without their backing and conviction that this reference source was needed, we might have stopped many times when the mails failed to carry or the progress seemed slow and uncertain.

STOCK

INTERNATIONAL
COMMODITY
EXCHANGE
DIRECTORY

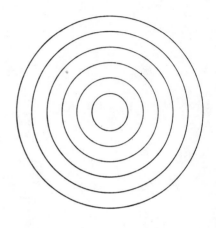

SECTION 1

PROFILE DATA
ON
EXCHANGES

ARAB REPUBLIC OF EGYPT

CAIRO

CAIRO STOCK EXCHANGE

Before President Gamal Abdel Nasser nationalized most of Egypt's large companies in 1961 there were some 400 stocks listed on the Cairo Stock Exchange. Thereafter the exchange barely functioned until 1973 when Egypt eased its socialist policy and began to bid for foreign investment. At the same time domestic companies were encouraged to list their shares on the exchange and at year end, according to the *Wall Street Journal,* approximately thirty stocks were listed.

In the spring of 1974 President Anwar Sadat declared that the public sector of the economy will continue to be strong and important but that the private sector will also be active although Egypt will not have an open capitalist system. Arab and foreign capital will be welcomed and with money flowing back into Egypt it was hoped that the exchange's activity and importance would be revived.

Registered letters sent to the Minister of Finance, Economy and Foreign Trade and to the Cairo Stock Exchange were neither acknowledged nor returned.

ARGENTINA

THE STOCK EXCHANGES OF ARGENTINA

The Mercado de Valores de Buenos Aires is the largest stock exchange in Argentina. A much smaller exchange in Rosario ranks second in size and importance; still lesser exchanges are in Cordoba and Mendoza.

A lack of earlier communication with the Mercado prior to press time for this volume, or with the Bolsa de Comercio de Buenos Aires, a private, non-profit organization which supervises the activities of the Mercado as well as those of more than 20 diversified markets and associations operating in Buenos Aires, precludes further information on these Argentine exchanges. With respect to commodities markets, in 1965 the Buenos Aires Grain Futures Market (Mercado de Cereales a Termino de Buenos Aires, S.A.) became independent of the Bolsa de Comercio, but as of press time additional information on futures markets was not received.

BUENOS AIRES STOCK EXCHANGE

Title: Mercado de Valores de Buenos Aires Socieded Anonima.

Address: 25 de Mayo 305, Buenos Aires, Republica Argentina.

Telephone: 32-6262; 32-6446; 32-8334

Telex: 0121709

Cable Address: AR BOLSA

Officers:

President: Carlos J. R. Sosa
Vice-President: Eduardo C. Perez Iturraspe
Secretary: Julio A. Macchi
Treasurer: Alberto M. Gianni

Nominal Directors:	Substitute Directors:
Roberto Blanco	Carlos S. Caballero
Jorge H. B. Dellepiane	Osv Ido Larrea
Hugo J. J. Grondona	Roberto Arana
Ricardo L. Mascaretti	J. J. Rodolfo Soucarros
Enrique Segota	Adolfo Casal
	Carlos A. Porzio
Nominal Fiscal Commissioners:	Substitute Fiscal Commissioners:
Wenceslao Urdapilleta	H. J. Aldabe
Domingo G. Maggiotti	Andres Moar Vieites
Nilda M. E. Formoso	R. J. Fernandez

Hours of Business: The trading floor (La Rueda de Titulos, or "Wheel of Shares") is open for business from 1:00 P.M. to 3:00 P.M. on weekdays.

Regulatory Laws:

1. Law No. 17,811 — pertaining to the public offering of securities on the exchange or on the commercial markets;
2. Internal regulations of the Mercado de Valores, approved by various commissions in December, 1969; April and June, 1971;
3. Ordinance approved by the Ministry of Finance in December, 1969, and recorded in the National Court of Justice, March 11, 1970.

Issues Traded and Volume:

1. No. listed Companies (December 31):

1967	516	1971	370
1968	482	1972	363
1969	454	1973	342
1970	414		

2.

	Volume (shares)	Market Value (all securities) Pesos Ley 18,188
1967	211,725,735	31,116,400,000
1968	145,757,220	29,769,100,000
1969	215,542,190	57,622,068,086
1970	237,555,348	62,874,561,957

1971	297,078,032		96,731,552,546
1972	281,696,901		128,879,445,655*
1973	387,519,563		255,924,641,190

*includes subscription rights.

Unit of Trading:

1. 100 shares.
2. Transactions effected in amounts of less than 100 shares (odd-lots) are not recorded on the blackboards which normally carry the price and volume of all trades executed. However, every trade is cleared and guaranteed equally by the Mercado de Valores, regardless of number of shares involved.
3. The same fixed commissions apply to all transactions.

Memberships:

1. Regular Members: Membership is limited to 250.
2. Members are obligated to own one share of stock in La Bolsa, whose capital is authorized at $100,000,000 — divided into 250 common shares at $400,000 each.
3. Membership (share) Prices:

	High	Low		High	Low
1960	$30,500	$ 9,000	1967	$35,000	$15,000
1961	40,000	22,500	1968	27,000	19,500
1962	22,000	15,800	1969	30,000	18,800
1963	30,500	17,000	1970	20,100	17,000
1964	30,000	27,000	1971	65,000	18,000
1965	28,500	15,500	1972	48,000	36,000
1966	30,000	14,500	1973	80,000	45,500

Commissions (buying or selling)*:

1. For public securities —
   a. paying up to 3% interest
      i. shares and bonds paying no more than 2½% interest 1½%
      ii. shares and bonds paying interest greater than 2½%, but no more than 3% 2%
      iii. other types of transactions .... 1½ - 2½%
   b. paying interest from 3% to 5% 2½%
   c. paying more than 5% interest 5%
2. For private securities —
   a. cash transactions 5%
   b. margin transactions 5%
3. Minimum Commission: except for sales made at auction, the minimum commission in all cases is $5.

*based on money involved in each purchase or sale.

Historical Background:

1929   (March 9) The Market for Shares and Letters of Exchange of the Commercial Exchange of Buenos Aires ("El Mercado de Titulos y Cambios de la Bolsa de Comercio de Buenos Aires") was created. It took over the management of the securities business, which previously had been limited to the local Bolsa de Comercio.

1950   (July 3) Decree No. 12,793 became operative, relating to Law No. 15,353 of 1946, under which the Central Bank of the Argentine Republic assumed control of all national exchanges. The Mercado then became known officially as the Mercado de Valores de Buenos Aires S.A.

1959-60 The Mercado de Valores experienced its greatest change and growth during this period.

1969   Legal requirements regulating the public offering of securities were modified under Decree No. 17,811 in 1968. In January the following year, the Mercado adopted its own statutes and regulations, and assumed a greater responsibility in governing and operating the exchange.

CORDOBA

CORDOBA STOCK EXCHANGE

Title: Cordoba Stock Exchange
Address: Cordoba, Argentina

MENDOZA

MENDOZA STOCK EXCHANGE

Title: Mendoza Stock Exchange
Address: Mendoza, Argentina

ROSARIO

ROSARIO STOCK EXCHANGE

Title: Rosario Stock Exchange
Address: Rosario, Argentina

AUSTRALIA

AUSTRALIAN ASSOCIATED STOCK EXCHANGES

Address: 60 Martin Place, Sydney N.S.W. 2000, Australia

Telephone: 25-5261

Telex: AA24628

The Association was formed in Sydney in 1937 and consists of the following Member Exchanges.*

The Stock Exchange of Adelaide Limited,
55 Exchange Place, Adelaide, South Australia 5001

The Brisbane Stock Exchange,
344 Queen Street, Brisbane, Queensland 4000, Australia

The Hobart Stock Exchange,
86 Collins Street, Hobart, Tasmania 7000

The Stock Exchange of Melbourne Limited
351 Collins Street, Melbourne, Victoria 3000, Australia

The Stock Exchange of Perth Limited,
86 St. George's Terrace, Perth, Western Australia 6000

The Sydney Stock Exchange Limited,
20 O'Connell Street, Sydney, N.S.W. 2000, Australia

*For more detailed information, consult the individual exchanges reviewed separately.

These Member Exchanges have certain things in common. For example, they all must follow the same basic rules and regulations. On January 3, 1962 uniform listing requirements were established by the association. Units of trading ("marketable parcels") are also identical; as are minimum bids, stamp duties, commission rates, order fees, etc.

The following information, relating to some of these factors, is intended only as a guide and is not exhaustive. Moreover, it is subject to variation from time to time. For more precise details, therefore, it is recommended that direct contact be made with the member exchange involved, or with the Australian Associated Stock Exchanges.

Unit of Trading: Normally 100 shares, subject to the following:

Marketable Parcels

1. Shares, Share Options or Convertible Loan Securities
   1,000 where the price does not exceed 25c
    500 where the price exceeds 25c but does not exceed 50c
    100 where the price exceeds 50c but does not exceed $5
     50 where the price exceeds $5   but does not exceed $10
     20 where the price exceeds $10   but does not exceed $25
     10 where the price exceeds $25   but does not exceed $50
      5 where the price exceeds $50   but does not exceed $100

2 where the price exceeds $100 but does not exceed $250
1 where the price exceeds $250

2. Rights to a New Issue
    100 where the price does not exceed $5
     50 where the price exceeds $ 5 but does not exceed $10
     20 where the price exceeds $10 but does not exceed $25
     10 where the price exceeds $25 but does not exceed $50
      5 where the price exceeds $50

3. Company Loan Securities (non-convertible), Commonwealth Loans and Public Securities - $100

Odd-lots: Handled by odd-lot specialists at the following rates:

Full Market Price	Margin
Under 10c	1c
10c and under 30c	2c
30c and under 50c	3c
50c and under $1.00	4c
$1.00 and under $1.50	5c
$1.50 and under $3.00	8c
$3.00 and under $5.00	10c
$5.00 and under $10.00	15c
$10.00 and over	25c

Commissions or Fees:

Rates of Brokerage —

1. Listed Companies:
    a. On shares, capital stock, rights to new issues, share options or convertible loan securities in companies listed on a recognized stock exchange (except as hereinafter provided)
        i. on the first $10,000 of consideration ... 2%
        ii. on the next $40,000 of consideration ... 1½%
        iii. on that amount by which the consideration exceeds $50,000 ... 1%
        The concessional rates in (ii) and (iii) above apply only to a single instruction given at any time to buy or sell on behalf of one beneficial interest an issue of securities by a company of the same class and paid-up value on that part of the order completed within one calendar month from the date of the order.

2. Unlisted Companies:
    The rate is double that for listed companies for transactions up to $20,000 consideration.

3. Order Fee:
    On each order comprising a single instruction given at the one time to buy or sell on behalf of the one beneficial interest, securities in the one company of the same class and paid-up value in addition to the brokerage payable an order fee of $5.00 shall be charged PROVIDED THAT in the case of a selling order, when the consideration is less than $25.00, a fee of $2.00 shall be charged in place of both the order fee and the appropriate brokerage.

4. Commonwealth Loans:
    On securities issued by the Commonwealth of Australia on the face value of the security —

a. Short Term:
   When the date of the sale or purchase is within five years immediately preceding the maturity date of the security
   i.   on the first $10,000 face value ... ¼%
   ii. on that amount by which the face value exceeds $10,000 ...⅛%
   iii. provided that on any one order with any client which is not less than $25,000 in face value and of the same series, no fixed rates of brokerage shall apply.

b. Long Term:
   When the date of sale or purchase is not within five years immediately preceding the maturity date of the security
   i.   on the first $50,000 face value ... ¼%
   ii. on the next $50,000 face value ... ⅛%
   iii. on the next $100,000 face value ... 1/20%
   iv. on that amount exceeding $200,000 face value ... 1/40%
   The concessional rates in (a) (ii) and (iii) and (b) (ii), (iii) and (iv) above, apply only in respect of any sale or purchase when there is a single instruction given at the one time on behalf of the one beneficial interest, and when the date of the transaction is within ten business days after the date on which the order was placed, and when the total value of sales or purchases of securities aggregated is not less than $100,000, provided that short term securities and long term securities shall be aggregated separately.

c. Minumum
   When the value of the securities of any one issue in either clause (a) or (b) above is not more than $80, 10c for each $20.

5. Public Securities:
   On securities classified as "Public Securities" within the meaning of the Income Tax and Social Services Contribution Assessment Act (other than securities issued by the Commonwealth of Australia) on the paid-up value of the security.

   a. Short Term
      When the date of the sale or purchase is within one year immediately preceding the maturity date on the first $10,000 ... ¼% on any amount exceeding $10,000 ... ⅛%

   b. Long Term
      When the date of sale or purchase is not within one year immediately preceding the maturity date ... ¼%

   c. On any one transaction with any client which involves a sale or purchase of semi-government securities which are approved investments by the Reserve Bank for Authorized Short Term Money Market Dealers with a maturity within five years and which is not less than $25,000 in face value and of the same series, no fixed rates of brokerage shall apply.

6. Company Loan Securities (Non-Convertible)
   When the date of sale or purchase is within one year immediately preceding the maturity date ... ¼% When the date of sale or purchase is not within one year immediately preceding the maturity date ... ½%

ADELAIDE STOCK EXCHANGE

Title: The Stock Exchange of Adelaide Limited

Address: 55 Exchange Place, Adelaide, South Australia (G.P.O. Box 547, Adelaide, South Australia 5001)

Telephone: 87 3702

Telex: STOCKEX AA82186

Branches and Affiliates: See "The Australian Associated Stock Exchanges."

Officers:
Chairman and Director: William George Fraser McCulloch
Vice-Chairman and Director: Thomas Nash Phillips
Director: Maurice Thiem
Director: Ian Howard Lloyd
Director: Harold Nevill Sprod
Director: Richard Lloyd Collison

_____

Manager: Frank Lindon Wray
Assistant Manager: Stanley Errol Banks
Secretary: Maurice Edmund Longden

Hours of Business (trading):
9:30 A.M. - 12:00 noon (weekdays)
1:45 P.M. - 3:00 P.M.

Regulatory Laws: The Sharebrokers Act (1945)

Issues Traded and Volume:
1. All listed companies and issues are common to all member exchanges of the Australian Associated Stock Exchanges.
2. Unlisted or "other issues"; no records are kept.
3. (a) Volume of listed shares:

Year*	Tot. Volume	Year*	Tot. Volume
1962/63	20,612,622	1968/69	59,547,512
1963/64	23,366,167	1969/70	125,615,119
1964/65	19,105,140	1970/71	73,619,308
1965/66	18,537,362	1971/72	51,650,420
1966/67	23,494,707	1972/73	45,530,483
1967/68	52,654,633		

*Fiscal years ending June 30.

(b) Records achieved:

Highest daily share volume:	2,075,060	(11/24/69)
Lowest daily share volume:	14,795	(12/29/65)
Highest value of shares traded:	$1,976,522	(1/15/70)
Lowest value of shares traded:	$16,454	(12/29/65)
Most transactions in one day:	2,320	(1/12/70)
Fewest transactions in one day:	56	(12/29/65)

Unit of Trading:
1. Shares are normally traded in "marketable parcels" according to price. See "The Australian Associated Stock Exchanges" for specific data.
2. There are no odd-lot specialists or dealers on the Stock Exchange of Adelaide. However, odd-lots are traded relative to the ruling market price. See "The Australian Associated Stock Exchanges."

Memberships:
1. Regular Members: 60
2. Non-member partners: 1
3. Mean prices of "seats" (memberships):

1963	$7,200	1969	$16,000
1964	8,100	1970	21,250
1965	8,900	1971	15,000
1966	8,000	1972	8,000
1967	7,250	1973	8,000
1968	10,625		

4. Record high price: $22,500 (1/30/70)

Commissions or Fees:
The only basis of payment between client and sharebroker is the commission and order fee paid on stock actually bought or sold on behalf of the client. See "The Australian Associated Stock Exchanges" for specific data.

Historical Background:
1867 Green's buildings on King William Street became a favorite location for trading in shares.

1887 (Sept. 2) The Adelaide Stock Exchange and the Stock Exchange of South Australia amalgamated to form the Stock Exchange of Adelaide. Henry Bellingham elected president. Membership limited to 65. The newly formed exchange took premises on Pirie Street, Adelaide.

1890 Membership increased from 65 to 70 (entrance fee for first 50 members - $50). The price of the five seats created in 1890 was fixed at $2,000.

1891 (Nov. 30) A building on King William Street, where the Commonwealth Banking Corp. stands now, was acquired.

1899 (Mar. 16) The present site in Exchange Place was acquired.

1901 Present building was erected.

1904 The exchange was formed into a limited liability company with 72 shares of $400 each.

1938 (June 6) Fire caused considerable damage to the interior of the Exchange. Rebuilding carried out - sound proof ceiling in call room and vestibule; heating, cooling plant and elevator installed.

1954 (May 7) Number of seats reduced to 60 by cancelling 12 seats held by the estates of deceased members.

1960 (Sept. 7) Nominal capital of the Stock Exchange of Adelaide Limited increased to 100 shares of $400 each. Issued and paid up capital of 60 shares of $400 each.

1961 (Jan. 17) The Stock Exchange Transfer Marking Service was established.

1962 (Jan. 3) After using the "call" method of trading for 60 years, the "post" system was introduced. Uniform listing requirements established by the Australian Associated Stock Exchanges.

1964 (Feb. 3) Noting Services commenced.
1966 (Feb. 14) A central clearing house was introduced to facilitate delivery and settlement between members.
1967 (July 1) New transfer system introduced.
1968 (Aug. 14) Dial-a-Quote commenced.
1972 (Jan. 4) National listing and quotations introduced.
1972 (March) Appointment of first executive president of Australian Associated Stock Exchanges, Mr. M. I. McAlister, and a National Secretariat established.
1972 The various Exchange's Journal replaced by the national publication, "The Australian Stock Exchange Journal."

BRISBANE

BRISBANE STOCK EXCHANGE

Title: The Brisbane Stock Exchange

Address: 344 Queen Street, Brisbane, Queensland 4000, Australia

No information furnished by the exchange. See "The Australian Associated Stock Exchanges."

HOBART

HOBART STOCK EXCHANGE

Title: The Hobart Stock Exchange

Address: 86 Collins Street, Hobart, Tasmania

Telephone: 347333 (STD 002)
Telex: AA58111

Branches and Affiliates: See "The Australian Associated Stock Exchanges."

Officers: Chairman: T. K. Shadforth
Secretary/Manager: A. K. Wertheimer

Hours of Business: Two calls daily. 11:30 A.M. and 3:00 P.M.

Regulatory Laws: Australian Associated Stock Exchanges Uniform Rules and Listing Requirements apply.

Issues Traded: All companies listed on any member exchange of the Australian Associated Stock Exchanges are listed automatically.

Unit of Trading: See "The Australian Associated Stock Exchanges" for specific data.

Membership: Regular Members: 17

Commissions or Fees: See "The Australian Associated Stock Exchanges" for specific data.

Historical Background: 1891 The Stock Exchange was founded by Act of the Tasmanian Parliament.

MELBOURNE

MELBOURNE STOCK EXCHANGE

Title: The Stock Exchange of Melbourne Limited

Address: 351 Collins Street, Melbourne, Victoria 3000, Australia (Box 1784 Q, G.P.O., Melbourne, 3001)

Telephone: (03) 62 0241

Telex: 30611

Branches and Affiliates: See "The Australian Associated Stock Exchanges."

Officers: Chairman: J. C. Johnston
Vice-Chairman: H. W. Nankervis
General Manager: R. B. Lee
Manager, Operations: I. K. Aston
Manager, Investment Service: E. L. Grimwood
Manager, Nominee Services: N. K. Matthews
Manager, Data Processing: J. H. Molony
Manager, Listings: K. J. Quinlan
Manager, Personnel: C. F. Smitten
Manager, Public Relations: C. Wilson (Mrs.)
Secretary to the Committee: I. N. Davidson

Hours of Business: 10:00 A.M. - 12:30 P.M. (weekdays) 2:00 P.M. - 3:00 P.M. (weekdays) (Eastern Standard Summer Time—no changes in other seasons)

Regulatory Laws: Companies Act of the State of Victoria (No. 6839 of 1961—Fourth Reprint dated 1st March, 1972)—relates principally to prospectuses and financial reports by listed companies.

Marketable Securities Act of the State of Victoria (Nos. 7970 of 1970 and 8038 of 1970)—these relate principally to forms for the transfer of securities.

Securities Industry Act of the State of Victoria (No. 7962 of 1970—Reprint dated 22nd March, 1971)—Relates to licensing of Stock Exchanges, authorised dealers, advisers and representatives, accounts and Audit, Trust Funds, Fidelity Funds and trading in securities.

Currently the Australian (Federal) Government has not legislated on a national basis for either companies or the securities industry, but a Senate Committee has considered these questions—no report yet submitted.

Issues Traded and Volume:

1. Listed Issues*:

	Equities		Fixed	
Year	Ind.	Mining	Interest	Total
1963	791	138	1,942	2,871
1964	809	139	1,956	2,904
1965	824	135	1,981	2,940
1966	809	121	2,048	2,978
1967	775	130	2,014	2,919
1968	776	155	2,072	3,003
1969	790	261	2,186	3,237
1970	799	361	2,207	3,367
1971	764	438	2,219	3,421
1972	1,200	562	2,712	4,474
1973	1,174	490	2,627	4,291

*1. Includes an undefined number of issues not traded.
2. No trading is recorded in unlisted or "other" issues.
3. 1963-1969 years to September; 9 months to June, 1970; thereafter years to June.

2. Volume (000,000)*

Year	Ind.	Mining	Preference	Total
1963	144.0	28.0	1.3	173.3
1964	153.1	33.2	2.5	188.8
1965	111.4	29.4	1.7	142.5
1966	120.4	46.0	2.6	169.0
1967	152.1	81.0	2.0	235.1
1968	250.0	248.6	2.7	501.3
1969	273.2	296.0	3.3	572.5
1970	245.0	1,122.6	2.2	1,369.8
1971	260.5	788.5	1.7	1,050.7
1972	368.1	406.0	5.7	779.8
1973	355.3	280.7	2.0	638.0

*1963-1969 years to September; 9 months to June, 1970; thereafter years to June.

Unit of Trading:

1. Shares are normally traded in "marketable parcels," according to price. See "The Australian Associated Stock Exchanges" for specific data.
2. Odd-lots: See "The Australian Associated Stock Exchanges."

Memberships:

1. Full Members: 162
2. Non-member partners: 55
3. Seat Prices: 1966-1970: High—$35,000; Low—$16,000
   1971-1973: Not available.

Commissions or Fees: See "The Australian Associated Stock Exchanges."

Historical Background:

1852 First known publication of share list.
1859 Australia's first organisation of brokers formed in Melbourne, meeting at the Hall of Commerce, Collins Street.

1861 First Melbourne Stock Exchange formed.
1884 Stock Exchange of Melbourne established.
1888 Turnover exceeded 2 million pounds ($4 m.) on January 20.
1891 Stock Exchange moved to 388 Collins Street. Public, press admitted as observers.
1903 First Interstate Conference of stock exchanges.
1913 First comprehensive listing rules issued to companies.
1914 Outbreak of World War I. Australian stock exchanges closed for eight weeks.
1924 Stock exchange moved to 422 Little Collins Street.
1939 Outbreak of World War II. Stock exchange closed for 1½ days.
1942 National Security (Economic Organisation) Regulations restricting share sales and limiting prices.
1947 Share price ceilings removed.
1962 Introduction of post trading.
1968 Stock Exchange House opened at 351 Collins Street on October 14.
1969 Computer communication service installed.
1970 Year of records and of mining boom; 107 companies added to official list; mining turnover increased by 280% to 1,123 million units. Peak trading day (February 17) when total transactions numbered 10,450. Total value of year's turnover was $1,369 million.

PERTH

PERTH STOCK EXCHANGE

Title: The Stock Exchange of Perth Limited.

Address: 68 St. George's Terrace, Perth, W.A. 6000, Australia

Telephone: 22 5066

Telex: AA92159

Cable Address: STOCKEX, Perth, Western Australia.

Branches and Affiliates: See "The Australian Associated Stock Exchanges."

Officers: Chairman: R. A. Black
             Vice-Chairman: D. G. Maloney
             General Manager: P. J. Unsworth

Hours of Business:

Winter 8:30 A.M. - 10:30 A.M.	Summer 8:00 A.M. - 9:30 A.M.
12:00 Noon - 1:00 P.M.	11:00 A.M. - 12:00 Noon
2:30 P.M. - 3:00 P.M.	2:00 P.M. - 2:30 P.M.

Regulatory Laws: The Companies Act; Securities Industry Act; Marketable Securities Transfer Act—Acts of the Western Australian Parliament.

Issues Traded and Volume:
1. The Official List*:
   (a) Companies issuing shares: Industrial—1,109; Mining—314; Oil—44.

(b) Companies issuing debentures: 114
(c) Companies issuing unsecured notes: 34
(d) Number of loans listed: debenture stock—924; unsecured notes—115
(e) Trustee securities listed: 100
(f) Transferable deposits listed: 24
(g) Commonwealth loans: 96
(h) Semi-Government loans listed: 1,175
(i) Tax-free semi-Government loans listed: 15

2. Volume:

Fiscal Year	Shares	Value
1967/68	46,771,953	$94,897,525
1968/69	83,708,890	98,244,727
1969/70*	133,139,000	91,587,000
1970/71	221,377,161	149,887,114
1971/72	107,343,003	58,872,189
1972/73**	110,991,740	65,584,835

*Eight months only, as fiscal year changed from October 31, to June 30.
**As of June 30.

Unit of Trading:
1. Trading on the Exchange is in "marketable parcels." The number of shares in a parcel depends upon the market price of the security involved. See "The Australian Associated Stock Exchanges" for specific data.
2. Odd-lots: See "The Australian Associated Stock Exchanges."

Memberships: Regular Members: 32

Commissions or Fees: See "The Australian Associated Stock Exchanges."

Historical Background:

1889 (July)	The Stock Exchange of Perth was formed. It occupied an auction mart in St. George's Terrace.
1890 (July)	First annual general meeting. Turnover was $9,000 for the year, versus almost $150 million in 1970-1971.
1960 (July)	"Call" room on 5th floor, C.M.L. Building was enlarged.
1962 (September)	First Chairman's Conference of the Australian Associated Stock Exchanges held in Perth.
1963 (October)	Limited form of post trading introduced.
1965 (October)	First full time secretary appointed.
1967 (July)	Total post trading introduced.
1968 (December)	Moved to present premises—Exchange House.

SYDNEY

SYDNEY FUTURES EXCHANGE LIMITED

Title: Sydney Futures Exchange Limited.

Address: 7th Floor, Tower Building, Australia Square, Sydney 2000, Australia

Telephone: 241 - 1077

Cable Address: "WOOLFUTURES" Sydney.

Officers: Floor Member Directors: R. O. Newman—Chairman, G. E. Green —Deputy Chairman, D. H. Goode, C. M. Hall.

Associate Member Directors: W. G. Davies, A. J. M. McConnel
Executive Officer and Secretary: A. C. Robson

Hours of Business: 11:00 A.M. - 12:30 P.M. (weekdays) 2:30 P.M. - 4:00 P.M. (weekdays)

Regulatory Laws: There are no specific Federal or State Acts regulating the exchange at the present time.

Issues Traded and Volume:
1. Eight contract months: March, May, July, October, December, New March, New May, New July.
2. Volume:

1963	82,034	contracts	1969	37,055	contracts
1964	130,703	contracts	1970	65,074	contracts
1965	77,356	contracts	1971	44,807	contracts
1966	62,147	contracts	1972	103,284	contracts
1967	66,597	contracts	1973	186,011	contracts
1968	56,330	contracts			

Unit of Trading: Unit of Contract is the greasy equivalent of 1,500 Kg. clean weight of combing wool. The Standard Wool is 64's quality Good Topmaking Merino Fleece Wool of Good to Average Length—C.W.C. Type 78.

Membership:
1. Floor Members: 12
2. Associate Members: 114
3. Membership Costs:
   a. Floor Members: $10,000 deposit with the exchange partially refundable after two years. The size of the deposit is variable at the discretion of the board of the exchange. Floor membership applications must be recommended by the board and approved by a ballot of two-thirds of the floor members.
   b. Associate Members: original memberships purchased from the exchange at $1,000 each. Subsequent sales by transfer have varied from $50 (January, 1971) to $6,000 (1973).

Commissions or Fees:
1. Deposits: Minimum $350 per contract (refunded on termination of contract).
2. Margin: as required.
3. Brokerage:
   a. Non-Members: $20 per contract to buy and $20 per contract to sell. $40 per contract round turn.
   b. Associate Members: One-half the above rates.
Clearing House Charges: $1.30 per contract bought and $1.20 per contract sold.

Historical Background:
As Australia is the world's major wool producer, producing more than half

the world clip of Merino wool, it seemed logical that a local wool futures market should be established.

In November, 1959, advice was received from the Australian Federal Treasurer that payments would be permitted to a non-resident in the currency of his country, or its equivalent, of amounts accruing to him from the settlement by residents of contractual obligations, or from earnings arising out of participation in a futures market in greasy wool in Australia. In addition, exchange would be provided to enable floor members to engage in appropriate arbitrage operations in wool futures markets overseas.

A meeting of interested companies was accordingly held to discuss the formation of the Sydney Exchange. This meeting agreed on a general framework for the exchange based on existing wool futures markets, particularly the London Wool Terminal Market Association, and resolved that the Sydney Greasy Wool Futures Exchange Limited, a non-profit company limited by guarantee, should be established. The company was incorporated under the Companies Act of New South Wales on January 25, 1960, and began trading on May 11 of that year.

All trading is by "Open Outcry" on the exchange floor; trades are recorded by the exchange staff. Registration is effected by the clearing house and only contracts executed within the rules of the exchange will be so registered.

In September 1972, the name of the exchange was changed from Sydney Greasy Wool Futures Exchange Limited to Sydney Futures Exchange Limited, as progress developed on the research and investigation of new futures markets, such as the proposed Sydney Currency Futures Market and Sydney Beef Futures Market. On January 18, 1974, the one millionth greasy wool futures contract was traded on the exchange.

SYDNEY STOCK EXCHANGE

Title: The Sydney Stock Exchange Limited.

Address: G.P.O. Box 1360, Sydney, N.S.W. 2001, Australia

Telephone: 28 - 0421

Telex: AA20630 - AA22273

Cable Address: STOCKEX, Sydney

Branches and Affiliates: See "The Australian Associated Stock Exchanges."

Officers:
    Chairman: J. H. Valder
    Vice-Chairman: C. P. Curran
    Honorary Treasurer: P. C. Hains
    Committee: I. P. Buckle   I. T. S. Reid
              B. C. France   W. J. Tilley
              G. T. Kryger   R. G. Utz
              K. C. Phillips
    General Manager: D. M. Butcher

Hours of Business (Trading): 10:00 A.M. - 3:00 P.M. (weekdays)

Regulatory Laws:
Companies Act 1961, as amended.
Securities Industry Act 1970, as amended.
Marketable Securities Act 1970, as amended.
Stamp Duties Act 1920-65, as amended.
The Sydney Stock Exchange Limited—Memorandum & Articles of Association, By-Laws & Regulations.
Australian Associated Stock Exchanges, Official List Requirements.

Issues Traded and Volume:
1. Listed Companies:

	Mining	Industrial		Mining	Industrial
1963	96	835	1969	146	796
1964	94	840	1970	255	788
1965	90	845	1971	346	790
1966	83	837	1972*	382	1,169
1967	88	821	1973	355	1,101
1968	98	800			

*In January, all public companies in Australia were listed on all Member Exchanges of the Australian Associated Stock Exchanges.

2. Volume*(000,000,000)

	Mining	Industrial	Total
1965	30	121	151
1966	43	137	180
1967	73	148	221
1968	304	283	587
1969	649	335	984
1970	2,870	325	3,195
1971	2,025	244	2,269
1972	852	299	1,151
1973	653	383	1,036

*As of June 30, each year.

Unit of Trading:
1. Shares are normally traded in "marketable parcels," according to price. See "The Australian Associated Stock Exchanges" for specific data.
2. Odd-lots: See "The Australian Associated Stock Exchanges."

Membership:
1. Full Members: 145
2. Partners: 131
3. Firms: 65
4. From February, 1966, when Australia converted to decimal currency, until August, 1968, seat prices fluctuated between $20,000 and $30,000. The price rose to $36,000 in September and continued advancing to a peak of $85,000 in April, 1970. After leveling off at around $70,000, seats dropped to $55,000 in August, 1971, and are currently changing hands at approximately $25,500.

Commissions or Fees:
See "The Australian Associated Stock Exchanges."

Historical Background:
1829   Matthew Gregson, first known stockbroker in Australia.

1850's	Gold discoveries developed securities business.
1871	Sydney Stock Exchange (Australia's oldest) was founded; rules and regulations instituted.
1872	Gold and copper mining boom. Meetings of brokers moved from Greville's Rooms at 388 George Street to the Sydney Stock Exchange Building on Bridge Street.
1887-88	Broken Hill silver boom.
1892-93	General financial collapse of the Sydney and Melbourne stock markets.
1896	Exchange moved to temporary premises in Mutual Life Building, Martin Place.
1900	Formation of the Commonwealth of Australia.
1901	Exchange moved into its own building at 113 Pitt Street.
1911	First paid secretary appointed.
1914	Exchange closed six weeks for World War I.
1925	Great Britain returned to the gold standard.
1937	Australian Associated Stock Exchanges formed in Sydney. Research and Statistical Department formed at Sydney Stock Exchange.
1942-47	Stock market controlled by the Government (World War II).
1959	Post trading system adopted.
1960	Exchange moved to 20 O'Connell Street.
1963	Computer Department established.
1964	Sydney Stock Exchange became a corporate body.
1966	A single day's trading exceeded 38 million shares.
1970	Securities Industry Act.
1973	Member firms required to comprise two or more partners, thus eliminating the individual trader.

AUSTRIA

VIENNA

VIENNA COMMODITIES EXCHANGE
(a branch of the Vienna Stock Exchange)

Title: Wiener Böerse

Address: Wipplingerstrabsse 34, A-1010 Vienna, Austria

Telephone: 0222/63 - 37 - 66

Teletype: wbk

Telex: 074693

Officers:
      President: Heinrich Treichl

Vice Presidents: Franz Ockermuller, Friedrich Schoeller-Szuts, Franz Josef Mayer-Gunthof

Secretary General: Harald Eichler

Hours of Business:
1. Timber Exchange: 11:00 A.M. - 1:00 P.M. (Wednesday)
2. Chemicals, Colonial Products and Textiles Exchange: 12:00 noon - 1:00 P.M. (Thursday)
3. Skins and Leather Exchange: 12:00 noon - 1:00 P.M. (Tuesday)

Memberships:
1. 244 firms.
2. Fee: AS 200 per year.

Commissions or Fees: 0.5% of the agreed price; at least AS 50.

Historical Background:
1873: Vienna Commodities Exchange was founded, as an independent exchange.
1876: Merged with the Vienna Stock Exchange.

Supplementary Information: The importance of the commodities exchange for Austrian trading associations is based on
1. The publication of quotations in the "Official List of the Vienna Commodities Exchange," which appears weekly for timber and colonial products and fortnightly for leather and skins;
2. On the publication of exchange rules; and
3. On the proceedings of the Court of Arbitration, which may also be appealed to for business transactions other than commodities exchange dealings.

VIENNA STOCK EXCHANGE

Title: Wiener Boerse

Address: Wipplingerstrasse 34 A-1010 Vienna, Austria

Telephone: 0222/63-37-66

Teletype: wbk

Telex: 074693

Branches: Stock Exchange, Foreign Exchange, Commodity Exchange.

Officers:
President: Heinrich Treichl
Vice-presidents: Franz Ockermuller, Friedrich Schoeller-Szuts, Franz Josef Mayer-Gunthof
Secretary General: Harald Eichler

Hours of Business: 11:30 A.M. - 1:00 P.M.

Regulatory Laws:
1. Stock Exchange Law of April 1, 1875, No. 67/1875, amended 1903, newly issued 1948, No. 160/1948
2. Official Broker's Law of October 13, 1948, No. 3/1949

Issues Traded (12/31/72)

Fixed Interest Securities	822	(including 16 foreign currency bonds)
Convertible Bonds	8	(including 2 foreign)
Shares (issued by 95 companies)	104	(including 23 foreign)
Investment Certificates	7	(including 3 foreign)
Warrants	5	
	946	

Volume: (in million Austrian Schillings)

1. Official trading and semi-official market

Year	Bonds	Shares	Investment Certificates	Total
1960	309	582	. . .	891
1961	382	789	. . .	1,171
1962	476	703	28	1,207
1963	592	251	12	855
1964	604	227	9	840
1965	614	204	10	828
1966	572	195	13	780
1967	708	189	16	913
1968	840	229	25	1,094
1969	830	299	24	1,153
1970	926	333	21	1,280
1971	830	251	19	1,100
1972	1.205	432	37	1,674
1973	1.431	667	53	2,151

In Austria, since there is no obligation to trade securities through a stock exchange, only a part of the business in listed securities is so transacted.

2. Listed Austrian securities (excluding new issues and block trades)

Year	Bonds	Shares	Investment Certificates	Total
1970	3,336	858	182	4,376
1971	3,106	548	156	3,810
1972	4,728	1,182	379	6,289
1973	5,321	1,423	384	7,128

Memberships: 258 members of sixty-two firms. The firms pay an annual fee according to the amount of business they transact.

Commissions or Fees: For brokers: 0.1% (bonds); 0.175% (shares); 0.175% (investment certificates)

For bankers: 0.5% (bonds); 0.775% (shares); 0.425% (investment certificates). Only half the banker's commission is charged for foreign banks.

Stock exchange turnover tax: 0.125% (bonds); 0.19% (shares); 0.15% (investment certificates). The tax is lower for foreigners.

Historical Highlights:

The Vienna Stock Exchange was founded in 1771, as a governmental institution for trading in government bonds. The first shares admitted to trading were those of the Austrian National Bank in 1818.

The exchange was reorganized as an independent corporation after the market panic in the 1870's. It maintained its leading position in southeastern

Europe during the early part of this century. Many of Austria's foremost companies today, as well as those of neighboring countries, were financed originally through the Vienna Stock Exchange.

The exchange was organized according to German stock exchanges after Austria was occupied in 1938. It did not reopen in its present form until November 15, 1948. The Vienna Stock Exchange is the only securities exchange in Austria.

BELGIUM

Although the Brussels Stock Exchange is the most important in that country, it was in Antwerp that the nation's first bourse appears to have been built during the fifteenth century. There are presently three other exchanges: the Antwerp Stock Exchange, the Ghent Stock Exchange, and the Liege Stock Exchange.

There are no commodity exchanges in Belgium.

ANTWERP

ANTWERP STOCK EXCHANGE

Title: Fondsen en Wesselbeurs van Antwerpen

Address: Korte Klarenstaat 1, 200 Antwerp, Belgium

BRUSSELS

BRUSSELS STOCK EXCHANGE

Title: La Bourse de Bruxelles

Address: Palais de la Bourse, Brussels, Belgium

Telephone: 12 - 51 - 10

Telex: 374

Officers:
President: Jean Reyers
Vice-Presidents:
   Marcel Dineur
   Emile Leclercq
   Raymond Hombergen
Secretary: Charles Timmermans
Secretary Assistant: Daniel Bernaerts
Treasurer: Paul Rampelbergs

Members:
Pierre Drugmand
Leon Flament
Christian Goeminne
Desire Hicter
Jacques Leleux
Jules Migeot
Roger Sterckx
Henri Van Den Bosch

Regulatory Laws: The Commercial Law Code (Book 1, Chapter 5). The Commercial Code has been amended by various by-laws, but its basic measures apply to all national stock exchanges: Brussels, Antwerp, Ghent, Liege.

Issues Traded and Volume:
1. Official List (April 30, 1974)
   a. State bonds—Belgian: 281; Foreign: 3.
   b. Industrial debentures—Belgian: 41; Foreign: 20.
   c. Shares—Belgian: 321; Foreign: 143.
   d. Belgium has no restrictions for investing in foreign securities, but foreign share listings must be authorized by the Minister of Finance.
2. Main Figures 1973 (francs, millions):

	12/31/72	12/31/73
Total volume transactions	68,104.3	97,555.6
Fixed Interest	20,240.8	31,571.4
Equities	47,863.5	65,984.2
General Index		
(base) 12/30/63 = 100)		
Cash Market Belgian Companies	121.5	125.39
Forward Market	152.65	144.81
Capitalization of Belgian Companies	415,963.9	424,001.2
New Admissions during 1973		
State, Province, Town and Public	——	137,804.8
Service Bonds	——	
Industrial Debentures	——	5,310.7
Belgian Shares	——	1,707.8

Unit of Trading:
1. There is no minimum for dealings on the cash market but on the forward market, a minimum number is fixed for each security by the Commission de la Bourse. It varies between five and one thousand shares depending upon the effective value of the security and approaches 50,000 BF.
2. There are two types of markets (cash and forward), where three trading or quotation methods are employed: open outcry; auction; rack or pigeon-hole ("cashier").

Memberships:
1. Broker's associations: 418, as of January 1, 1974.
2. a. Brokers may deal for their own account.
   b. They may have no other profession without the authorization of the Stock Exchange Commission.
   c. They must charge commissions at the official rate.
   d. The Stock Exchange Committee in Brussels has 15 members. Among its other duties, the committee is responsible for preparing and amending the stock exchange rules.

Commissions or Fees (determined by the Ministry of Finance):
1. Minimum brokerage per contract, depending upon the type of security and the market:

a. 3 francs per 1,000 of the effective value, plus the interest for spot transactions in government stocks;
b. 7.50 francs per 1,000 for spot transactions in Belgian and foreign company stocks;
c. 6 francs per 1,000 for forward transactions;
d. an additional fixed duty of 60 francs per bargain (transaction).
2. Stock Exchange Tax; Government Tax:
a. 0.70 franc per 1,000 for government securities;
b. 3.50 francs per 1,000 in the spot market for Belgian and foreign company shares;
c. 1.70 francs per 1,000 for forward transactions; it is reduced to 1.40 francs per 1,000 for forward transactions in certificates issued in Belgium to represent Belgian or foreign shares.
3. Quotation Charge:
a. 0.25 franc per 1,000 on the total of transactions on the cash market;
b. 0.1 franc per 1,000 on the total of transactions on the forward market.
c. 0.10 franc per 1,000 on the total of transactions for government securities.

Historical Background:

1867 The law of December 30 completely abolished the provisions then in force for controlling the profession of broker, the organization of the exchange and the operations transacted there.

1901 The Bourse de Bruxelles was founded July 8. The word "Bourse" is derived from "van der Buerse," the surname of the man whose inn in Bruges became the headquarters for merchants and brokers in 1360.

1930 A committee was appointed to study measures to be taken to afford greater protection to investors and to improve the working of the market in quoted securities.
The commission's report inspired in large measure the legislation incorporated into the Commercial Code of 1935, which still generally controls the organization of the stock exchanges and the stockbroking profession in Belgium. The law provides that each stock exchange be administered by a Stock Exchange Commission and that a government representative, nominated by the Minister of Finance, be attached to each exchange to ascertain that all the rules and laws are observed.

1967 The Belgian clearing system (C.I.K.) was formed. In the first stage, C.I.K. limited its activity to Belgian securities and members; it is now open also to foreign securities and members.

GHENT

GHENT STOCK EXCHANGE

Title: Fondsen en Wesselbeurs van Ghent
Address: Kouter, 29, 9000 Ghent, Belgium

LIEGE

LIEGE STOCK EXCHANGE

Title: Bourse de Fonds Publics de Liege
Address: Rue de Bex, 4000 Liege, Belgium

BRAZIL

THE STOCK EXCHANGES OF BRAZIL

The majority of trading volume (over 95%) is concentrated on Brazil's two leading stock exchanges situated in Rio de Janeiro and Sao Paulo. Markets in Rio Grande do Sul, Minas Gerais, and Recife are runners-up in size, but a company's shares may be traded on any of Brazil's thirteen bolsas, according to a system of national registration.

New tax incentives, higher dividend payments, and favorable corporate earnings have sparked a growing interest in the nation's bourses. Efforts have been made to discourage speculation and to attract and retain capital which formerly was sent abroad or channeled into foreign currencies. More and more companies are "going public" and the stock market is gaining prominence as a pillar of the capital system. The expansion of mutual funds has contributed also; there are now about 200 in operation, compared with only seven early in 1966.

It is not easy for a foreigner to participate in the growth of Brazil. For one thing, he can purchase Brazilian stocks only if he forms a local company and registers its entire capital, plus possible future increases, with the Central Bank. Profits realized and "plowed back" into the business cannot be repatriated without being registered as reinvestment. Currency fluctuations are an added risk; taxes are a problem. Foreigners are liable to a 25% withholding tax on profits from a Brazilian investment company. Moreover, once the capital of a business has been expanded, it cannot be contracted for five years without a possible tax penalty.

BELO HORIZONTE - MINAS GERAIS

MINAS GERAIS STOCK EXCHANGE

Title: Minas Gerais Stock Exchange
Address: Rua Carijos, 126, Belo Horizonte - Minas Gerais, Brazil.

CURITIBA-PARANA

PARANA STOCK EXCHANGE

Title: Parana Stock Exchange

Address: Rua XV de Novembro, 621 - 4° and., Curitiba - Parana, Brazil.

FLORIANOPOLIS - SANTA CATARINA

FLORIANOPOLIS STOCK EXCHANGE

Title: Florianopolis Stock Exchange

Address: Rua Saldanha Marinho, 2 - 1° and., Florianopolis - Santa Catarina, Brazil.

GOIANIA - GOIAS

GOIAS STOCK EXCHANGE

Title: Goias Stock Exchange

Address: Avenida Goias, 759 - Lojas A e B, Goiania - Goias, Brazil.

NATAL - RIO GRANDE DO NORTE

RIO GRANDE DO NORTE STOCK EXCHANGE

Title: Rio Grande do Norte Stock Exchange

Address: Rua Camara Cascudo, 184, Natal - Rio Grande do Norte, Brazil.

NITEROI - EST. DO RIO DE JANEIRO

ESTADO DO RIO DE JANEIRO STOCK EXCHANGE (NITEROI)

Title: Estado do Rio de Janeiro Stock Exchange (Niteroi)

Address: Rua Col. Gomes Machado, 165, Niteroi - Est. do Rio de Janeiro, Brazil

PORTO ALEGRE - RIO GRANDE DO SUL

RIO GRANDE DO SUL STOCK EXCHANGE

Title: Rio Grande do Sul Stock Exchange
Address: Rua dos Andradas, 1234 - 4°. and., Porto Alegre - Rio Grande do Sul, Brazil.

RECIFE - PERNAMBUCO

RECIFE STOCK EXCHANGE

Title: Recife Stock Exchange
Address: Praca Rio Branco, 18, Recife - Pernambuco, Brazil.

RIO de JANEIRO

RIO DE JANEIRO STOCK EXCHANGE

Title: Bolsa de Valores do Rio de Janeiro (GB)
Address: Praca XV de Novembro, 20 - Rio de Janeiro (GB), Brazil
Telephone: 231 - 5854
Teletype: BOLVALORES RIO
Telex: 031875
Cable Address: BOLVALORES
Branches and Affiliates:
  Rua dos Carijos no. 126, S/204 Belo Horizonte - MG, Brazil
  Rua Boavista no. 254, S/417 Sao Paulo - SP, Brazil
Officers:
  Chairman: Fernando Souza Ribeiro de Carvalho
  Counselors:

Carlos de Almeida Liberal	Geraldo Tosta de Sá
Adolpho Ferreira de Oliveira	Octávio Dyckerhoff
Roberto Vianna Pinto	Laerte Mazza
Eduardo dos Guimarães Bonjean	Cesar Ribeiro Barrozo
Ignácio Hisbello Correia de Mello	Arnaldo Borges Tavares
Aloysio de Souza Bastos	Raymundo José Gomes Frias
Althemar Dutra de Castilho	Victório Bhering Cabral

  General Supt.: Althemar Dutra de Castilho
  Operational Supt.: Guilherme Augusto Cardoso Furtado

Administrative Supt.: Francisco Xavier Sandee Castro Salgado
General Secretary: Luis Tapias

Hours of Business: 10:00 A.M. - 1:00 P.M. (weekdays)

Regulatory Laws: The principal laws which provide for and regulate stock exchanges in Brazil:
1. Law No. 4595 (December 31, 1964) created the National Monetary Council.
2. Law No. 4728 (July 14, 1965) governs the capital markets.
3. Law No. 5589 (July 3, 1970)
4. Law No. 5710 (October 7, 1971)

Issues Traded and Volume:
1. Listed Issues:
   a. Regional Market: 28
   b. National Market: 277 (Open capital) 15 (closed capital)
   c. No unlisted issues traded.
   d. Corporate dividends are fixed in relation to the nominal value of the share (normally Cr$ 1.00) and in the form of a percentage.
2. Volume:

a.

	Shares (000)		Shares (000)
	1963	30,161	1959	588,264
	1964	54,510	1970	1,023,304
	1965	128,716	1971	2,592,703
	1966	119,353	1972	2,070,288
	1967	201,898	1973	1,967,586
	1968	198,692		

b.

	High Day (Cr$ 000)		Low Day	
1970	32,200	(12/9)	3,989	(6/15)
1971	168,620	(5/18)	25,084	(11/24)
1972	109,620	(8/29)	10,718	(11/16)
1973	100,173	(8/22)	9,274	(3/2)

Unit of Trading:
1. Standard Lot: 1,000 shares.
2. Odd-lots are traded separately; no extra fee or commission is charged.

Membership:
1. Regular Members: 91
2. Cost of membership (1973): Cr$ 94,700

Commissions or Fees:
Stocks: up to Cr$ 10,000 . . . . 1½%
      from Cr$ 10,000 to Cr$ 60,000 . . . . 1%
      over Cr$ 60,000 . . . . ½%

Historical Background:
1843	All stock brokers required to obtain a license.
1850	A Broker's Board was organized.
1876	Creation of a trading floor centralized all operations.
1893	The Chamber of Public Funds Brokers was created; Stock Exchange of the Republic established; new legislation was introduced.
1930	The exchange was integrated and came under State control. A central

stock exchange building was constructed, trading in foreign debt securities was permitted and brokers were included in the Technical Economic and Financial Council.

1953 Brokers permitted to trade in foreign exchange futures (import licenses).

1962-65 The exchange reorganized internally: certain old departments were changed and new ones introduced (legal, general service, technical, public relations, accounting).

1972 Central Bank of Brazil specified standards for auditing of accounting statements of enterprises dealing on the stock exchange. General standards of auditing and principles of accounting for publicly-held companies were laid down. Requirements for registration of companies and share listings were issued.

1973 A presidential decree issued in August stimulated dividend payments by publicly-owned corporations, reestablished equilibrium in taxation levied on investment income, and created conditions for developing a debenture market, particularly convertible debentures.

SALVADOR - BAHIA

BAHIA STOCK EXCHANGE

Title: Bahia Stock Exchange

Address: Rua da Argentina 1 - 30 and., Salvador - Bahia, Brazil.

SANTOS - SAO PAULO

SANTOS STOCK EXCHANGE

Title: Santos Stock Exchange

Address: Rua XV de Novembro, 95 - 1° and., Santos - Sao Paulo, Brazil.

SAO PAULO

SAO PAULO STOCK EXCHANGE

Title: Bolsa de Valores de Sao Paulo

Address: Rua Alvares Penteado, No. 151/185, Sao Paulo, Brazil

Telephone: 33 - 7181; 37 - 7561

Teletype: BOVALORES SPO

Telex: 021 - 225
Officers: Administrative Council:
  President: Alfredo Nagib Rizkallh
  Vice-President: Ivan Martins Motta
  Councilors:
    Paulo Roberto Ferreira Levy
    Raymundo Magliano
    Evandro Oliveira Puggina
    Paschoal Geraldo da Silveira Isoldi
    Eduardo Duarte Leopoldo e Silva (Representing the Societies of Open Capital)
    Reynaldo Borges Affonso (General Superintendent)
  Substitute Councilors:
    Fernando Luiz Nabuco de Abreu
    Luiz Carlos Azevedo Vieira
    Mauricio Figueiredo Magalhaes (Representing the Societies of Open Capital)

Hours of Business: 10:00 A.M. - 1:00 P.M. (weekdays)
Regulatory Laws:
1. Law No. 4595—Bank Reform—(December 31, 1964)
2. Law No. 4728—Capital Markets—(July 14, 1965) It established regulatory and operating procedures and gave tax breaks to those who invested in new issues or mutual funds.
3. Resolution No. 39 (October 20, 1966), which defined the principal characteristics, tasks and prerogatives of the stock exchange. It stipulated that "only firms consisting of practicing brokers, or broker's associations, may be admitted as members of the stock exchange . . . . . and that broker's associations may be associated with one or more stock exchanges, as long as they assume the corresponding patrimonial title and fulfill the necessary requirements of membership of each exchange."

Issues Traded and Volume:
1. No. of issues: 317 in 1973, versus 50 in 1968. About 60 of these issues account for 85% of the trading volume.
2. Volume:

	Shares Traded	Value (Cruzeiros)
1960	#	391,180,947
1961	#	725,232,965
1962	#	758,566,700
1963	#	640,169,117
1964	#	1,344,075,952
1965	#	939,556,412
1966	#	346,010,841
1967	#	299,980,926
1968	855,065,436	545,139,575
1969	383,125,678	1,576,969,716
1970	691,755,305	2,272,108,242
1971	2,447,555,210	11,543,396,934
1972	3,525,740,685	10,412,340,337
1973*	4,029,968,534	9,338,239,265

#Not available
*Eleven months only.

Unit of Trading:
1. 100 shares.
2. No "differential," or extra commission, is involved when dealing in odd-lots.

Memberships:
1. 134 "Sociedades Corretoras"—stock broker's associations.
2. Membership prices:

1967	Cr$ 30,000
1968	39,000
1969	57,000
1970	101,000
1971	139,000
1972	272,000
1973	324,000

Commissions or Fees:
Stocks:

from Cr$ 0.01 to Cr$ 10,000 .... 1.5%
from Cr$ 10,000.01 to Cr$ 30,000 .... 1.0%
Cr$ 30,000.01 and above 0.5%

Historical Background:
1890 Emilio Rangel Pestana founded a free market for stocks in Sao Paulo on August 23, about nine months after Brazil became completely independent of Portugal.

1895 The market became known officially as "La Bolsa de Fundos Publicos de Sao Paulo."

1935 The exchange adopted a new title—Bolsa Oficial de Valores de Sao Paulo.

1967 On March 7, the present title was adopted—Bolsa de Valores de Sao Paulo.

Volume of Trading on all Brazilian Exchanges
1971

Exchanges	Shares Traded (000)	Value (Cr.$ 000)	%
Bahia	11,150	41,251	0.15
Niteroi	12,669	63,885	0.24
Esp. Santo	—	—	—
Florianopolis	3,429	6,215	0.02
Goias**	189	1,069	—
M. Gerais	138,697	860,627	3.17
Parana	23,273	67,430	0.25
Recife***	3,792	53,759	0.20
R. G. Norte	360	2,215	0.01
R. G. Sul	74,075	295,923	1.09
R. Janeiro	2,697,732	14,185,917	52.23
Santos	9,598	41,221	.15
Sao Paulo	2,447,555	11,543,397	42.50
	5,442,519	27,162,909	100

Exchanges	1972* Shares Traded (000)	Value (Cr. $ 000)	%
Bahia	12,408	41,094	0.23
Niteroi	5,984	15,559	0.09
Esp. Santo	675	2,189	0.01
Florianopolis	5,177	9,179	0.05
Goias**	526	1,716	0.01
M. Gerais	156,538	691,595	3.84
Parana	7,639	14,759	0.08
Recife***	6,509	32,797	0.18
R. G. Norte	146	876	—
R. G. Sul	58,515	123,240	0.68
R. Janeiro	1,956,710	7,399,669	41.00
Santos	10,819	24,538	0.14
Sao Paulo	3,156,414	9,690,555	53.69
	5,378,060	18,047,766	100

*1972 totals from Jan. - Nov. only
**Opened in May, 1971
***Includes letters of exchange which accounted for about 50% in 1971 and 70% in 1972 of the volume in cruzeiros.
Note: Local commodities exchanges do not trade in futures.

VICTORIA-ESPIRITO SANTO

ESPIRITO SANTO STOCK EXCHANGE

Title: Espirito Santo Stock Exchange
Address: Rua Jeronimo Monteiro, 240 - s/603, Victoria-Espirito Santo, Brazil.

CANADA

THE STOCK EXCHANGES OF CANADA

Canada has five stock exchanges: Calgary, Montreal, Toronto, Vancouver, and Winnipeg. The Toronto Stock Exchange is largest in terms of number and value of shares traded, followed by Montreal. The volume in Toronto first topped that of Montreal in 1948. Most Canadian exchanges trade heavily in mining issues. Calgary is principally an oil exchange; its rules and regulations are modeled on those of Toronto.

The Winnipeg Commodity Exchange (formerly called the Winnipeg Grain Exchange) is Canada's only commodity exchange, and a wide variety of commodities are traded here. The exchange has gained world-wide fame as a gold-futures market, although Winnipeg has long been known as the center of the

Canadian wheat industry. Canada, as the third largest producer of gold, fittingly has an exchange which has grown to be the third largest in the world in terms of volume of metal trade, with only the London and Zurich markets surpassing it.

On July 12, 1974, the major Canadian stock exchanges announced that they were proposing to add a 17½% surcharge to all commissions on orders over $20,000.

CANADIAN STOCK EXCHANGES
1972, 1973

	Share Volume	
Exchange	1972	1973
Calgary Stock Exchange	12,208,365	10,215,318
Montreal Stock Exchange	330,125,289	N.A.
Toronto Stock Exchange	635,885,589	663,856,327
Vancouver Stock Exchange	906,053,892	592,744,506
Winnipeg Stock Exchange	521,025	1,457,706

	Dollar Value	
Exchange	1972	1973
Calgary Stock Exchange	$6,492,516	$7,123,466
Montreal Stock Exchange	2,057,293,935	N.A.
Toronto Stock Exchange	6,258,151,656	N.A.
Vancouver Stock Exchange	784,102,576	483,271,028
Winnipeg Stock Exchange	840,634	N.A.

CALGARY

CALGARY STOCK EXCHANGE

Title: Calgary Stock Exchange

Address: Anglo American Building, 330 - 9th Avenue S.W., Calgary, Alberta T2P 1K7, Canada

Telephone: (403) 262 - 7791

Telex: 038-21793 (answer back CSE CGY)

Officers: The exchange is governed by a Board of Governors, consisting of not less than nine nor more than fifteen members. The President is the Chief Executive Officer and is appointed by the Board of Governors.
Chairman: W. R. Fulton
Vice-Chairman: G. H. Powis
President: J. R. Thomson
Secretary-Treasurer: A. S. Hawkins

Hours of Business: The trading floor is open from 7:00 A.M. - 1:30 P.M. (local time), to coincide with the openings of the New York and the Toronto Stock Exchanges.

Regulatory Laws: The exchange was incorporated under the Calgary Stock Exchange Act, Chapter 45 of the Statutes of Alberta, 1913, and operated under the regulations of the Alberta Securities Act, Chapter 333, Statutes of Alberta, 1970, as amended.

Issues Traded and Volume:

	Issues	Volume	Value
1964	116	29,008,812	$ 5,905,374.77
1965	113	34,753,974	9,484,850.15
1966	113	74,494,261	32,003,950.53
1967	123	54,231,804	29,326,345.24
1968	133	49,917,554	27,782,974.00
1969	160	81,136,616	76,554,674.00
1970	163	26,350,124	17,044,534.99
1971	156	21,255,342	11,827,435.00
1972	161	12,208,365	6,492,516.00
1973	145	10,215,318	7,123,466.00

Unit of Trading:
1. Stocks selling below 10c .... 1,000 shares
   Selling from 10c to 99c .... 500 shares
   Selling from $1.00 and over .... 100 shares
2. Odd-lots:
   a. Trading in odd-lots is subject to a schedule of maximum allowable odd-lot and "broken-lot" premiums or discounts, as follows:

All Securities	Odd-lot	Broken-lot
Selling under $0.50	2c	4c
Selling at $0.50 and under $1.00	3c	6c
Selling at $1.00 and under $2.00	5c	10c
Selling at $2.00 and under $5.00	10c	20c
Selling at $5.00 and under $60.00	12½c	25c
Selling at $60.00 and under $100.00	25c	50c
Selling at $100.00 and over	50c	$1.00

   b. Fees and commissions for buying and selling odd-lots are identical to those of the Toronto Stock Exchange.

Memberships:
1. Regular Members: 31
2. Seat (membership) prices:

1960-1964	$ 500	1969	$4,000
1965	2,500	1970	5,000
1966	1,500	1971	2,000
1967	3,500	1972	4,800
1968	3,000	1973	6,000

Commissions or Fees: Same as those of the Toronto Stock Exchange.

Historical Background:

1913   The exchange was incorporated under the Calgary Stock Exchange Act, following a petition by various Calgary residents and business-men. The chaotic conditions derived from oil discoveries in Alberta was a principal reason for the petition being made.

1914   The exchange opened for business.

1917-26 The exchange was closed, partly as a result of World War I.

1974	The exchange has always been the principal oil exchange in Canada, so that activity reflected the varying interests in oil, peaking with each new discovery. In recent years, concentrated effort has been made to diversify listings to enable the exchange to contribute and participate more fully in the industrial development of the province and of junior companies in Canada.

The rules and regulations of the exchange are modeled on those of the Toronto Stock Exchange. This facilitates the stated policy of the exchange to list junior companies and to impose upon them the same regulatory control as is expected on the senior Toronto Stock Exchange.

The majority of members of the Calgary Stock Exchange are also members of the Toronto Stock Exchange. The similarity of trading practices and operation contributes to the unification of stock exchange business. This is further enhanced by the fact that the Toronto Stock Exchange carries quotations and trades of the Calgary Stock Exchange on its ticker and, further, all clearing and settling of trades is carried out through the facilities of the Toronto Stock Exchange.

MONTREAL

MONTREAL STOCK EXCHANGE

Title: The Montreal Stock Exchange

Address: 800 Victoria Square, Montreal (Quebec) H4Z 1A9, Canada

Telephone: 871 - 2424 (general number)

Telex: 012841

Branches and Affiliates: Associated Stock Exchanges:
Boston Stock Exchange
53 State Street
Boston, Massachusetts 02109 U.S.A.
PBW Stock Exchange, Inc.
17th Street and Stock Exchange Place
Philadelphia, Pennsylvania 19103 U.S.A.

Officers:
Chairman: Pierre Brunet
Vice Chairman: Dominik Dlouhy
President: Michel Belanger
Regular Members:

George H. Garneau	H. A. Jones
Richard H. Stevenson	Ronald G. Campbell
Derek W. Taylor	E. G. Cleather
Paul J. Deslauriers	Charles Rouleau
E. B. Newcomb	

Public Governors:
  Clifford S. Malone
  Antoine Turmei
  Robert Després

Hours of Business (trading): 9:00 a.m. - 3:30 p.m. (weekdays)

Regulatory Laws: By-Laws and Rules of the Montreal Stock Exchange are available at a cost of $25.00.

Issues Traded and Volume:
1. Listed and Unlisted issues: not available.
2. Volume:

	No. of Shares		No. of Shares
1960	77,962,014	1967	260,145,340
1961	144,024,637	1968	323,431,186
1962	157,108,427	1969	304,307,536
1963	179,840,283	1970	268,284,668
1964	322,301,903	1971	304,829,541
1965	427,866,040	1972	330,125,289
1966	297,353,537	1973	296,474,634

Unit of Trading:
1. Size of the trading unit depends upon the price of the security involved.
   1,000 shares - stocks selling under 10 cents.
     500 shares - stocks selling at 10 cents but under $1.00.
     100 shares - stocks selling at $1.00 but under $100.
      10 shares - stocks selling at $100 and above.
2. Orders to buy or sell in an amount that is less than a board-lot (see 1. above) are called odd-lots, or broken lots. They are given to the specialist to whom the stock involved has been allocated, or they may be "put-through" without interference in cases when buy and sell orders are entered simultaneously.* The odd-lot specialist system is supervised by the floor committee, which may allocate or reallocate stocks to and between the odd-lot specialists.
3. Following are the maximum allowable premiums and discounts on odd-or broken-lot bids and offers:

Price Range of Stock	Maximum Allowable Premium or Discount
0 - .49½	2 cents
.50 - .99	3 cents
1.00 - 1.99	5 cents
2.00 - 4.95	10 cents
5.00 - 60.00	12½ cents
60.00 and over	25 cents

There is no extra fee for buying and selling odd-lots, other than the regular commission.

*A "put-through" is a transaction made by a broker who has a sale order from a client for one stock and at the same time has a purchase order from another client for the same stock. The exchange's by-laws provide that this transaction can be completed on the exchange floor on the regular limit of price of the stock at the moment of the transaction, without intervention from another member except for confirmation by initials on the sales slip.

Memberships:
1. Regular Members: 85
2. Associate Members (stock exchanges): 2 - Boston and Philadelphia.
3. Non-member brokers: 26
4. Membership prices ("seats"):

1964	$32,000	1969	30,000
1965	45,000	1970	30,000
1966	43,000	1971	35,000
1967	14,000	1972	25,000
1968	15,000	1973	18,000

Commissions or Fees: The bases for calculating commissions on all orders with values of $20,000 or less are as follows:
1. On shares selling under $14.00: The base rate is 2.50% of the value of the order.
2. On shares selling at $14.00 up to and including $30.00: The base rate is 0.8875% of the order value, plus 22.575 cents per share.
3. On shares selling over $30.00: The base rate is 1.64% of the value of the order.

The applicable base rates apply to the first $20,000 of each order. For orders over $20,000, the base rates are tapered on a value basis, as follows:
   a. for that portion of the order between $20,000 and $40,000, the rate is 70% of the applicable base rate.
   b. for that portion of the order between $40,000 and $60,000, the rate is 50% of the applicable base rate.
   c. for that portion of the order over $60,000, the rate is 30% of the applicable base rate.

Minimum Commission Charges:
1. When the total amount involved in an order is less than $10.00 the charge shall be at the member's discretion.
2. When the total amount involved in an order is between $10.00 and $50.00, the charge shall be discretionary, except that a minimum of $2.00 shall be charged. The minimum charge is $1.00 with such an order on rights, warrants or fractional shares.

Historical Background:
   1832 Trading in stocks began about this time at the Exchange Coffee House, operated by a Mr. Goodenough, on St. Paul Street.
1849-1850 First organization of brokers was formed.
   1863 Board of Brokers was formed.
   1867 Board of Brokers reorganized, adopted new rules and set commissions at ½% of par value.
   1871 Board of Brokers raised entrance fee to $500; then to $1,000 a few months later.
   1872 Board of Brokers began calling itself the Montreal Stock Exchange.
   1874 Montreal Stock Exchange came into being by charter of the Government of Quebec. Seats cost $800. Forty-two companies were listed, of which 21 were banks.
   1880 Bell Telephone of Canada was listed.

1883 Canadian Pacific Railroad was listed. Seats cost $4,650.

1894 Listings dropped to 51 from 64 in 1884.

1901 Five new seats ("reluctantly" created) were sold for an average of $12,850. For many years prior to this, the number of seats had been limited to forty. This prompted the impatient applicants for Exchange membership to call them "the Forty Thieves."

1904 Montreal Stock Exchange moved to its new building on St. Francois Xavier Street, June 29.

1914 The Stock Exchange was closed at 1:55 P.M. on July 28, for World War I. It reopened early in September with certain controls, such as minimum price limits. Short selling was banned. The restrictions were relaxed slightly on October 15. Members ready to buy securities for cash might send a list to the Governing Committee. Bids must not be below minimum prices. Members wishing to sell might follow the same procedure, but only "in order to relieve the necessities of themselves or their clients."

1915 Trading resumed in all stocks on April 6, and in bonds selling above the minimum prices previously set, but short selling was still banned.

1916 All minimum prices were removed, June 23.

1917 Free trading was again suspended, October 30. Reasons: tight money, unfavorable war news, etc.

1919 Minimum prices and other war restrictions were not fully removed until June 2. Volume for the year totaled 915,000 shares.

1924 The Stock Exchange had 147 listings.

1926 Montreal Curb Market formed. Most of its stocks had previously been traded in the Unlisted Department of the Montreal Stock Exchange. Membership was established at 100. Montreal Stock Exchange members were given an opportunity to join for $100; most of them did. Remaining seats were sold for $1,000 each. Within 2½ years, Curb seats sold as high as $50,000.

1929 Curb Market moved into an extension of the Montreal Stock Exchange building on May 1. A Montreal Stock Exchange seat was sold for $225,000 in February. On October 24, reflecting the panic in New York, 382, 521 shares were traded.

1931 British Government's decision to abandon gold standard prompted Montreal Stock Exchange to ban short selling (September 21), and rule that all transactions be made at prices equal to or above the last sale of board lots prior to that date.

1932 Volume for the year: 4,170,845 shares.

1933 Montreal Stock Exchange introduced a long series of reforms. Margins were revised upward - previously, the amount had been left to each exchange member.

1934 Audit provisions were strengthened, an Advisory Committee was set up, a 2-day settlement system was inaugurated . Also the trading floor was modernized and enlarged; ticker service was provided from New York; loud speakers were installed.

1939 Short selling banned when World War II began.

1940 Short selling reinstated during the summer.

1953 Montreal Curb Market renamed Canadian Stock Exchange on March 30.

1956 Henry G. Norman, first president of the Montreal and Canadian Exchanges, took office.

1965 Final trading session held at old (1904) building on St. Francois Xavier Street (October 21); the Montreal Stock Exchange moved into the new Stock Exchange Tower at Place Victoria.

1969 Under a new law issued January 1, aimed to increase disclosure, all companies listed on both exchanges were required to issue quarterly statements to the exchanges and to the press within ninety days of the end of the period to which the information related.

1970 A system of insurance was set up for investors on December 22.

1973 Michel Belanger appointed president January 1. Montreal Stock Exchange charter amended to give the president, as well as public governors, the right to vote. A market surveillance department was established.

1974 Montreal and Canadian Stock Exchanges merged, January 1.

TORONTO

Title: The Toronto Stock Exchange

Address: 234 Bay Street, Toronto, Ontario, M5J IR1, Canada

Telephone: 363 - 6121

Teletype: TSE TOR

Telex: 02 - 2755

Officers:
Chairman: R. T. Morgan
President: J. R. Kimber
Vice-Chairman: E. S. Miles
Executive Vice-President: W. L. Somerville
Vice-President, Stock List: Lester Lowe
Vice-President, Research and Market Development: H. W. F. McKay
Secretary: Ailsa M. Currie
Treasurer: R. J. Buckley

Hours of Business (trading): 10:00 A.M. - 3:30 P.M.

Regulatory Laws:
1. The Securities Act 1970
2. The Toronto Stock Exchange Act 1968-1969

Listed Issues and Volume:
1. No. issues listed:

a.	Inds.	Mining & Oil	Total		Inds.	Mining & Oil	Total
1948	493	357	850	1966	684	414	1,098
1950	513	402	915	1967	702	377	1,079
1955	534	536	1,070	1968	742	364	1,106
1960	617	501	1,118	1969	794	361	1,155

1961	620	497	1,117	1970	817	360	1,177
1962	642	479	1,121	1971	829	343	1,172
1963	641	457	1,098	1972	873	312	1,185
1964	657	452	1,109	1973	929	317	1,246
1965	673	435	1,108				

   b. In 1973, 68 newly listed companies posted, between them, 73 issues for trading on the Toronto Stock Exchange. Of the issues listed, 52 were industrial stocks, 6 mining stocks, 12 oil stocks and 3 trust units. Fifty-eight of the 68 companies listed are Canadian-based. The total number of shares listed in 1973 was 327.9 million. Quoted market value of these shares, at listing date, was $4.4 billion.

2. Volume: No. shares traded:

a.	Industrials	Mines & Oils	Total Vol.	No. of Transactions
1934	8,409,395	332,911,578	341,320,973	948,547
1936	12,691,600	438,157,105	450,848,705	1,280,436
1940	4,182,092	70,748,529	74,930,621	312,226
1945	10,273,777	431,490,617	441,764,394	888,818
1950	21,428,113	485,167,352	506,595,465	1,087,111
1955	30,342,201	1,482,273,228	1,512,615,429	2,643,863
1960	43,978,216	425,713,327	469,691,543	1,209,541
1961	101,914,135	617,406,841	719,320,976	1,845,100
1962	77,649,288	726,848,908	804,498,196	1,664,848
1963	93,119,898	715,732,200	808,852,098	1,611,809
1964	114,531,141	1,200,124,991	1,314,656,132	2,267,142
1965	109,807,370	824,432,577	934,239,947	2,084,085
1966	94,437,937	877,003,727	971,441,664	2,014,759
1967	130,314,717	688,832,403	819,147,120	2,044,836
1968	251,918,368	659,773,415	911,691,783	2,584,089
1969	272,382,405	599,549,356	871,931,761	2,548,810
1970	193,203,259	329,705,528	522,908,787	1,601,077
1971	239,335,620	306,432,331	545,767,951	1,746,174
1972	314,311,352	321,574,237	635,885,589	1,940,750
1973	313,287,831	350,568,496	663,856,327	1,902,629

   b. Volume Records: Highest Daily Turnover: 28,704,246 shares (April 17, 1964) Lowest Daily Turnover: 711,080 shares (January 3, 1972)

Unit of Trading:

1. Minimum Quotation Spreads:
   a. All Securities
      Selling under $0.50 . . . . .½ cent
      Selling at $0.50 and under $3.00 . . . . .1 cent
      Selling at $3.00 and under $5.00 . . . . .5 cents
      Selling at $5.00 and over . . . . .12½ cents
   b. Rights and Warrants (same as above).
2. Board Lots and Special Board Lots:
   a. An offer to buy or sell without stating the number of shares embraced therein shall be open for acceptance for such number of shares as the exchange may from time to time specify as a Board Lot.
   b. Until altered by the exchange the following shall constitute board lots: In respect of all securities:
      i. on securities selling under $0.10 . . . . 1,000 shares

    ii. on securities selling at $0.10 and under $1.00 ......   500 shares
   iii. on securities selling at $1.00 and under $100.00 ...   100 shares
   iv. on securities selling at $100.00 and over ....   10 shares

  c. The exchange may from time to time specify special board lots for particular securities.

3. Schedule of maximum allowable odd-lot and broken-lot premiums or discounts:

All Securities	Posts 1 - 9		Posts 10 - 11	
	Odd-lot	Broken-lot	Odd-lot	Broken-lot
Sellings under $0.50	2c	4c	2c	4c
Selling at $0.50 and under $1.00	3c	6c	3c	6c
Selling at $1.00 and under $2.00	5c	10c	5c	10c
Selling at $2.00 and under $5.00	10c	20c	10c	20c
Selling at $5.00 and under $60.00	12½c	25c	25c	50c
Selling at $60.00 and under $100.00	25c	50c	50c	$1.00
Selling at $100.00 and over	50c	$1.00	$1.00	$2.00

4. Transactions shall be considered as broken lots when they are
   — less than 100 shares where a board lot is 1,000 or 500 shares.
   — less than 10 shares where a board lot is 100 shares.
   — less than 5 shares where a board lot is 10 shares.

5. Odd-lots may be traded in two ways at the option of the broker with the odd-lot order:
  i. by entering into the auction;
  ii. by requiring the registered trader to take the other side at a specified discount or premium from the board lot quotation.

Memberships:

1. Regular Members: 90
2. Associate Members: 0
3. Authorized non-member brokers entitled to split commission privileges.
4. Membership ("Seat") prices:

a.	Price Range	Seats Sold		Price Range	Seats Sold
1935	50,000-29,000	N.A.*	1967	92,000- 65,000	7
1940	20,000-12,000	N.A.	1968	98,000- 98,000	1
1945	60,000-44,000	7	1969	125,000-125,000	14**
1950	40,000-35,000	4	1970	132,500-115,000	4
1955	100,000-75,000	7	1971	95,000- 80,000	2
1960	90,000-90,000	1	1972	90,000- 60,000	7
1965	105,000-90,000	3	1973	90,000- 87,000	3
1966	105,000-90,000	2			

   *N.A. — Not Available.
   **Includes issue of 13 treasury seats.
  b. All-time high — 1929; all-time low — 1924.

Commissions or Fees:

1. The bases for calculating commissions on all orders with values of $20,000 or less:
  a. On shares selling under $14.00: the base rate applicable to the first $20,000 of each order is 2.50% of the value of the order;
  b. On shares selling over $30,000: the base rate applicable to the first

$20,000 of each order is 1.64% of the value of the order;

    c. On shares selling at $14.00 up to and including $30.00: the formula applicable to the first $20,000 for each order is as follows — 0.8875% (0.008875) of the order value plus 22.575c per share.

2. Minimum Charges:

    a. When the total amount involved in an order is less than $10.00 the charge shall be at the member's discretion;

    b. When the total amount involved in an order is $10.00 or more but less than $50.00 the charge shall be discretionary except that a minimum of $2.00 shall be charged, but in connection with such an order in rights, warrants or fractional shares the minimum charge shall be $1.00;

    c. When the total amount involved in an order is $50.00 or more, the minimum charge shall be $5.00 except in connection with such a trade in rights, warrants or fractional shares when the minimum charge shall be $1.00.

3. For calculating commission charges on orders where the value is over $20,000, reference must be made to the actual rate schedule or other material such as the "Manual on New Canadian Commission Rates," which incorporate tapering factors allowed on orders over $20,000.

Historical Background:

1852 Toronto Stock Exchange was founded.

1878 The exchange was incorporated by the Canadian Government.

1934 The exchange and the Standard Stock and Mining Exchange merged to become The Toronto Stock Exchange.

1961 Quotation broadcast of 70 Toronto Stock Exchange listed stocks to Europe initiated, January 30.
Trial period of one year trading privileges by Toronto Stock Exchange members on Mid-West Stock Exchange. No reciprocal privileges for Mid-West members on Toronto Stock Exchange, September 20.

1962 April 23 — Toronto Stock Exchange trading arrangements with Mid-West Exchange finalized. Payment of initiation fee and a net commission fee. Toronto Stock Exchange Curb on unlisted section eliminated after 28 years as an entity of the exchange, August 7. October 23 — Dial Quotation System approved by members.

1963 August 22 — "Z" market inaugurated on Toronto Stock Exchange to allow U. S. investors to trade Canadian stocks between themselves to avoid 15% tax on Americans who buy foreign securities. Toronto Stock Exchange launched its new 19 indices, making a 113 stock Toronto Stock Exchange index, November 4.

1964 Volume at record high: 28.7 million shares, with a value of $21.3 million and representing 19,600 transactions, April 17. August 17 — Share volume of Montreal and Canadian Stock Exchange reached 3,533,900 shares, surpassing Toronto Stock Exchange for first time since 1940's. November 24 — first stock table transmitted via high-speed punched tape from Toronto Stock Exchange to a newspaper published the following day.

1965 January 19 — Category of Registered Trader created. Minimum capital investment of $10,000 must be maintained by partners and directors in their firm. August 17 — Market Surveillance Department established to enforce more stringent disclosure policies in respect to listed companies.

1966 Registered traders required to fill public orders in odd-lots whether it is profitable or not, June 15.

1967 Toronto Stock Exchange suspended "Z" market, because of amendments of U. S. Government pertaining to Interest Equalization Tax Act, July 17.

Toronto Stock Exchange members formally approved new commission rates. All orders of less than $500,000 to be completed on trading floor, August 15.

1968 February 1 — Toronto Stock Exchange Index enlarged by 60% to over 200 stocks in the four major groups, from 108 stocks when index first introduced in 1963.

November 18 — Montreal, Canadian, Toronto and Vancouver Stock Exchanges and Investment Dealers Association agreed in principle to establish a National Contingency Fund. Funds set aside totaled $1.5 million.

November 28 — Companies seeking to list shares after January 1, 1969, in industrial section required to meet higher standards.

1969 Thirteen new seats approved, raising total to 126, January 14.

1971 April 19 — Toronto Stock Exchange implemented negotiated commission rates on portion of any order exceeding $500,000 in value.

1972 Exchange proposed new commission rates to members. Volume discounts incorporated into rate; increased rates on small orders; more equitable with U. S. rates, April 27.

October 12 — Inclusion of Calgary Stock Exchange data on Toronto Stock Exchange ticker and the use of the Toronto Stock Exchange clearing system by Calgary.

December 11 — Board of Governors of Montreal, Canadian, Toronto and Vancouver exchanges announced recommendation of new national commission schedule for members. New rates resulted in 5% aggregate commission increase.

1973 The Toronto Stock Exchange in conjunction with other major exchanges in Canada instituted a new commission rate schedule.

VANCOUVER

VANCOUVER STOCK EXCHANGE

Title: Vancouver Stock Exchange

Address: 536 Howe Street, Vancouver, British Columbia V6C 2E1, Canada

Telephone: (604) 685 - 0331

Teletype: VSE EXEC VCR

Telex: 04 - 55480

Officers:
Chairman: Ernest C. Drake
President: Cyril White
Vice-Chairman: George D. Sherwood
Hon. Secretary-Treasurer: Robert B. E. Samis
Vice-President
Administration: K. Maxwell Fleming
Vice-President
Listings: Christopher C. Caulton
Vice-President
Membership & Compliance: Jack E. Grant

Hours of Business: 7:00 A.M. - 2:00 P.M. Pacific Time (opening coincides with New York Markets.)

Regulatory Laws: (Provincial jurisdiction in Canada)
1. British Columbia Securities Act, 1967
2. Vancouver Stock Exchange Act, 1907

Issues Traded and Volume:

	Listed Issues	Volume (shares)	Dollar Value
1964	350	263,289,883	$219,784,049
1965	371	300,502,360	302,201,821
1966	416	303,930,085	319,017,975
1967	442	351,800,663	337,617,964
1968	442	502,214,258	633,311,634
1969	690	753,727,906	1,147,735,011
1970	745	518,779,497	454,367,618
1971	800	606,552,554	488,440,880
1972	789	906,053,892	784,102,576
1973	812	592,744,506	483,271,028

Unit of Trading:
1. Mines and Oils
   On securities selling under $1.00 .... 500 shares
   On securities selling at $1.00 and over .... 100 shares
   Industrials
   On securities selling at $1.00 .... 500 shares
   On securities selling at $1.00 and under $25.00 .... 100 shares
   On securities selling at $25.00 and under $100.00 .... 25 shares
   On securities selling at $100.00 and over .... 10 shares

   2. Odd-lots are normally handled by a specialist in the company stock; no extra fee or commission is involved. However, the selling price will be lower, and the buying price will be higher, than the price prevailing in the market at the time the order is executed.

Memberships:
1. Regular members: 63
2. More than one seat may be held by a single member. There is no limit to the total number of seats; they may be purchased from an existing member, or from the exchange treasury.

3. Seat prices:

	High	Low		High	Low
1960	$ 8,500	$ 6,180	1967	$35,000	$35,000
1961	10,000	8,500	1968	47,500	35,000
1962	12,000	11,000	1969	65,000	55,000
1963	15,000	12,000	1970	45,000	45,000
1964	20,500	16,000	1971	35,000	35,000
1965	30,000	24,500	1972	30,000	30,000
1966	32,500	32,500	1973	25,000	25,000

Commissions or Fees: Basis for calculating commissions on all orders with values of $20,000 or less:

1. On shares selling under $14.00: Base rate is 2.50% of the value of the order.
2. On shares selling at $14.00 up to and including $30.00: Base rate is 0.8875% of the order value plus 22.575c per share.
3. On shares selling over $30.00: Base rate is 1.64% of the value of the order.

Tapering Schedule for Base Rates:

The following percentages of the basic rates apply for orders over $20,000 in value:

On the first $20,000	—	100% of the base rates
On the next $20,000	—	70% of the base rates
On the next $20,000	—	50% of the base rates
On the remainder	—	30% of the base rates

Historical Background:

1907 Vancouver Stock Exchange incorporated April 25, by special act of British Columbia Legislature. First business transacted, August 1. There were twelve charter members; initial price of a seat was $250.

1965 Present exchange headquarters at 536 Howe Street opened on December 10.

1969 Seat sold for record $65,000 on June 24. Vancouver, Montreal and Toronto stock exchanges and the Investment Dealers Association of Canada, established a National Contingency Fund to assist public clients who may suffer a financial loss due to the failure of a Member.

1970 Expanded trading floor facilities were opened.

1972 Record day's trading volume of 11,413,752 shares (April 10).

1973 Board of Governors enlarged to fourteen with appointment of two Public Governors.

WINNIPEG

WINNIPEG COMMODITY EXCHANGE

Title: The Winnipeg Commodity Exchange
Address: 678 - 167 Lombard Avenue, Winnipeg, Manitoba, R3B 0V7, Canada
Telephone: (204) 942-6401 office; 943-0661 trading floor.

Officers:
President: R. S. Ennis
Chairman: K. B. MacMillan
Vice-Chairman: D. W. Elliott
Vice-Chairman: W. A. Robertson
Secretary-Treasurer: P. K. Huffman

Hours of Business (futures trading):
1. Oats, barley, flaxseed, rapeseed, rye, live beef: 9:30 A.M. - 1:15 P.M.
2. Gold: 8:45 A.M. - 1:00 P.M.

Commodities traded: 7 - Oats, barley, rye, flaxseed, rapeseed, gold, live beef.

Trading Units:
1. Oats, barley, rye, flaxseed, rapeseed: Board lot 5,000 bushels; Job lot 1,000 bushels.
2. Gold: (Standard) — 400 fine ounces troy; (Centum) — 100 fine ounces troy.
3. Live Beef: 25,000 lb.

Delivery Months:
1. Oats, barley, rye: October, December, May, July.
2. Flaxseed: October, November*, December, May, July.
3. a. Thunder Bay rapeseed: October, November*, December, May, July.
   b. Vancouver rapeseed: September, November, January, March, June.
4. Grains futures markets deal with contracts for delivery "in store" at a forward date. Grains are deliverable at Thunder Bay. There is also a futures contract for rapeseed deliverable at Vancouver, alternate delivery points are at Saskatoon, Edmonton or Calgary under certain conditions. Gold futures are traded for delivery in Toronto.
5. Gold: (Standard) — January, April, July, October in each year; (Centum) — February, May, August, November in each year.
6. Live Beef: May, July, September, November, January, March.
7. Live finished beef cattle may be delivered at par to the Alberta Stockyards, Calgary. Delivery to Union Stockyards, Winnipeg at a premium over par of $1.00/cwt. and to the Ontario Stockyards, Toronto at a premium over par of $1.00/cwt.
   Deliveries can be made only on a Tuesday, Wednesday or a Thursday in any week of the contract month, following one day's irrevocable Notice of Intent to Delivery.
   *November is a short delivery month (21/11) for flaxseed and Thunder Bay rapeseed.

Price Quotations — Fluctuation Units:
1. Grains and Oilseeds: Either one-eighth (⅛c) cent per bushel or one-quarter (¼c) cent per bushel, at the trader's discretion. Thus a quotation of 312 ⅜ is $3.12 ⅜ per bushel; or 95 ⅝ is $0.95 ⅝ per bushel.
2. Gold: (Standard and Centum) Not less than one (1c) cent U.S. and not more than five (5c) cents U.S. per fine ounce, at the trader's discretion. Fluctuations of twenty (20c) cents U.S. per fine ounce allowed during first ten (10) minutes of trading session or during fast market conditions.
3. Live Finished Beef Cattle: Two and one-half (2½c) cents per cwt.

Daily Trading Limits:

1. Oats 8 cents, barley 10 cents, rye 15 cents, flaxseed 30 cents and rapeseed 20 cents per bushel, up or down from the previous (clearing) closing price; or, when trading in a new futures month is authorized, 8 cents, 10 cents, 15 cents, 30 cents and 20 cents, respectively, up or down from the price of the board lot quotation of the first actual trade for the month.
2. Gold: (Standard and Centum) — $5.00 per fine ounce up or down from the previous (clearing) closing price, except that there will be no such limit on the final day of trading.
3. Live Beef: $1.50 per cwt., up or down from the previous (clearing) closing price.

Contract Deliverable Grades:

1. Oats: No. 2 Canada Western Oats with the privilege of delivering:
   a. Higher grade Oats;
   b. Extra No. 3 Canada Western Oats at a discount of 3 cents per bushel;
   c. No. 3 Canada Western Oats at a discount of 3 cents per bushel;
   d. Extra No. 1 Feed Oats at a discount of 3 cents per bushel;
   e. No. 1 Feed Oats at a discount of 5 cents per bushel.
2. Barley: No. 1 Canada Western Six-Row Barley; or No. 1 Canada Western Two-Row Barley; with the privilege of delivering:
   a. No. 2 Canada Western Two-Row Barley at a discount of 3 cents per bushel;
   b. No. 2 Canada Western Six-Row Barley at a discount of 3 cents per bushel;
   c. No. 1 Feed Barley at a discount of 4 cents per bushel;
   d. No. 2 Feed Barley at a discount of 8 cents per bushel.
3. Flaxseed: No. 1 Canada Western Flaxseed with the privilege of delivering: No. 2 Canada Western Flaxseed at a discount of 5 cents per bushel.
4. Rapeseed: No. 1 Canada Rapeseed, with the privilege of delivering: No. 2 Canada Rapeseed at a discount of 15 cents per bushel.
5. Rye: No. 1 Canada Western Rye or No. 2 Canada Western Rye with the privilege of delivering: No. 3 Canada Western Rye at a discount of 5c per bushel.
6. Gold: (Standard and Centum)
   a. Minimum 995 parts per 1,000 fine gold.
   b. Bars shall:
      1. be serially numbered;
      2. be stamped by a Melter and Assayer declared acceptable for good delivery on the London Gold Market.
   c. 1. (Standard): — each bar shall conform in all respects as to size and weight to requirements for good delivery on the London Gold Market as at the date of delivery — amount of gold to be delivered by an issuing Bank on the surrender of a gold certificate shall be the amount indicated on the certificate plus or minus not more than 2%.
      2. (Centum): — amount of gold to be delivered by an issuing Bank on the surrender of a gold certificate shall be the amount indicated on the certificate plus or minus not more than 5%.

7. Live Finished Beef Cattle: Dry fed choice quality steers appraised to grade "Canada A-1 Beef Carcasses", and "Canada A-2 Beef Carcasses", minimum yield, cold weight 57% with the privilege of delivering:
   a. up to six (6) steers per contract "Canada A-3 Beef Carcasses", at a discount of 1½c per lb.;
   b. steers appraised to yield less than 57% cold weight at a discount of ¼c per lb. for each ½% below 57%.
   c. steers appraised to yield 58% or more, cold weight, shall be at a premium of ¼c per lb. for each ½% over 57½%.

Discounts and premiums shall be computed basis the number of head of such steers times the average weight of the lot.

(Addition at presstime: During August 1974, the exchange anticipates changing oats and barley contracts to feed oats and feed barley contracts, as well as adding a feed wheat contract and an eastern corn contract.)

Memberships: The exchange has 323 members; holding 340 seats; 112 companies are registered for trading privileges.

Commissions on Futures Contracts: Minimum non-member commission rates.
   1. Oats, Barley, Rye:
      a. Regular—$20.00 per 5,000 bushel board lot or $4.50 per 1,000 bushel job lot, for buying and selling (round turn).
      b. Day Trades—$12.50 per board lot, or $2.50 per 1,000 bushel job lot, round turn.
      c. Spreads—$25.00 per board lot, or $5.00 per 1,000 bushel job lot, all four sides.
   2. Flaxseed and Rapeseed:
      a. Regular—$25.00 per 5,000 bushel board lot, or $5.50 per 1,000 bushel job lot, round turn.
      b. Day Trades—$17.50 per board lot, or $3.50 per 1,000 bushel job lot, round turn.
      c. Spreads—$35.00 on board lots, or $7.00 on 1,000 bushel job lots, all four sides.
   3. Gold: per unit of trade.

	(Standard) (Centum)
a. Regular	$75.-U.S.-$35. round turn
b. Day Trades	$50.-U.S.-$25. round turn
c. Intra-Market Spread	$50.-U.S.-$25. ea. round turn
d. Making Delivery	$15-U.S.-$10. in addition
e. Receiving Delivery	$20.-U.S.-$15. to the above
f. Same Day Transfer from Executing Clearing Member to Another Clearing Member	$10-U.S.-$ 5 charge extra to brokerage

   4. Live Beef:
      a. Regular—$25.00 per contract, round turn.
      b. Day Trades—$17.00 per contract, round turn.
      c. Spreading—$25.00 per contract, all four sides.

Margins:

1. Oats, barley, rye, flaxseed, rapeseed: The Exchange's By-laws do not specify minimum rates of customer's margins. Therefore, the amount of margins to be deposited by the customer with the member carrying his account is left to the member's discretion, and may depend upon prevailing market conditions.
2. Gold:
   a. (Standard)

	Initial	Maintenance
Regular	$6,000. - U.S. -	$4,000.
Spread (each side)	$1,200. - U.S. -	$ 800.
Hedge	$3,000. - U.S. -	$2,000.

   b. (Centum)

	Initial	Maintenance
Regular	$2,000. - U.S. -	$1,500.
Spread (each side)	$ 500. - U.S. -	$ 400.
Hedge	$1,000. - U.S. -	$ 750.

3. Live Beef: Minimum initial margin to be maintained is $300 per contract. Maintenance level is $200 per contract.

The above are subject to amendment by the Board of Governors. The member carrying a customer's account may call for higher rates at his discretion.

Historical Background:

1883 An unsuccessful attempt was made to organize a grain and provision exchange.

1887 The Winnipeg Grain & Produce Exchange was organized November 24; operations began in December. The Exchange was incorporated in 1891.

1889 A call market, forerunner of the modern futures market, was established.

1903 Wheat futures market established.

1904 Oats and flaxseed futures markets established.

1908 Exchange reorganized as The Winnipeg Grain Exchange, a voluntary, unincorporated, non-profit association; it moved to its present location on Lombard Avenue.

1913 Barley futures introduced.

1917 Wheat futures trading suspended due to World War I. Rye futures market established.

1920 Wheat market reestablished.

1935 Government appointed a Wheat Board to provide a guaranteed minimum support price for producers.

1943 Wheat trading suspended due to World War II.

1963 Trading began in Vancouver rapeseed futures.

1967 Live beef futures commenced trading.

1968 Facilities provided for trading in Maritime potato futures.

1970 A Thunder Bay rapeseed contract was introduced.

1971 Maritime potato futures withdrawn.

1972 New title adopted: The Winnipeg Commodity Exchange.
     Gold Futures (Standard 400 ounce Contract) Market established.

1974 Centum (100 ounce) Gold Futures Contract established.

WINNIPEG STOCK EXCHANGE

Title: The Winnipeg Stock Exchange

Address: 420 - 167 Lombard Avenue, Winnipeg, Manitoba R3B OT7, Canada

Telephone: (204) 942 - 4831

Officers:
President: R. W. Richards
Vice-President: A. R. Maxwell
Secretary-Treasurer: F. W. Buchanan

Hours of Business (trading):
1. 10:00 A.M. - 12:00 noon (shares listed solely on the Winnipeg Stock Exchange).
2. 10:00 A.M. - 4:00 P.M. (shares interlisted with other Canadian exchanges).

Regulatory Laws: Brokers in Manitoba are licensed by the Manitoba Securities Commission which administers the Manitoba Securities Act. All brokers conducting a general securities business within the Province of Manitoba are members of the Winnipeg Stock Exchange and as such, are governed by the by-laws, rules and regulations of the exchange, in addition to the provisions of the Securities Act.

Issues Traded and Volume:
1. No. of issues: not available.
2. Volume:

1960	488,037	1967	2,440,298
1961	1,266,137	1968	4,615,824
1962	499,987	1969	4,745,947
1963	461,594	1970	865,821
1964	766,481	1971	1,314,216
1965	2,255,598	1972	521,025
1966	3,023,861	1973	1,457,706

3. The exchange does not operate a clearing house. Selling members make delivery to the office of the buyer on the day of settlement.

Unit of Trading:
1. The same as the Toronto Stock Exchange.
2. Odd-lots are traded the same as board-lots; no extra fee or commission is involved for buying or selling.
3. There are no open trading sessions, with all members present, such as on other exchanges. Rather, all trades are executed by telephone, cleared by the exchange and reported back to the brokers concerned.

Memberships:
1. Shareholder Members: 20. They have full trading privileges. Memberships are registered in the name of the individual; the firm he represents is registered as a member firm.
2. Non-shareholder Members: 3. They have no trading privileges. Their transactions on the exchange are effected through a member, who charges one-half commission rates.
3. Seats (memberships) have ranged in price from $300 to $1,000 over the past several years.

Commissions or Fees: Same as the Toronto Stock Exchange.

Historial Background:
1903 The Winnipeg Stock Exchange was incorporated under the laws of the Province of Manitoba in March.

CEYLON

See Sri Lanka

CHILE

SANTIAGO

SANTIAGO STOCK EXCHANGE

Title: Bolsa de Comercio

Address: Bandera 63, Santiago, Chile

Telephone: 82001 to 82009

Teletype: B. Comercio

Cable Address: Casilla 123-D, Santiago, Chile

Officers: Board of Administration:
President: Eugenio Blanco Ruiz
Directors:
Manuel Jose Ureta M.   Leonidas Larrain Vial
Alfredo Larrain G.   Luis Felipe Mujica M.
Alamiro Valdes C.   Jaime Vial Rozas
Manager: Carlos Carvallo Stagg
Treasurer: Sergio Araya B.
Analyst: Jorge Marty Berthelon

Hours of Business: 10:30 A.M. - 1:00 P.M. (weekdays)

Regulatory Laws:
1. Codigo de Comercio (Trade Code)
2. DFL. 251 de Mayo de 1931 (Code for incorporated enterprises, insurance companies, stock exchanges)
3. Reglamento No. 4705 (Ordinance for incorporated enterprises and securities trading)

Issues Traded and Volume:

	Listed Issues	Value of Shs. Traded*		Listed Issues	Value of Shs. Traded*
1960	347	27,201.0	1967	345	57,035.2
1961	353	28,068.0	1968	354	80,173.5
1962	334	51,296.3	1969	352	126,528.2
1963	339	91,325.6	1970	353	162,587.7
1964	374	101,320.0	1971	343	81,621.4
1965	375	106,740.6	1972	334	145,411.2
1966	334	62,711.3	1973	338	2,217,251.3

*Escudos (000).

Unit of Trading:

1. Usually 100 shares. However, there are special cases where the accepted trading unit, or "Board Lot" is one share: Bolsa de Comercio, Bolsa de Corredores, Club Hipico, Sporting Club and Hipodromo de Chile. Three shares is the trading unit for Club de Polo and Club de Golf.
2. Odd-lots are traded informally; no extra fee or commission is involved.

Memberships: Regular Members:

1. Actual membership: 43 brokerage firms.
2. Maximum allowable: 60 brokerage firms.
3. Membership Prices:

	Value of 1 Share*		Value of 1 share*
1960	16,000	1967	30,000
1961	16,000	1968	60,000
1962	16,050	1969	60,000
1963	35,000	1970	60,000
1964	35,000	1971	50,000
1965	40,000	1972	400,000
1966	40,000	1973	5,000,000

*Escudos

Commissions or Fees:

1. Broker's commission: 2% above market value
2. Stock fees: 1% above market value
3. Taxes:
   a. 20% above broker's commission and stock fees (impuesto de prestacion de servicios)
   b. 0.75% above market value (impuesto de transferencia; paid only by the buyer).

Historical Background:

1893 La Bolsa de Comercio was established in November.
1973-74 Trading volume expanded sharply under a free economy. The value of shares traded in January 1974 was more than 1 billion escudos.

VALPARAISO

VALPARAISO STOCK EXCHANGE

Name: Valparaiso Stock Exchange
Address: Valparaiso, Chile

CHINA

See Republic of China

DENMARK

COPENHAGEN

COPENHAGEN STOCK EXCHANGE

Title: Københavns Fondsbørs (Copenhagen Stock Exchange)
Address: Nikolaj Plads 6, 1067 Copenhagen K., Denmark
Telephone: (01) 121985 (Administration and information)
Telex: 16496 COSTEX DK.
Officers:
   Chairman (Management Committee): J. Kobbernagel
   Director: Børschef Erik Ravn
   Information Officer and Secretary: Torben Krogh
Hours of Business:
   Main Exchange—Bonds: 10:30 A.M. - approx. 1:00 P.M. (weekdays)
      Shares: 10:30 A.M. - approx. 11:30 A.M. (weekdays)
      To be quoted on this Exchange a corporation's share capital must be at least
      5 million Dkr.
   After Exchange—A quotation session is held at approx. 11:30 A.M. on week-
      days, after the closing of the Main Exchange.
      Shares may be quoted on the After Exchange if the share capital of the
      corporation is at least 1 million Dkr.
Regulatory Laws: The Copenhagen Stock Exchange Act (June 7th, 1972), The
   Copenhagen Stock Exchange Order (November 16th, 1972)

Issues Traded and Turnover:
1. No Issues Traded:
   a. Bonds: 1,345 (1973), 1,322 (1972)
      Shares: Main Exchange—148 (1973), 144 (1972)
              After Exchange—192 (1973), 197 (1972)
   b. Apart from a more or less private organized market for private mortgage bonds, there are no organized markets for unlisted or other issues, according to a spokesman for the Exchange.
2. Turnover: (1,000 Dkr. nominal value)
   Bonds: 7,419,200 (1973), 6,909,081 (1972)
   Shares: Main Exchange—361,870 (1973), 204,115 (1972)
           After Exchange—16,282 (1973)
3. Volume: Main Exchange
   a. Bonds—Dkr. (000)

1964	33,015,495	1969	72,971,501
1965	39,606,910	1970	83,118,039
1966	45,216,102	1971	96,572,227
1967	52,077,523	1972	112,867,810
1968	60,641,973	1973	136,129,020

   b. Shares

1964	2,169,788	1969	3,668,869
1965	2,499,633	1970	4,120,305
1966	2,766,130	1971	4,449,947
1967	2,938,958	1972	4,969,998
1968	3,214,976	1973	6,745,976

Unit of Trading:
1. Bonds: Main Exchange—20,000 Dkr. (nominal value)
   Shares: Main Exchange—4,000 Dkr. (nominal value)
           After Exchange—2,000 Dkr. (nominal value)
2. Odd-lot orders are executed on the After Exchange during the course of regular trading.

Memberships:
1. Regular Members: 33 memberships, divided among 24 firms.
2. Associated Members: There are no such memberships in the American sense of the term. However, the majority of regular members have co-partners or clerks, who are legally empowered to participate in quotations on the member's behalf and assume his responsibilities.
3. Memberships are granted only by the Minister of Commerce and there are no direct membership prices. Among the qualifications required for membership, the applicant must have insurance to cover a possible loss of 100,000 Dkr. and a minimum capital of 250,000 Dkr. Ten percent of the exchange's overall annual budget is charged to members to offset operating and other expenses. Therefore, only a negligible amount is paid for an actual seat.

Commissions or Fees:
Main Exchange: Bonds—15% of the purchase price.
               Shares—5% of the purchase price.
After Exchange: Shares—1% of the purchase price.
               These same rates apply also to odd-lots.

Profile Data

Historical Background:

1684 First traces of the Copenhagen Stock Exchange in the form of written rules for trading in stocks.

1787 The King decreed regulations for trading on two weekdays.

1817 Merchant's Guild took over the supervision of quotations.

1870 Stock Exchange became independent and self-governing. Stock Exchange organized through cooperation between brokers and the Merchant's Guild.

1919 First Copenhagen Stock Exchange Act.

1930 Second Copenhagen Stock Exchange Act.

1967 Copenhagen Stock Exchange Index introduced.

1969 Weekly indices of the effective interest rate on bonds introduced.

1972 Highest all-time volume in bonds: 97 million Dkr. nominal value. Membership in the EEC, affirmed by national referendum, initiated boom in the stock market. Third Copenhagen Stock Exchange Act.

1974 Removal of the Exchange from its almost 300 year-old domicile to new and modern headquarters in the center of Copenhagen.

DOMINICAN REPUBLIC

At the present time there is no stock exchange in the Dominican Republic. Law No. 3553 (7564 G.O.) dated May 15, 1953, is known as the Organic Law of the National Stock Exchange and provides regulation for such activities in the event that one or more stock exchanges should be established.

FINLAND

HELSINKI

HELSINKI STOCK EXCHANGE

Title: Helsingin Arvopaperiporssi (The Helsinki Stock Exchange)

Address: Fabianinkatu 14, 00100 Helsinki, 10, Finland

Telephone: 627116   629688

Officers:
Chairman: Raimo Ilaskivi
Deputy Chairmen:
Tapani Mantysaari
Matti Tolonen

Hours of Business: 9:45 A.M. - 11:30 A.M. (approx.)

Regulatory Laws: Parliament has never passed an act governing the activities of the Helsinki Stock Exchange. The exchange is controlled and administered by a 12-member Stock Exchange Committee. The committee decides whether new bonds and securities will be listed; it also appoints members of the exchange.

Issues Traded and Volume:

1. Listed Issues: about 100, consisting of 46 company shares; 52 bonds; 4 debentures. Shares may not be bought on margin.

Share Capital of listed companies in marks (000,000,000)

	1950	1960	1970	1973
Banks	34.71	82.50	298.50	648.75
Insurance companies	1.82	13.25	27.45	51.60
Trade	3.18	43.88	85.75	179.91
Industrial Companies	125.44	487.56	1,200.93	1,615.50
Total	165.15	627.19	1,612.63	2,495.76

2. Volume:

Volume in marks (000,000,000)

	1965	1970	1971	1972	1973
Shares	24.22	53.16	66.10	109.47	204.00
Subscription Rights	4.81	9.24	5.64	36.54	61.37
Bonds	5.26	12.94	18.35	16.50	19.50
Debentures	0.54	1.93	2.40	4.38	6.17
	34.83	77.27	92.49	166.89	291.04

Unit of Trading:

1. One to five shares, depending upon value.
2. Odd-lots are traded during the after-session, or period of "free dealing," and not during the price determination period, which precedes it. No extra fee or commission is charged for odd-lots.
3. The Helsinki Stock Exchange and the Stockholm Stock Exchange are "silent" exchanges. Brokers have their own desks with two sets of numbered buttons: one for buying, one for selling. The buttons connect with a panel which dominates the entire exchange hall. The panel lights up when a button is pushed, indicating that a broker is ready to trade. The panel identifies the broker and indicates the priority of bids or offers in different colors. After the list has been "called," there is a period of "free dealing," when the brokers bargain within the quotation limits and give written notice of their transactions to the exchange manager.

Memberships:

1. Regular Members: 12 members pay an entrance fee of 1,200 marks and a stock exchange fee for each transaction effected there.
2. Associated, or Outside Brokers: They pay an entrance fee of 240 marks and an annual subscription of 30 marks.

Commissions or Fees: One percent for shares and on bonds of the Second Compensation Loan. One-half percent for other bonds. Stamp tax for shares is one percent and is split between buyer and seller.

Historical Background:
- **1862**   Leading merchants met to discuss the formation of a stock exchange and a stock exchange association. The first meetings were held Wednesdays and Saturdays in the "House of the Nobility."
- **1883**   The Senate gave permission to hold stock exchange auctions.
- **1911**   Dissatisfaction with stock exchange auctions led to reviving the idea of organizing a stock exchange.
- **1912**   A committee completed its proposals for rules and regulations, which formed the basis for the Helsinki Stock Exchange.
- **1935**   An electromechanical system for signaling bids and offers was introduced.
- **1936**   The last amendment to the Stock Exchange Rules was made.
- **1939-40**   The exchange was closed during the Winter War.
- **1971**   A ten percent limit on daily quotations, that came into being during the post-war inflationary boom, was removed.

FRANCE

THE STOCK EXCHANGES OF FRANCE

The Paris Bourse is the father, the grandfather, even the great-great-grandfather of all French stock exchanges. There are six provincial exchanges (Bordeaux, Lille, Lyon, Marseille, Nancy, Nantes), but they account for only 3% of total trading volume.

France has several markets "of national interest" which are not commodity exchanges for agricultural products. The principal markets which deal in futures contracts are located in Le Havre and Paris.

BORDEAUX

BORDEAUX STOCK EXCHANGE

Title: Bourse des Valeurs de Bordeaux
Address: 13, Palais de la Bourse, 33000 Bordeaux, France
Telephone: 15/56 44.70.91. - 15/56 44.70.92
President Delegate: Pierre Fonade

LE HAVRE

LE HAVRE COMMODITY EXCHANGE

Title: Bourse de Commerce du Havre

Address: Chambre de Commerce et d'Industrie du Havre Palais de la Bourse, 76 067, Le Havre Cedex, France.

Telephone: (35) 42 - 68 - 67

Officers:
President of the Trade Syndicate of Coffee and Spices in Havre: J. Dumont
President of the Syndicate of Authorized Coffee Brokers in Havre: R. Le Fur
President of the Association of Recognized Commission Agents associated with the Paris Board of Trade: G. Maurer
President of the Technical Committee, International Market for Robusta Coffee of Paris and Havre: G. Wiart
Vice-president of the Technical Committee, International Market for Robusta Coffee of Paris and Havre: J. Dumont

Hours of Business: Quotations periods are determined by the Technical Committee. Business is conducted by open outcry in trading rings, or circles.

Regulatory Laws:
1. Articles 1 to 20 and 25 to 30 of the General Ordinance — Market Regulations of the Paris Board of Trade.
2. General Ordinance of Futures Markets of the Bourse de Commerce du Havre.
3. Rules of the Technical Committee of the International Market for Robusta Coffee of Paris and Havre.

Basic Grade Deliverable:
1. Coffee originating from the Ivory Coast Republic, comprising no more than 60 imperfections for each 300 gram sample, where the size of the beans corresponds with 14 screen coffee with a weight allowance of 8%. The Technical Committee determines the variations that will be applied to different qualities and sources.
2. Admission requirements:
   a. good quality, marketable and with a natural taste;
   b. compliance with rules of the Committee, respecting delivery outlets;
   c. packaging in original bags and of good quality with no spoilage;
   d. storage under supervision of customs in a warehouse specified by the Committee.

Contract Unit: Ten Metric tons.

Delivery Points: Marseille, Bordeaux, Le Havre, Rotterdam, Amsterdam. The addition of others depends upon the Technical Committee.

Price Quotations:
1. Trading is conducted for delivery during the current month and fourteen succeeding months.
2. Quotations are based on a scale of one franc per 100 kilograms.

3. Margins, fixed by the Technical Committee, are based on closing quotations each day.

Daily Trading Limits: 15 francs per 100 kilograms, based on margin reports of the preceding day.

Commissions (buying and selling):
1. 1.60 francs per 100 kilos when the price equals or exceeds 361 francs, but is less or equal to 440 francs.

   2.40 francs for 100 kilos when the price equals or exceeds 441 francs, but is less or equal to 520 francs.
2. a. The commission increases by 40 francs for any part of 80 francs above 521 francs;

   b. Commissions are reduced by 50% for Day Trades (buying — selling the same day).
3. Members are entitled to a 50% reduction on commissions.

Fees:
1. Members pay an admission fee of 2,500 francs and an annual assessment of 500 francs.
2. A recording fee of 18 francs (for each purchase or sale) is paid to the Fund for Payment of Merchandise in Havre, or to the Fund for the Sale of Merchandise in Paris.

Historical Background:
1786 The Bourse was founded in October. Business was transacted for one hour daily: 12:00 noon to 1:00 P.M.

1793 Operations were suspended by a decree of June 25 and were not resumed openly until September 28, 1880.

1862 The Bourse was demolished to accommodate an enlargement of the Harbor.

1880 The second Bourse, bearing the same title, was inaugurated September 29. Markets were operated in coffee, cocoa, cotton, grain and other merchandise until September 1939.

1944 The Bourse was destroyed during an air raid on September 4.

1954 The cornerstone for the third Bourse was laid June 26.

1957 Offices of the Chamber of Commerce were installed July 22.

1958 A market in coffee futures opened, June 2.

1959 The Bourse was inaugurated officially, July 25.

1966 A new futures market for Robusta Coffee opened on April 21, with the agreement of the Chamber of Commerce and under a ruling ratified by the Minister of Finance and Economic Affairs.

1972 The markets in Robusta Coffee in Paris and Havre merged on December 14 to become the "Marché International des Cafes Robusto de Paris et du Havre." From this date until November 30, 1973 trading totaled 16,840 tons.

LILLE

LILLE STOCK EXCHANGE

Title: Bourse des Valeurs de Lille
Address: 38, rue Thiers, 59000 Lille, France
Telephone: 16/20 57.07.75
President Delegate: Bernard Boone

LYON

LYON STOCK EXCHANGE

Title: Bourse des Valeurs de Lyon
Address: Palais du Commerce, Place de la Bourse, 69289 Lyon Cedex 1, France
Telephone: 15/78 42.54.71 - 15/78 42.54.72
President Delegate: Andre Krucker

MARSEILLE

MARSEILLE STOCK EXCHANGE

Title: Bourse des Valeurs de Marseille
Address: Compagnie des Agents de Change, Palais de la Bourse, 13215 Marseille Cedex 1, France
Telephone: 15/91 39.70.32

NANCY

NANCY STOCK EXCHANGE

Title: Bourse des Valeurs de Nancy
Address: Chambre de Commerce et d'Industrie, 40, rue Henri Poincare, 54000 Nancy, France
Telephone: 15/28 52.85.15
President Delegate: Roger Kempf

NANTES

NANTES STOCK EXCHANGE

Title: Bourse des Valeurs de Nantes

Address: Palais de la Bourse, 44000 Nantes, France

PARIS

PARIS COMMODITY EXCHANGE

Title: La Bourse de Commerce de Paris

Address: 2, rue de Viarmes, 75040 Paris Cedex 01, France

Telephone: 233 - 44 - 01

Telex: PUB CCIP Paris 68 522

Officers:

1. Management: M. Furet, Head of the Department of the Bourse de Commerce de Paris, Chambre de Commerce et d'Industrie de Paris 27, avenue de Friedland 75382 Paris Cedex 08 (Tel. 720 - 52 - 00)
2. Information: Secretary: Mme. Argyris (Tel. 720 - 52 - 00)
3. Controller of Regulated Markets: M. Aubert, 2, rue de Viarmes, 75040 Paris Cedex 01 (Tel. 231 - 00 - 67)
4. Property and Locations of Offices and Departments: Mme. Coulet, 140, boulevard Haussmann 75008 Paris (Tel. 227 - 98 - 10)
5. Communications Center: M. Matran (Tel. 233 - 44 - 01)
6. Protection and Maintenance: M. Lesieur

Hours of Business:

1. Every weekday, except national holidays. Trading hours are fixed by the Technical Committee for each commodity, which also determines the months to be quoted.
2. Quotations:

	Opening	Intermediate	Second	Closing
Cocoa	10:00 A.M.	11:45 A.M.	2:45 P.M.	4:30 P.M.
Sugar	10:40 A.M.	12:30 P.M.	2:30 P.M.	5:10 P.M.
Coffee	Le Havre:	Paris:	Le Havre:	Paris:
	10:20 A.M.	12:05 P.M.	2:30 P.M.	5:10 P.M.

Regulatory Laws:

1. The Law of August 9, 1950 relating to the organization of the Company of Brokers of the Commercial Exchange of Paris.
   a. By-law of September 16, 1968 — general regulations;
   b. By-law of October 16, 1969 — statutes.
2. The Bourse is supervised and administered by the "Commission Adminis-

trative de la Bourse de Commerce et des Marches," and governed by the regulations of the terminal markets and the Clearing House.

Commodity Markets of France:

1. Cash Markets. They exist in Paris and in the main cities for cereals, meals, sugar, cocoa, coffee; hides and skins (in Paris only). Cash markets are expected soon for barley, oats, potatoes, silver.
2. Futures Markets:
   a. Commodity Exchange of Lille-Roubaix-Tourcoing: combed wool.
   b. Commodity Exchange of Le Havre: international market for "Robusta" coffee; operates conjunctively with Paris.
   c. Commodity Exchange of Paris:
      1. international market for cocoa in broad bean:
      2. international market for white sugar;
      3. international market for "Robusta" coffee; operates conjunctively with Le Havre.
      4. linseed oil and peanut meal futures markets and international futures markets for soymeal are under reorganization.
      5. studies are being made for opening a domestic market for white sugar.

Paris Futures:

1. Cocoa in broad bean: A very active market. Cocoa price changes are naturally based upon variable crop conditions. In fact, it is very difficult to know in advance the importance of a crop, as seasonal influences are always changing. The majority of African cocoa is harvested between October and February; Brazilian cocoa comes on the market during an intermediate period, although it cannot completely take the place of West African cocoa.

   Price fluctuations affect greatly the users of cocoa, especially the chocolate business; they try to buy judiciously when prices are low. That is why the majority of cocoa users, in trying to cover their requirements in advance, resort to arbitrage in the Paris market. In order to minimize the price risks involved they make equal, but opposing commitments in the cash and futures markets, i.e. they sell futures against a purchase of spots, or vice versa. This practice, known as "hedging," is applied in some form to virtually all commodities today.

Basis of the Market: To be admitted to the Paris market, cocoa (in broad bean) must be

1. of sound, fair and marketable quality; no unpleasant taste or odor;
2. must not contain more than 5% defective beans for "good" quality, nor more than 10% for "fair" quality;
3. packed in original sacks, in good condition;
4. stored in customs warehouses, agreed upon by the Technical Committee, in France, or abroad;
5. ready for delivery through the usual clearing house channels.

Unit of Trading:
1. the contract unit is 10 metric tons.
2. prices are quoted in francs and centimes on a minimum scale of 0.50F.
3. the maximum fluctuation during a call is 45F per 100 kilograms, up or down, scaled in relation to margin prices set during the preceding day. However, this maximum can be attained only in steps of 15F.

Commissions: Per 100 kilograms for buying and selling.

Price	Commissions
at or below 350F	1.50F
350.50F to 450F	2.00F
450.50F to 550F	2.50F
and so on pro rata	

1. White Sugar: The international market reestablished in 1964 (operations were suspended in 1939), succeeded a market that began in Paris, July 1881. This international market existing in white sugar today is the only one in the world; the New York market trades only in cane sugar originating from American, African, and Asian countries, and prices are quoted at parity FOB Grand Caribbean. The London market trades in cane sugar originating from Commonwealth countries and prices are quoted CAF United Kingdom. On the Paris market prices are quoted in francs per metric ton net FOB packed. FOB represents the best common price measure. It is outside of all custom's authority, and it enables business to be transacted internationally from all sources and to all destinations. Sugar from any source is admissible. This pliability makes the market truly international. Thus, there is no need for anxiety about the cash market in France for beet, cane or pure sugar; the futures market involves international prices.

    To help the market to function more smoothly and to widen its international scope, a Number 2 Contract was introduced in 1966. This authorized a form of FOB delivery which by-passed dealings with a bonded warehouse and proved very popular. The market serves as a reference for business and other contracts in many countries.

Basis of the Market: white beet or cane crystal sugar of any origin —
1. dry, of regular size grains, free running;
2. of sound, fair and marketable quality;
3. polarization minimum 99.7°;
4. humidity maximum 0.08%;
5. the color shall not be below type color No. 6 of the Brunswick Institute for agricultural technology and the sugar industry.

Unit of Trading:
1. the contract unit is 50 metric tons. Every transaction must be registered with the Clearing House;
2. quotations move in steps of one franc per ton;
3. the maximum fluctuation allowed during a call is scaled in relation to the prices fixed during the previous calls as an obligatory basis for the calling of margins:

Price per ton	Maximum fluctuation
at or below 250 Frs.	25 Frs.
from 251 to 450 Frs.	35 Frs.

from 451 to 650 Frs.	55 Frs.
from 651 to 850 Frs.	75 Frs.
from 851 to 1,050 Frs.	95 Frs.
from 1,051 to 1,250 Frs.	115 Frs.
and so on pro rata	

Commissions: Per metric ton net for purchase and resale, or for sale and re-purchase.

Price per ton	Commision
at or below 450 Frs.	5 Frs.
from 451 to 850 Frs.	6 Frs.
from 851 to 1,250 Frs.	7 Frs.
from 1,251 to 1,650 Frs.	8 Frs.
and so on pro rata	

1. In case of supply against delivery order (No. 1 Contract), or against delivery note (No. 2 Contract), a handling commission is also payable — calculated at the rate of 0.25% of the selling price and 0.25% of the buying price.
    a. "Robusta" Coffee:
        1. Basic Grade Deliverable:
        Coffee originating from the Ivory Coast Republic, comprising no more than 60 imperfections for each 300 gram sample and where the size of the beans correspond to 14 screen coffee with a weight allowance of 8%. The Technical Committee of the Paris Commodity Exchange determines the variations that will be applied to different qualities and sources.

Admission requirements:
    a. good quality, marketable and with a natural taste;
    b. complies with rules of the committee, respecting delivery outlets;
    c. packed in original bags and is of good quality with no spoilage;
    d. stored under supervision of customs in a warehouse specified by the committee.

2. Contract unit: 10 metric tons.
3. Delivery points: Marseille, Bordeaux, Le Havre, Rotterdam, Amsterdam. Others may be added at the committee's discretion.
4. Price quotations:
    a. Trading is conducted for delivery fourteen months ahead, including the current month;
    b. Quotations are based on a scale of one franc per 100 kilograms;
    c. Margins, fixed by the technical committee, are based on closing price quotations each day.
5. Daily trading limit: 15 francs per 100 kilograms, scaled in relation to margin prices set during the preceding day.
6. Commissions (buying and selling):
    a. 1.60 francs per 100 kilos when the price is less or equal to 360 francs;
    b. 2.00 francs for 100 kilos when the price equals or exceeds 361 francs, but is less or equal to 440 francs.
    c. 2.40 francs for 100 kilos when the price equals or exceeds 441 francs, but is less or equal to 520 francs.

Profile Data

d. 1. the commission increases by 40 francs for any portion of 80 francs above 521 francs.
   2. commissions for "day trading" are reduced by 50%.
e. Members are entitled to a 50% reduction in commissions.
7. Fees:
   Professional members pay an admission fee of 2,500 francs and an annual assessment of 500 francs.

Memberships: There are 36 members of the "Compagnie des Commissionnaires Agrees Pres la Bourse de Commerce de Paris."

Historical Background:
1961 Markets in flax and linseed oil were instituted, April 26.
1963 The cocoa market in the broad bean was opened, February 11.
1964 The international market in white sugar was inaugurated, May 28, based on a Number 1 contract: a Number 2 contract was authorized July 1, 1966.
1967 The international market in soya beans was opened, March 15.
1972 The international market for "Robusta" coffee of Paris and Le Havre opened on December 14.

Volume of Business (tons)

	Cocoa	Sugar	Coffee
1969	336,040	243,500	——
1970	787,310	292,950	——
1971	776,080	656,100	——
1972	613,060	4,415,400	790*
1973	1,143,840	7,074,550	17,270

*December only

PARIS STOCK EXCHANGE

Title: Bourse de Paris (Compagnie des Agents de Change)

Address: 4, place de la Bourse, 75080 PARIS CEDEX 02, France.

Telephone: 231 - 92 - 00

Telex: 23 844

Cable Address: SYNAGEN

Syndic (President of Stock Exchange Committee): Yves Meunier

Affiliated Exchanges: Apart from the Paris Stock Exchange, there are six provincial exchanges in France: Bordeaux, Lille, Lyon, Marseille, Nancy, Nantes, Securities of national importance and foreign issues are traded in Paris. Securities of local importance are traded on the nearest provincial exchange. 98.5 percent of the trading volume for all of France is concentrated on the Paris Bourse.
Provincial exchanges:
1. Bourse des Valeurs de Bordeaux
   Secretariat: 13, Palais de la Bourse, 33000 Bordeaux

Telephone: 15/56 44-70-91; 15/56 44-70-92
President Delegate: Pierre Fonade
Trading volume:

1964	44,934	1969	47,114
1965	27,780	1970	60,081
1966	21,527	1971	49,969
1967	27,525	1972	110,352
1968	37,618	1973	159,677

2. Bourse des Valeurs de Lille
   Secretariat: 38, rue Thiers, 59000 Lille
   Telephone: 16/20 57-07-75
   President Delegate: Bernard Boone
   Trading volume: Value of securities traded (000 francs)

1964	42,437	1969	78,051
1965	38,315	1970	67,659
1966	34,308	1971	126,822
1967	38,134	1972	184,320
1968	67,352	1973	134,707

3. Bourse des Valeurs de Lyon
   Secretariat: Palais du Commerce, Place de la Bourse, 69289 Lyon Cedex 1
   Telephone: 15/78 42-54-71; 15/78 42-54-72
   President Delegate: André Krucker
   Trading volume: Value of securities traded (000 francs)

1964	112,390	1969	204,226
1965	90,185	1970	133,349
1966	107,261	1971	122,368
1967	99,006	1972	211,776
1968	129,347	1973	255,179

4. Bourse des Valeurs de Marseille
   Secretariat: Compagnie des Agents de Change, Palais de la Bourse, 13215
   Marseille Cedex 1
   Telephone: 15/91 39-70-32
   Trading volume: Value of securities traded (000 francs)

1964	49,529	1969	123,564
1965	45,068	1970	58,552
1966	30,332	1971	81,014
1967	45,756	1972	77,485
1968	97,454	1973	138,292

5. Bourse des Valeurs de Nancy
   Secretariat: Chambre de Commerce et d'Industrie, 40, rue Henri Poincare
   54000 Nancy
   Telephone: 15/28 52-85-15
   President Delegate: Roger Kempf
   Trading volume: Value of securities traded (000 francs)

1964	44,415	1969	198,609
1965	40,613	1970	120,576
1966	51,345	1971	84,239
1967	53,457	1972	149,188
1968	65,660	1973	231,484

6. Bourse des Valeurs de Nantes
   Secretariat: Palais de la Bourse 44000 Nantes
   Trading volume: Value of securities traded (000 francs)

1964	23,842	1969	53,281
1965	22,247	1970	59,546
1966	32,937	1971	43,917
1967	40,297	1972	66,612
1968	32,834	1973	104,690

7. Total trading volume—Total value of securities traded on all provincial exchanges (000 francs)

1964*	327,993	1969**	704,845
1965*	272,250	1970	499,763
1966*	288,797	1971	508,329
1967*	305,417	1972	799,733
1968	430,265	1973	1,024,029

   *includes la Bourse de Toulouse, dissolved in 1967.
   **from 1969, totals include over-the-counter market for provincial exchanges.

Officers: The French Stockbroker's Company has an administrative staff of about 500, headed by a Secretary-General.
Secretary-General: Daniel Petit
Deputy Secretary-General and Director of the Stock Exchange Department: Bernard Mirat
Deputy Secretary-General and Director of Technical Services: Michel Perier
Director of Legal Services: Jacques Pinat
Director of Information and Public Relations: Bruno Montier

Hours of Business:
   1. 11:30 A.M. - 12:30 P.M. Bonds and gilt-edged securities (cash market).
   2. 12:30 P.M. - 2:30 P.M. All other listed securities (official cash and future market); over-the-counter issues.
   3. 3:00 P.M. - 4:00 P.M. (variable). Additional session for foreign securities quoted on the forward market.
   4. The Paris market is open from Monday to Friday.

Regulatory Laws: The Bill of Trade (1807) of Napoleon I. This basic law provides for the organization of French exchanges and confirms the rights of stockbrokers. The functioning of the market itself depends upon "The General Regulations of the Stockbrokers' Company," which must be approved by the Minister of Finance. The last issue is dated August 8, 1973.

Issues Traded and Volume:
   1. Officially listed: 2,677 issues on the cash market. Of this number, 231 are traded also on the future market.
   2. Volume (000): Official and over-the-counter market.

	No. Shares	Daily Average		No. Shares	Daily Average
1964	101,784	405	1969	225,939	900
1965	108,102	430	1970	200,141	803
1966	112,929	453	1971	201,776	813
1967	118,777	479	1972	270,480	1,095
1968	159,157	683	1973	275,680	1,125

3. Value of shares traded (000 francs):

(a)	Official Market	Over-The-Counter		Official Market	Over-The-Counter
1964	18,072,969	192,245	1969	42,107,811	470,319
1965	17,163,946	218,423	1970	34,234,244	385,131
1966	19,272,410	251,094	1971	36,316,894	400,983
1967	19,569,110	264,605	1972	56,711,903	864,041
1968	29,254,085	238,249	1973	67,540,929	839,763

(b)	French Issues	Foreign Issues		French Issues	Foreign Issues
1964	15,681,469	2,391,500	1969	36,720,927	5,386,884
1965	15,333,980	1,829,966	1970	30,098,441	4,135,803
1966	17,446,512	1,825,898	1971	30,963,938	5,352,956
1967	17,305,904	2,263,206	1972	50,711,567	6,000,336
1968	24,415,682	4,838,403	1973	58,640,594	8,900,335

4. Records: all markets since 1962

Maxima Minima	Value (in 000 francs)	Date
Year:		
Strongest	68,380,692	1973
Weakest	17,382,369	1965
Quarter:		
Strongest	21,854,676	2nd. 1973
Weakest	3,324,302	3rd. 1966
Month:		
Strongest	8,455,106	May, 1973
Weakest	932,983	August, 1966
Week:		
Strongest	2,186,821	ending 5/26/72
Weakest	192,653	ending 8/5/66
Day:		
Strongest	975,720	5/23/72
Weakest	35,578	1/3/66
Daily Average (on the year):		
Strongest	279,105	1973
Weakest	69,252	1965

Unit of Trading:
1. Future market: 10, 25, 50, 100 or 200 shares, depending upon the price of the security involved.
2. Cash market: Securities are traded in any quantity desired.

Membership: The "seat-owner" system of stock exchange membership is not practiced in France, where 113 stockbrokers represent 80 offices. Paris has 91 stockbrokers representing 61 offices. There are three methods, regulated by law, in which stockbroker offices can be organized: a "société de personnes"; a "société en commandite simple"; a limited company.

Stockbrokers are public officers, appointed by the Minister of Finance. They represent a unique national company—"Compagnie des Agents de Change."

The company is headed by a committee—"Chambre Syndicale"—which is elected annually and consists of one "Syndic" (comparable to the President of the Stock Exchange) and seven assistants (equivalent to a board of directors). All new stockbrokers must be accepted and approved by the others.

Commissions or Fees:

1. The commission rate is variable. It depends upon the nature of the stocks traded and the kind of market chosen. Example: cash market transactions require a higher commission than those of the future market. In general, the rates are between 0.2% and 0.7% of the volume in listed securities traded on the Paris Stock Exchange, and between 0.45% and 0.85% for securities listed on the provincial exchanges. The purchase or sale of a security traded on a foreign exchange involves an extra commission.

2. Taxes:
   a. The "Droit de Timbre," or "Impôt de Bourse," concerns all taxable securities. It represents: 3% on trades valued from 0 to 1 million francs; 0.15% on trades valued at more than 1 million francs and 0.15% on all trades for carry-over transactions.
   b. Taxes account for 17.6% of the total commission or brokerage.
   c. It is estimated that commissions and taxes represent about 1% of the trading volume.

Historical Background:

1141 King Louis VII established the "changeurs" on the Pont du Change in Paris.

1301 A royal decree prohibited the "courtiers" from trading with the same goods that they used for negotiating over loans and stocks.

1572 Royal permission was required to deal in securities—the first stock market regulation.

1724 Sixty stockholders were granted the privilege of transacting business in loans and stocks.

1807 Through the "Bill of Trade," Napoleon I confirmed the rights of the profession. He also ordered construction of the Palais Brongniart in which the stock exchange has been domiciled since 1827.

1962 An over-the-counter market was created, where only stockbrokers could trade in issues that were not officially listed.

1967 The previously independent exchanges of France were combined to form a national stockbrokers' company. It consisted of seven exchanges after the Toulouse Exchange was dissolved. Stockbrokers were permitted to manage securities portfolios for private clients.

1972 Stockbrokers were enabled to create limited companies to maintain and manage their offices.

1973 On March 6, stockbrokers were given the opportunity to deal in securities at any time. Clients' orders could be executed at a higher price on the buy side and a lower price on the sell side, when such transactions were effected outside of the official trading hours.

GERMAN FEDERAL REPUBLIC

See West Germany

GREECE

ATHENS

ATHENS STOCK EXCHANGE

Title: Athens Stock Exchange

Address: 10 Sophokleous Street, Athens, 121, Greece

Telex: 215820 BURS G.R.

Officers: Stock Exchange Committee:
President: D. Kokorinos
Vice-President: Chr Theodorides
Cashier: E. Komninos
Members: K. Komninos
　　　　　 J. Pantelakis

Director: G. Kotitsas
General Government Commissioner: G. Passias

Hours of Business: 10:00 A.M. - 12:00 noon (weekdays)

Regulatory Laws: Law 3632 of 1928

Issues Traded and Volume:
1. Listed Securities:

1971 Post War II Loans	No. of Loans or Co.s	No. Bonds or Shares Quoted	Face Value Drachmae (000)	Market Value Drachmae (000)
Government Bonds	12	33,980,712	13,555,882	12,882,358
Public Power Co.	12	27,267,960	7,323,744	7,185,628
Corporation Bonds	7	1,935,968	581,636	576,366
Total	—			
Shares	31	63,184,640	21,461,262	20,644,352

Banks	10	7,357,483	2,693,711	21,949,891
Industrials				
Communications	2	· 1,600,000	157,475	987,750
Chem. Products	4	1,141,804	218,435	2,849,441
Spinning-Weaving	12	2,480,084	685,824	1,459,279
Building	6	3,105,767	415,957	3,752,195
Food-Wine	18	2,655,370	461,857	1,789,951
Miscellaneous	17	2,521,408	566,789	3,285,362
Tot. (Ind. Co's.)	59	13,504,433	2,506,337	14,123,978
Comm. - Ins.	10	24,597,107	530,494	4,558,267
	—			
Total all shares	79	24,597,107	5,730,542	40,632,136

1972 Post War II Loans	No. of Loans or Co.s	No. Bonds or Shares Quoted	Face Value Drachmae (000)	Market Value Drachmae (000)
Government Bonds	13	38,443,812	15,940,274	14,876,458
Public Power Co.	13	31,236,060	8,725,659	8,438,220
Corporation Bonds	6	2,043,955	504,240	469,202
Total	—			
Shares	32	71,723,827	25,170,173	23,783,880
Banks	10	7,371,233	2,695,773	52,912,379
Industrials				
Communications	2	1,600,000	149,444	1,959,250
Chem. Products	4	1,271,656	273,808	7,359,622
Spinning-Weaving	14	3,384,067	927,764	4,454,996
Building	7	5,333,457	680,401	12,281,510
Food-Wine	18	3,250,306	620,990	3,747,611
Miscellaneous	19	4,048,448	686,581	7,954,974
Tot. (Ind. Co's.)	64	18,887,934	3,338,988	37,757,963
Comm. Insur.	15	7,941,631	1,179,192	16,516,501
	—			
Total all shares	89	34,200,798	7,213,953	107,186,843

2. Volume (bonds and shares)

1971 Post War II Loans	Amount of Bonds and Shs.	Val. in Drachmae	% Ratio
Government Bonds	1,755,706	758,470,860	29.20
Public Power	2,154,016	603,294,949	23.22
Corporation Bonds	78,100	24,979,045	0.96
Pre-War II Loans	133,949	86,241,189	3.32
Total of Bonds	4,121,771	1,472,986,043	56.70
Banks-Insurance	192,640	628,833,307	24.20
Industrials	579,849	496,351,203	19.10
Total all Shares	772,489	1,125,184,510	43.30
Grand Total	4,894,260	2,598,170,553	100.00

1972 Post War II Loans	Amount of Bonds and Shs.	Val. in Drachmae	% Ratio
Government Bonds	1,513,123	675,830,155	9.17
Public Power	1,239,902	342,660,212	4.65
Corporation Bonds	84,194	24,970,747	0.34
Pre-War II Loans	107,594	89,905,581	1.22
Total of Bonds	2,944,813	1,133,366,695	15.38
Banks-Insurance	934,749	3,350,029,586	45.44
Industrials	2,644,632	2,888,253,207	39.18
Total all shares	3,579,381	6,238,282,793	84.62
Grand Total	6,524,194	7,371,649,488	100.00

Unit of Trading: 25 shares on most stocks, but some issues are traded in units of 1,5, or 10 shares.

Memberships:
1. Regular Members: 30-35
2. There are no membership prices in the general sense of the term. But each member puts a variable sum of money into a Common Fund.

Commissions:
1. Bearer securities: 0.5%
2. Registered securities: 0.8%

HONG KONG

HONG KONG STOCK EXCHANGE

Title: The Hong Kong Stock Exchange

Address: 801 Edinburgh House, Ice House Street, Hong Kong

Telephone: 5 - 221639

Cable Address: STOCKS HONG KONG

Officers:
Secretary & General Manager: R. A. Witts
Assistant Secretary: Mok Chiu Shun
Assistant Secretary (Research): Miss Annabella Wong

Hours of Business: 10:00 A.M. - 12:30 P.M.; 2:30 P.M. - 3:30 P.M.

Regulatory Laws: Hong Kong Government Ordinance No. 24 of 1970 (Securities Bill 1973 and Protection of Investors Bill are being processed).

Issues Traded and Volume:
1. Listed Issues - 183
2. There are no unlisted or "other" issues.

3. Total volume (HK$ Million):

1960	875	1967	297
1961	1,414	1968	943
1962	701	1969	2,523
1963	520	1970	3,051
1964	747	1971	4,738
1965	389	1972	10,610
1966	349	1973	12,285

Unit of Trading:

1. Different "board-lots" apply to different companies. A board-lot (number of shares) is often 1,000.
2. Odd-lots are usually traded at a small discount from the price of board-lots.
3. No extra commission or fee is charged for an odd-lot.

Memberships:

1. Local members - 129
2. Overseas members - 12. These are established brokerage firms of recognized stock exchanges, which have an associated membership arrangement with the Hong Kong Stock Exchange.
3. There are no "other" members.
4. Membership Prices:
1960	HK$ 30,000
1965	HK$ 50,000
1970	HK$ 100,000
1972	HK$ 500,000
1973	HK$ 600,000

Commissions or Fees:

1. a. 1% on new issues
   b. 0.5% on a normal trade
   c. HK$25 minimum on any single transaction
2. Government Taxes: 0.4% ad valorem on purchases and sales. The instrument of transfer must bear a HK$5 embossed stamp before being signed.

Historical Background:

Before 1890 an association of stockbrokers was formed; on February 3, 1891, it was incorporated as the "Association of Stockbrokers in Hong Kong." The association functioned under that name until February 21, 1914, when it was changed to the Hong Kong Stock Exchange.

The Hong Kong Stock Exchange, which includes the Stockbrokers Association of Hong Kong, carried on its activities at various locations, until the members purchased land and erected the Stock Exchange Building at 10 Ice House Street in 1934.

From 1891, members of the Hong Kong Stock Exchange met twice daily (10:00 A.M. and 2:30 P.M.) for call-overs. They then gathered in small groups adjacent to the exchange, or dashed off in rickshaws to visit clients.

Until 1925, an active business was transacted for monthly settlements; shares were bought and sold three months ahead. This led to a certain amount of gambling. However, all brokers were later affected by the general strike and were liquidating their contracts, or attempting to do so, for many months.

For a considerable time thereafter, business was transacted on a cash basis: when forward business was resumed it never reached its former volume. Trading today is conducted on a daily settlement basis.

The Hong Kong Stockbrokers Association was incorporated in 1921. It had the same objectives as the Hong Kong Stock Exchange, and virtually all dealings were transacted by members of these organizations. However, it was apparent that two organizations, each with its own Committee of Control, was unsatisfactory. It was not until the re-occupation of the Colony that any serious steps were taken to remedy the situation. Merger negotiations were initiated in 1946 by a few members of both organizations in the Colony. On October 7, 1946. resolutions were passed appointing liquidators to achieve this.

The Hong Kong Stock Exchange Ltd. was incorporated March 11, 1947. Members of the Hong Kong Stock Exchange and the Hong Kong Stockbrokers Association were eligible for membership without ballot or entrance fee.

Membership on the Hong Kong Stock Exchange was limited to 60 for many years, but this ceiling was raised to 200 in 1973.

The largest daily turnover on the Exchange occurred February 8, 1973, when shares valued at HK$ 204,000,000 changed hands.

Market Index: The Hang Seng Index is the accepted barometer of share prices in Hong Kong. On July 31,1964, it stood at 100. The Index topped 500 initially on July 26, 1972, and 1,000 on February 2, 1973. Its all-time high was 1,774.96 on March 9, 1973.

ICELAND

REYKJAVIK

REYKJAVIK STOCK BROKERAGE FIRM

There are no stock exchanges in Iceland despite information to the contrary on file with the New York office of the Consulate General of Iceland.

The stock brokerage firm of Kauphollin is located at Laekjargata 2, Reykjavik, Iceland. The owner and managing director is Aron Gudbrandsson. Telephone is 11710-11712; Cable Address: KAUPHOLLIN. Hours of business are 9 A.M. - 4 P.M. A commission of 2% is charged for trading securities.

INDIA

THE STOCK EXCHANGES OF INDIA

Eight stock exchanges are recognized by the Government of India under the Securities Contracts (Regulations) Act: Bombay, Calcutta, Ahmedabad, Madras, Delhi, Hyderabad, Indore, and Bangalore. The first exchange to be recognized was the Bombay Stock Exchange on August 31, 1957; the eighth exchange was the Bangalore Stock Exchange on February 16, 1963.

The governing body of a recognized exchange has extensive powers of government and administration and, subject to government approval, to make, amend, and suspend the operation of the rules, by-laws, and regulations of the exchange. It also has complete jurisdiction over all members and in practice its powers of management and control are almost absolute.

The regulations relating to the qualification and admission of members to the recognized stock exchanges are uniform and common under the provisions of the Securities Contracts (Regulation) Rules of 1957. These statutory rules prescribe that a person to become a member should have attained the age of 21, should be a citizen of India, should not have been adjudged bankrupt or declared insolvent, or guilty of having compounded with his creditors, or have suffered conviction for fraud or dishonesty.

He should also not engage himself as principal or employee in any other business, other than that of securities, which may involve him in financial loss. Firms and companies are not eligible for membership on a recognized stock exchange, and individuals are not ordinarily deemed to be qualified to become a member, unless they have had at least two years market experience as an apprentice, or as a partner, or authorized assistant to a member. Partnership of individual members is allowed and members are also permitted to trade with business names subject to the approval of the governing board. Every member must keep a specified sum of money as security deposit with the stock exchange, a sort of financial guaranty to cover his business risks and obligations to the investing public, in addition to the payment he must make to acquire a membership card, or share.

Three government directors are nominated to the boards of stock exchanges to maintain day-to-day contact with the activities of the exchanges and to give guidance and advice in carrying out their functions. Besides, the exchanges are called upon to have on their board a public representative nominated from among eminent persons of standing and position unconnected with the securities business, and a full-time executive director vested with the executive function and administration of the exchange.

The by-laws and regulations and mode of trading are uniform for all exchanges. Besides routine procedural matters relating to trading and the settlement of transactions in securities, these by-laws and regulations specify the terms and conditions under which shares of public companies can be listed for trading, the types of contracts in which securities can be dealt in, and the method of settlement. Also, the procedure for the completion of contracts in cleared securities through the clearing house, the manner in which disputes are to be settled, the action to be taken in a time of emergency, the different types of penalties — such as fines, suspension, or expulsion — for breaking by-laws, regulations, etc.

The main purpose of government regulation is to control speculation and to encourage bona fide investing. The listing requirements imposed by government and the stock exchanges are intended to encourage and to facilitate public investments in joint stock enterprises and to protect the interests of investors. The most important of these is the requirement that any company which seeks to have its shares listed on the stock exchange must offer 60% of each class of its issued capital to the public, and to allot the same among the applicants fairly and unconditionally. This has resulted in a wide distribution of shareholders and has evoked a keen interest in joint stock enterprises by public investors. The stock exchanges today have the necessary mechanism, through statutory regulations, for checking speculative price fluctuations, as well as routine procedures for determining a good or bad delivery of shares and documents. They can also provide lower units of trading to facilitate dealings by small investors and standard methods of transfering securities.

Source: *Madras Stock Exchange Official Year-Book,* 1973-1974

No. of Stock Issues Listed
(As of December 31, 1972)

Stock Exchange	No. of Cos. Listed	Total	Equity	Pref.	Deb.
Bombay	614	1,113	657	396	80
Calcutta	629	1,063	660	329	74
Madras	356	666	384	219	63
Ahmedabad	131	271	132	124	15
Delhi	215	400	223	164	13
Hyderabad	41	75	41	27	7
Indore	17	26	19	7	..
Bangalore	73	118	81	37	..
TOTAL	2,076	3,752	2,197	1,303	252
Less: Common	454	809	489	352	38
ALL EXCHANGES	1,622	2,943	1,708	951	214

Stock Exchange	Paid-up Capital (Cr. Rs.)		
	Equity	Pref.	Total
Bombay	959.83	139.92	1,099.75
Calcutta	596.56	82.49	679.05
Madras	270.85	31.57	302.42
Ahmedabad	166.71	33.25	199.96
Delhi	239.22	52.11	291.33
Hyderabad	43.41	7.25	50.66
Indore	16.49	2.35	18.84
Bangalore	52.83	6.55	59.38
TOTAL	2,345.90	355.49	2,701.39
Less: Common	879.18	152.44	1,031.62
ALL EXCHANGES	1,466.72	203.05	1,669.77

Stock Exchange	Deb. Amt. Outstanding (Cr. Rs.)	Total Capital Employed (Cr. Rs.)	Market Value of Capital Employed (Cr. Rs.)	
			Equity	Pref.
Bombay	168.02	1,267.77	1,626.74	123.66
Calcutta	82.86	761.91	958.83	62.16
Madras	135.50	437.92	323.41	27.48
Ahmedabad	36.47	236.43	.331.39	26.18
Delhi	23.43	314.76	355.29	45.99
Hyderabad	2.69	53.35	50.25	5.87
Indore	..	18.84	31.86	2.13
Bangalore	..	59.38	73.12	5.51
TOTAL	448.97	3,150.36	3,750.89	298.98
Less: Common	125.09	1,156.71	1,460.75	134.08
ALL EXCHANGES	323.88	1,993.65	2,290.14	164.90

Stock Exchange	Market Value of Capital Employed (Cr. Rs.)		Average per Company (Lakh Rs.)		
	Deb.	Total	Share Capital	Total Capital	Market Value of Total Capital
Bombay	160.63	1,911.03	179	206	311
Calcutta	81.01	1,102.00	108	121	175
Madras	132.63	483.52	85	123	136
Ahmedabad	36.13	393.70	153	180	301
Delhi	23.38	424.66	136	146	198
Hyderabad	2.66	58.78	124	130	143
Indore	..	33.99	111	111	200
Bangalore	..	78.63	81	81	108
TOTAL	436.44	4,486.31	130	152	216
Less: Common	122.71	1,717.54			
ALL EXCHANGES	313.73	2,768.77	103	123	171

Source: The Stock Exchange, Bombay, *Present Position of The Stock Market in India,* 1973.

BOMBAY

BOMBAY STOCK EXCHANGE

Title: The Stock Exchange
Address: Dalal Street, Bombay 400 001, India
Telephone: 252221/22
Cable Address: SHERATION, Bombay

Officers:
President: Jayant Amerchand
Chairman: P. J. Jeejeebhoy
Vice-President: Mathradas Samaldas
Hon. Treasurer: Vasantlal Champaklal
Governing Board:

Laldas Jamnadas	Vasantlal Kantilal
Rasiklal Maneklal	B. M. Gandhi
Jasvantlal Chhotalal	N. C. Kampani
Hiralal Girdharlal	B. N. Khandelwal
Vasantlal Jivatlal	Ashokkumar G. Fozdar
J. R. Motishaw	Chhotalal Devchand
A. R. Mahadevia	P. G. Ruia

Secretary: A. J. Shah

Hours of Business: 12:00 noon - 2:00 P.M. (weekdays)

Regulatory Laws: The Securities Contracts (Regulation) Act, 1956

Issues Traded and Volume:

	No. Listed Companies	No. Listed Stocks	Tot. Paid-up Value (Cr. Rs.*)	Mkt. Value Total Capital (Cr. Rs.*)
1946	197	271	123	
1961	297	538	381	645
1965	502	891	689	841
1972	614	1,133	1,268	1,911
1973	680	1,257	1,472	N.A.

*One crore equals 100 million rupees; 10 lakhs equal 1 million rupees.
Volume: Not Available.

Unit of Trading: Varies according to face value and market price of the security concerned. Generally accepted units: 1, 5, 10, 25, and 50 shares.

Memberships:
1. Regular Members: 504
2. Membership prices: "Card" is synonymous with "Seat" in Bombay.

	High	Low		High	Low
1960	Rs. 28,000	Rs. 18,000	1967	Rs. 19,500	Rs. 18,000
1961	37,000	26,500	1968	18,000	14,000
1962	32,500	30,000	1969	25,500	17,750
1963	32,000	26,750	1970	25,000	19,000
1964	32,000	29,000	1971	21,000	20,000
1965	22,000	17,000	1972	21,000	19,000
1966	20,000	16,000	1973	22,250	18,500

Commissions or Fees

Description	Brokerage (Rs.) On Face Value
1. Securities of the Government of India and State governments of face value ---	
a. under Rs. 25,000	0.50%
b. Rs. 25,000 or over	0.25%

2. Loans and Debentures of Port
Trusts, Municipal Corporations
and similar other bodies   0.50%
3. Debentures of Joint Stock
Companies   1.00%
4. Share of Joint Stock Companies
when the contract price
per share

Exceeds Rs.		Does Not Exceed Rs.	Per Share	
0	—	2.50	0.10	
2.50	—	5	0.20	
5	—	10	0.30	
10	—	15	0.40	
15	—	20	0.50	
20	—	25	0.60	
25	—	30	0.70	
30	—	40	1.00	
40	—	50	1.20	
50	—	60	1.50	
60	—	80	2.00	
80	—	100	2.50	
100	—	400	2.50	plus 0.50 for every Rs. 25 or part thereof in excess of Rs. 100.
400			8.50	plus 0.50 for every Rs. 50 or part thereof in excess of Rs. 400.

5. The lowest charge per contract shall be Rs. 5.
6. The scale prescribed in 1 to 4 above is exclusive of service charge and does
not apply to underwriting or the placing of new issues.

Historical Background:

1840-50 A half dozen brokers were recognized by the banks and merchants.

1850   The Companies Act introducing limited liability was enacted; thus
        began the era of modern joint stock enterprise in India.

1860   The acknowledged leader of the brokerage business was the legen-
        dary Premchand Roychand-the first broker who could speak and write
        English.

1865   Hundreds of time bargains matured July 1, which no one could fulfill
        and a disastrous slump followed. Special legislation - Act XXVIII had
        to be enacted to deal with the mass failures.

1875   The Bombay Stock Exchange was founded with 318 members on the
        list, September 7.

1887   At a meeting held in Broker's Hall on February 5, it was resolved to
        execute a formal deed of Association, constitute the first Managing
        Committee and appoint the first trustees.

On December 3, the Articles of Association were drawn up and the exchange was thus formally established in Bombay as a society to be called "The Native Share and Stock Brokers' Association." The word "native" in the original title was a sign of exclusiveness and pride. Article II of the Articles of Association specifically declares "that no other persons except natives of India shall be admitted as members of said Association."

1899 The new Brokers' Hall opened January 18, on Dalal Street.
1914 There were three stock exchanges in India: Bombay, Calcutta, Ahmedabad.
1925 The Bombay Securities Contracts Control Act was passed.
1938 A rival stock exchange was established in Bombay in February. It is now defunct.
1956 The Bombay Exchange became one of eight stock exchanges recognized by the Government of India under the Securities Contracts (Regulation) Act. It was the first to be recognized and the only one that has been granted the privilege of permanent recognition.

CALCUTTA

CALCUTTA STOCK EXCHANGE

Title: The Calcutta Stock Exchange Association, Ltd.

Address: 7, Lyons Range, Calcutta 700001, India

Telephone: 22-1641 (Exchange Hall); 22-6136 (President); 22-1646 (Vice-President); 22-8636 (Executive Director); 22-1488 (Secretary); 22-9366 (Asst. Secretary & Research Officer).

Officers:
President: G. S. Mantry
Vice-President: A. K. Bose
Executive Director: B. B. Ghosh
Research Officer: P. K. Ray
Secretary: B. Mazumdar
Asst. Secretary: P. K. De

Hours of Business (trading): 12:00 noon - 2:30 P.M. (weekdays) 12:00 noon - 1:00 P.M. (Saturdays)

Regulatory Laws:
1. The Securities Contracts (Regulation) Act—1956, enacted by the Government of India.
2. The Stock Exchange Association is controlled and managed by a committee composed of 15 elected members, 2 additional members, 3 government nominees, 1 public representative and the Executive Director.

Issues Traded and Volume:
1. Listed Issues: 1,237 (12/31/73)
2. Securities traded on the Calcutta Exchange must be listed. To become

eligible for listing, a company must make a public offering of at least 60% of each category of its shares, by advertising in newspapers and keeping the subscription list open for at least three days. However, this requirement may be relaxed in certain instances by the Stock Exchange authorities, with the approval of the Central Government.

3. Volume: Not available.
4. Value: Nominal value of securities quoted on exchange as of 12/31/73; Rs 709,30,83,912-50.

Unit of Trading:

1. Shares of companies listed after February 26, 1965:
   a. where nominal value per share is Rs. 10 - 50 shares;
   b. where nominal value per share is Rs. 100 - 5 shares.
2. The trading unit in all other cases:
   a. shares of Rs. 10 nominal value - 100 shares;
   b. shares of Rs. 100 nominal value - 25 shares;
   c. Government securities and debentures of joint stock companies are traded in lots of Rs. 25,000 face value.
3. The majority of business on the Calcutta Stock Exchange is transacted for "cash delivery."
4. Four kinds of "bargains" (transactions between or on behalf of exchange members) are usually permissible:
   a. Spot Delivery—delivery and payment on the same day, or the following day;
   b. Hand Delivery—delivery and payment within 14 days of the contract date;
   c. Clearing—clearance and settlement through the Clearing House;
   d. Special Delivery—delivery and payment at any time exceeding 14 days from the contract date.

Membership:

1. Regular Members: 650, of which about 350 are active.
2. Cost of Membership Card:

1960	Rs. 8,500	1965	Rs. 6,100
1961	Rs. 8,400	1966	Rs. 6,000
1962	Rs. 7,500	1967	Rs. 5,500
1963	Rs. 7,250	1968-1973	Rs. 5,000
1964	Rs. 7,100		

Commissions or Fees:

Description		Brokerage (Rs.) On Face Value
1. Securities of the Government of India and State Governments of face value -		
a. Under Rs. 25,000	. . . . .	0.50%
b. Rs. 25,000 or over	. . . . .	0.25%
2. Loans and Debentures of Port Trusts, Municipal Corporations and similar other bodies	. . . . .	0.50%

3. Debentures of Joint Stock
   Companies 1.00%
4. Shares of Joint Stock Companies
   when the contract price per share -

Exceeds		Does Not Exceed		Per Share	
Rs.		Rs.			
0	. . . .	2.50	. . . .	0.10	
2.50	. . . .	5.00	. . . .	0.20	
5.00	. . . .	10.00	. . . .	0.30	
10.00	. . . .	15.00	. . . .	0.40	
15.00	. . . .	20.00	. . . .	0.50	
20.00	. . . .	25.00	. . . .	0.60	
25.00	. . . .	30.00	. . . .	0.70	
30.00	. . . .	40.00	. . . .	1.00	
40.00	. . . .	50.00	. . . .	1.20	
50.00	. . . .	60.00	. . . .	1.50	
60.00	. . . .	80.00	. . . .	2.00	
80.00	. . . .	100.00	. . . .	2.50	
100.00	. . . .	400.00	. . . .	2.50	plus 0.50 for every Rs. 25 or part thereof in excess of Rs. 100.
400.00	. . . .	. . . .	. . . .	8.50	plus 0.50 for every Rs. 50 or part thereof in excess of Rs. 400.

5. The lowest charge per contract shall be Rs. 5.
6. The scale prescribed in 1 to 5 above is exclusive of service charge and does not apply to underwriting or the placing of new issues.

Historical Background:

1836 Stockbroking in Calcutta began about this time, although old records show that government securities and securities of the East India Company were traded around the end of the 18th century.

1864 Ninety-one joint stock companies were traded, including 38 tea companies, 5 coal companies, and 5 steam tug companies. The center of activity was near a "Neem" tree, where the Chartered Bank and James Finlay & Co., Ltd. are situated today.

1894 Calcutta brokers shifted their open-air headquarters to the vicinity of the present Allahabad Bank.

1908 The Calcutta Stock Exchange Association was formed at 2, New China Bazaar Street, with 150 founding members.

1923 The Association was registered as a limited liability concern, with an authorized capital of Rs. 300,000 composed of 300 shares of Rs. 1,000 each.

1927 The present headquarters building of the Association was erected at the corner of Lyons Range and Royal Exchange Place and opened for business in 1928.

1957 With the enactment of the Securities Contracts (Regulation) Act—1956, the Calcutta Exchange was officially recognized on October 10.

1958 Calcutta Stock Exchange celebrated its Golden Jubilee.

Profile Data

1959 The 300, Rs. 1,000, shares of the Association were split four-for-one and allotted only to members.

1968 The Calcutta Stock Exchange celebrated its Diamond Jubilee.

1969 The Central Government banned forward trading in scrips in the Clearing Schedule.

DELHI

DELHI STOCK EXCHANGE

Title: The Delhi Stock Exchange Association Ltd.

Address: 3 & 4/4B, Asaf Ali Road, New Delhi, India

Telephone: 279000, 271302, 272493

Member's Telephone: 271038

Cable Address: UPKARI, New Delhi

Officers:
Executive Director: H. C. Verma
Assistant Secretary: Ramesh Chander Goel

Hours of Business: 12:00 noon - 2:30 P.M. (Weekdays) 12:00 noon - 2:00 P.M. (Saturdays)

Regulatory Laws: The Securities Contract (Regulation) Act of 1956; Securities Contract (Regulation) Rules of 1957.

Issues Traded and Volume: During 1972 3,131,083 shares of 233 issues were traded. The total value of stocks listed on the Delhi Stock Exchange is Rs. 2,856,598,726.

Unit of Trading:
1. 50 shares, when the face value is Rs. 10; 5 shares, when the face value is Rs. 100.
2. No extra fee or commission is charged for executing an odd-lot order. However, orders to buy and orders to sell are executed at prices which are slightly above or below the market price prevailing at the time of execution.

Membership:
1. Active Members: 89
2. Inactive Members: 11
3. Representative Members. Close relatives of existing members may be admitted as partners and treated as constituent members.
4. Membership costs:
   a. members must purchase two qualification shares in the paid-up capital of the association. The face value per share is Rs. 2,000; the market value is about Rs. 11,000 per share.
   b. New members pay an admission fee of Rs. 1,000. A security deposit of Rs. 10,000 must be maintained to retain trading rights.

Commissions or Fees:
1. Normal brokerage charges vary from 3 to 2.5% based on the value of a contract. The minimum brokerage charged is Rs. 5 per contract. This brokerage charge excludes service charges. Brokers generally give concessions to their clients if the business is large or there are cross transactions.
2. In the case of public issues brokerage is paid at the rate of 1% on the face value of the business procured by the companies offering new or additional issues.
3. Underwriting commissions are charged at the rate of 2½% of the face value of the shares underwritten. All capital issues are generally fully underwritten.

Historical Background:
1947 On June 25 the Delhi Stock Exchange Association Ltd. was incorporated as a limited company under the Indian Companies Act of 1913. It acquired and took over the activities, functions, and business of the then existing Delhi Stock and Share Exchange Ltd. and The Delhi Stock and Share Brokers Association Ltd.

1948 On April 1 the new company commenced operations.

1950 A new set of by-laws was adopted effective July 7 and covered all aspects of the business and for the first time business was transacted under a set of rules.

1955 Present exchange building completed.

1956 Securities Contracts (Regulation) Act of 1956 adopted.

1957 The Securities Contracts Act became applicable to the Union Territory of Delhi effective December 9. The stock exchange adopted new by-laws and regulations. Underlying object was to create confidence in minds of investing public and encourage savings and investment in corporate sector.

MADRAS

MADRAS STOCK EXCHANGE

Title: Madras Stock Exchange, Ltd.

Address: Stock Exchange Building, 16/17 Second Line Beach, Madras 600001, India

Telephone: 22145; 22237; 23081

Cable Address: MASTEX

Officers: Management Council:
President: M. S. Sivasubramanian
Vice-President: K. Krishnamoorthy
Treasurer: V. K. Padmanabhan

Council Members:
J. V. Somayajulu
M. Sankaran
S. Ramaswami

Government Nominees:
   S. C. Bafna
   R. P. Dobe
Public Representative: C. R. Pattabhi Raman
Executive Director: E. R. Krishnamurti
Secretary: Y. Sundara Babu

Hours of Business (trading): 12:00 noon - 2:00 P.M., every day except Saturday.

Regulatory Laws:
   1. Securities Contracts (Regulation) Act, 1956
   2. Securities Contracts (Regulation) Rules, 1957

Issues Traded and Volume:
   1. Listed Shares:

Year		Bank	Insurance	Electric	Sugar
1968	1 Half	10	3	9	15
	2 Half	10	3	6	16
1969	1 Half	8	2	7	16
	2 Half	10	3	5	15
1970	1 Half	11	2	7	16
	2 Half	10	3	7	12
1971	1 Half	9	3	7	12
	2 Half	9	2	5	13
1972	1 Half	10	2	5	14
	2 Half	7	2	3	16
1973	1 Half	5	—	6	14
	2 Half	4	—	6	15

Year		Planting	Textile	Miscellaneous
1968	1 Half	68	32	73
	2 Half	68	32	79
1969	1 Half	69	33	79
	2 Half	67	29	78
1970	1 Half	68	40	95
	2 Half	71	38	99
1971	1 Half	62	32	92
	2 Half	58	29	87
1972	1 Half	63	30	89
	2 Half	61	29	86
1973	1 Half	58	31	89
	2 Half	56	40	87

   2. Unlisted or "Other" Issues:

	1 Half-year		2 Half-year	
	Number	Volume	Number	Volume
1968	11	8,933	18	13,097
1969	10	31,835	10	16,242
1970	2	850	5	467
1971	9	27,682	3	824
1972	9	13,190	5	1,945
1973	10	17,037	5	6,274

   3. Volume (all shares):

	1 Half-year	2 Half-year
1968	818,058	921,738

1969	1,304,117	1,161,553
1970	2,094,272	1,499,314
1971	975,082	982,585
1972	1,125,096	804,312
1973	1,311,631	2,452,423

Unit of Trading:

1. 50 or 100 share units for Rs. 10 - face value shares and below.
2. 5 share unit for Rs. 100 - face value shares and below.
3. Odd-lots involve no extra commission or fee; nor are they handled by special dealers. Odd-lot sell orders are executed at a price slightly lower than the prevailing market price; buy orders are executed at a price that is slightly higher.

Memberships:

1. Member Firms: 17
2. Individual Members: 33
3. Membership Prices: The cost of membership, or a seat, on the exchange has ranged from Rs. 2,000 to Rs. 5,000 in recent years.

Commissions or Fees:

Description	Brokerage Rs. On Face Value
1. Securities of the Government of India and State Governments of face value —	
a. under Rs. 25,000	0.50%
b. Rs. 25,000 or over	0.25%
2. Loans and debentures of Port Trusts, Municipal Corporations and similar other bodies.	0.50%
3. Debentures of Joint Stock Companies	1.00%

4. Shares of Joint Stock Companies when the contract price per share -

exceeds	does not exceed	Per Share	
Rs.	Rs.		
0	2.50	0.10	
2.50	5	0.20	
5	10	0.30	
10	15	0.40	
15	20	0.50	
20	25	0.60	
25	30	0.70	
30	40	1.00	
40	50	1.20	
50	60	1.50	
60	80	2.00	
80	100	2.50	
100	400	2.50	plus
		0.50	for every Rs. 25 or part thereof in excess of Rs. 100
400		8.50	plus
		0.50	for every Rs. 50 or part thereof in excess of Rs. 400

5. The lowest charge per contract shall be Rs. 5.
6. The scale prescribed in 1 to 5 above is exclusive of service charge and does not apply to underwriting or the placing of new issues.

Historical Background:

1920 The Madras Stock Exchange was founded in April with about 100 members. Trading was predominantly in textile shares and in shares of foreign-owned South Indian plantation companies, plus those of companies listed on the Bombay and Calcutta Stock Exchanges.

1923 The Exchange was forced to close for lack of business.

1927 Only two brokerage firms were in Madras: one European, which closed in 1934, and one Indian. Another European firm soon opened and the two existing firms did about 12 to 25 transactions a day.

1933 Interest in the share market broadened gradually, stimulated by the establishment of trunk telephone facilities.

1937 A private company was organized August 12 in the name and style of Madras Stock Exchange Association Ltd. The Exchange was inaugurated officially September 4. Seven firms were founding members, of which five were signatories to the Memorandum of Association.
About 84 scrips were listed, apart from Government and other securities; listing requirements were introduced. A unique feature of the Madras market: shares were dealt in only for cash.

1957 In order to meet Government requirements, the Exchange was reorganized as a new company limited by guarantee on April 29, under the name Madras Stock Exchange Limited. The Exchange was recognized by the Government of India in October.

1958 A Clearing House was established in July.

1969 The foundation stone was laid for a new Exchange Building on August 22.

1971 The new building opened - October 9 - at 16/17 Jehangir Street, better known as Second Line Beach.

INTERNATIONAL FEDERATION OF STOCK EXCHANGES

INTERNATIONAL FEDERATION OF STOCK EXCHANGES

Title: Federation Internationale des Bourses de Valeurs

Address: 129, rue de Courcelles, 75017 Paris, France

Telephone: 231 - 10 - 71

Cable Address: FEDINTERBO PARIS

Officers:
President: M. Pedro Rodriguez Ponga (Chairman of Madrid Stock Exchange)
Vice President: James J. Needham (Chairman of New York Stock Exchange)
Secretary General: M. Louis Delanney

Memberships:
1. The Federation has fourteen members which include:
   a. The following stock exchanges: Amsterdam, Brussels, Johannesbourg, London, Luxembourg, Madrid, New York, Paris, Tokyo, Toronto, Vienna.
   b. The following stock exchange associations: Association of German Exchanges, Union of the Committee Directors of Italian Stock Exchanges, Association of Swiss Stock Exchanges.
2. In addition to the regular members, there are the following associate members: American Stock Exchange, the Buenos Aires Stock Exchange, the Copenhagen Stock Exchange, the Hong Kong Stock Exchange, the Mexico Stock Exchange, the Stockholm Stock Exchange, the Osaka Stock Exchange.

Organization:
The purpose of the Federation is to promote collaboration among its members within the traditional relations which they maintain with each other.

The four divisions of the Federation include the General Assembly, the Presidency, the Working Commission, and the Secretariat.

Typical of questions dealt with by the Working Committee are: listing of foreign securities on national exchanges; exchange membership; international cooperation in the clearing and settlement of securities; use of automation among the world's stock exchanges; and issues posed by the growth of institutional investors.

Historical Background:
1961 Organized in October to succeed the Association of European Stock Exchanges which was formed in 1957.
1973 Held first General Assembly in the United States.
1974 General Assembly scheduled to meet in Madrid.

IRAN

TEHRAN

TEHRAN STOCK EXCHANGE

Title: Tehran Stock Exchange

Address: Taghinia Building, 521 Lower Saadi Avenue, Tehran, Iran

Telephone: 311149; 311150; 318488; 393858

Cable Address: MARKAZBANK

Officers:
Governor of the Central Bank of Iran, Chairman of the Council of the Stock Exchange, which consists of eleven members: M. Yeganeh
Deputy Governor of the Central Bank of Iran, Chairman of the Acceptance

Committee, which consists of seven members: J. Shoraka
President of the Industrial and Mining Development Bank of Iran and Head of
the Board of Directors of the Broker's Organization, which consists of twenty
members: A. Kheradjou
Director of the Secretariat of the Council of the Stock Exchange and Securities
Acceptance Committee: N. F. Larijani
Secretary of the Broker's Organization: D. K. Allam

Hours of Business: 10:00 A.M. - 12:00 noon, every day except Thursday and
Friday.

Regulatory Laws: Law for the Establishment of the Stock Exchange; Securities
Acceptance Committee By-Laws; Brokers Organization By-Laws; Administrative By-Laws (Stock Exchange Council); Articles of Association.

   3. Broker's Organization By-Laws.

Issues Traded and Volume:
   1. Listed Issues:
      a. Shares:

Year*	No. of Cos.	Val. Shs. Traded**	Val. Bds. Traded**	Total**
1968	2	15.3	——	15.3
1969	6	31.4	92.4	123.8
1970	9	89.0	44.4	133.4
1971	12	106.6	14.5	121.1
1972	17	134.2	254.2	388.4
1973	23	334.2	865.3	1,199.5
1974	34	1,322.7	1,450.9	2,773.6

      *Year ending March 20; **000,000 Rials
      b. Bonds: Twelve different kinds and series of Government issues are
         traded.
   2. Volume (March 29, 1973 - March 20, 1974): 591,126 shares.

Unit of Trading: One share.

Memberships:
   1. Regular Members: 20
   2. There are no membership fees. Members have to deposit one million rials at
      the time of their appointment. Memberships are not transferable.

Commissions or Fees: For share transactions below 1 million rials, up to a
maximum of 1% of the amount involved charged to each party. On the excess
over 1 million rials, maximum is 0.5%.

Historical Background:
   1346 (1967) The Tehran Stock Exchange was founded. Trading volume has
               increased in each year.
   1351 (1972) The program for "Wider Share Ownership of Individual Units"
               gave volume a further impetus.

IRELAND

DUBLIN

DUBLIN STOCK EXCHANGE

Title: The Stock Exchange—Irish Unit.

Address: 24-28 Anglesea, Dublin 2, Ireland.

Telephone: 778808 (office); 776841 (market)

Telex: 4537

Cable Address: STOCK EXCHANGE, Dublin, Ireland

Branches and Affiliates: 12 Marlboro Street, Cork. Telephone: Cork - 20875

Officers:
President: Michael F. Dillon
Vice-President: John A. Garvey
General Manager: J. S. Leeson

Hours of Business: 10:45 A.M. and 2:15 P.M. (weekdays)

Regulatory Laws: The stock exchanges of Great Britain and Ireland amalgamated with London to form The Stock Exchange in March, 1973. The rules and regulations governing this exchange therefore apply also to The Stock Exchange—Irish unit. See "London Stock Exchange."

Issues Traded and Volume:
1. Listed Issues: 424, representing 14 different categories: Government Funds, Land Bonds, British Funds, Corporate Stock and Public Boards, etc.
2. Volume: Not available.

Membership:
1. Regular Members: 95
2. Associate Members: 11
3. Membership costs: Current yearly subscription: 300 pounds.

Commissions or Fees:
1. British Government Securities
   a. Bargains up to £ 50,000 consideration:

	Under 5 years to redemption	5-10 years	Over 10 years
first £ 2,000	at discretion	0.5 %	0.5 %
on the next £ 2,000	at discretion	0.1 %	0.2 %
on the next £ 10,000	at discretion	0.05 %	0.2 %
on the next £ 36,000	at discretion	0.05 %	0.1 %

   b. Bargains over £ 50,000 consideration

on the first £ 250,000	at discretion	0.07 %	0.14 %
on the excess	at discretion	0.0625%	0.125%

2. Debentures, Bonds, etc.:
   a. Registered*

0.75%	on the first	£	5,000	consideration
0.375%	on the next		15,000	consideration
nil	on the next		5,000	consideration
0.375%	on the next		25,000	consideration
0.325%	on the next		50,000	consideration
0.3%	on the next		150,000	consideration
0.25%	on the next		500,000	consideration
0.2%	on the next		1,000,000	consideration
0.125%	on the excess			

   *Including New Issues passing by delivery in scrip form, or by letters of renunciation.

   b. Bearer:

0.5%	on the first	£	5,000	consideration
0.25%	on the next		15,000	consideration
nil	on the next		5,000	consideration
0.25%	on the excess.			

3. Stocks and Shares: Registered or Bearer, whether partly or fully paid.

1.25%	on the first	£	5,000	consideration
0.625%	on the next		15,000	consideration
nil	on the next		5,000	consideration
0.625%	on the next		25,000	consideration
0.5%	on the next		50,000	consideration
0.4%	on the next		150,000	consideration
0.3%	on the next		500,000	consideration
0.2%	on the next		1,000,000	consideration
0.125%	on the excess			

4. American and Canadian shares:
   Shares of companies incorporated in the United States or Canada (whether dealt in London on a dollar or sterling basis), with the exception of shares which are deliverable by transfer.

0.75%	on the first	£	5,000	consideration
0.375%	on the next		15,000	consideration
nil	on the next		5,000	consideration
0.375%	on the excess			

Historical Background:

1799 Dublin Stock Exchange formed.
1971 Name changed to Irish Stock Exchange (March).
1973 Name changed to The Stock Exchange—Irish Unit (March).

ISREAL

TEL-AVIV

THE TEL-AVIV STOCK EXCHANGE LTD.

Title: The Tel-Aviv Stock Exchange Ltd.

Address: 113 Allenby Road, Tel-Aviv 65127, Israel.

Telephone: (03) 614301

Cable Address: TASTOCKEX

Branches and Affiliates: The Stock Exchange Clearing House Ltd.

Officers:
Chairman: E. Lehmann
Vice Chairman: D. Recanati
Executive Director: D. Ottensooser

Hours of Business: 9 A.M. to approximately 2 P.M.
 Trading in the stock exchange is conducted Sunday through Thursday (except holidays and the eves of holidays). There are two sessions daily in the share market, of which the first is conducted by roll call and the second as a continuous auction market. Members are not expected to bring all their deals to the floor, but use its facilities to execute those buy and sell orders which they are unable to match individually. Prices and volume of transactions are reported in the Official Quotations List. Share prices as well as those of bonds are in percent of par values.

Regulatory Laws:
1. Securities Law 1968 and Regulations promulgated by virtue thereof;
2. Stock Exchange Regulations;
3. Stock Exchange Rulings.

Issues Traded and Volume:
1. a. Number of issues listed (end of year)

	1968	1969	1970	1971	1972	1973
Shares*	165	157	156	154	147	144
Debentures	629	668	731	808	807	1,125

*Number of companies listed:

95	95	98	99	93	93

   b. "Other" issues (traded but not listed):

3	3	3	3	3	3

2. Capital listed (end of year, IL mill., rounded figures)

	1968	1969	1970	1971	1972	1973
Shares						
Nominal value	830	960	1,040	1,100	1,210	1,540
Market value	960	1,080	1,080	1,420	2,830	2,780
Debentures						
Nominal value	2,700	3,100	3,600	4,700	5,500	8,020
Market value	3,000	3,600	4,400	6,100	7,300	11,044

3. Annual volume (money proceeds, IL mill.)

	1968	1969	1970	1971	1972	1973
Shares	112.4	107.1	52.3	105.4	763.0	633.0
Debentures	284.5	349.4	337.5	519.4	908.3	1,221.6

Unit of Trading:

1. Debentures: IL 1,000 nom. value.
2. Shares: First Session: IL 100 nom. value; Second Session: IL 1,000 nom. value
3. Odd-Lots:
   a. Shares—Trading takes place once monthly between members. Customers may sell odd-lots at any time.
   b. Debentures—Matched by members in the ordinary course of business.

Memberships: Number of regular members:

1. Banks: 19
2. Non-Banks (Brokers and financial institutions): 9
   Membership prices: There is an entrance fee payable upon admission of a new member and a membership fee which is voted annually. There is no membership price.

Commissions or Fees: Commissions for trading securities (maximum rates, percent of money proceeds):

Shares: 1%
Debentures: 0.7%
Short Term Paper: 0.15%

Income tax on all listed shares and most bonds is limited to a maximum of 25%, deducted at source. Foreign investors may claim exemption from this tax, provided -

1. that they benefit from the exemption and
2. that their investment was paid from the proceeds of foreign currency or certain State of Israel Bonds cashed at the official rate of exchange.

Income and proceeds from the sale of investment made in this manner may be repatriated in foreign currency at the official rate of exchange.

Historical Background:

The Tel-Aviv Stock Exchange is the only organized stock market in Israel. Founded in 1935, it was incorporated in 1953 as a company limited by guarantee. In 1969 it was licensed by the Ministry of Finance under the Securities Law of 1968. Governed by a Board of Directors, the exchange makes its own rules, subject to the provisions of the above mentioned law.

Affiliated with the Tel-Aviv Stock Exchange is the Stock Exchange Clearing House Ltd., the members of which must be members of the exchange. In Israel it is not customary for the public to keep their own securities; they usually leave them with their bank or broker who, in turn, keeps them in safe custody with the Clearing House. Purchases and sales of listed securities are cleared daily as book entries and the necessity of delivery of certificates is thereby avoided. The Clearing House also clears dividend and interest payments, capital repayment, etc.

ITALY

THE STOCK EXCHANGES OF ITALY

(Bologna, Firenze, Genoa, Milan, Naples,
Palermo, Rome, Turin, Trieste, Venice)

Italy has ten stock exchanges—public institutions set up by decree of the Chief of State on proposal of the local Chamber of Commerce. The exchange in Milan is the most important for here the bulk of the nation's trading is conducted. The exchanges are governed by law and supervised by:

1. The Treasury
2. The Chamber of Commerce
3. The Deputazione di Borsa, appointed annually by ministerial decree. It consists, according to the importance of the exchange, of 3, 5, or 7 members, who supervise the proper functioning of the exchange and ensure that its laws and regulations are observed. In addition to extensive advisory functions, the Committee is vested with police and disciplinary powers.
4. The Comitato Direttivo degli Agenti di Cambio, a body installed by law to supervise broker's activities and to represent registered brokers. Its 4 or 8 members, depending upon the importance of the exchange, are elected among stockbrokers every two years at the stockbrokers' general meeting. The Committee also arbitrates disputes arising out of business transactions on the exchange and acts in an advisory capacity.

   A Treasury representative attends stock exchange sessions, presides over the commission entrusted with preparing the official list, attends meetings of the above-mentioned committees without effective vote and has powers to inspect stockbrokers' activities. Each exchange is under special jurisdiction of the Chamber of Commerce.

Stock Exchange Dealers

1. Stockbrokers ("Agenti di Cambio") are appointed by decree of the Chief of State. The appointment is effected exclusively by means of a competitive examination sponsored by the Treasury, which may be taken by those who have met certain requirements regarding age, nationality, education and previous training for the brokerage profession. Upon appointment the stockbroker must post a security bond (500,000 to 1 million lire depending upon the stock exchange).

   The number of stockbrokers is fixed by law in proportion to the requirements of each exchange. Stockbrokers may not deal for their own account, either directly or through an intermediary.
2. Stockbrokers' Representatives. Each stockbroker may employ a maximum of 2 representatives who may act for him on the floor ("alle grida") under the direct responsibility of their principal. Their appointment must be approved by the Comita Direttivo degli Agenti di Cambio with the consent of the Deputazione di Borsa and must be communicated to the Treasury.
3. Representatives of Banks. Banks with a paid-up capital of at least 100 million lire and registered in a Register kept by the Banca d'Italia may be authorized to have their representatives attend trading on the floor as observers.

Securities Admitted to Listing: All bonds and debentures are, in general, to the bearer but they may be also in registered form, while shares are required by law to be in registered form.
1. Admitted by Law:
   a. Government securities.
   b. Government-guaranteed securities.
   c. Bonds secured by mortgage of real property and similar.
2. Admitted on Government Proposal:
   a. Securities issued by provincial and municipal authorities.
   b. Securities issued by legally recognized non-profit organizations.
   c. Securities issued by Italian companies.
   d. Securities issued by foreign governments.
   e. Securities issued by foreign companies and foreign non-profit organizations.

Types of Transactions
1. Cash transactions ("operazioni a contanti") concluded in respect of all fixed interest securities, with settlement on the first business day following the day on which the transaction was concluded;
2. Future delivery contracts ("operazioni a termine"), concluded in respect of shares with monthly settlement on the day and hour fixed by the calendar of the stock exchange. This type of transaction also includes options;
3. "Riporti." A "riporto" is a contract in which a party sells a certain number of securities to another party (broker, bank, etc.) at a price and assumes the obligation of repurchasing from the same party an equivalent number of securities of the same kind on the maturity date of the contract, by paying the price previously agreed upon plus a fee.
4. Foreign exchange transactions (concluded solely by banks acting as agents of Banca d'Italia, through authorized brokers in conformity with the exchange control regulations in force).

Minimum Amounts (established by the Comitato Direttivo degli Agenti di Cambio in agreement with the Deputazione di Borsa.)
1. In lots of 1 to 10 for consolidated and redeemable government bonds with a par value from 100,000 to 1 million lire.
2. In lots of 10 to 1,000 for bonds of public law agencies and real property mortgage bonds, with a par value from 250,000 to 1 million lire;
3. In lots of 50 to 500 for corporate bonds with a par value of 500,000 lire;
4. Shares are traded in lots of 25 to 5,000 depending upon their market value.

Commissions. Brokerage rates are fixed by decree of the Treasury uniformly for all Italian stock exchanges:
1. for consolidated and redeemable government bonds: 0.15 per 100 of market value;
2. for corporate debentures with market value up to 600 lire: 2 lire each; over 600 lire: 4 lire each;
3. for shares with market value:
from 1 to 1,000 lire:	from 1 to 6 lire each
from 1,001 to 3,000 lire:	from 10 to 20 lire each

from 3,001 to 5,000 lire:	from 24 to 34 lire each
from 5,001 to 7,000 lire:	from 38 to 48 lire each
from 7,001 to 10,000 lire:	from 50 to 70 lire each
over 10,000 lire:	7 per 1,000

Prices and the Official Lists The ascertainment of prices and the compilation of the list are carried out by the Official List Commission at the close of each session of the stock exchange, on the basis of written declarations or reports made daily by stockbrokers in respect of all transactions concluded by them. The quotation of the securities may be entered on the official list only upon declaration of both the seller and the buyer. The official list is published daily by the Chamber of Commerce.

Quotation Methods Prices are determined exclusively "alle grida" (by calling out). The quotation of shares is expressed in lire and refers to a unit (no particular par value is prescribed) and to fully paid up securities; while quotations in bonds and debentures are expressed in percent of their nominal value.
Prices may be "a contante" i.e. for immediate delivery of the securities, for fixed-interest securities, and for variable-yield securities: "per fine corrente," i.e. for delivery of the securities on the current settlement day and "per fine prossimo," i.e. for delivery on the subsequent settlement day; a price for options ("operazioni a premio") is also recorded.
The prices of government annuities, redeemable bonds and of shares are "tel quel," i.e. they contain accrued interest or the portion of dividend pertaining to the current coupon, while the prices of Treasury and corporate bonds are "plus," i.e. net of accrued interest from the due date of the last coupon paid.

Note: Although the list of Commodity Exchanges was furnished by an official government agency and efforts were made to reach each of the exchanges included, it is possible that some, like the Genova Commodity Exchange, no longer deal in futures trading, despite information to the contrary.

BARI

BARI COMMODITY EXCHANGE

Title: Borsa Merci
Address: Corso Cavour, 2, 70121 Bari, Italy
Telephone: 216600

BOLOGNA

BOLOGNA COMMODITY EXCHANGE

Title: Borsa Merci
Address: Via Ugo Bassi, 2, 40121 Bologna, Italy
Telephone: 229911

BOLOGNA STOCK EXCHANGE

Title: Borsa Valori
Address: Via Ugo Bassi, 2, 40121 Bologna, Italy
Telephone: 223684

FIRENZE

FIRENZE COMMODITY EXCHANGE

Title: La Borsa Merci di Firenze
Address: Florence, Italy
Telephone: 27.71
Officers: President: Giancarlo Cassi
The Exchange is disciplined by a delegation and a committee.
1. Delegation Members:

Guiseppe Belsito	Agostino Allegri
Guido Tosato	Vieri Balboni
Renzo Lenzi	Mario Borgioli
Giovanni Fanfani	

2. Committee Members:

Arduino Borghi	Franco Faraoni
Alfonso Francheschini	Italo Petroni
Agostino Archilli	

Hours of Business: The market is open two days each week—Tuesday and Friday.

Regulatory Laws: The existence and status of the exchange were established by decree of the President of the Republic on July 16, 1951 and a supplementary regulation approved a ministerial decree of August 28, 1954.

Commodities Traded: In addition to products typical of certain areas, such as wine (Chianti), the principal commodities traded are vegetable oil, flour, wheat, cereal, fertilizer.

FIRENZE STOCK EXCHANGE

Title: Borsa Valori
Address: Piazza Mentana, 2, 50122 Firenze, Italy
Telephone: 276807

GENOVA

GENOVA STOCK EXCHANGE

Title: Borsa Valori
Address: Via G. Boccaccio, 1, 16121 Genova, Italy
Telephone: 564441

MILAN

MILAN STOCK EXCHANGE

Title: Borsa Valori di Milano
Address: Piazza degli Affari, 6, 20123 - Milan, Italy
Telephone: 87 00 33 - 87 07 16 - 89 79 48
Teletype: COMITATO BORSA MILANO
Telex: MicomBSA 35430
Cable Address: COMITATO BORSA MILANO
Officers: General Secretary: Achille Boretti
Hours of Business:
1. Shares and Bonds: 10:00 A.M. - 1:45 P.M. weekdays. The exchange is defined as a "call market." The opening call lasts until 10:25. Then, after a five-minute interval, the closing call starts. Only the most representative shares are dealt in during the opening call.
2. The currency exchange market opens at 1:15 P.M.

Regulatory Laws:
The principal sources of law governing stock exchanges in Italy:
1. Law of March 20, 1913, concerning the organization of the Commerce Stock Exchange, the method of transacting business, etc. and the fees on stock exchange contracts.
2. Royal Decree of August 4, 1913. Regulations for the execution of the above-mentioned law.
3. Law on Stock Exchange contract fees, issued by Royal Decree on December 30,1923.

4. Royal Decree Law of March 7, 1925. Reorganization of the Stock Exchanges.
5. Royal Decree Law of April 9, 1925. Measures taken on the reorganization of the Stock Exchanges.
6. Royal Decree of April 9, 1925. Regulation of the Stock Exchanges.
7. Royal Decree Law of June 30, 1932. Changes to some of the regulations regarding the Stock Exchanges and stockbrokers.
8. Royal Decree Law of October 25, 1941. Compulsory registration of the shareholder's name on the share certificate.
9. Royal Decree of March 29, 1942. Regulations for the interpretation, integration and complementation, regarding the compulsory registration of the shareholder's name on the share certificate.
10. Particular orders are found in the fourth (debentures) and fifth (work) books of the Civil Code.

Issues Traded and Volume:

1. Listed Issues: 161 stocks representing 146 corporations; 559 bonds; 27 government stocks. There is also an "unofficial market," which presently is not under the jurisdiction of the Executive Committee. As of December 31, 1973, 111 stocks of 109 companies were traded there.
2. Volume:
   a. Milan Stock Exchange

Year	Shs. Traded (000,000)	Market value Lire (000,000,000)	Nom. Value Gvt. Stk. Traded Lire (000,000)	Nom. Value Bonds Traded Lire (000,000)
1963	272.6	722.7	28,539	103,570
1964	258.5	612.7	31,102	109,734
1965	356.0	786.0	31,107	139,935
1966	541.3	1,256.7	48,699	175,082
1967	570.5	1,125.0	50,270	251,579
1968	424.6	1,109.2	63,670	282,814
1969	606.4	1,825.7	108,730	466,578
1970	497.7	1,478.3	72,548	332,540
1971	525.8	996.9	33,686	324,101
1972	885.1	1,468.2	34,686	472,909
1973	1,441.0	2,485.0	N.A.	N.A.

   b. Milan Unofficial Market

Year	Shares Traded	Value - Lire (000,000)
1963	2,357,694	8,397.7
1964	2,779,736	9,000.5
1965	2,178,614	4,424.7
1966	2,407,179	10,511.8
1967	2,202,220	5,332.9
1968	2,139,773	7,288.0
1969	4,826,082	20,963.0
1970	8,428,731	23,727.5
1971	5,713,142	22,209.4
1972	14,207,232	66,584.5
1973	19,257,052	146,630.5

Unit of Trading: Minimum amounts:
1. Shares: units of 25 to 5,000 depending upon market value.
2. Bonds:
   a. Consolidated and redeemable government issues, with a par value from 100,000 to 1 million lire, are traded in units of 1 to 10;
   b. Public law agencies and real property mortgage issues, with a par value from 250,000 to 1 million lire, are traded in units of 10 to 1,000;
   c. Corporate issues, with a par value of 500,000 lire, are traded in units of 50 to 500.
3. Odd-lots are not handled in the rings ("corbeilles") like round-lots. Buyers and sellers mark their orders on special boards. However, experiments are currently being conducted to match odd-lot orders electronically. There is no extra commission for executing odd-lots, but prices are naturally less favorable than those for round-lots.

Membership: Regular Members: 103. The number is fixed by law in proportion to the requirements of each stock exchange. It varies from a minimum of 8 in Venice and Bologna to a maximum of 130 at the Milan Stock Exchange. Brokers may not deal for their own accounts. They are entitled to a commission for their services, which is fixed by the Treasury upon consultation with the Italian Association of Stockbrokers.

Commissions or Fees:
1. Shares with market value of:

1	to	1,000	lire	—	from	1	to	6	lire each
1,001	to	3,000	lire	—	from	10	to	20	lire each
3,001	to	5,000	lire	—	from	24	to	34	lire each
5,0001	to	7,000	lire	—	from	38	to	48	lire each
7,001	to	10,000	lire	—	from	50	to	70	lire each
over		10,000	lire	—	from	7	lire	per	1,000

2. Bonds:
   a. consolidated and redeemable government issues: 0.15 per 100 of market value;
   b. corporate debentures with market value up to 600 lire: 2 lire each; over 600 lire: 4 lire each.
3. The same rates apply to all Italian stock exchanges: Bologna, Florence, Genoa, Milan, Naples, Palermo, Rome, Trieste, Turin, Venice.

Historical Background:
1808 (February 6) The Viceroy Eugene Napoleon founded the Milan Stock Exchange. It was inaugurated February 15 on the premises of the Monte di Pieta (Pawn Brokers).

NAPOLI

NAPOLI COMMODITY EXCHANGE

Title: Borsa Merci
Address: Via Mercato dei Grani, 80133 Napoli, Italy
Telephone: 321969

PADOVA

PADOVA COMMODITY EXCHANGE

Title: Borsa Merci
Address: P. Insurrezione, 35100 Padova, Italy
Telephone: 42245

PARMA

PARMA BOARD OF TRADE

Title: La Borsa Merci di Parma
Address: Camera di Commercio Industria ed Agricoltura, Parma, Italy
Telephone: 0521/44341 - 2-3-4-5
Telex: PARMATEL 51059
Officers: Governing Committee:

1. Active Members:
   Luigi Ruffino
   Luciano Bertoni
   Rolando Fava
   Guido Guareschi
   Maurizio Piazza

   Umberto Savi
   Giuseppe Ziliotti
2. Substitute Members:
   A. Vittorio Artoni
   Renato Ghersetich
   Antonio Savi

Hours of Business: The market is open on Wednesday and Saturday.

Regulatory Laws: The Borsa is regulated by Law 272 of March 20, 1913, by Law 1068 of August 4, 1913, and by successive modifications thereof, as well as by its own special rules.
The market is administered by the Chamber of Commerce, which elects a surveillance committee each year to enforce various rules and regulations, supervise trading and prices. In addition, each commodity traded has its own active and substitute committees, composed of farmers, dealers, producers, brokers and others.

Commodities Traded:

	Contract size (tons)
1. Dairy Produce	
a. Butter	4,000
b. Cheese	20,000
2. Cured Hams and Salami	50-70,000
3. Extract of Tomato	30,000
4. Cereal, Flour and by-products	250-300,000
5. Potatoes, Vegetables and Grapes	
a. Potato)	
b. Onion)	
c. Tomato)	80-120,000
d. Grape)	
6. Pork	300,000
7. Poultry and Eggs	130,000

Historical Background:
1970 La Borsa Merci di Parma opened for business June 14.

ROME

ROME STOCK EXCHANGE

Title: Borsa Valori
Address: P. di Pietra, Palazzo Camera di Commercio, 00186 Rome, Italy
Telephone: 674541

TORINO

TORINO COMMODITY EXCHANGE

Title: Borsa Merci
Address: Via A. Doria, 15, 10123 Torino, Italy
Telephone: 553121

TORINO STOCK EXCHANGE

Title: Borsa Valori
Address: Via S. Francesco di Paola, 28, 10123 Torino, Italy
Telephone: 547743

JAMAICA

KINGSTON

JAMAICA STOCK EXCHANGE

Title: The Jamaica Stock Exchange

Address: P.O. Box 621, 31½ Olivier Place, Kingston, Jamaica

Telephone: 93 - 22536 : 92 - 23662

Officers:
General Manager: V. H. O. Mendez
Assistant General Manager: K. B. Whyte
Secretary: Joyce Woodham (Mrs.)

Hours of Business: 10:00 A.M. - 12:00 noon

Regulatory Laws: Securities Act Legislation pending

Issues Traded: Forty-three companies comprising: 41 ordinary (common) stocks, 10 preference shares, 10 corporate bonds.

Volume:

Year	Total Volume (shs.)
1969	7,450,000
1970	5,070,000
1971	8,418,000
1972	12,133,000
1973	9,450,000

	Date	Volume (000)	Value ($000)
Aug.	1969-High	915	753
Nov.	1969-Low	283	263
	Total-1969	7,450	$6,501
Jan.	1970-High	841	869
Aug.	1970-Low	209	116
	Total-1970	5,070	$3,907
July	1971-High	1,746	1,660
Oct.	1971-Low	327	248
	Total-1971	8,418	$6,493
May	1972-High	2,761	2,478
Feb.	1972-Low	526	453
	Total-1972	12,133	$11,465
Jan.	1973-High	3,037	1,631
Oct.	1973-Low	273	226
	Total-1973	9,450	$7,811

Unit of Trading (Board-Lots):
1. 500 units up to 50 cents per unit
   200 units from 51 cents to $1.00 per unit
   100 units from $1.01 to $5.00 per unit
   50 units from over $5.00 per unit
2. Odd-lots may be dealt in provided such transactions are done at prices not lower than the established "Bid," nor higher than the established "Offer."
3. Odd-lot commissions are set at the broker's discretion.

Memberships:
Regular Members   4
Associated Members   12
"Other" Members   0

       Upon being accepted for membership a prospective member is required to take up one share in the Jamaica Stock Exchange Limited, a company whose sole function is to operate The Jamaica Stock Exchange. The cost of such a share is $200.

       The company may issue its share at a premium, in addition to the nominal value of $200. In 1969 the premium assessed on each share was $1,000. Since. then no new shares have been issued.

Commissions or Fees:
a. Stocks and Shares
   1. Regular Commission
     2% on the first $10,000 involved
     1½% on the next $20,000 involved
     1% on the next $20,000 involved
     ½% on the excess over $50,000 involved
   2. Minimum Commission

Amount	Commission Chargeable
Under $25.00	At member's discretion
$25.00 and under $50.00	At member's discretion but not less than $1.00
$50.00 and over	At regular commission but not less than $2.00

   3. Block Transactions (Minimum $30,000)
     ½% on the first $50,000 involved
     ¼% on the next $50,000 involved
     ⅛% on the next $100,000 involved
     1/16% on the excess over $200,000 involved
b. Debentures/Loan Stock
     1% on the first $10,000 involved.
     ½% on the next $40,000 involved.
     ¼% on the excess over $50,000 involved.

Historical Background:
       The Jamaica Stock Exchange Limited was incorporated in August 1968 for the purpose of operating stock exchanges in Jamaica. Prior to this there was a fairly active over-the-counter market in shares and other securities of resident

Jamaican companies, which was supervised by the Kingston Stock Market Committee.

Members of the Committee comprised four stock brokers, seven commercial banks, four trust companies and the Bank of Jamaica (the Central Bank). The Committee, which was chaired by the Bank of Jamaica, met on Thursday of each week to hear reports of prices at which shares had been traded during the course of the preceding five business days. On this basis, closing bid and asked prices were published in the press each Friday morning.

On February 3, 1969, The Jamaica Stock Exchange was formally opened with 23 companies listed. By year's end (1969) 34 companies were listed.

JAPAN

THE STOCK EXCHANGES OF JAPAN

Japan has eight stock exchanges: Fukuoka, Hiroshima, Kyoto, Nagoya, Niigata, Osaka, Sapporo, Tokyo.

The first securities markets were organized in 1878 when exchanges were founded in Tokyo and Osaka. The Nagoya Stock Exchange (third largest today) was established in 1886; other smaller markets began operating in various cities.

The rapid expansion of business and industry—most notably the "Zaibatsu" (powerful industrial and financial combines)—was naturally reflected by higher security prices, both during and after World War I. The Sino-Japanese conflict in 1937 brought wartime controls and regulations, but the most significant changes occurred in 1943; a) the Cooperation Securities Co. and the Wartime Financial Bank were inaugurated in an attempt to stabilize securities prices; b) most importantly, Japan's eleven stock exchanges were consolidated into one government-controlled corporation—the Japan (Nippon) Securities Exchange.

The corporation suspended operations at war's end in August, 1945, and Japan was left without an organized stock market. For the next few years the only trading was over-the-counter. In 1947, after the Japan Securities Exchange was formally dissolved and the Zaibatsu liquidated, a mass release of stocks was made through the Securities Coordination Liquidation Committee. Investors took advantage of this to drastically increase their securities holdings, thus completely changing the character of the Japanese stock market.

On May 16, 1949, as the result of a new Securities Exchange Law enacted in 1948, stock exchanges founded on the membership system were inaugurated in Tokyo, Osaka and Nagoya. They were followed by exchanges in Kyoto, Hiroshima, Fukuoka, Niigata and Sapporo. The financial organization of Japan was properly reestablished in 1951-1952, when the Mutual Financing Bank Law, the Credit Bank Law, the Long-Term Credit Bank Law, and the Loan Trust Law were enacted.

Increased productivity put Japan on the paths of rapid economic growth and rising stock prices during the years 1955-1961. Indeed, the market expanded so rapidly and profits were so easily harvested during the "Jinmu Boom" and the "Iwato Boom" that stockbrokers generally greeted one another: "Good Morning securities companies, bye-bye banks." The banks had some revenge, however, when tighter money temporarily pricked the prosperity bubble in July, 1961, and stocks tumbled.

The basic underpinnings of the stock market and the economy nevertheless remained strong. The upward trend was resumed after a bottoming out phase in the fall of 1965 and the securities market strengthened its foundations under the licensing system. The Securities Exchange Law was amended, revisions aimed at strengthening the public character of the exchanges were introduced, the disclosure system was enforced, and investments by foreigners assumed boom proportions.

The popular stock averages moved to all-time peaks as volume soared. On November 14, 1972, a record 359,874,000 shares changed hands in Osaka; turnover in Tokyo the same day reached an astounding 1,066,524,400 shares (First Section).

Volume (%):

	Tokyo	Osaka	Nagoya	Other Exchanges
1963	68.98	23.65	3.90	3.47
1964	70.22	23.29	3.53	2.96
1965	69.01	24.58	3.17	3.24
1966	69.06	24.71	3.20	3.03
1967	68.32	25.31	3.88	2.44
1968	71.43	23.66	3.27	1.64
1969	74.05	21.38	3.26	1.30
1970	74.88	20.63	3.14	1.35
1971	74.68	21.79	2.44	1.09
1972	74.08	22.16	2.56	1.20
1973	74.66	21.17	2.73	1.44

Memberships:

1. Membership on a Japanese stock exchange is limited to corporations. A corporation seeking entry into the securities business must first obtain one of four kinds of licenses from the Ministry of Finance. The licenses permit:
   a. dealing for one's own account;
   b. brokerage activity;
   c. underwriting and distributing securities;
   d. selling securities as a member of a syndicate which distributes securities.

   Capital stock requirements vary according to the categories in which the securities company wants to operate. For example, a broker-dealer member of the Tokyo Stock Exchange, whose business involves neither underwriting nor distributing, must possess ¥ 100 million or more capital. To obtain a license for all categories, a minimum capital of 200 million yen is required.
2. Members are classified as "regular" or "saitori" (called "nakadachi" members in Osaka). All are licensed securities companies.
   a. most regular members are not only dealers and brokers but also underwriters and distributors of securities. Moreover, they provide such incidental services as safeguarding securities and acting as "standing proxy" for foreign clients.
   b. the saitori member serves as a middleman in transactions between regular members, i.e., he is a kind of broker's broker. He does not trade

for his own account as do New York Stock Exchange "specialists" or "jobbers" on the Stock Exchange in London.

Listed Securities: Stocks listed on the big exchanges are divided into two classes: First Section and Second Section. They are traded in different areas of the trading floors. The principal criteria which determine the section to which they are assigned are capital amount, distribution of shares, dividend, and trading volume. In general, the stocks of most large companies are traded in Section One; stocks of the smaller companies are in Section Two.

Foreign Investors: The Government of Japan has been easing the restrictions for foreigners investing in Japanese securities. Though restraints are still strict on formation of joint ventures and other direct investment, restrictions on acquisition by non-Japanese of securities through the stock market have been markedly reduced. It is now quite easy for non-residents to operate in Japanese securities, except for trading on margin. (The Minister of Finance has authority to set the margin rate; margin transactions must be settled within six months).

However, foreign investment is still limited to "restricted industries." Total foreign holdings, in principle, may not exceed 15% of the outstanding shares of companies in 18 designated industries, including electric power, railroads, banks, airlines. Foreign investment in other industries is, as a rule, limited to 25% of the outstanding shares of each company. A non-resident intending to invest in Japanese stocks must comply with procedures set forth by the Foreign Investment Law and other related rules and regulations.

A foreign investor who has used the designated foreign currencies for his investment may sell his stocks at any time and repatriate the proceeds freely in any of the designated currencies. He may also leave the sales proceeds in his account and reinvest in other Japanese securities, while retaining the remittance privilege on the proceeds of such reinvestment. Also, a regular member of an exchange acting as a standing proxy may repatriate dividends after collection.

In the case of investment in bonds or beneficiary certificates of investment trusts, the procedure is somewhat different. The principal of bonds or the sales proceeds of beneficiary certificates may be freely recovered by the investor in the designated foreign currency, provided they have been held by him for six months or more. However, if he sells such securities before six months have elapsed he may not repatriate the proceeds, even though he is permitted to reinvest in another security and maintain a balance in a non-resident deposit account. In this way, recovery of capital is assured.

Taxes: No tax is levied on capital gains under Japanese tax laws. There is a transfer tax of 0.15% on the sales proceeds of stocks. It is deducted from sales proceeds by the broker at the time he collects his brokerage commission. Taxes levied on dividends vary in accordance with the tax agreements between Japan and the country in which the investor resides. Residents of the U.S., the U.K., Canada, France, and other countries with whom Japan has concluded a tax treaty pay a dividend tax of 15%; investors in countries other than the above pay a 20% tax.

Commissions: General Commission Rates* (as of June, 1974):
1. Stocks and Subscription Warrants.

Price per Sh.**	Less than 30,000 shs.	30,000 shs. or over but less than 50,000 shs.	50,000 shs. or over but less than 100,000 shs.	100,000 or over
¥10 or less	¥0.90	¥0.80	¥0.70	¥0.60
25	1.10	1.00	0.90	0.80
50	1.30	1.20	1.00	0.90
75	1.50	1.30	1.20	1.00
100	1.70	1.50	1.40	1.20
150	1.90	1.70	1.50	1.30
200	2.00	1.80	1.60	1.40
250	2.20	2.00	1.80	1.50
300	2.40	2.20	1.90	1.70
350	2.60	2.30	2.10	1.80
400	2.70	2.40	2.20	1.90
450	2.90	2.60	2.30	2.00
500	3.10	2.80	2.50	2.20
600	3.40	3.10	2.70	2.40
800	4.00	3.60	3.20	2.80
1,000	5.00	4.50	4.00	3.50

* For the purpose of computing general commission rates, the number of shares shall mean those shares involved in one order for one account, of a single security, on the same day.

** Applies only to Subscription Warrants.

Price per Sh.	Less than 30,000 shs.	30,000 shs. or over but less than 50,000 shs.	50,000 shs. or over but less than 100,000 shs.	100,000 or over
In cases exceeding ¥1,000 for every ¥200, or less, plus stated amounts	1.00	0.90	0.80	0.70

2. Bonds (per ¥100 par value in case of straight bonds and a percentage of contract value on convertible bonds)

Contract Value (Par Value)	Govt. Bond	Govt. Gtd. Bond	Municipal Bond & Bank Debenture	Corporate Bond and others	Convertible Bond
Less than ¥0.5 mils					1.0%
¥0.5 mils- less than ¥1 mils.	¥0.20	¥0.30	¥0.40	¥0.50	0.9
¥1 mils. less than ¥3 mils.					0.8

(Continued)

Contract Value (Par Value)	Govt. Bond	Govt. Gtd. Bond	Municipal Bond & Bank Debenture	Corporate Bond and others	Convert- ible Bond
¥3 mils.- less than ¥5 mils.					0.7%
¥5 mils.- less than ¥10 mils.	0.15	0.20	0.30	0.40	0.6
¥10 mils.- less than ¥100 mils.	0.10	0.15	0.20	0.30	
or over ¥100 mils.	0.05	0.10	0.15	0.20	0.5

The investment bankers/brokers which dominate the industry and have offices in New York City as well as in Japan are Daiwa Securities Co., Ltd., Nikko Securities Co., Ltd., Nomura Securities Co., Ltd., and Yamaichi Securities Co., Ltd. The leading security analyst society is the Security Analysts Association of Japan.

(Source of most of this material: The Tokyo Stock Exchange).

FUKUOKA

FUKUOKA STOCK EXCHANGE

Title: Fukuoka Stock Exchange

Address: Fukuoka, Japan

HIROSHIMA

HIROSHIMA STOCK EXCHANGE

Title: Hiroshima Stock Exchange

Address: Hiroshima, Japan

KYOTO

KYOTO STOCK EXCHANGE

Title: Kyoto Stock Exchange
Address: Kyoto, Japan

NAGOYA

NAGOYA STOCK EXCHANGE

Title: Nagoya Stock Exchange
Address: 3 - 17 Sakae-Sanchome, Naka - ku, Nagoya, Japan.
Telephone: (052 - Nagoya) 241-1521
Telex: 442-2193
Officers:
    Chairman and President: Takumi Yoshihashi
    Senior Executive Director: Isamu Inagaki
    Executive Directors:
      Atumu Okuyama
      Shigeo Iwamiya
    Departmental Managers:
      Eizaburo Ishiwara   Eiichi Ito
      Norimasa Ishii   Kazuo Morita
    Vice Controller: Kunio Asai
Hours of Business:
  1. Stocks and Convertible Bonds:
     9:00 A.M. - 11:00 A.M. (Saturdays - weekdays)
     1:00 P.M. - 3:00 P.M. (weekdays)
  2. Bonds: At 9:30 A.M. and 2:30 P.M.
  3. In addition to Sundays and national holidays, all trading floors are closed on the third Saturday of each month and the first three and last three days of the year.
Regulatory Laws: The Securities Exchange Law (1948)
Issues Traded and Volume:

Year	Listed Issues (000)	Trading Volume (000)
1963	51,127,960	2,308,440.0
1964	57,476,761	1,475,951.0
1965	58,527,810	1,602,551.0
1966	59,489,300	1,664,700.8
1967	62,402,105	1,636,321.2
1968	65,777,219	2,144,859.8
1969	72,098,725	2,247,054.1

(Continued)

Year	Listed Issues (000)	Trading Volume (000)
1970	78,717,110	1,793,972.9
1971	83,343,427	1,987,912.9
1972	87,057,922	3,473,472.6
1973	93,259,176	2,168,854.3

Unit of Trading:

1. 1,000 share unit for stocks with par value of 50 or 100 yen.
2. 100 share unit for stocks with par value of 500 yen.
3. Odd-lots are traded in the over-the-counter market, with no extra commission or fee involved.

Memberships: Regular Members: 30; Special Members: 1; "Saitori" Members: 3; Saitoris are broker's brokers. They may not trade for their own account.

Commissions or Fees: Commission rates are the same for all Japanese stock exchanges. See "The Stock Exchanges of Japan" at the beginning of this section.

Historical Background:

1866 (March)	The Nagoya Stock Exchange Corp. was established.
1889 (October)	The Nagoya Stock Exchange Corp. was dissolved.
1893 (October)	The Nagoya Stock Exchange Corp. was reestablished under a new law.
1943 (June)	Japan Co-operation Securities Co. and Wartime Financial Bank were established in order to stabilize stock prices. They were followed by a quasi-public corporation: Japan Securities Exchange. The Nagoya Stock Exchange became the Nagoya Branch of this exchange.
1945 (August)	Trading was suspended on all exchanges at the end of World War II.
1948 (May)	A new securities law, patterned after the American law was enacted. Based upon this, a new stock exchange, the Nagoya Stock Exchange, founded on the membership system, was organized and opened in 1949.
1961 (December)	Second Section* Trading started.
1966 (June)	The Certified Public Accountant Law was amended and the disclosure system was enforced.
1970 (December)	The Asian Development Bank offered the first post-war issue of yen-based foreign bonds.
1971 (February)	A convertible bond market was opened.
1972 (March)	A market for municipal and corporate bonds and bank debentures was opened.
1972 (July)	Trading was opened to foreign securities on the over-the-counter market.
1973 (January)	A government bond market was opened.

*The trading floors have two sections: First and Second. The stocks of most large companies are traded on the former; smaller companies are on the latter.

NIIGATA

NIIGATA STOCK EXCHANGE

Title: Niigata Stock Exchange
Address: Niigata, Japan

OSAKA

OSAKA STOCK EXCHANGE

Title: The Osaka Securities Exchange

Address: Kitahama 2-Chome, Higashi-Ku, Osaka 541, Japan

Telephone: Osaka (06) 203 1151

Teletype: OSASE J

Telex: 5225118

Officers:
President and Chairman: Minoru Tomita
Executive Governors:
Michio Miyauchi
Yasuhiro Komatsu
Haruo Sawada
Rikichi Ohashi
Standing Auditor: Shizuo Kobayashi

Hours of Business:
9:00 A.M. - 11:00 A.M. (weekdays)
1:00 P.M. - 3:00 P.M. (weekdays)
9:00 A.M. - 11:00 A.M. (Saturday)

Regulatory Laws: Securities Exchange Act Law (1948). The General Meeting of Members is the highest decision-making body. The Board of Governors performs the same function in matters pertaining to management and control of the exchange.

Issues Traded and Volume:
1. Issues Traded:
a. Stocks:

Year	Companies	Issues	Listed Shs. (000,000)	Market Value* Yen (000,000)
1963	867	947	62,853	6,688,192
1964	870	938	71,586	6,711,224
1965	861	882	73,169	7,733,901
1966	853	878	75,330	8,459,124
1967	853	896	80,142	8,356,493

(Continued)

Year	Companies	Issues	Listed Shs. (000,000)	Market Value* Yen (000,000)
1968	856	884	85,431	11,362,620
1969	862	912	93,615	16,234,984
1970	892	958	104,169	14,488,527
1971	921	963	111,475	20,041,453
1972	940	985	119,380	43,526,273
1973	975	1,000	130,021	34,965,773

*Market value prior to 1966 is calculated by the closing prices of the last business day of the first week in December; and, since 1967, by those of the last business day in December.

  b. Bonds (See also "Japanese Stock Exchanges" at beginning of this section):

Year	Issuers	Issues	Amt. Issued Yen (000,000)	Amt. Listed Yen (000,000)	Market Value* Yen (000,000)
1963	9	28	137,506	136,020	76,611
1964	9	31	263,225	261,295	156,089
1965	9	34	416,773	414,244	290,479
1966	26	54	822,827	816,421	702,257
1967	26	61	1,697,438	1,682,372	1,499,317
1968	26	68	2,644,924	2,614,525	2,390,369
1969	27	76	3,366,540	3,291,051	3,029,688
1970	42	99	4,167,845	4,051,152	3,745,824
1971	62	126	5,005,082	4,815,917	4,612,179
1972	87	161	6,806,214	6,501,581	6,574,284
1973	163	271	8,237,704	8,050,231	7,152,573

*Aggregate market value, from 1963-1965, is only for that of Tel. & Tel. bonds, because current prices of other bonds are unavailable.

  2. Volume and Value: Stocks

Year	Volume Shs. (000)	Daily Av. Shs. (000)	Value Yen (000)	Transactions Number	Daily Av.
1963	13,981,651	46,761	1,909,494,496	4,554,329	15,232
1964	9,734,195	32,447	1,096,217,045	2,671,788	8,906
1965	12,406,632	41,218	1,425,113,309	3,089,251	10,262
1966	12,859,563	43,152	1,831,885,045	3,515,504	11,797
1967	10,668,789	35,681	1,554,335,939	3,003,062	10,043
1968	15,528,819	51,419	2,715,679,712	5,083,890	16,834
1969	14,719,216	49,559	3,987,619,141	5,191,966	17,482
1970	11,777,930	39,656	2,397,307,606	3,878,345	13,058
1971	17,746,053	59,351	4,282,632,318	4,975,262	16,640
1972	30,021,300	101,081	6,367,670,718	6,870,463	23,133
1973	16,799,261	58,534	4,437,214,431	4,559,923	15,886

Trading floors of the exchange are divided into the First Section and the Second Section. In general, stocks of relatively large companies are traded in the First Section; those of medium-sized or small companies are traded in the Second Section.

Unit of Trading:

  1. Stocks: 1,000 shares for all issues, except those with a par value of 500 yen for which the trading unit is 100 shares. Also, certain issues designated by the exchange have 100-share units. The minimum price variation is 1 yen, but when the price of the stock is 1,000 yen, or more, the bid or offer is made at a variation of 10 yen.

2. Bonds: 100,000 yen at par value for convertible bonds and 1 million yen at par value for other bonds. The minimum price variation is 5 sen per 100 yen at par value (1 yen equals 100 sen).
3. Rights: 1,000. Hand signals are used frequently on the trading floors. With few exceptions, off-floor transactions in listed securities are prohibited by law.

Memberships:
1. 53 companies are Regular Members, who execute customer's orders to buy or sell. They may trade for their own account and underwrite new issues after obtaining a license.
2. Five companies are Nakadachi Members. They act as brokers for Regular Members. They differ from "specialists" or "jobbers" and cannot trade for their own account.
   Exchange members must have a minimum capital of 100 million yen.

Commissions or Fees: See "The Stock Exchanges of Japan" at the beginning of this section.

Historical Background:
1878 Osaka Stock Exchange established.
1943 Exchange became the Osaka Division of the Nippon Securities Exchange, when Japan's eleven stock exchanges were consolidated into one Government-controlled corporation during World War II.
1945 Nippon Securities Exchange suspended operations in August.
1947 Nippon Securities Exchange dissolved in April.
1948 A new Securities and Exchange Law (Shoken Torihiki Ho) was enacted.
1949 Osaka Securities Exchange was established in April, with 361 companies and 1 billion of listed shares. Average daily trading volume for the year: 0.6 million shares.
1956 Bond market reopened.
1961 The Second Section was established.
1967 Subscription warrants admitted to trading in January.
1970 Convertible bond market opened in May.
1972 Highest daily stock volume: 359,874,000 shares - November 14.

SAPPORO

SAPPORO STOCK EXCHANGE

Title: Sapporo Stock Exchange
Address: Sapporo, Japan

TOKYO

TOKYO STOCK EXCHANGE

Title: Tokyo Stock Exchange

Address: 6, Nihombashi-Kabuto-cho, I-chome, Chuo-ku, Tokyo, 103 Japan

Telephone: Tokyo (666) 0141

Telex: 0252 - 2759

Officers:
President: Hireshi Tanimura
Executive Vice-President: Shoichiro Aihara
Senior Managing Director: Yasuo Nakanishi
Managing Directors:
Takashi Hoshino
Kenzo Takahashi
Tatsuzo Inoue
Standing Auditor: Yukio Uehara

Hours of Business: 9:00 A.M. - 11:00 A.M. (weekdays and Saturday)
1:00 P.M. - 3:00 P.M. (weekdays)

Regulatory Laws: Securities Exchange Law (1948). The Tokyo Stock Exchange is under the direction of the Minister of Finance.

Issues Traded and Volume:

1. Listed Issues: All stocks traded on the exchange are listed. They are assigned to one of two sections according to capital amount, distribution of shares, dividend, trading volume. The First Section comprises stocks listed before October, 1961. The Second Section includes most stocks formerly traded over-the-counter. Inter-sectional reassignment of stocks is frequent.

a. Stocks (as of March 1, 1974)

	First Section	Second Section
Listed Companies	875	500
Listed Issues	902	520
Capital of Listed Shares (in mill. yen)	8,028,757	358,842
Listed Shares (in mill.)	138,080	7,017
Market Value (in mill. yen)	39,578,981	1,795,100

b. Bonds (as of 1/31/74)

Listed Issues	290
Listed Issuers	188

2. (a) Volume:

Year	First Section	Shares (000,000) Second Section	Value-Yen (000,000) First Section	Second Section
1963	39,375	1,403	5,428,458	319,987
1964	28,578	766	3,328,748	101,043
1965	33,952	886	3,906,891	97,660
1966	34,466	1,471	5,036,141	230,378
1967	27,697	1,107	4,158,550	152,482

1968	45,105	1,780	8,138,047	295,581
1969	48,246	2,739	13,186,417	704,897
1970	41,043	1,709	8,753,458	398,996
1971	59,033	1,785	13,505,112	475,188
1972	97,346	3,011	20,612,434	822,800
1973	57,883	1,363	14,532,174	372,298

(b) Volume (%)

Year	Tokyo	Osaka	Nagoya	Other Exchanges
1963	68.98	23.65	3.90	3.47
1964	70.22	23.29	3.53	2.96
1965	69.01	24.58	3.17	3.24
1966	69.06	24.71	3.20	3.03
1967	68.32	25.31	3.88	2.44
1968	71.43	23.66	3.27	1.64
1969	74.05	21.38	3.26	1.30
1970	74.88	20.63	3.14	1.35
1971	74.68	21.79	2.44	1.09
1972	74.08	22.16	2.56	1.20
1973	74.66	21.17	2.73	1.44

Unit of Trading:

Stocks: 1,000 shares, when par value is less than 500 yen. 100 shares, when par value is 500 yen, or above.

Bonds: One million yen (par value); convertible bonds, 100,000 yen (par value). Securities may be traded in four different ways, according to the day of delivery. Regular Way: delivery on the third business day after the date of trade; Cash: delivery on the same day, or a date agreed upon; Seller's Option: delivery within fifteen days dependent upon the seller's option; When Issued: delivery on a future date determined by the exchange.

Membership:

1. Limited to corporations; individual membership is not permitted. Members are classified as Regular (limited to 83) and "Saitori" (limited to 12). All are licensed securities companies. A Saitori member serves as a middleman between regular members—a kind of broker's broker. However, he does not trade for his own account.

2. The Minister of Finance issues four kinds of licenses which permit: 1. dealing for one's own account; 2. brokerage activity; 3. underwriting and distributing securities; 4. selling securities as a member of a syndicate, which distributes securities. Capital stock requirements vary for each category. A license for all categories requires a minimum capital of 200 million yen.

Commissions or Fees: Commission rates are the same for all Japanese stock exchanges. See "The Stock Exchanges of Japan" at the beginning of this section.

Historical Background:

1878 (May)   Tokyo Stock Exchange Co. Ltd., a profit making organization, was established. It was superseded by the Nippon Securities Exchange, a semi-governmental organization, at the start of World War II.

1945	(August)	Nippon Exchange dissolved. The only remaining market was over-the-counter.
1949	(May 16)	Stock exchanges inaugurated in Tokyo, Osaka, Nagoya and, later, in Kyoto, Hiroshima, Fukuoka, Niigata, Sapporo.
1948	(April)	A new Securities Exchange Law was enacted, providing for reorganization of the exchanges.
1961	(October)	The "dual section" system was initiated.
1962	(July 17)	Record daily volume: 31,322,600 shares (Second Section).
1965		Securities Exchange Law was amended.
1966		Rules and procedures for trading in rights were adopted. Government bonds were listed on the exchange.
1970		Convertible bonds were listed.
1972	(November 13)	A new system for simplifying securities deliveries was introduced.
1972	(November 14)	Record daily volume: 1,066,524,400 shares (First Section).

KENYA

NAIROBI

NAIROBI STOCK EXCHANGE

Title: Nairobi Stock Exchange

Address: P.O. Box 43633, Nairobi, Kenya, East Africa.

Telephone: 22296

Officers:
Chairman: Francis M. Thuo
Secretaries: Africa Registrars Limited

Hours of Business: 8:30 A.M. - 5:00 P.M. (weekdays and Saturday)

Regulatory Laws: The Societies Act, and Rules and Regulations, which govern the members.

Issues Traded and Volume:

1. Listed: over seventy companies, plus government stocks of East African countries: Kenya, Uganda, Tanzania. A few City Council of Nairobi stocks are also quoted.
2. Unlisted or "other" issues: approximately 5.
3. Volume: about 80 million U. S. dollars annually.

Unit of Trading:
1. 100 shares. There is no extra fee or commission for buying or selling odd-lots.
2. The exchange has no trading floor. Brokers meet across a table each morning, where quotations and trades are made under the call system.

Membership:
1. Regular Members: 5
2. Membership Prices: 200 shillings (1960-1963)
   2,000 shillings (1964-1968)
   4,000 shillings (1969-1974)

Commissions or Fees:

1. Where the consideration (amount involved) is shillings	Commission (brokerage) per share is
Up to 1/	3 cents
1/ to 2/50	5 cents
2/50 to 5/	10 cents
5/ to 7/50	15 cents
7/50 to 10/	20 cents
10/ to 15/	25 cents
15/ to 20/	30 cents
over 20/	1½% on consideration

2. Government and Municipal stocks: $\frac{3}{8}$% on the nominal amount of the stock up to £ 10,000 on any one deal and thereafter at $\frac{1}{4}$%. On stocks with one year or less to redemption date, the brokerage is $\frac{1}{8}$% on the nominal amount.
3. Minimum commission: Twenty shillings on any one deal where the consideration is from Shs. 200/ to Shs. 600/; on deals over Shs. 600/ the minimum is Shs. 40/. Deals below Shs. 200/ are charged at the discretion of the broker.

Historical Background:
1954 The Nairobi Stock Exchange was founded at the initiative of the then British Colonial Government, and has been supported by the present government for the role it is playing in the economic life of the country.

KOREA

SEOUL

KOREA STOCK EXCHANGE

Title: Korea Stock Exchange

Address: 199, 2-ka Ulchi-ro, Chung-ku, Seoul, Korea

Telephone: (23) 0071 - 7

Branches and Affiliates: Pusan Stock Exchange, 38-1, 1-ka Kwang-bock dong Chung-ku, Pusan, Korea.

Officers:
President: Yong Kap, Kim
Vice-President: Jong Seung, Pai
General affairs director: Sung Kuk, Kang
Operations director: Jae Chol, Chang
Research director: Yun Kun, Oh
Auditor: Seung Man, Cho

Hours of Business:
Morning session: 9:40 A.M. - 11:40 A.M.
Afternoon session: 1:20 P.M. - 2:30 P.M.
Odd-lots sessions: 1:20 P.M. - 2:30 P.M.
The morning session opens with "gavel matching" (a type of "Call system", where trades are executed at one price). This soon gives way to a continuous auction market. "Gavelling" takes place only once each day, at the start of the morning session.

Regulatory Laws: Securities Transaction Law; Capital Market Promotion Law; and Public Corporation Inducement Law.

Issues Traded and Volume:

1.	Listed Co's.	Listed Shs.	Capital of Listed Stocks (000 won)	Market Value (000 won)
1964	17	27,021,126	22,228,116	17,084,500
1965	17	28,933,103	23,162,409	15,566,077
1966	24	42,963,070	32,450,943	19,507,981
1967	24	59,446,277	46,083,353	38,475,664
1968	34	114,861,833	96,585,361	64,323,410
1969	42	141,041,810	119,902,298	86,569,423
1970	48	158,965,146	134,292,367	97,922,555
1971	50	170,211,718	141,356,684	108,706,133
1972	66	209,755,045	174,338,694	245,980,705
1973	104	305,053,433	251,620,053	426,246,648
1974*	111	343,928,471	275,228,500	446,796,290

*As of March 31, 1974.

2. Volume:	Stocks (000 shs.)	Bonds (000 won)	3. Value: Stocks (000 shs.)	Bonds (000 won)
1964	316,617	1,050,940	27,038,985	708,448
1965	43,047	214,468	9,271,092	165,769
1966	48,684	114,727	11,160,405	85,609
1967	72,029	44,698	24,916,661	36,345
1968	76,342	32,243	19,984,212	26,446
1969	98,325	412,220	41,942,109	320,408
1970	78,384	4,200,870	42,142,031	3,566,705
1971	49,852	10,957,201	33,775,150	7,181,495
1972	83,963	9,837,992	70,268,753	8,390,936
1973	113,543	8,552,850	160,129,277	7,417,739

Unit of Trading:
1. 10, 50, or 100 shares.
2. Odd-lots are executed on the over-the-counter market, or in a separate afternoon session on the regular stock exchange.
3. The over-the-counter market in Korea is quite inactive; almost all transac-

tions are effected on the regular exchange.
4. Exchange contracts are settled on the second full business day following the date of trade.
5. The Seoul market consists of two sections: newly listed small companies; better grade and bigger companies.

Memberships: At the present time the number of exchange members is 30. All of them are joint stock companies under the Securities Transaction Law. In case an exchange member intends to act only as a broker/dealer, his capital stock shall be no less than W200 million. If he intends to act as not only a broker/dealer but also an underwriter, his capital stock shall be not less than W300 million. An exchange member shall own shares of the exchange totaling not less than W30 million, which must be deposited in the custody of the exchange as his guarantee.

Commissions or Fees:

Purchase or Sales Value	Rates
Less than 1 million won	8/1000
From 1 to 5 million won	7/1000
5 million won or more	6/1000
Odd-lots	10/1000

Historical Background:

1956 The Daehan Stock Exchange, a forerunner of the present Korea Stock Exchange, was established February 11, by the joint contribution of banks, insurers and brokers. From the opening date to the end of 1961, 76.7% of the total trading value was that of national bonds.

1961 Stock transactions gradually exceeded transactions in national bonds.

1962 On April 1 the form of the exchange was changed to a joint stock company under the Securities Transaction Law enacted on January 15, 1962. A notorious boom and crash engulfed the market during 1962.

1963 The exchange was changed into a government-operated corporation under the Securities Transaction Law amended on April 27. Until 1968 the market was inactive and made no contribution to capital fund raising.

1968 On November 22 the Capital Market Promotion Law was enacted. On December 14 the Korea Investment Corporation was established under which the Investment Deliberation Committee was authorized.

1969 The Pusan Stock Exchange opened on March 5, Korea's initial regional exchange and a branch of the Korea Stock Exchange.

1971 Continuous market system introduced in October.

1973 Public Corporation Inducement Law adopted January 5. Thanks to sharp decrease in bank interest rate, a moratorium on usury, and prosperity of overall business, the stock market has shown a remarkable expansion. Korean Stock Exchange introduced Central Certificate Service System in November.

LUXEMBOURG

LUXEMBOURG STOCK EXCHANGE

Title: Société de la Bourse de Luxembourg S.A.

Address: 11, avenue de la Porte neuve, P.O. Box 165 Luxembourg, (Grand Duchy of Luxembourg).

Telephone: 2-92-17

Teletype: LUXSTOK L

Telex: 559 LUXSTOK L

Cable Address: Bourse de Luxembourg

Branches and Affiliates: The Exchange is a member of the International Federation of Stock Exchanges.

Officers: Management is in the hands of the "Conseil d'Administration de la Bourse" (Board of Directors), which presently is composed of thirteen members elected at the annual meeting of shareholders.

1. President: Paul Weber
   Vice-President: Pierre Guill
   Administrators:

Gilbert Bochaton	Camille Lamboray
E. W. Frank	Joseph Leydenbach
Constant Franssens	Robert Reckinger
Xavier Harmel	Victor Reyter
Jean d'Huart	George S. Schwall
Fernand Koster	

2. Stock Exchange Committee:
   Assisting the Board in an advisory function, the "Commission de la Bourse," consists of eleven members, elected annually among the authorized dealers.

Remy Kremer	Joseph Rebhuhn
Yves Charpentier	Aloyse Reiff
Andre Coussement	Alphonse Schmit
Patrick Delcourt	Henri Servais
Edmond Israel	Marc Weinand
Francois Karpen	

   General Secretary: Marcel Lamboray

Hours of Business:
1. 11:00 A.M. - 1:00 P.M.
2. A very active over-the-counter market functions all day.

Regulatory Laws:
1. Law of December 30, 1927 - defines strict rules for brokers and other intermediaries.
2. Decree of March 22, 1928 - enforces the Law of 1927 and entrusts a private company, the "Société de la Bourse de Luxembourg," with operating and managing the stock exchange for 99 years (until 2027), subject to proroga-

tion. The Société complies with self-imposed rules and regulations, which are countersigned by the Minister of Finance. A Government Commissioner oversees control on behalf of the Luxembourg Government.

The Decree emphasizes and enforces the requirements that determine which institutions and individuals may have access to the exchange and which may not. There is no clause which forbids access to foreigners.

3. The Law on Commercial Companies (August 10, 1915) and the Grand Ducal Decree (June 19, 1965) — define public offering and listing procedures and the information the prospectus must contain. The same regulations apply to foreign and domestic corporations.

Issues Traded and Volume:
1. Listed issues:

1969	556	1972	806
1970	644	1973	842
1971	724		

2. Unlisted or "other" issues: Exchange brokers maintain local markets in virtually all international securities, through specialized departments.
3. Volume shares traded: Most transactions in listed and unlisted international securities are handled over-the-counter. No official volume figures are available.

Unit of Trading:
1. Minimum 10 shares, or FLUX 5,000
2. Odd-lots:
   a. The minimum size for "firm" quotations equals the nominal value of $US 10,000 — in the over-the-counter market. Dealers are free to deal on both sides of a nominal value of $US 10,000 — with or without price adjustments. The built-in pressures of the market itself determine the trend.
   b. No official fee or commission is charged for dealing in odd-lots.

Memberships:
1. Regular Members: 25, mostly Luxembourg-based international banks.
2. Membership Prices (unchanged since 1960):
   a admission fee: FLUX 50,000
   b. annual fee: FLUX 10,000

Commissions or Fees: Brokerage rates are established pursuant to Article 103 of the Rules and Regulations of the Stock Exchange.
1. Luxembourg Government and bonds of supernational organizations, 4%
2. All other types of bonds, 5%
3. Shares, including those of investment and mutual funds, 8%
4. Contracts to buy and sell are not subject to stamp duty or other fiscal charges, in addition to the above rates.
5. Non-registered brokers and bankers are entitled to a refund of ⅜ths of the official brokerage fee. For transactions involving the 5% rate, the reallowance is 2½%.

Historical Background:
1927 (December 30)   Luxembourg Stock Exchange created under special laws.

1929 (May 6)	The Exchange was officially opened.
1929 (July 31)	Luxembourg Government extended to investment funds the favorable tax treatment accorded to Luxembourg holding companies.
1965 (June 19)	Public offering and listing procedures for both foreign and domestic corporations became regulated by Grand-Ducal Decree.
1969 (October)	The new trading floor opened for business.
1970 (September 28)	A group of banks from 11 countries of CEDEL S.A., an international clearing system for Euro-bonds, enabled the settlement through that system of transactions carried out on the Luxembourg Stock Exchange in such international securities admitted within CEDEL.
1973	The Stock Exchange and a number of financial institutions are conducting studies to create a computerized trading system for Euro-securities, called "Eurex." The Eurex Study Syndicate held its inaugural meeting in Luxembourg, September 21, 1973. The main functions of the system will be matching, confirming, issuing clearing instructions and performing other back-office work, yet it will also provide the participants with information, such as high/low prices, yields and similar market data.

MALAYSIA

KUALA LUMPUR

MALAYSIAN RUBBER EXCHANGE AND LICENSING BOARD

Title: Malaysian Rubber Exchange

Address: P.O. Box 531, Hong Kong Bank Building, Leboh Pasar Besar, Kuala Lumpur 01 - 23, Malaysia

Telephone: 87961/4

Cable Address: PASGETAH

Note: At presstime the Exchange was being reorganized and therefore preferred not to furnish additional information.

MALAYSIAN STOCK EXCHANGE

Title: Malaysian Stock Exchange

Address: 4th Floor, Block C, Damansara Centre, Damansara Heights, Kuala Lumpur, Malaysia

Note: This information was furnished by the Embassy of Malaysia but by presstime no contact had been made with the Exchange.

MAURITIUS

PORT LOUIS

"MAURITIUS STOCK EXCHANGE"
(there is no proper stock exchange, but trading sessions are held at auction, or "Bourse", on specific days each week)

Title: Mauritius Chamber of Brokers.

Address: 6 Sir William Newton Street, Port Louis, Island of Mauritius.

Telephone: (New number unavailable at press time)

Officers:
President: Pierre Leclezio
Vice President: F. G. S. de la Hogue
Committee Members:
I. N. Roy
L. M. Mungur
C. Regnard
G. Gujudhur
G. Ramet
Secretary: L. Ramburn
Treasurer: B. Daruty de Grandpre

Hours of Business: Auction sales: 12:00 noon - 1:00 P.M. (Monday, Wednesday, Friday)

Regulatory Laws:
1. Brokers Ordinance, 1945
2. The Bourse is governed by a seven-member administrative committee elected each year.

Issues Traded and Volume: Not available.

Unit of Trading: Orders accepted in any size, any quantity.

Membership:
1. Regular Members: 48, of whom about 20 are fulltime stock brokers; the others deal mainly in sugar.
2. Associate Members: 13
3. Member's Subscription Fee: Rs. 150 annually.
4. Every broker must be a member of the corporation. Before exercising his functions, he must furnish a bond, or a mortgage, of Rs. 20,000. He must also pay Rs. 1,500 each year for a trade license.

Commissions or Fees: ½% on securities traded.

Historical Background:
1804 The Bourse was created.
1810 The British flag replaced the French flag in this year, but existing basic laws remained in force. Indeed, the Bourse today is the only exchange of the former British Empire that is still governed by the principles of French law.
1816 The first exchange building was destroyed by fire.
1866 A stock brokers association was incorporated.
1946 Brokers were permitted to deal in securities for their own account.

MEXICO

There are three stock exchanges in Mexico: Bolsa de Valores de Mexico; Bolsa de Valores de Monterrey: Bolsa de Valores Guadalajara. The latter is perhaps better known as Bolsa de Occidente (Guadalajara) at the same address. Unfortunately, we were unable to open contact with them.

All exchanges are supervised by the National Securities Commission, known as Comision Nacional de Valores, Av. Paseo Reforma 77, Mexico, D.F. and the Ministry of Finance and Public Credit, known as Secretaria de Hacienda y Credito Publico, Palacio Nacional, Mexico D.F.

The Mexican counterpart of the Commodity Credit Corp. in the U.S.A. is Cia. Nacional de Subsistencias Populares (abbreviated to "Conasupo"), Av. Juarez 92, Mexico D.F.

Commission rates are identical in Mexico. Six principal types of fixed income securities are traded. The major categories of stock are industrial, banking, insurance, and finance.

GUADALAJARA

GUADALAJARA STOCK EXCHANGE

Title: Bolsa de Valores de Guadalajara, S.A. de C.V.

Address: Sec. Juarez Calle 17-A #865, Guadalajara, Jal., Mexico.

MEXICO CITY STOCK EXCHANGE

Title: Bolsa de Valores de Mexico, S.A. de C.V.

Address: Uruguay 68, Mexico 1, D.F.

Telephone: 10-46-20

Officers:
Chairman: Arturo Alonso C.
Vice-Chairman: Rafael Blumenkron
President: Lic. Manuel Caso Bercht
Secretary: C. P. Guillermo Lecuona Saiz

Hours of Business: 11:30 A.M. - 3:30 P.M.

Regulatory Laws: Operations of the Stock Exchange and of its members fall under the jurisdiction of the Ministry of Finance, the National Banking Commission and the National Securities Commission.

Issues Traded and Volume:
1. Listed Companies: 474
2. Listed Securities: 863
   a. Most stocks are issued to bearer ("portador"). The certificates carry coupons to facilitate dividend payments, rights issuance, etc.
   b. Other stock, called "nominativa," is issued to a specific person; his name appears on the certificate.
3. Volume

	No. Shares	Value (pesos)
1935	44,575	1,747,007
1940	88,472	5,050,396
1945	278,067	16,747,590
1950	160,843	54,296,096
1955	387,157	227,522,699
1960	1,324,379	5,103,730,110
1965	9,945,412	21,416,675,000
1966	10,893,965	23,062,694,590
1967	12,695,467	22,541,192,582
1968	20,010,071	27,972,826,279
1969	18,176,969	35,208,256,050
1970	8,895,077	33,752,534,941
1971	11,077,634	38,864,839,078
1972	18,205,650	55,620,780,329
1973	24,361,030	75,389,708,768

Unit of Trading:
1. Stocks: usually in round-lots; 100 shares, or a multiple thereof.
2. Mortgage certificates, mortgage bonds, financial bonds are traded at par value, usually 100 pesos plus accrued interest.
3. Odd-lots ("picos") are seldom traded. One reason: the difficulty of exchanging round-lot certificates for odd-lot certificates. However, when they are

traded, the brokerage fee is about two points above or below the prevailing market price.

4. La Bolsa is a public auction market. Only the "agentes de bolsa" (brokers) do the trading. There are no specialists, dealers or jobbers. The dealings are made on a fixed price base, or on the better price base. Fixed price base dealings are recorded on blackboards as the bid price and the asked price. Trading on the better price base is made by shouting the bid and asked prices until a transaction is effected.

Memberships: Regular Members: 83. They may not trade for their own account, and may not hold more than one share of capital stock of the stock exchange.

Commissions or Fees:

1. Bonds: 0.25% on the full value of the trade. Minimum commission is $25 pesos per deal. ($ means Mexican pesos).
2. Stocks:
   a. Commission is charged on each round-lot; it depends upon the full value of the round-lot as follows:

Round-lot Value	Commission*
From $1 to $499.99	$5 plus 4%
From $500 to $7,999.99	$20 plus 1%
From $8,000 to $99,999.99	$60 plus 0.50%
$100,000 and above	$460 plus 0.10%

   *Minimum is $25 per deal

   b. Commission on odd-lots will be in proportion to the number of shares involved and the round-lot price. It can never be less than the $25 minimum.
3. Coupons and Rights: Commissions are calculated in the same way as on stocks, but the minimum is $5.
4. Futures: Commissions are calculated the same way as cash dealings and must be paid on the same day the deals are made. The maximum commission the "agentes de bolsa" can charge for dealings on the trading floor can be no more than 10% of the full value of each deal; thus the "agente" should charge as his commission the lowest amount in comparison with the fees.
5. Government Taxes: Companies add their capital gains to other revenues. Private investors do not have to pay taxes on capital gains derived from dealings made on the exchange.

Historical Background:

1895 The Bolsa de Valores de Mexico was founded. Mining stocks were the main trading vehicles.

1926 An unsuccessful attempt was made to initiate federal government controls over stock and mining exchanges.

1928 It was established that the stock exchange was subject to inspection by the National Banking Commission.

1932 Law of Credit Institutions made the exchange part of the federal government credit system.

1933 Basic laws controlling and regulating the stock exchange came into being.

1946 A National Securities Commission was created by presidential decree.

1956 Nacional Financiera S.A. first started to register all its transactions on the Bolsa de Valores.

MONTERREY

MONTERREY STOCK EXCHANGE

Title: Bolsa de Valores de Monterrey, S.A. de C.V.

Address: Escobedo Sur 733, Planta Baja, Monterrey, Mexico

Telephone: 42 - 47 - 50; 43 - 32 - 90

Telex: 038 - 736

Officers:
Administrative Council
President: Don Cayetano Santos G.
Secretary: Don Augusto Trigos J.
Propietary Counselors:
Lic. Adrián G. Sada, Jr.   Don Bernabé A. del Valle N.
C. P. Salvador F. Albo T.   Lic. Ignacio Martínez G.
Substitute Counselors:
Lic. Juan S. Farías V.   Don César G. Lozano
Don Federico Velazco R.   Don Eduardo A. Zambrano
Lic. Francisco Garza Calderón   Don Arturo Garza Treviño
Commissioners:
C. P. Humberto Llovera A., Propietary
Don Sergio L. Gutiérrez, Substitute
Director: Augusto Trigos J.
Assistant Manager: Fernando A. Sánchez H.

Hours of Business (trading): 12:30 P.M. - 1:30 P.M.

Regulatory Laws: "Law of the Stock Exchanges"; "Law of the National Securities Commission"; "Law of Bonds and Credit Transactions"; "Law to Promote Mexican Investment and Regulate Foreign Investment."

Volume:

1. Value of all securities traded (pesos)

1963	$ 51,480,000	1969	$ 3,192,627,000
1964	172,413,000	1970	3,693,046,000
1965	796,117,000	1971	5,599,920,000
1966	1,384,325,000	1972	8,463,258,000
1967	1,518,666,000	1973	14,343,900,000
1968	2,410,386,000		

2. Value of shares traded (pesos)

1963	$ 873,000	1969	$102,686,000
1964	5,448,000	1970	83,958,000
1965	20,161,000	1971	44,521,000
1966	41,403,000	1972	160,802,000
1967	77,556,000	1973	285,111,000
1968	84,918,000		

Unit of Trading:
1. 100 shares.
2. Odd-lots are traded, but prices are not recorded on the boards of the trading room. There is a minimum odd-lot commission and the price of execution is three points less than for round-lots of the same stock.

Membership:
1. Associate Members: 43; maximum allowable is 50.
2. Cost of Membership: One share - $24,000 (pesos), plus a monthly fee of $200 (pesos).

Commissions or Fees:
1. Fixed income securities: 0.25% of the value involved. Minimum commission: $25 (pesos).
2. Shares: for each 100 share unit:

Amount (pesos)	Commission (pesos)
$0.00 to 499.99	$5.00 plus 4%*
500.00 to 7,999.99	20.00 plus 1%
8,000.00 to 99,999.99	60.00 plus 0.5%
100,000.00 and above	460.00 plus 0.1%

*Based on the value of 100 shares.
Minimum commission per trade: $25
3. Odd-lots: minimum commission $25 (pesos).
4. Rights and Coupons: minimum commission $5 (pesos).

Historical Background:
1949 The Monterrey Stock Exchange was established August 27, but the start of trading was postponed by delays connected with arranging the site of the Exchange.
1950 When operations began April 17, the Exchange anticipated that quotations would include about 49 issues, actually there were 314. The value of securities traded in this first year totaled $1,006,900 (pesos). In 1973, the value was $14,343,900,000 (pesos).

NETHERLANDS

AMSTERDAM

AMSTERDAM STOCK EXCHANGE

Title: Amsterdam Stock Exchange
Address: Beursplein 5, Amsterdam — 1001, The Netherlands
Telephone: 020 - 23 97 11
Teletype: EFBEU NE
Telex: 12302

Cable Address: COMBOURSE

Officers:
Chairman: J. Ph. Korthals Altes
Secretary: J. G. N. de Hoop Scheffer

Hours of Business: 11:30 A.M. - 1:15 P.M. Outside of official hours, trading takes place in securities usually in response to arbitrage.

Regulatory Laws: Beurswet 1914 (Exchange Law): Beschikking beursverkeer 1947 (Stock Exchange Decree).

Issues Traded and Volume:
1. Listed Securities (1973): Dutch bonds — 1,272; Foreign bonds — 187; shares in investment trusts: Dutch — 31, foreign — 44; Dutch shares and certificates of them — 309; Foreign shares and certificates of them — 292. Total securities listed: 2,135. Number of listed Dutch companies: 256
2. Volume (1972): Stocks — 19,144.1 (Dfl. m.);
   Bonds — 6,531.7 (Dfl. m.).
   Total — 25,675.8 (Dfl. m.).

Unit of Trading: Quotations must be made in percentages of nominal value for bonds, and in guilders, or in dollars, for shares and fractions thereof. Share trading is always on a cash basis. Each listed security is traded at one of the eighty-two imaginary "hoeken" (pitches or corners) into which the exchange floor is divided. The trading unit is not necessarily 100 shares, as on some other exchanges. An order to buy or sell is not regulated as to size.

Membership: 212 companies. Annual cost of exchange membership is 500 florins. Individuals are members only by reason of their function with a member firm of the exchange. At the end of 1973, there were about 425 individual members.

Commissions of Fees: Commission rate was increased on March 1, 1974 from 6.3% to 6.8%.

Historical Background:
1602 Dutch East India Co. founded; it was the first company in the world to issue shares by public offering; its shares were the first to be traded on a public exchange.
1876 The Association of the Amsterdam Stock Exchange was founded by Amsterdam brokers to direct the development of stock trading.
1914 The Exchange Act gave the Minister of Finance the right to decide which securities will be listed and to fix the days on which the exchange will be closed.
1947 A ministerial decree ruled that all buying and selling of securities must be done through a member of the stock exchange.

ROTTERDAM

ROTTERDAM STOCK EXCHANGE

Title: Vereeniging van Effectenhandelaren te Rotterdam
Address: Rotterdam, The Netherlands
Note: This exchange was being liquidated during the Spring of 1974.

NEW ZEALAND

THE AFFILIATED STOCK EXCHANGES OF NEW ZEALAND

AUCKLAND

AUCKLAND STOCK EXCHANGE

Address: Box 3251, Auckland.
Telephone: Auckland 379247
Telex: 2329
Officers: Chairman: H. M McElroy (1974)*
Vice Chairman: M. I. Harriman
Secretary: D. S. Wright

CHRISTCHURCH

CHRISTCHURCH STOCK EXCHANGE

Address: Box 639, Christchurch
Telephone: Christchurch 64554
Telex: 4226
Officers: Chairman: J. B. Hindin (1974)*
Vice Chairman: J. R. Wignall
Secretary: P. F. Maples

* Term expires in November of year shown.

DUNEDIN

DUNEDIN STOCK EXCHANGE

Address: Box 483, Dunedin
Telephone: Dunedin 88826
Telex: 5638
Officers: Chairman: H. R. Wilson (1974)*
Secretary: K. Sellar

INVERCARGILL

INVERCARGILL STOCK EXCHANGE

Address: Box 1203, Invercargill
Telephone: Invercargill 4345
Telex: 5355
Officers: Chairman: G. D. McCrostie (1974)*
Vice Chairman: L. J. Lamb
Secretary: R. J. Cuthill

WELLINGTON

WELLINGTON STOCK EXCHANGE

Address: Box 767, Wellington
Telephone: 40316
Officers: Chairman: W. R. Hocking (1975)*
Vice Chairman: R. C. Pearson
Secretary: D. McTaggart

STOCK EXCHANGE ASSOCIATION OF NEW ZEALAND

Address: Box 2959, Wellington
Telephones: 43291 45655
Telex: NZ3424 (Answer Back STOCKNZ)
Cables: Affiliated

* Term expires in November of year shown.

Officers: President: D. G. Whyte (1976)**
           Vice-President: R. J. Riley (1976)**
           General Secretary: I. D. McAllister
     * Term expires in November of year shown.
    ** Term expires in February of year shown.

Affiliated Stock Exchanges: Auckland, Christchurch, Dunedin, Invercargill, Wellington.
The following information, provided by The Stock Exchange Association of New Zealand, applies to all of these exchanges.

Hours of Business: 8:30 A.M. - 5:00 P.M. (weekdays)

Regulatory Laws: The Stockbroker's Act (1908), under which Stock Exchange rules are officially listed.

Issues Traded and Volume: The listed issues of 296 New Zealand companies and 85 overseas companies are traded, but no volume statistics are available. Unlisted issues are not traded on the exchanges.

Unit of Trading: "Marketable parcels" represent 1,000 units at a price of 1 — 9 cents, decreasing to 100 units at 50 cents — $3.99, and down to 2 units at $100, or above.
Odd-lots are handled by brokers, who are appointed for specific companies under the association's odd-lot regulations. Ordinary brokerage is charged, plus a graduated margin of 5 cents up to a price of $2, and 20 cents for a price above $10.

Memberships: Total membership is 218, of which 84 are Country Members. A seat may cost up to $10,000, depending upon the stock exchange involved.

Commissions or Fees: Buyers and sellers each pay:
a. For New Zealand Government and Local

Authority securities	—	
On the first $5,000	—	½%
On the next $5,000	—	¼%
On the next $40,000	—	12%
On the excess over $50,000	—	6%

b. For Listed shares —

On the first $10,000	—	2%
On the next $40,000	—	1½%
On any amount above $50,000	—	1%

The concessional rates of brokerage apply to only one buying or selling order.

Historical Background:
1915 The association was established to regulate dealings between exchanges, between members and between members and the public. It determines the basis of trading for all the affiliated stock exchanges.

NICARAGUA

MANAGUA

MANAGUA STOCK EXCHANGE

Title: Actividades Bursátiles de Fomento, S. A. (ABF)

Address: Apartado Postal No. 4126, Managua, D.N., Nicaragua, Central America

Telephone: No. 3112, Managua

Telex: INFONAC 375-1050

Cable Address: INFONAC, ABF — Managua, Nicaragua

Officers: Manager: J. Román González

Hours of Business: 9:00 A.M. - 4:00 P.M. (Weekdays)

Regulatory Laws: There are no special laws regulating stock exchanges in Nicaragua.

Issues Traded and Volume: Ordinary shares for C29.8 million (US $4.3 million). This is a new exchange. Operations began in January, 1974.

Unit of Trading: No limitation

Membership: No limitation

Historical Background: The Exchange was founded in June, 1973, by Instituto de Fomento Nacional, the national state owned development finance corporation, and opened for business in January, 1974.

NIGERIA

LAGOS

LAGOS STOCK EXCHANGE

Title: The Lagos Stock Exchange

Address: 114 Yakubu Gowon Street, P.O. Box 2457, Lagos, Nigeria

Telephone: Lagos 24979

Cable Address: STOCK LAGOS

Officers:
Chairman: T. A. Odutola
Deputy Chairman: T. A. Braithwaite
Executive Director: M. A. Odedina

Hours of Business: 7:30 A.M. - 4:00 P.M. Call-over: Every weekday at 2:30 P.M.

Regulatory Laws: The Lagos Stock Exchange Act, 1961.

Volume and Issues Traded:

1. Listed Issues

Period*	Volume (naira)	No. of Trades	Listed Issues Traded
1961-62	4,370,000	667	14
1962-63	8,492,482	795	21
1963-64	12,506,416	876	28
1964-65	16,143,604	1,084	32
1965-66	16,846,430	1,032	37
1966-67	12,379,676	911	41
1967-68	12,886,976	661	45
1968-69	17,433,114	547	49
1969-70	15,856,280	638	54
1970-71	33,624,360	884	61
1971-72	28,042,042	906	70
1972-73	36,797,054	859	77

*Fiscal year ending September 30.

2. Unlisted and "other" issues traded: Security Deposit Receipts: 5

Unit of Trading:

1. Unit of Trading: 100 shares.
2. Odd-lots are traded the same as 100 share (round-lot) orders.
3. No extra commission or fee is involved with an odd-lot.

Membership: There are 20 shareholding members, of whom 3 are dealing members. There are no associated or "other" members. The price of each membership is 100 naira.

Commissions or Fees:

1. For Government Municipal Statutory Corporation and other Local Authority securities.
   a. Maturing in less than five years — ⅜% of nominal value;
   b. Maturing in more than five years — ½% of nominal value;
   c. Matching transactions involving the Central Bank of Nigeria and the National Provident Fund — 1/32% of nominal value.
2. Other quoted securities — 1¼% of the money involved.
3. No less than two naira can be charged for a single transaction. There is also a Statutory Duty of 15k for every 200 naira involved.

Historical Background:

The Lagos Stock Exchange was incorporated September 15, 1960, under the Companies Act, with an authorized capital of 10,000 naira, divided into 500 shares of 20 naira each.

The Lagos Stock Exchange Act, passed in the Nigerian Houses of Parliament on June 6, 1961, controlled the stock brokerage business and restricted it only to registered agents of the Lagos Stock Exchange.

The Stock Exchange is a limited liability company, limited by shares and guaranty. It is a non-profit organization, the excess of income over expenditure is not distributed, hence, the word "limited" after its title is unnecessary.

NORWAY

As opposed to earlier days when Norway had ten bourses, only three are currently in operation: Oslo, Bergen, Trondheim. Of these, the Oslo Stock Exchange is by far the largest, handling about 85% of all trading volume. On the Trondheim Bourse, for example, securities are quoted but once a week.

We found no evidence of any commodity futures market in Norway. The closest facsimile is Oslo Fur Auctions, Ltd., which conducts public sales.

BERGEN

BERGEN STOCK EXCHANGE

Title: Bergen Bors
Address: Bergen, Norway

OSLO

OSLO FUR AUCTIONS LTD.

Title: Oslo Skinnauksjoner (Oslo Fur Auctions Ltd.)
Address: Ø Slottsgate 3, Oslo 1, Norway
Telephone: 22.41 50
Telex: 16724
Cable Address: OSLOSKINN

Information is included about the Oslo Fur Auctions Ltd. because the nature of its operations may lead some to think that it deals in futures contracts. The auction provides a public sale for the production of Norwegian farm raised mink, fox skins, and some wild furs. There are no quoted prices for future delivery but all bidding takes place on the condition that the goods will be shipped 21 days after the closing date of each sale.

OSLO STOCK EXCHANGE

Title: Oslo Bors
Address: Tollbugt. 2, Oslo, Norway
Telephone: 423888
Officers: Bourse Commissioner: Hans Arnessen.

The exchange is governed by a Bourse Committee, composed of 5 businessmen including a stockbroker from the City of Oslo and a Bourse Commissioner, who is the daily Administrative Manager of the Bourse.

Hours of Business: 10:30 A.M. - 12:30 P.M.

Regulatory Laws: The exchange is controlled by the Ministry of Commerce, which approves the Rules for the Quotations of Securities. The original Law of September 6, 1818, upon which the Oslo Bourse was founded, was superseded by the revised law of June 19, 1931, relating to bourses, which is in force today, with some amendments.

Volume and Issues Traded:
1. Listed share issues: 160
2. Listed bond issues: 300
3. Applications for listing are submitted to the Stockbrokers Association for expression of opinion. Bond issues must total at least Nkr. 2 million. Regarding share issues, a company must have existed for at least one year and have paid a dividend, although this condition may be waived by the Bourse Committee in special cases. Also, its share capital must be at least Nkr. 1 million.

   In general, bond applications must be accompanied by information concerning the amount of the loan, interest rate and dates, amortization etc. Share applications must include data concerning capital, nominal share value, number of shareholders, dividends, and two copies of the by-laws and income statement for the last two years.

   If listing permission is granted, the Bourse Committee will decide whether the security shall be quoted on List A (quoted five times weekly), or List B (quoted twice weekly). Securities may be transferred from one list to the other at any time at the Committee's discretion.

   Annual quotation fees for securities are paid in advance to the Bourse. No fee is charged for Norwegian Government bonds, or those issues guaranteed by Norwegian counties and municipalities.

   Four foreign securities currently are quoted; permission depends upon the Ministry of Commerce which controls the exchange.

Unit of Trading:
1. Shares — about Nkr. 5,000 (market value)
   Bonds — Nkr. 10,000 (minimum nominal amount)
2. Odd-lots are traded the same as round-lots.
3. There is no extra fee or commission for odd-lots.
4. Trading is conducted under the auction system. When a security is called by the presiding official, the brokers immediately state their buying or selling prices. The prices of shares are quoted in kroner; bonds in percent of the sum specified in the transaction.

Membership: All stock brokers in Oslo are members of the Bourse. They number twenty, including the brokerage departments of banks. Broker-candidates must be Norwegian citizens and be twenty-five years of age. They are required to pass an examination, and must have been a broker's assistant for at least three years. They are authorized by the Ministry of Commerce. Membership dues or fees are Nkr. 1,000 annually; each individual broker or firm has a fixed seat in the quotation room. Exchange members are fully responsible for the settlement of transactions. The settlement period is seven days.

Commissions: 1.5 per thousand Norwegian Government bonds, municipality and county bonds, bank bonds, bonds guaranteed by the Norwegian Government, or by Norwegian municipalities and counties and bonds issued by Norwegian authorized credit and mortgage associations. ¼% — all other bonds, debentures and shares guaranteed by the Government. ¾% — all other shares.

Historical Background: The Bourse was founded in 1818, but did not begin operating until the following year. It has occupied the same building since 1828 (enlarged in 1910), where its main original function was quoting rates on foreign exchange. Commodity prices were quoted later on, but such activity today is heavily restricted. Securities were not quoted until 1881.

The exchange was a small affair in the early years. There were only two brokers and once-a-month quotations were based on written statements from banks and brokers, derived from verbal information that the brokers supplied.

Fixed rules for admission to the quotation list were introduced in 1897. Subsequently, quotations took place twice monthly; then once a week, until daily quotations began in World War I.

The Bourse was closed from April 9 to May 21, 1940, during World War II. When it reopened it was put under quite rigid restrictions, which were not completely removed until the war ended.

According to the Oslo Stock Exchange, dividend regulations initiated by the Government in 1940 have been partly repealed. "However, a limited company still has to transfer to its reserve fund an amount equaling the amount by which the dividend declared exceeds 5% of the sum of the company's paid up capital and reserve fund at the beginning of the fiscal year."

Investments in Norwegian shares by non-residents are subject to license from the Bank of Norway, as is the repatriation of the funds invested. Foreign shareholders in Norwegian joint-stock companies are liable to a dividend withholding tax of 25%.

TRONDHEIM

TRONDHEIM STOCK EXCHANGE

Title: Trondhjems Bors
Address: Trondheim, Norway

PAKISTAN

The stock exchanges of Pakistan, located in Karachi and Lahore, are closely coordinated. Their rules are aligned; they are linked by a telex machine installed in the trading hall of the Lahore Stock Exchange; they handle jointly all problems or decisions involving the government. The initial listing fee for companies already listed on the Karachi Stock Exchange for a certain time period is waived by Lahore, and both exchanges are in constant and active communication on important matters.

Pakistan has one commodities exchange, which we have attempted to contact without result: Karachi Cotton Association, Ltd.

KARACHI

KARACHI COTTON ASSOCIATION

Title: Karachi Cotton Association, Inc.

Address: Cotton Exchange Building, I. I. Chundrigar Road, Karachi-2, Pakistan

KARACHI STOCK EXCHANGE

Title: The Karachi Stock Exchange Limited

Address: Stock Exchange Building, Kallian Road, Karachi — 2, Pakistan.

Telephone: 238761, 233581, 233361, 234338

Telex: KR 746

Officers: Secretary: M. I. Chaudhry
Assistant Secretary: Abdul Saeed Khan Ghori

Hours of Business: 10:15 A.M. — 1:30 P.M. (Monday through Saturday, except Friday) 10:00 A.M. — 12:00 noon (Friday)

Regulatory Laws:
1. Security Exchange Ordinance (1969)
2. Security Exchange Rules (1971)

Issues Traded and Volume:
1. Listed Issues:

1964	164	1969	249
1965	182	1970	291
1966	191	1971	313
1967	208	1972	263*
1968	226	1973	272

*The 60 companies registered in East Pakistan have been excluded from the year 1972.

2. Volume:

1964	4,804,650	1969	16,086,860
1965	4,366,530	1970	25,837,680
1966	5,437,525	1971	15,428,150
1967	5,534,810	1972*	12,233,542
1968	17,448,420	1973	32,127,078

*Market was closed due to war from December 4, 1971 — May 24, 1972.

Unit of Trading:
1. 5, 10, 25, 50, or 100 share lots.
2. Odd-lots are not traded on the Exchange.

Membership:
1. Regular Members: 200.
   The Memorandum and Articles of Association of the exchange provide that the directors may, by resolution from time to time, determine the maximum number of members. This number currently is fixed at 200.
2. Seat or membership prices:

	Members	Price per Seat
1960	167	Rs. 5,000
1961	170	Rs. 20,000
1962	175	Rs. 20,000
1963	180	Rs. 20,000
1966	200	Rs. 22,500

Commissions or Fees:
1. a. Government and interest bearing securities: Paisas 12% on face value.
   b. Municipal or Port Trust debentures: Paisas 25%
   c. Joint stock debentures: Paisas 50%
2. Shares (based on contract prices):

	0	to Rs.	5	. . .	12 Paisa per share
above Rs.	5	to Rs.	25	. . .	25 Paisa per share
above Rs.	25	Rs.	50	. . .	50 Paisa per share
above Rs.	50	Rs.	75	. . .	75 Paisa per share
above Rs.	75	Rs.	100	. . .	Rs. 1 per share
above Rs.	100	Rs.	200	. . .	Rs. 1.50 per share
above Rs.	200	Rs.	300	. . .	Rs. 2 per share

and an additional 50 Paisas for every Rs. 1,000 — or part thereof above Rs. 3,000

Historical Background:
1949 (March 10): The Karachi Stock Exchange Limited was incorporated.

LAHORE STOCK EXCHANGE

Title: Lahore Stock Exchange Ltd.

Address: 17 Bank Square, Lahore, Pakistan

Telephone: 55550 (51) 57265

Telex: LAHORSTOK LH-821

Cable Address: LAHORSTOK

Officers: President: Mian Tajammal Hussain
Member on Special Duty: Mohammad Aziz-ur-Rehman

Hours of Business: 10:15 A.M. - 1:30 P.M. (Saturday to Thursday; closed Sunday) 10:00 A.M. - 12:00 noon (Friday)

Regulatory Laws: Companies Act 1913; Capital Continuous Act 1949; Securities & Exchange Ordinance 1969; Securities & Exchange Rules 1971.

Issues Traded and Volume:
1. Listed Issues (1973): 151 companies, with paid-up capital of Rs 297.34 crores (a unit of value equal to 10 million rupees).
2. Unlisted or "other" issues: National Investment Trust units.
3. Volume (1973): "Two Lacs" — 200,000 shares.

Unit of Trading:
1. Five shares, or a multiple thereof.
2. Odd-lot dealings are not officially reported. However, an extra commission is charged for such transactions.

Memberships:
1. Regular Members: 0
2. Associate Members: 84
3. "Other" Members: 0
4. Entrance fee: Rs 7,500
   Annual Subscriptions: Rs 200

Commissions or Fees:
1. The minimum charge for each transaction is one rupee.
2. a. Government securities: Annas 2% of face value.
   b. Municipal or Port Trust debentures: Annas 4% of face value.
   c. Joint stock debentures: Annas 8% of face value.
3. Commissions on shares (preference, ordinary preferred, ordinary, deferred) are based on contract prices:

Up to Rs 5	2 Annas per share
Above Rs 5 to Rs 25	4 Annas per share
Above Rs 25 to Rs 50	8 Annas per share
Above Rs 50 to Rs 75	12 Annas per share
Above Rs 75 to Rs 100	Rs 1 per share
Above Rs 100 to Rs 200	Rs 1½ per share
Above Rs 200 to Rs 300	Rs 2 per share

An additional 8 Annas is charged for every Rs 100, or any part thereof, above Rs 300. The above does not apply to underwritings, or the placement of new issues.

Historical Background: The Lahore Stock Exchange was incorporated in October, 1970, with the object of providing a closer capital market to investors and industries in northern Pakistan. Operations began May 11, 1971 with 130 listed companies which had a paid-up capital of Rs 250.20 crores (1 crore equals 10 million rupees).

PANAMA

There is no stock exchange in Panama at the present time and all stocks and bonds are traded over-the-counter. Further information may be obtained through the office of the Consulado General de Panama, 1270 Avenue of the Americas, New York, NY 10020.

PERU

LIMA

LIMA STOCK EXCHANGE

Title: Bolsa de Valores de Lima

Address: A. Miró Quesada 265, Lima, Peru

Telephone: 286 - 280

Officers:
Executive President: Fernando Vidal Ramirez
Authorized General Accountant: Roberto Montoya Pavicich
Director of Trading: Jose Almenara Battifora

Hours of Business (trading): 12:45 P.M. - 1:30 P.M.

Regulatory Laws: Decrees-Laws Nos. 18302 (June 2, 1970) and 18353 (August 4, 1970) and connected measures.

Issues Traded and Volume:
1. Issues Traded:
   a. Total public debt issues, mortgage bills, bonds outstanding (12/31/73): 4,296,474,120*
   *10,722,716 of this amount in U.S. dollars, balance in soles.

b. Stocks: 77 companies. Total paid-in capital: 30,405,834,495 soles (12/31/73), vs. 14,459,438,749 soles (1/1/73)

2. Value of Securities Traded (soles)

	Bonds	Stocks	Total
1970	533,410,794.07	651,895,005.87	1,185,305,799.94
1971	592,401,490.95	723,208,000.10	1,315,609,491.05
1972	486,887,228.26	932,357,014.10	1,419,244,242.36
1973	556,419,695.46	819,346,294.85	1,375,765,990.31

Memberships: Regular members — 18. The Lima Stock Exchange is a civil association, integrated solely for its members. To transact business, exchange members must be certified by the National Supervisory Commission of Securities, before taking certain examinations and furnishing relative documents. They must also subscribe 50,000 soles to the exchange as an entrance fee.

Commissions or Fees:

1. Bonds:

1% on the first	300,000 soles
¾% up to	600,000 soles
½% up to	1,000,000 soles

2. Stocks:

1% on the first	500,000 soles
¾% up to	1,000,000 soles
½% up to	2,000,000 soles
¼% above	2,000,000 soles

3. Minimum commission, stocks and bonds: 10 soles.

Historical Background:

1860 La Bolsa Comercio de Lima was created, December 31.

1951 La Bolsa Comercio became a stock company, with the title, Bolsa de Comercio de Lima.

1971 Exchange operations were taken over by the Bolsa de Valores de Lima in January — currently the only exchange in Peru. It has no branches or affiliates.

PHILIPPINES

There are two stock exchanges in the Philippines, the Makati Stock Exchange, Inc. and the Manila Stock Exchange. Although there have been no commodity exchanges in operation, the Greater Manila Terminal Food Market (South Superhighway, Paranaque, Rizal, Philippines) has been developing into an organization similar to a commodity exchange. However, it is our understanding that there has been no trading in futures as yet.

MAKATI STOCK EXCHANGE

Title: Makati Stock Exchange, Inc.

Address: Makati Stock Exchange Building, Ayala Ave., Makati, Rizal, Philippines

Telephone: 88-64-11; 88-78-71

Cable Address: MAKATSTOCK

Officers:
President: Miguel Campos
Vice-President: Eduardo Lim
Treasurer: Irving I. Ackerman
Asst. Treasurer: Jose T. Flores, Jr.
Governors:
H. B. Reyes
M. V. Quintana
Alejandro T. de Castro
Executive Secretary: Juan B. Francisco

Hours of Business: 9:00 A.M. - 1:00 P.M., (weekdays).

Regulatory Laws: Philippines Securities Act.

Issues Traded and Volume:
1. Total Listed Issues: 177 stocks; 2 bonds
   Total Listed Shares: 204,099,996,809
   Total Authorized Capital: ₱5,375,678,000
2. Volume (mil. pesos)

Year	Volume	Year	Volume
1966	20.2	1970	1,234.9
1967	55.2	1971	149.4
1968	251.0	1972	194.0
1969	2,121.6	1973	2,289.1

Unit of Trading:
1. Transactions are based on board-lots, or units of trading. Following are price ranges, board-lots and minimum fluctuations for various types of securities:

Common Stocks:

Price Range		Board Lot No. of Shares	Minimum Fluctuation
.001	— .006	50,000	.0001
.006	— .01	50,000	.0002
.01	— .024	20,000	.0005
.024	— .05	10,000	.001
.05	— .15	5,000	.0025
.15	— .30	2,000	.0025
.30	— .50	1,000	.0025
.50	— 1.00	1,000	.005
1.00	— 2.00	500	.01
2.00	— 5.00	100	.02
5.00	— 10.00	100	.10

(Continued)

Profile Data

Price Range			Board Lot No. of Shares	Minimum Fluctuation
10.00	—	20.00	50	.10
20.00	—	30.00	20	.10
30.00	—	100.00	10	.25
100.00	—	250.00	5	.50
250.00	—	500.00	2	1.00
500.00	—	UP	1	2.00
Preferred Stocks:				
80.00	—	200.00	5	0.50
201.00	—	1,000.00	2	1.00
1,001.00	—	UP	1	5.00
Bonds or Debentures (Commerical):				
80.00	—	200.00	5	0.25
201.00	—	1,000.00	2	0.25
1,001.00	—	UP	1	0.25

On a price range below ₱80.00, the fluctuation rates on common stocks apply.

2. Odd-Lots: Any amount of stock that is less than the accepted trading unit (board-lot) is sold at a price lower than the prevailing market price. Ordinarily, no extra fee is charged for buying or selling odd-lots.

Membership: Regular members: 43 (seats are limited to 50 maximum)
Associate members: 25
Membership Prices:

1963	₱ 5,000	to	₱ 10,000
1964-69	10,000	to	30,000
1970	80,000	to	250,000
1973	750,000	to	805,000

Commissions or Fees: 1% on the value of shares traded

Historical Background:

1963 (May 27)	Makati Stock Exchange formally organized and incorporated.
1965 (June 30)	Supreme Court rendered a decision permitting securities to be dually listed on the Makati and Manila Stock Exchanges.
1965 (November 16)	Trading began officially on the Makati Stock Exchange.

MANILA

MANILA STOCK EXCHANGE

Title: Manila Stock Exchange

Address: M S E Building, Prensa St. Corner Muelle de la Industria, Binondo, Manila, Philippines

Telephone: 47-11-25; 47-97-04

Cable Address: MANSTOCK

Officers:
Chairman: Jose Ma. Barcelon
President: Antonio Garcia, Sr.
Executive Vice-President: Anthony Dee K. Chiong, Jr.
Secretary: Simplicio J. Roxas
Treasurer: Mariano U. Godinez
Asst. Treasurer: Martin Q. Dee
Governor: Roberto L. Recio
Governor: Enrique Santamaria
Governor: Fred C. Hagedorn, Jr.

Hours of Business: 9:00 A.M. - 1:00 P.M.

Regulatory Laws: The Stock Exchange is a non-stock, non-profit organization. Government is vested in a board of governors, which is the policy-making body of the exchange.

Issues Traded and Volumes:
1. Listed issues:*
   a. No. issues: 187
   b. No. shares: 3,471,550,825 preferred; 249,267,189,650 common.
   c. Nominal capital (pesos): 7,382,378,000 Common; 97,800,000 Preferred.
   *December 31, 1973
2. Volume:

Year	Shares (mill.)	Value (Thous. pesos)
1963	4,516	118,183
1964	4,715	188,962
1965	3,150	110,766
1966	3,332	132,101
1967	2,133	188,605
1968	4,417	423,101
1969	26,581	1,112,577
1970	34,170	2,090,568
1971	34,622	982,666
1972	12,583	312,350
1973	87,102	3,642,000

Unit of Trading:
1. Common Stocks:

Price Range (pesos)	Board Lot No. of shares	Minimum Fluctuation
0.001— 0.006	50,000	0.0001
.006— .01	50,000	.0002
.01 — .024	20,000	.0005
.024— .05	10,000	.001
.05 — .15	5,000	.0025
.15 — .30	2,000	.005
.30 — .50	1,000	.005
.50 — 1.00	1,000	.01
1.00 — 2.00	500	.02

(Continued)

Price Range (pesos)	Board Lot No. of Shares	Minimum Fluctuation
2.00 — 5.00	100	.05
5.00 —10.00	100	.10
10.00 —20.00	50	.25
20.00 —30.00	20	.50
30.00 —50.00	10	.50
50.00 — up	10	1.00

2. Preferred Stocks, Bonds or Debentures (corporate)

Price Range (pesos)	Board Lot No. of Shares	Minimum Fluctuation
80.00— 200.00	5	0.50
201.00—1,000.00	2	1.00
1,001.00— Up	1	5.00

On a price range below 80 pesos, the fluctuation rates on common stocks apply.

3. Odd-lots: Odd-lot transactions are posted on a separate quotation board. A stock offered in an amount that is less than the normal "board-lot" is usually sold at a price lower than the prevailing market price.

Membership:
1. Regular members: 45. No corporation or partnership can own a seat.
2. The last seat was sold for 1 million pesos on January 9, 1974.

Commissions or fees: Listed and unlisted stocks: 1%. The minimum charge on each transaction with a value of 2,000 pesos or less, is 20 pesos.
Government bonds: One-half of 1%, with a minimum charge of 5 pesos.

Historical Background: The stock exchange was organized on August 8, 1927. Its physical facilities consist of the building which houses the trading floor and communications facilities, administrative offices, and visitors' gallery.

PORTUGAL

LISBON

LISBON STOCK EXCHANGE

Title: Bolsa do Lisboa
Address: Praca do Comercio, Torreao Oriental, Lisbon, Portugal

PORTO

PORTO STOCK EXCHANGE

Title: Bolsa do Porto
Address: Palacio da Bolsa, Rua Ferreira Borges, Porto, Portugal

PUERTO RICO

There are no stock or commodities exchanges in Puerto Rico, although, several American stock exchange firms have offices on the Island. For information contact the Financial Service Bureau, Box 9584, Santurce, P.R. 00908 or the Department of Commerce, Box 4275, San Juan, P.R. 00905

REPUBLIC OF CHINA

TAIWAN

TAIWAN STOCK EXCHANGE

Title: Taiwan Stock Exchange
Address: City Building, 85 Yen-Ping South Road, Taipei, Taiwan, Republic of China.
Telephone: 313238 - 9
Cable Address: TSECTAIPEI
Officers:
Chairman of the Board: K. P. Chao
President: T. Y. Tsai
Vice-President: C. W. Hsu
Vice-President and Concurrent Chief Secretary: C. K. Pei
Director, Business Division: C. W. Hu
Director, Finance Division: S. C. Chien
Chief Auditor: S. Y. Ho
Hours of Business: 9:00 A.M. - 12:00 noon (Monday-Saturday)
Regulatory Laws: Securities Exchange Law of the Republic of China.

Issues Traded and Volume:

Year	Listed Issuers	Volume Shs. (000)	Value of Shares Traded (NT$ mill.)
1962	18	58,339	446
1963	24	241,239	9,902
1964	31	712,556	35,501
1965	37	479,247	10,960
1966	39	664,350	4,563
1967	39	797,017	5,429
1968	41	667,077	7,670
1969	42	422,449	4,214
1970	42	1,350,415	10,866
1971	45	1,275,462	23,598
1972	49	1,896,942	54,051
1973	62	3,997,807	87,091

Unit of Trading:

1. Stocks with a par value per share of NT$1: 10,000 shares;
2. Stocks with a par value per share from NT$1 to NT$10: 1,000 shares;
3. Stocks with a par value per share from NT$10 to NT$99: 100 shares;
4. Government bonds and corporate bonds: NT$1,000 of par value;
5. Odd-lots are traded on the floor of the Stock Exchange by a designated dealer. No extra fee, or commission, is charged for buying or selling. However, the price of odd-lots is 1% higher for buying and 1% lower for selling, than the prevailing market prices.

Membership: The exchange is organized in the form of a corporation. At present, 17 brokers and 12 traders participate in trading securities on the floor of the exchange.

Commissions or Fees: For stocks and corporate bonds, brokers may charge a commission at the rate of 0.15% to 0.2% of the executed price for each transaction; for government bonds at 0.1%.

Historical Background: The Taiwan Stock Exchange was inaugurated on November 23, 1961, and formally began operations on February 9, 1962. It was originally located in the Industrial and Mining Building but moved to the City Building on July 1, 1972.

SINGAPORE

RUBBER ASSOCIATION OF SINGAPORE

Title: The Rubber Association of Singapore

Address: Chinese Chamber of Commerce Building, 47 Hill Street, Singapore 6.

Telephone: 39836; 39839; 39323; 31278; 39724

Cable Address: RASINGA Singapore

Officers: Chairman: Tan Eng Joo
Executive Secretary: Gnoh Chong Hock

Hours of Business (Auctions):

1. 10:30 A.M. - 12:30 P.M. and 2:30 P.M. - 4:30 P.M. on days determined by the Management Committee.
2. Ordinary Members and Associate Members are entitled to buy and sell at these auctions. Non-members may apply for annual permits with a payment of $100*, together with a cash deposit or banker's guaranty for $15,000. They can buy only at auctions. The validity of such permits is left to the discretion of the committee.
   * Singapore dollar.
3. Members who wish to sell rubber at an auction must notify the secretary. In order to be catalogued for sale, each lot of rubber must exceed 1,000 pounds. All rubber is sold by the lot; each lot is sold separately at a certain price per pound. The Clearing House arranges for payment to the seller when delivery of the rubber is effected.

The Corporation: The Rubber Association of Singapore (RAS) is the legislative, administrative and judicial center for the rubber trade in Singapore. Its facilities include a clearing house, weekly auction sales, official price-fixing, endorsement for Certificates of Origin for Rubber, preparation and sales of International Copy Samples, arbitration.

1. The Clearing House:
   The Corporation's FOB contract (with or without variations) is the basis upon which all market operations in Singapore are carried out. It can also be linked to the FOB contract of the Malaysian Rubber Exchange and the CIF contracts of the Rubber Trade Associations of London and New York. When the RAS FOB contracts are linked to the latter, they are treated as "further contracts" and provisions for their enforcement and settlement are stipulated in the Corporation's rule book.

   The RAS Clearing House provides a system whereby purchases may be cleared against sales through the use of "tenders." FOB contracts are settled by means of the FOB Tender Form. Under this FOB contract, the seller tenders (offers) an amount of rubber to his buyers on or after the first working day of the contract period for delivery, but before the Tender Clearing Day in the contract period.

   In the case of "Prompt" or "Named Steamer" shipment, it complies with the regulations. A seller completes the particulars of the rubber to be tendered and the name of his buyer on a Tender Form. The form is then signed and forwarded to the Clearing House for registration, after which it is returned to the first seller, not later than noon the following working day. The tender is then circulated during working hours until its date of expiration. After it expires, the last member named on the form becomes the last buyer.

   Every buyer and every seller is required to submit forms with the particulars of tenders registered, received, forwarded or retained by him, to the Clearing House not later than noon on the working day following the handling of the tenders.

   The Tender Clearing Day marks the expiration date of the tender. On this day, usually the seventeenth of each month, members send their representatives to the Clearing House, bringing with them a completed list of unfilled FOB contracts, as well as tenders amounting to the quantity by which unfulfilled sales exceed unfulfilled purchases. These tenders are circulated among the buyers. Each buyer fills in the price of the sale contracts.

The tender is actually a means by which the first seller of a specified amount of rubber is put in touch with the last buyer of this same amount, through a series of intermediaries, who neither deliver nor take delivery of the rubber, but who merely wish to clear their obligations.

2. Price Fixing:

Price fixing is carried out twice daily—at noon and at 5 P.M.—on regular working days. Working in close association with the Clearing House, the Price Fixing Panel, consisting of dealers and brokers, submits prices for the RSS-1 grade of natural rubber for the various delivery dates, as well as for the lower grades. Prices are obtained from three members of the Price Fixing Panel. These prices are declared by the Clearing House Manager as official prices for the day if they are agreed upon by the three members. However, when varying opinions regarding prices arise, the Manager of the Clearing House initiates special procedures which are complied with.

3. Arbitration:

Arbitration is a valuable facility provided by the corporation to both members and non-members. Under reciprocal agreements with the Malaysian Rubber Exchange, the Panel of Arbitrators is comprised of twenty members. Ten are ordinary members elected annually by the Committee of the Corporation; ten are nominated by the Malaysian Rubber Exchange. Disputants may appoint any one of the twenty arbitrators to authenticate (assure, ratify, endorse, certify) their rights, duties, obligations, or liabilities under a contract. If an agreement on the appointment of a sole arbitrator cannot be reached, the two disputants may each appoint his own arbitrators from the panel. When these two appointed arbitrators cannot agree, the dispute is referred to an umpire chosen from the panel by the two arbitrators.

Memberships (12/31/73):

1. Class "A" (Estate Selling Agents): 4. They act as agents for marketing estate rubber and they supply equipment to the estates.

   Class "B" (Brokers): 8. They effect most transactions by putting the buyers in touch with the sellers.

   Class "C" (Manufacturer's Buying Agents): 5. They are buyers appointed by the manufacturing company to deal directly with the producers, as well as maintain their own "godowns" (warehouses) in Singapore.

   Class "D" (Dealers): 94. Representing agents throughout the world, the larger dealers distribute rubber to where it is needed, so that supplies are available to cover commitments. They also buy from producers when the manufacturers are not in the market.

2. Associate Members: 30

   Overseas Members: 3

STATISTICS (In Metric Tons)

	1970	1971	1972	1973
Clearing House-Tonnage	436,537	358,035	258,515	562,380
Weekly Auctions				
a. Tonnage-Offered	2,513.80	2,241.33	2,323.61	2,421.63
b. Tonnage-Sold	1,870.39	1,591.03	1,781.96	2,105.96
c. Fees	$3,201.09	$4,687.09	$4,997.34	$6,050.97
West Malaysian & Singapore				
Production-Tonnage	1,215,736	1,276,331	1,277,007	1,489,636
Rubber Imports-Tonnage	78,597	71,712	103,518	167,890
(including imports from Indonesia)				
Imports From Indonesia				
Tonnage	4,062	2,901	1,411	1,024
Exports-Tonnage	1,792,688	1,835,187	1,785,057	2,119,501
Latex Exports-Tonnage	169,422	191,598	202,387	196,531
Stocks At Year End-Tonnage	209,352	218,934	246,639	257,188

Exports To Main Destinations

	1970 Tonnage	1971 Tonnage	1972 Tonnage	1973 Tonnage
a. U.S.A. and Canada	352,604	419,175	365,457	398,773
b. United Kingdom	127,965	131,088	123,976	128,938
c. West Germany, France & Italy	326,267	313,382	320,514	338,779
d. Japan	120,298	100,901	71,398	147,935
e. U.S.S.R.	232,306	197,518	169,827	244,650
f. China	101,859	104,453	131,167	195,360

Historical Background:

1910   The Signapore rubber market began about this time.

1910-11   The Singapore Chamber of Commerce Rubber Association came into being.

1911   First rubber auction was held, September 12.

1922   The "Stevenson Restriction Scheme" emerged in November. It proposed to increase rubber production when prices were high and decrease production when they were low. It proved to be impractical, because it required absolute cooperation between the rubber producing countries and it was abandoned in 1928.

1934   The International Rubber Regulation Scheme, a "voluntary" measure, was introduced June 1, with the cooperation of the major rubber producing countries, each of which was granted an export quota. The scheme helped to improve the price until World War II erupted.

1972   Completion of a $77.6 million container port complex transformed Singapore into the most up-to-date trans-shipment port in the region.

SINGAPORE STOCK EXCHANGE

Title: Stock Exchange of Singapore Limited.

Address: 6th Floor, Clifford Centre, Raffles Place, Singapore 1.

Telephone: 92550, 70730, 912247, 982454

Telex: 21853

Cable Address: "SHARESTOCK" Singapore

Officers:
   Chairman: Ng Soo Peng
   Deputy Chairman: Ong Tjin An
   Committee Members:
      Joseph Chin
      Freddy Lee Thiam Yew
      Yau Meng Fai
   General Manager (Administration & Finance): Lim Choo Peng
   General Manager (Operation Research/Publications): Lim Hua Min
   General Secretary/Accountant: Yeo Eng Swee

Hours of Business (trading): 10:00 A.M. - 11:00 A.M. (weekdays)
                              11:15 A.M. - 12:30 P.M. (weekdays)
                              2:30 P.M. - 4:00 P.M. (weekdays)

Regulatory Laws: Securities Industry Act.

Issues Traded and Volume:
   1. Companies Traded:

1964	204	1969	242
1965	191	1970	256
1966	177	1971	260
1967	187	1972	264
1968	208	1973	N.A.

   2. Volume (000)

	Units	Value		Units	Value
1964	N.A.	$ N.A.	1969	587	$ 1,147.5
1965	89	N.A.	1970	455	746.5
1966	169	N.A.	1971	577	934.7
1967	259	419.0	1972	938	2,163.3
1968	472	857.5	1973	N.A.	N.A.

   N.A.—Not available

Unit of Trading:
   1. Dollar Stock

	50c	to	$10	..... 1,000 shares or units
over	$10	to	$20	..... 100 shares or units
				500 shares or units
				1,000 shares or units
	over	$20		..... 100 shares or units
				500 shares or units
				1,000 shares or units

   2. Sterling Stock (p. - pence)

0 to 50p.	.....	1,000 shares or units
over 50p. to 200p.	.....	500 shares or units
over 200p.	.....	100 shares or units

Membership:
   1. Regular Members: 71
   2. Cost of Membership: $1 million (1973)

Commissions or Fees: By-law 3(i) of the Stock Exchange sets the following minimum scales of brokerage payable by both buyer and seller.

1. Stocks, ordinary shares and preference shares.

Local		Sterling
Ready contracts Price	Brokerage per share	Ready contracts
Under 50c	½ cent	1%
At or over 50c	1 cent	
At or over $1.00	1%	Time Bargains and Arrival Contracts 1½%

Time	
Bargain contracts	Brokerage per share
Under 50c	¾ cent
At or over 50c	1½ cent
At or over $1.00	1½%

2. Government loans and municipal debentures:
   Up to $20,000—nominal value, ⅜% on nominal value. On nominal value in excess of $20,000, ¼% on excess over $20,000.
   Other debentures (non-convertible).
   Under $50,000—1%, $50,000-$100,000—½%, above $100,000—¼%. Options arranged in London—half the above rates applicable to the security. Minimum brokerage payable by both buyer and seller on loan transactions $2.00; on any other transactions $5.00.

3. Stamp Duty: Singapore—20c for every $100, or fractional part of $100, where the transfer bears a certificate signed by the transferor that the name of the transferee was filled in prior to the execution of the transfer by the transferor. 30c in every other case.

Historical Background:

1930	Singapore Stockbrokers Association founded.
1937	Malayan Stockbrokers Association founded.
1946	Name changed to Malayan Sharebrokers Association.
1959	Name changed to Malayan Stock Exchange.
1964 (June)	Organizations merged; became Stock Exchange of Malaysia & Singapore.
1973 (June 4)	Stock Exchange of Singapore Limited was incorporated.
1973 (June 16)	Inauguration of the Stock Exchange of Singapore Limited.

SOUTH AFRICA

JOHANNESBURG

JOHANNESBURG STOCK EXCHANGE

Title: The Johannesburg Stock Exchange

Address: Stock Exchange Building, Hollard Street, Johannesburg, South Africa

Telephone: 834 - 5711

Telex: 7663 SA

Cable Address: JOSTOCKEX

Officers:
 President: R. Luire
 Vice-President: E. Mc Kie
 General Manager: R. Clarke

Hours of Business: 9:15 A.M. - 3:30 P.M. (weekdays)

Regulatory Laws: The exchange is controlled externally by Act of Parliament —The Stock Exchanges Control Act of 1947 (as amended)—and internally by its own rules and regulations, which are based on those of the London Stock Exchange.

It has to apply annually to the Minister of Finance for its operating license. Control is vested in the Financial Institutions Office, which is a division of the Treasury.

Issues Traded and Volume:

1. Listed Issues: More than 1,300. Although there are four times as many industrial companies listed as mining companies, South Africa produces more than 70% of the free world's gold and the stock exchange has always been the greatest gold mining market in the world.

2. Volume and Value:

Year*	Volume	Value (in Rands)
1963	179,826,378	R 387,627,630
1964	254,000,000	775,799,945
1965	229,000,000	534,731,398
1966	154,877,037	355,931,759
1967	182,226,929	470,389,887
1968	253,701,469	663,638,984
1969	488,000,000	1,470,000,000
1970	544,000,000	1,699,826,482
1971	300,600,000	640,926,659
1972	360,200,000	636,643,718
1973	603,714,301	1,267,199,231

 * Fiscal years ending March 31.

Turnover in a busy week averages about 10 million shares.

Unit of Trading:
1. 100 shares.
2. Odd-lots are handled by odd-lot dealers, who charge a special commission.
3. Trading takes the form of a two-way oral auction between brokers.

Membership: Broking Members: 187 — Non-Broking Members: 75*
A member must buy and retain during his membership three proprietary rights on the Johannesburg Stock Exchange. These currently stand at about R 2,000 each. A member intending to trade must have R 20,000 of assets over liabilities in his stockbroking business. Where a member trades in partnership with others, the required assets over liabilities are at least R 20,000 for each of the first two partners, with an additional R 10,000 for each partner in excess of two. Entrance fee R 1,050: Annual subscription: R 200; Contribution to Guarantee Fund: R 400 (not annual).

Commissions or Fees: 0.85% ad valorem.

Historical Background:

1887 (Nov. 8)	The Exchange was founded by Benjamin Woollan in a building on Simmonds Street.
1889	The exchange building was demolished and a new headquarters erected on the same site.
1903	The exchange's third home was built in Hollard Street.
1957	The Hollard Street building was razed and a new one built on the site.
1960	Trading began in the new exchange in November. The Johannesburg Stock Exchange is the only exchange in South Africa.
1967	A computerized clearing system became operational in June.
1970	The exchange bought land in Newtown where a new headquarters will be erected.

*A non-broking member may not trade and must pay brokerage on his dealings. Usually he is an employee of a broking firm. Existing broking members may change their status to that of non-broking members on retirement or if changing to another field of activity, if they wish to retain their connections with the stock exchange.

SOUTH VIETNAM

SAIGON STOCK EXCHANGE

According to the United States Embassy, the Republic of Vietnam adopted a basic stock exchange law in February, 1972, but the necessary rules and regulations for such an exchange have not been formulated. It was expected that a modest stock exchange might be established by early 1975.

SPAIN

BARCELONA

BARCELONA STOCK EXCHANGE

Title: Bolsa Oficial de Comercio de Barcelona

Address: Paseo Isabel 11 s/n. Barcelona 3, Spain

Telephone: 319 62 00

Telex: 54601

Officers:
Board of Governors:
Chairman and President: Javier Garcon
Vice-President: Jose Pamies
Secretary: Miguel Cerezo

Hours of Business: 10:00 A.M. - 11:15 A.M. (Tuesday to Friday)

Regulatory Laws: Decree of 1506/1967 of June 30 — on which are based the rules and regulations of stock exchanges in Spain.

Issues Traded and Volume:
1. Listed companies: 406
2. Listed securities: 1,530
3. Volume (PTS 000,000):

		Public Securities	Bonds	Stocks	Total
1966	Nominal	1,351.2	1,095.6	1,350.1	3,796.9
	Actual	1,374.8	1,069.8	3,476.0	5,920.6
1967	Nominal	1,401.4	957.2	2,036.4	4,395.0
	Actual	1,483.4	924.2	4,343.9	6,751.5
1968	Nominal	1,950.1	1,310.5	2,408.1	5,668.6
	Actual	2,084.6	1,244.5	6,517.7	9,846.7
1969	Nominal	1,695.6	1,242.2	3,780.6	6,718.4
	Actual	1,854.5	1,178.7	3,357.3	14,603.5
1970	Nominal	1,644.6	1,199.7	11,572.2	6,201.6
	Actual	1,724.9	1,122.3	10,338.0	13,185.2
1971	Nominal	1,482.3	1,061.1	3,394.6	5,938.0
	Actual	1,601.7	1,020.1	9,931.6	12,553.4
1972	Nominal	1,792.5	1,522.3	7,261.2	10,576.1
	Actual	2,028.3	1,471.1	25,476.6	28,976.0
1973	Nominal	1,431.6	2,526.3	10,993.0	14,950.9
	Actual	1,521.8	2,630.0	39,209.5	43,361.3

Unit of Trading:
1. 25 shares.
2. Odd-lot business is usually transacted after the official market is closed ("outside trading hours"). No extra fee or commission is involved in the purchase or sale of odd-lots.

Memberships:
1. Regular Members: 45
2. Applicants for membership must:
   a. have certain qualifications (university degree, etc.);
   b. pass a rigid examination;
   c. be voted acceptable to existing Exchange members;
   d. be nominated by the Minister of Finance. This is mostly a formality; but it depends upon the candidate's success in meeting the other requirements.

Commissions or Fees:
1. Domestic Securities:
   a. Government and Treasury: 1.25 pesetas per 1,000 of principal, charged to both sides of the contract, with a minimum commission of 5 pesetas.
   b. Public Securities: 1.75 pesetas per 1,000 of principal, charged to both sides of the contract, with a minimum commission of 7.50 pesetas.
   c. Industrial and Commercial Stocks:

Amount involved in the order	Commission
up to 250 pesetas	.... 0.80 pesetas a share
250 pesetas to 500 pesetas	.... 1.50 pesetas a share
above 500 pesetas	.... 2.50 pesetas per 1,000 of value.

   Commissions must be collected on each side of a contract.
2. Foreign Securities:
   a. Public Securities: 3 pesetas per 1,000 of principal, charged to both sides of the contract, with a minimum commission of 15 pesetas.
   b. Industrial and Commercial Stocks: 5 pesetas per 1,000 of principal, charged to both sides of the contract, with a minimum commission of 20 pesetas.

Historical Background:

1251	Origins of the Bacelona Stock Exchange can be traced to this year, when a decree establishing certain fixed tariffs and regulations governing the brokerage on a series of commercial articles, was passed by the city councilors in February.
1271	New regulations were introduced with the purpose of fixing brokerage rates and avoiding fraud and deception. These regulations proclaimed on June 30, were replaced by new ones in 1372, 1491 and 1503.
1382	Work began on building the historic "Casa Llotja de Mar" (Maritime Exchange) where members of the Barcelona Stock Exchange now conduct their transactions.
1401	"Taula de Canvi" (Exchange Counter), the first regular bank for exchange, deposits and credits, made the Casa Llotja de Mar its first home on January 20. This early banking house lasted until 1865.
Mid-19th Century	Exchange brokers received their charter and became "Royal Exchange Brokers."

BILBOA

BILBOA STOCK EXCHANGE

Title: Bolsa de Bilboa
Address: Edificio de la Bolsa, Jose M. Olabarra 1, Bilboa, Spain

MADRID

MADRID STOCK EXCHANGE

Title: Bolsa de Comercio de Madrid

Address: Plaza de la Lealtad, No. 1; Madrid - 14, Spain

Telephone: 221 - 47 - 90

Telex: 27 - 619

Officers: Board of Governors:
   President: Pedro Rodriguez-Ponga y Ruiz de Salazar
   Vice-President: Enrique Jose de Benito y Rodriguez
   Secretary: Juan Jesus Roldan Fernandez
   Accountant: Leon Gutierrez Olea
   Treasurer and Director of Information and Service Studies: Jose Maria Fernandez Pirla
   Director of Building Management: Francisco Javier de Oyarzabal y Velarde
   Director of Business Operations: Manuel de la Concha y Lopez-Isla
   Director of Operations Settlement: Adolfo Ruiz de Velasco y del Valle
   Director of Mechanization and Organization Services: Jesus Maria Agurruza Aztarain
   Management:
   Director General: Fernando Ximenez Soteras
   Director of Technical Services: Manual Richi Bertran de Lis
   Director of Research: Marcial-Jesus Lopez Moreno

Hours of Business (trading):
   1. 10:00 A.M. - 11:15 A.M.
   2. The trading day consists of six ten-minute periods and three five-minute periods. The end of one period and the start of another is indicated by a bell. Securites may be traded/quoted only at the specific post, or ring, on the trading floor (seven in number) to which they have been assigned.

Regulatory Laws: Decree Number 1506/1967 of June 30 — on which are based the rules and regulations of stock exchanges in Spain.

Issues Traded and Volume:

1. Value of Issues Traded (PTS 000,000):

	Nominal Capital			Nominal Capital
1958	229,015		1966	491,391
1959	253,593		1967	548,987
1960	274,411		1968	613,934
1961	296,418		1969	715,583
1962	316,758		1970	812,479
1963	348,161		1971	932,795
1964	394,046		1972	1,040,110
1965	440,902		1973	1,177,231

2. Volume (PTS 000,000):

		Public Securities	Bonds	Stocks	Total
1961	Nominal	2,160.7	655.4	2,283.2	5,099.3
	Actual	2,145.7	622.5	5,095.0	7,863.2
1962	Nominal	2,269.2	905.5	2,577.6	5,752.3
	Actual	2,298.3	932.8	6,517.9	9,749.0
1963	Nominal	1,589.0	899.6	2,667.5	5,156.7
	Actual	1,619.5	913.1	7,545.0	10,077.6
1964	Nominal	1,878.6	1,337.9	2,427.6	5,644.1
	Actual	1,905.5	1,333.8	6,434.6	9,673.9
1965	Nominal	2,345.7	1,667.2	2,739.3	6,752.2
	Actual	2,395.0	1,642.4	8,307.3	12,344.7
1966	Nominal	2,869.5	1,965.5	3,218.6	8,053.6
	Actual	2,932.4	1,917.8	9,201.8	14,052.0
1967	Nominal	2,752.7	2,844.1	4,517.8	10,114.6
	Actual	2,889.0	2,706.1	13,723.0	19,318.1
1968	Nominal	3,151.8	3,922.8	5,733.7	12,808.3
	Actual	3,349.3	3,733.8	20,302.2	27,385.3
1969	Nominal	4,902.6	4,158.1	7,354.8	16,415.5
	Actual	5,317.2	3,930.4	28,908.1	38,155.7
1970	Nominal	3,157.0	4,616.4	6,439.9	14,213.3
	Actual	3,224.6	4,426.6	24,986.0	32,737.2
1971	Nominal	6,345.8	5,690.5	7,813.9	19,850.2
	Actual	6,963.9	5,414.3	26,349.2	38,727.4
1972	Nominal	8,630.9	5,620.9	13,063.3	27,315.1
	Actual	9,793.9	5,504.2	52,711.8	68,009.6
1973	Nominal	6,644.1	6,273.5	17,765.4	30,683.0
	Actual	7,098.8	6,284.9	86,680.3	100,064.0

Unit of Trading:

1. Officially Listed Issues and Rights:

Market Price					Trading Unit (PTS)
Up to			5,000	pesetas	5
From	5,000.01	to	30,000	pesetas	25
From	30,000.01	to	150,000	pesetas	125
From	150,000.01	to	250,000	pesetas	250
From	250,000.01	to	500,000	pesetas	500
From	500,000.01	to	1,000,000	pesetas	1,000

Above: ten pesetas per 10,000 or a fraction thereof.

2. Unlisted Issues and Rights:

	Market Price				Trading Unit (PTS)
Up to			5,000	pesetas	25
From	5,000.01	to	30,000	pesetas	125
From	30,000.01	to	150,000	pesetas	625
From	150,000.01	to	250,000	pesetas	1,250
From	250,000.01	to	500,000	pesetas	2,500
From	500,000.01	to	1,000,000	pesetas	5,000

Above: fifty pesetas per 10,000 or a fraction thereof.

Memberships: Regular Members:
1. 63, of whom 59 are active.
2. Candidates for membership must first pass rigid tests and meet specific entrance requirements. Their application is then voted upon by existing members of the stock exchange. If successful, the candidate will be nominated to membership by the Minister of Finance.

Commissions or Fees:
1. Domestic securities:
   a. Government and Treasury: 1.25 pesetas per 1,000 of principal, charged to both sides of the contract, with a minimum commission of 5 pesetas.
   b. Public Securities: 1.75 pesetas per 1,000 of principal, charged to both sides of the contract, with a minimum commission of 7.50 pesetas.
   c. Industrial and Commercial stocks:

Amount involved in the order		Commission
up to 250 pesetas	....	0.80 pesetas a share
250 pesetas to 500 pesetas	....	1.50 pesetas a share
above 500 pesetas	....	2.50 pesetas per 1,000 of value

   Commissions must be collected on each side of a contract.
2. Foreign Securities:
   a. Public Securities: 3 pesetas per 1,000 of principal, charged to both sides of the contract, with a minimum commission of 15 pesetas.
   b. Industrial and Commercial stocks: 5 pesetas per 1,000 of principal, charged to both sides of the contract, with a minimum commission of 20 pesetas.

Historical Background:
1649 A royal decree issued in this year, authorized twelve exchange brokers to deal in securities in Madrid.
1652 A Chamber of Commerce was established by decree of King Philip IV.
1709 A royal decree of November determined the membership and operations of exchange brokers.
1829 The Code of Commerce instituted this year ruled upon the activities of brokers, yet it had no part in arranging the affairs of the Bolsa de Comercio, which were regulated by royal decree on September 10, 1831, and which contained many rules that form the basis for the operation and administration of the Stock Exchange today.
1831 Madrid Stock Exchange founded, September 10.
1854 The "Quotation Price List" was first published on March 13.

VALENCIA

VALENCIA STOCK EXCHANGE

Title: Bolsa de Valencia
Address: Calle Pascual y Genis, 19 bjs, Valencia, Spain

SRI LANKA

COLOMBO

COLOMBO BROKERS' ASSOCIATION

Title: The Colombo Brokers' Association
Address: P.O. Box 101, Colombo 1, Sri Lanka
Telephone: 25545 - 25547
Cable Address: TURQUANDIA

The Colombo Brokers' Association functions as a stock exchange since there is no stock exchange in Sri Lanka (Ceylon).

Membership consists of the following firms: Bartleet & Co. Ltd.; De Silva, Abeywardena & Peiris; Forbes & Walker, Ltd.; John Keells, Ltd.; Somerville & Co., Ltd.

SWEDEN

STOCKHOLM

STOCKHOLM STOCK EXCHANGE

Title: The Stockholm Stock Exchange (Stockholms Fondbors)
Address: Kallargrand 2, S - 111 29 Stockholm, Sweden
Telephone: 08/10 56 38
Officers: Chairman, N. Erik Aqvist; Deputy Chairman, Rune Hermansson. The Council of the Stock Exchange consists of nine members and nine deputies.
Hours of Business: 9:30 A.M. - 2:30 P.M. (bonds), 10:45 A.M. - 2:30 P.M. (shares). Business is transacted on all weekdays during the year, except Midsummer Eve, Christmas Eve, New Year's Eve.

Regulatory Laws: The stock exchange legislation that was prepared in 1916 - 1918 was enacted by the Riksdag in 1919 and became operative in 1920. Since then no change has been made to the statutes and functions of the stock exchange; any revisions of the regulations have involved only details. Exchange regulations are valid for ten years. Those enacted in 1969 will be effective until the end of 1979. Government permission must be obtained to establish a stock exchange in Sweden.

Issues Traded and Volume:
1. Listed issues: 144 stocks of 104 companies and 1,176 bonds.
2. Volume: Shares: approximately Kr. 1,602 million in 1972 (a record high), versus Kr. 1,061.5 million in 1971.
   Bonds: Kr. 278.6 million in 1972, against 249.1 million in 1971.

Unit of Trading: Round-lots executed under the call-over system in an auction market. Transactions are for cash only. Brokerage firms may act either as brokers or jobbers and they usually may deal in their own shares.

Memberships: Number of members: 17, consisting of 6 brokerage firms and 11 banks, which account for about 75% of the total turnover.

Commissions or Fees: 0.45% ad valorem (shares); 0.10 - 0.25% ad valorem (bonds).

Historical Background:
- 1863 Securities auction markets were initiated in Stockholm.
- 1901 Stockholm Stock Exchange was established.
- 1907 The exchange was reorganized; banks were admitted to membership.
- 1912 The first official price list was published by the exchange.
- 1919 Legislation was enacted which became effective in 1920.
- 1971 A new and simplified system for handling shares, including a Securities Register Center, was adopted in Sweden on January 1.

SWITZERLAND

BASLE

BASLE STOCK EXCHANGE

Official Title: Chamber of the Basle Stock Exchange

Address: Freie Strasse, 3 P.O. Box 940, CH-4001 Basle, Switzerland

Telephone: 061 25 11 50

Telex: 62 719

Officers:
President: H. Guth
Vice-President: P. Stern

Assessors:
M. Ehinger   M. Lauchli
H. B. La Roche   A. E. Sarasin
R. Jeker
Executive Secretary: J.-B1. Treyvaud

Hours of Business: From Monday to Friday: 9:40 A.M. over-the-counter; 10:00 A.M. bonds; 10:15 A.M. shares. Trading is conducted until about 1 P.M.

Regulatory Laws: The Basle Stock Exchange operates under the Stock Exchange Law of February 17, 1944.

Issues Traded:

Year	Shares	Bonds	Year	Shares	Bonds
1960	137	501	1967	181	896
1961	143	537	1968	186	982
1962	155	562	1969	201	1,021
1963	156	607	1970	202	1,089
1964	163	658	1971	211	1,182
1965	169	736	1972	227	1,293
1966	176	819	1973	246	1,391

Dates and volumes of heaviest and lightest trading:

Year	Sw.Fr. (000,000)	Year	Sw.Fr. (000,000)
1898	792.3	1950	1,439.2
1905	1,679.3	1960	6,199.0
1916	327.3	1969	10,368.9
1928	2,627.1	1972	14,055.5
1934	462.2	1973	13,692.8
1940	261.0		

Unit of Trading:

	Cash Transactions	Forward Transactions
	Nominal Value	
a. for securities traded in percentages of their nominal value: (bonds)	Fr. 5,000. -	Fr. 25,000 -
b. for securities trades in francs apiece (shares)	Number of Securities	
price up to Fr. 500.-	25	50
price over Fr. 500.-and up to Fr. 1,000.-	10	20
price over Fr. 1,000.-and up to Fr. 5,000.-	5	10
price over Fr. 5,000.-and up to Fr. 10,000.-	2	5
price over Fr. 10,000.-	1	2

Odd-lots are handled at a slightly higher price.

Membership: 22 regular members; 22 associate members; no "other" members. No fees are charged for membership on the exchange.

Commissions or Fees: For shares brokerage is ⅝% of the combined market value. Brokerage amounts to ⅜% for Swiss bonds, ½% for foreign bonds, on the combined market value and accrued interests. Minimum of Sw.Fr. 10.-per type of security. This minimum may be reduced to Sw.Fr. 5. if the total amount is lower than Sw.Fr. 100.

Historical Background:

1503	First city stock exchange established.
1683	Brokerage regulations adopted and remained in force until 1854.
1871	First market quotations published.
1876	"Bourse à la criée" opened.
1897 (April 8)	Basle Stock Exchange Act adopted.
1908	Acquisition of new premises at the "Fish Market."
1929	Trading on the exchange forewarned of the coming crisis of the 1930's.
1945 (August)	Swiss stock and bond values underwent a sharp rise in value.
1960-70	Development of system to transmit prices via telex and TV.
1961	The cycle of stock market trends reach new, all-time high. Basle Stock Market prospered from the prosperity of the 1950's. Excellent development of the Basle market may be attributed in no small measure to the Swiss chemical stocks and the listing of U.S. blue chip securities. Basle is the scene of extensive international arbitrage dealings.
1972	Second trading floor opened.
1973	Electronic drawing machine installed.

BERN

BERN STOCK EXCHANGE

Title: Berner Borsenverein

Address: Aarbergergasse, 30, CH 3000, Bern, Switzerland

GRAIN AND PRODUCE EXCHANGE OF BERN

Title: Getreide-und Produktenborse Bern

Address: Bundesgasse 28, 3000 Bern, Switzerland

Telephone: 031 - 22 - 36 - 99

Officers:
President: Ernst Biedermann
Secretary: Werner Oesch

Hours of Business: Tuesday from 2:00 P.M. to 5:30 P.M.

Regulatory Laws: The Swiss Civil Code. A committee, elected by membership, is charged with managing and operating the bourse. Litigation arising from the settlement of contracts and disputes among members is handled by a special judiciary tribunal. The rules and regulations on which the decisions of the managing committee and the tribunal are based became effective January 1, 1959.

The Bourse: "Getreide-und Produktenborse Bern" has 269 regular members. Established in 1913 with headquarters in Bern, it has the following main objectives:

1. to create a central meeting place for transacting business in cereals, fodder and related products:
2. to regulate these operations by rules, practices and arbitration;
3. to defend the interests of the profession and of its members.

A large and varied business is carried on internationally in fish and farm products, and fertilizer.

GENEVA

GENEVA STOCK EXCHANGE

Title: Chambre de la Bourse de Geneve

Address: 8, rue Petitot, 1211 Geneva, Case postale No. 228, Switzerland.

Telephone: 022/28-06-84

Officers: Secretary: Pierre Jeanmonod

Hours of Business: 10:10 A.M. - 12:30 P.M. (approximately, on weekdays)

Regulatory Laws: Law of the Canton of Geneva (December 20, 1856). The Exchange is a member of The Association of Swiss Stock Exchanges. It is managed by an eight-member "Conseil d'Administration."

Issues Traded and Volume: Not available.
The secretary of the exchange maintains the official quotation list, which consists of securities approved for trading by the Chambre de la Bourse.
A quotation handbook, made out and supervised by the state commissioner, is referred to in the event of litigation about a price.

Unit of Trading: Not available.
Trading is conducted "à la criée" (the call system). Trades are made on the basis of "cash"; "end of the current month"; "end of the next month"; or "at a premium."

Memberships: 30 regular members and 3 associate members, 16 of whom are represented at the "Corbeille" (trading ring).

Commissions or Fees:
1. Bonds: 3.75% (based on price, plus current interest).
2. Foreign bonds: 5% (based on price, plus current interest).
3. Shares and Rights (based on price):
   a. 0 to Sfr. 150—1%.
   b. above Sfr. 150—⅝%.
   c. minimum for each transaction Sfr. 10; on stocks priced below Sfr. 100—Sfr. 5.

Historical Background:
    1850 The Bourse was founded.
    1944 Up to and including this year, the Bourse was essentially for stockbrokers.
    1945 On January 1, the banks were represented directly at the "Corbeille."

LAUSANNE

LAUSANNE STOCK EXCHANGE

Title: Bourse de Lausanne

Address: Place Bel-Air 4, 1003, Lausanne, Switzerland

Officers:
    Chairman of the Board: Jean de Roguin, co-proprietor of the Bank Chollet, Roguin & Cie.
    Commissioner: Bernard Hofstetter, co-proprietor of the Bank Hofstetter, Landolt & Cie.

Hours of Business: 10:30 A.M. - 12:30 P.M. (approx.) on weekdays.

Regulatory Laws: Swiss Civil Code, Art. 60 and following.

Unit of Trading: Bonds: Sfr. 5,000
    Shares: under Sfr.   200 -   : 20 units
               from Sfr.   200 - to Sfr. 1,000 - : 10 units
               from Sfr. 1,000 - to Sfr. 5,000 - : 5 units
               over Sfr. 5,000 -   : 2 units

Membership: Fifteen Regular Members.

Commissions or Fees: Same as those charged by the Zurich Stock Exchange.

Historical Background: The Bourse de Lausanne, founded in 1873, is a private association, whose members are local banks, plus some affiliates of other Swiss banks.

NEUCHATEL

NEUCHATEL STOCK EXCHANGE

Title: Bourse de Neuchatel

Address: 24 rue du Coq d'Inde, Neuchatel, Switzerland

ST. GALL

ST. GALL STOCK EXCHANGE

Title: St. Gall Stock Exchange

Address: % Swiss Bank Corporation, 9001 St. Gall, Switzerland

Officers: The Swiss Bank Corporation serves as presidency of the exchange for current (1974) term. New premises for the exchange are under construction.

Hours of Business: Representatives of the ten principal banks meet daily at 9:30 A.M. to buy and sell securities.

Memberships: Local banks are members. There is no cost for a seat on the exchange but the member banks defray all operating costs of the exchange.

Commissions: Same as Zurich Stock Exchange.

Historical Background:
1888 Origins of this small provincial exchange date back to this year.
1932 Formal exchange created.

ZURICH

ZURICH STOCK EXCHANGE

Title: Zurich Stock Exchange

Address: Bleicherweg 5, CH-8021 Zurich, Switzerland.

Telephone: 01 - 27 - 14 - 70

Telex: 57065

Officers:
President: R. Rahn
Vice-President: E. Studer
Treasurer: E. Roesle
Other Members:
R. Schait
H. C. Kessler
N. J. Bar
Manager: A. Rossi
Secretary: R. T. Meier

Hours of Business:
1. Pre-market dealings (9:40 A.M. - 10:00 A.M.); transactions in securities which have been proposed for exchange trading privileges, but have not yet been officially accepted. Prices and executions are not registered officially, nor has the cantonal exchange commissioner any control over them.

2. Official bond trading starts at 10:00 A.M.; dealings in Swiss shares begin at 10:15 and in foreign shares at 11:00. There are no regular closing times; hours subject to change on short notice.

Regulatory Laws: "Wertpapiergesetz". The Stock Exchange Association of Zurich, a legal corporation formed in 1877, is responsible for operations of the exchange.

Issues Traded and Volume:
1. Securities quoted (December 31, 1973):
   a. bonds: 1540
   b. shares and investment trust certificates: 262.
2. Volume (000,000 Sfr.):

1913	1,657	1965	19,046
1945	2,986	1970	35,703
1950	4,969	1971	54,516
1955	13,262	1972	74,003
1960	19,484	1973	65,408

Unit of Trading:
1. Varies according to price, but generally about Sfr. 10,000—market value.
2. Odd-lots are traded "off the floor"; no extra fee or commission is charged.

Memberships:
1. Regular members ("Ringbanken"): 26
2. "Other" members (OTC dealers): 124
3. There is no fixed number of members.
4. Membership deposit: Sfr. 330,000 plus annual fee based on business volume.
5. Firms which engage in stock exchange business must have a minimum basic capital of 1 million Sfr.

Commissions or Fees: As members of the Association of Swiss Stock Exchanges, the exchanges of Basle, Berne, Geneva, Lausanne, Neuchatel, St. Gall and Zurich charge the following minimum rates for all transactions. The association does not recognize discounts and will apply sanctions if the rates are violated.
1. Bonds: There is a distinction between Swiss and foreign bonds. For Swiss bonds, brokerage amounts to ⅜% of said total. Brokerage on foreign securities is calculated on the same principle, but at a rate of ½%.
2. Shares: No distinction is made between Swiss and foreign shares. Also, there is no difference between the rates applying to spot and forward transactions. In option deals, the commission is calculated on the market price, not on the premium. If a purchaser operating on an option basis withdraws from the transaction on the fixed date, this will not produce a new situation for computing the commission on the premium to be paid. Brokerage rates are graded according to price and at present are as follows:

Market Price Sfrs.	Brokerage (per share)
up to 150 - incl.	⅝% of market price
above 150 -	1% of market price

Minimum brokerage per transaction is Sfrs. 10.

3. Stamp Duty and Fees: Both the Confederation and the Canton of Zurich benefit from the stock exchange. The Federal Stamp Duty on Swiss securities is Sfrs. - .15 per Sfrs. 1,000. On foreign securities it amounts to Sfrs. - .50 per Sfrs. 1,000. The Canton of Zurich draws a fee of Sfrs. - .10 per Sfrs. 1,000 - regardless of whether the security is of Swiss or foreign origin. The stock exchange fee is Sfrs. - .05 per Sfrs. 1,000.
4. Different charges are again made for transactions done through a Zurich bank in securities not quoted in Zurich, but traded on some foreign exchange.

Historical Background:

1877	Zurich Stock Exchange Association established.
1883	Citizens passed "law concerning the trades of brokers and representatives operating in the Stock Exchange." It provided for a stock exchange commissioner to supervise what had previously been a private market and it raised the levy on exchange transactions. "Evening markets" were held daily, as of November 3, from 3:30 P.M. to 4:30 P.M., in addition to regular sessions from 11:15 A.M. to 12:15 P.M.
1884	Stock exchange members went on strike January 1, to avoid this law. When this produced nothing, trading was resumed April 1, with only six members attending. The stock exchange has been supervised ever since by the State.
1904-05	First American securities traded on the exchange.
1912	New stock exchange law passed on December 22.
1914	Trading suspended for World War I.
1915	Bond trading resumed.
1921	Forward dealings resumed after having been halted seven years on account of World War I.
1929-33	Wall Street crash, German financial crisis, collapse of Austrian Creditanstalt and devaluation of British pound caused unsettlement on Zurich Exchange.
1930	Exchange moved to present location where separate rings for bond and stock trading were inaugurated.
1940	Swiss exchanges closed from May 10 - July 8 when Germany invaded Low Countries.
1972	Volume set all-time record of $74,000 million Swiss francs.

TURKEY

ISTANBUL

ISTANBUL STOCK EXCHANGE

Title: Istanbul Menkul Kiymetler ve Kambiyo Borsasi
Address: 4 Vakit Han, Kat 1, Behcekapi, Istanbul, Turkey

UNITED KINGDOM

London is the headquarters of many kinds of exchanges, trade associations, terminal markets, clearing houses, etc. The information about them included here is based upon data received directly from these organizations.

The Stock Exchange (London) and its Administrative Departments (formerly provincial exchanges), the London Commodity Exchange and the Terminal Market Associations using the exchange, plus the International Commodities Clearing House, are reviewed; there is data also about trade associations. Even where no futures market exists, as with fur and tea (temporarily), an effort has been made to present as much up-to-date and accurate information as time and space limitations would permit.

BRADFORD

THE LONDON WOOL TERMINAL MARKET ASSOCIATION

Title: The London Wool Terminal Market Association

Address: Manor Buildings, Manor Row
Bradford 1, England

Telephone: Bradford 31461

Branches and Affiliates: London Offices:
Roman Wall House, 1-2 Crutched Friars
London E.C.3, England

Officers: Secretary: N. G. Cowley

Hours of Business (trading):
1. Trading sessions (weekdays): 11:15 A.M. - 11:30 A.M.; 3:15 P.M. - 3:30 P.M.; 4:15 P.M. - 4:45 P.M.
2. All trading is done by "open outcry" on the floor of the London Commodity Exchange.
3. Kerb trading is allowed after hours until 5:30 P.M. and contracts must be telephoned to the Clearing House by 5:45 P.M.

Regulatory Laws: Rules and regulations of the Association are enforced by the Management Committee, which consists of one representative from each floor member, plus an affiliate representative and three associate member representatives.

Contracts:
1. The Standard Top contract specifies Merino Wool grown and shorn from living animals in Australia. It must be drycombed and contain the standard allowance of grease and oil. The wool must be sorted, scoured and carded in accordance with methods prevailing in the wool textile industry.
The specifications of the Standard are as follows:
Fiber Fineness as expressed by the WIRA Fiber Fineness Meter 22.5 Microns.

Fiber length as expressed by the Almeter: —
Hauteur .... 6.2 cm
Barbe .... 7.7 cm
Coefficient of variation of hauteur 50%
2. Contract unit: 2,250 Kg.
3. Quoted months: March, May, July, October, December - up to 19 months ahead.
4. All contracts on the market must be registered with the International Commodities Clearing House Limited. The Clearing House guarantees the fulfillment of the contract to the person in whose name it is registered, in accordance with its rules and those of the Association.

Delivery (the physical delivery of the wool types from the warehouse):
1. Each 2,250 Kg. contract must be unit net conditioned weight, with a tolerance of not less than 2,150 Kg. and not more than 2,350 Kg. net conditioned weight, including allowance for fatty matter.
2. Type specifications:
   a. lowest tenderable: fiber fineness as expressed by the WIRA Fiber Fineness Meter — 24.5 Microns.
   Hauteur as expressed by the Almeter — 6.0 cm
   Barbe as expressed by the Almeter — 7.8 cm
   Coefficient of variation of hauteur — 55%
   The buyer pays the seller through the Clearing House, as agent, a fee of £ 5 for each lot tendered to him.
   b. highest deliverable: fiber fineness as expressed by the WIRA Fiber Fineness Meter — 21.0 Microns.
   Hauteur as expressed by the Almeter — 6.2 cm
   Barbe as expressed by the Almeter — 7.5 cm
   Coefficient of variation of hauteur — 45%
   c. deliverable range: Tops having specifications between the lowest and highest types may be delivered subject to appraisal, but the hauteur as shown by the Test Certificate must not be outside the following range of readings:

Fiber Fineness	Hauteur not less than
24.5 to 24 microns	6.0 cm
23.9 to 22.5 microns	5.8 cm
22.4 microns and finer	5.5 cm

3. Location: in warehouses as approved by the Committee from time to time. If the Tops come from overseas, a clean warehouse receipt must be obtained from the warehouse keeper before appraisal.

Prices and Minimum Fluctuations: Prices are quoted in new pence per kilogram, with a minimum fluctuation of 0.1 of a new penny.

Memberships:

	Entrance Fee	Annual Subscription
Floor Members:		
Affiliate Members:	£ 1,000	£ 105
Associate Members:	£ 300	£ 105

Commissions (including Clearing House Registration Fee and Levy):
From an Affiliate Member .... £ 3.50 buying and selling
From an Associate Member .... £ 6.00 buying and selling
From a non-member .... £ 9.00 buying and selling

Historical Background:
1953 The London Wool Terminal Market Association was founded.

LONDON

BRITISH FUR TRADE ASSOCIATION

Title: British Fur Trade Association

Address: 68 Upper Thames Street, London EC4V 3AN, England

Telephone: 01 - 248 5947

Officers: Acting Secretary: Mrs. E. Lockyer

There is no commodity exchange operating within the fur trade. The British Fur Trade Association represents and promotes the industry and may be contacted for information about its membership.

COFFEE IMPORTERS AND EXPORTERS ASSOCIATION OF LONDON

Title: The Coffee Importers and Exporters Association of London

Address: Coffee Exchange Building, 52/57 Mark Lane, London EC3, England

Since there are more than 30 coffee producing countries, each with its own diverse and varied range of qualities and grades, it follows that "trading in actuals" is a complex operation necessitating a great deal of accumulated knowledge.

Purchases and sales are mainly effected within three broad categories:

1. Sales made on quality description.

   This implies that the seller makes the offer by describing the quality in terms that are fully understood and recognizable within the trade, for instance:

   a. 1. The Grade — where it is customary to relate the quality to a pre-determined number of defects, i.e., "Santos New York 4" or "Uganda Standard Grade" or "Indonesian E.K. 1/35%", etc.

   or 2. The Brand or Type, which by itself is sufficiently identifiable so as not to need reference to a defect count, i.e., "Tanganyika F.A.Q." or "Guatemala Prime Washed" or "Colombian Medellin Excelso", etc.

   b. These descriptions may on occasions need to be amplified by reference to the size of bean, i.e., "Good to fine roast" and to cup quality, i.e., "Screen ... " or "Firsts and seconds only".

   c. Where necessary, further amplifications are made with respect to roast, i.e., "Good to fine roast" and to cup quality, i.e., "Strictly soft" or "Mild Taste" or "Clean cup" etc.

2. Sales made upon Type Sample.

   This implies that the seller has established with the buyer, by sending a representative sample, a quality and grade which he guarantees to deliver "about equal to" or "fully equal to" according to the terms of the contract. The type sample can be further amplified by adding to its number or name a description of its basic quality, e.g., "Salvador High Crown" or "Guatemala Hard Bean" or "Kenya A" etc.
3. Sales made on acutal stock-lot sample.

   This implies that the seller has sent to the buyer a sample of the coffee actually taken from the lot he has available to sell and he guarantees that he will deliver as per sample, conforming in all respects — grade, size, roast, cup, etc.

In general, trading in actuals rests absolutely upon confidence between seller and buyer that each knows precisely what is offered and what is bought, and that each is fully capable of honoring his part of the contract, there being no outside body guaranteeing performance of the contract.

THE COFFEE TERMINAL MARKET ASSOCIATION OF LONDON

Title: The Coffee Terminal Market Association of London

Address: Corn Exchange Building, 52/57 Mark Lane, London, EC3R 7NE, England.

Hours of Business:
1. 10:15 A.M. - 12:30 P.M.; 2:30 P.M. - 5:10 P.M.
2. Calls:
   a. Robusta: 10:30 A.M. - 12:20 P.M.; 2:30 P.M. - 4:50 P.M.
   b. Arabica: 10:15 A.M. - 12:05 P.M.; 2:45 P.M. - 5:05 P.M.

Unit of Trading:
1. Robusta: Five metric tons of sound Robusta quoted in sterling per metric ton with minimum fluctuation of 50p. Coffee must be stored in an approved warehouse in London/Home counties or in Bristol at contract price, or in Amsterdam/Rotterdam at a discount.

   Other grades are tenderable in accordance with CTMAL rules.
2. Arabica: 5865 kilos (5% more or less), equaling 85 bags of 69 kilos, of Sound Wet processed Arabica Coffee, quoted in dollars and cents with minimum fluctuation of 10 cents per 50 kilos. Coffee must be stored in an approved warehouse in Amsterdam, Rotterdam, or Hamburg at contract price, or in London at $1.50 per 50 kilos discount.
3. In both cases, a wide range of growth and qualities are tenderable and there are seven trading positions ranging over 14 months ahead.

   Actuals: In addition to futures, physical coffee is traded in London for home consumption and for consumption in markets all over the world. In particular, the London dealer houses take a large share in the world Robusta coffee trade based, obviously, on the use of the London Robusta Futures market which has become a major tool of their trade, and also on the London Foreign Exchange Market. In Robusta trading, a very large proportion of the business is based on the official grades and descriptions established in the various producing countries, but a certain amount of business is also based on acutal stocklot samples.

Arabica coffee of all origins is also traded by London dealer houses on an international basis. The quality definitions vary from origin to origin: official types and descriptions, private shippers' types or brands, stocklot samples, etc.

Home Trade: The vast proportion of coffee consumed in the U.K. is soluble or instant coffee. The proportion of total usage in soluble form varies from 85% upwards. Total imports for 1973 were a record at over 2 million bags of green coffee and over 32 million pounds weight of soluble powder. Approximately 60/65% of powder consumed is made in the U.K. from imported green coffee and the balance imported as ready made powder.

The large manufacturers import green coffee on their own account, buying from trade or sometimes official producer organizations. Smaller users buy through the green coffee traders on CIF or "landed" terms. Bigger buyers tend to buy on standard types, but smaller users tend to buy on a stocklot sample basis. The smallest buyers frequently buy only "spot" coffee from the green coffee dealers who have already imported the coffee and hold it in public warehouses.

Organization: There is now one organization embracing all types of companies interested in coffee: importers, dealers, roasters, soluble manufacturers, brokers, warehouses, etc. This is The Coffee Trade Federation, 69 Cannon Street, London, E.C.4.

The brokers normally function as go-betweens in the home trade, as between one company and another; often combined with business as commission houses on the futures market.

Memberships:

1. The representatives of 35 Floor Members do the actual trading by open outcry on the trading floor. Floor members accept orders from clients at fixed rates of commission.
2. An unlimited number of Associate Members divided into Home and Overseas are mostly active in the coffee trade either as producers, merchants, or manufacturers. Overseas clients may become associate members and secure reduced commissions.
3. The market is managed by a committee of twelve; eight represent the floor members and four the associate members.

Historical Background:

1958 Coffee Terminal Market opened in July.

1973 Trading in the Arabica Coffee contract began September 17, soon after the Terminal Market Association moved into new market premises in the Corn Exchange Building.

THE GENERAL PRODUCE BROKERS' ASSOCIATION OF LONDON

Title: The General Produce Brokers' Association of London

Address: Cereal House, 58 Mark Lane, London, EC3R 7HP, England.

Telephone: 01 - 480 5388/9

Officers: Committee 1974
President: P. J. Knight
Vice-President: L.A. Cowley
Members:

A. V. Andrews	P. C. Hart
J. E. Bowyer	P. Heppenstall
L. A. Cowley	S. C. Hudson
H. Geewater	J. V. Smith
G. E. Godfrey	N. E. Treliving
L. C. Grant	

Secretary: Mrs. M. V. Greene

Hours of Business: 9:30 A.M. - 5:30 P.M.

Regulatory Laws: Rules and regulations of the Association are supervised and enforced by a twelve-man Committee. Disputes are settled by a Panel of Arbitrators consisting of 87 members.

Memberships: There are 32 regular member firms and 4 individual Associate Members.

Historical Background:

The Association was founded in 1876 by brokers who met in the Subscription Room of the London Commercial Sale Rooms in Mincing Lane. Prior to this, the produce brokers each made their own terms and conditions of sale; holding auctions in their own "Sale Room," and there was no established method of handling disputes between buyers and sellers.

The auction method of doing business and the practice of selling spot goods by means of samples in broker's sale rooms were gradually eclipsed by transactions made by "private treaty," and by contracts made for shipment on C.I.F. or F.O.B. terms.

After World War II, a very large business was transacted in a wide variety of spices, essential oils and drugs and in other commodities, such as aromatic seeds, bristles, hair, gums, waxes, mica, etc. The Association's member firms handle more than one hundred commodities.

THE GRAIN AND FEED TRADE ASSOCIATION

Title: The Grain and Feed Trade Association, Ltd.

Address: Baltic Exchange Chambers, 24/28 St. Mary Axe, London EC3A 8EP, England.

Telephone: 01 - 283 5146

Telex: 886984

Cable Address: CONSIGNMENT London EC3

Officers:
President: L. Pullen
Deputy President: B. McC. Rutherford
U.K. Vice-President: C. J. Tilley
European Vice-President: H. Muus
Director General: J. C. S. Mackie
Secretary: W. J. Englebright

Hours of Business:
1. Futures ring for barley and wheat is open on weekdays from 11:00 A.M. - 12:30 P.M. and from 2:45 P.M. - 4:00 P.M.
2. Trading in the current month halts at 4:00 P.M. on the 22nd day of the month. However, if this is not a market day, at 4:00 P.M. on the market day prior to the 22nd of the month.
3. Trading is in the months of September, November, January, March and May, and it is possible to deal eleven months forward, in that when trading ceases on the 22nd day of the current month, the same delivery month a year hence is opened for trading on the first business day of the next month.

Regulatory Laws:
1. The Association maintains a committee which supervises and enforces — and may from time to time change — the rules and regulations stipulated in the by-laws, known as The London Grain Futures Market and Clearing House Regulations.
2. The conduct of the market is under the control of The Grain and Feed Trade Association and is managed by the London Grain Futures & Clearing House Committee of that Association. The registering of contracts is made at the Clearing House of that Association, where all other facets of the day-to-day business of the market are also dealt with.
3. The composition of the London Grain Futures & Clearing House Committee is as follows:
   a. 4 members elected by the market;
   b. 7 members nominated by the Council of The Grain and Feed Trade Association;
   c. 2 persons nominated annually by the British Association of Grain, Seed, Feed & Agricultural Merchants. The Committee appoints each year from among its own members a chairman who must also be a member of the Council of G.A.F.T.A. One elected member and one nominated member retires by rotation each year.

Contract Details:
Contract Grades:
1. Barley:
   a. sound and sweet and to contain not more than 3% heat damage;
   b. natural weight to be not less than 50 lbs. per bushel;
   c. moisture content not to exceed 15½% (by water oven test);
   d. total admixture of seeds and/or farinaceous grains (including wild oats) and dirt not to exceed 5%, of which dirt content not to exceed 1%.
   e. sprouted grains not to exceed 5%.

2. Wheat:
   a. sound and sweet and to contain not more than 3% heat damage;
   b. natural weight to be not less than 58 lbs. per bushel;
   c. moisture content not to exceed 15½% (by water oven test);
   d. admixture — (1) seeds and/or farinaceous grains (including wild oats) and dirt not to exceed 2%, of which the dirt content not to exceed 1%; (2) ergot and/or garlic not to exceed 0.001%;
   e. sprouted grains not to exceed 2%.

Contract Units: The unit of quantity for each contract is 100 long tons of 2,240 lbs. each.

Price Basis:

1. Offers are made in multiples of £0.05 per 2,240 lbs. and quotations of pounds and decimals thereof. There is no daily limit as to how prices may move.
2. The price of the barley or wheat is to include insurance cover and free rent for fourteen days from the date of tender, and delivery is free to buyers in bulk ex-store. At time of tender the grain must be stored in the premises to an Approved Service Operator on the list authorized and published by the Committee.

Value of Trades Registered — 1972/1973 (as of September 30).

Basis of calculations: On the basis that an equivalent number of trades was made in each of the five trading positions for barley and likewise for wheat, and that an average is taken between the lowest and highest prices during the period, the following totals are concluded:

E.E.C. Barley

	Lowest Price	Highest Price	Average	Trades @ 100T.	Value
Sept.	£27-00	£55-90	£41-45	6134	£25,425,430
Nov.	£29-20	£57-95	£43-50	6134	£26,682,900
Jan.	£31-65	£59-90	£45-80	6134	£28,093,720
Mar.	£33-30	£61-05	£46-25	6134	£28,369,750
May	£39-15	£62-15	£50-65	6134	£31,068,710
					£139,640,510

E.E.C. Wheat

	Lowest Price	Highest Price	Average	Trades @ 100T.	Value
Sept.	£32-25	£65-70	£49-00	6134	£30,056,600
Nov.	£35-00	£67-70	£51-35	6134	£31,498,090
Jan.	£37-15	£69-10	£53-15	6134	£32,602,210
Mar.	£38-85	£69-90	£54-40	6134	£33,368,960
May	£46-30	£70-70	£58-50	6134	£35,883,900
					£163,409,760

COMBINED Total: £303,050,270

NOTE: Trades as above = 10 x 6134 . . . . . . .61,340 Trades
      Actual Trades registered . . . . . . .61,346 Trades

Memberships:

1. Membership of the market entails qualifications as follow:
    a. London Members: To be members of G.A.F.T.A., members of the Baltic Mercantile & Shipping Exchange, to hold a certificate of membership of the London Grain Futures Market, and for their offices to be situated within a five-mile radius of London.
    b. Country Members: To qualify as above excepting that their place of business must be beyond the five-mile of London radius but within the United Kingdom;
    c. To hold a certificate of membership, costing £ 200, an applicant must fulfill conditions of qualification laid down by the Council of G.A.F.T.A.
    d. Additionally, there are the following categories of traders: Subscribers, and Subscriber Brokers. Each category requires approval of the Council and must pay an annual subscription of £ 200.
2. The Association holds a Reserve Fund, which has been built up from an allotted portion of the Clearing House registration fee. The use of this fund is governed by an article in the G.A.F.T.A. constitution which permits, at any one time, up to 50% of the fund to be used at the discretion of the Council for settling claims by members arising out of the default of a member or the insolvency of a storekeeper. Additionally, the Association holds a very large insurance cover.

Historical Background:

1929 The London Grain Futures Market was formed.

1974 Trading takes place across a ring on the Baltic Mercantile & Shipping Exchange. Business is by open cry and is never conducted through a chairman, as in certain other markets. The prices of all trades are marked on boards by an official of The Grain and Feed Trade Association who also enters the official opening and closing prices of each session. These latter prices are fixed by a member nominated each week from a panel approved by the Grain Futures and Clearing House Committee of the Association.

INTERNATIONAL COMMODITIES CLEARING HOUSE LTD.

Title: International Commodities Clearing House Ltd.

Address: Roman Wall House, 1-2 Crutched Friars, London EC3N 1AN, England

Telephone: 01 - 488 3200

Telex: 887234

Cable Address: LIBONOTUS London EC3

Branches and Affiliates:

International Commodities Clearing House, Ltd.
Level 6, Australia Square Tower
Sydney N.S.W. 2000, Australia
Telephone: 27 2841
Telex: AA 22142
Cable Address: LIBONOTUS Sydney

Officers:
Managing Director: C. J. J. Clay
Executive Directors:
  M. Stockdale
  I. W. T. McGaw

The Company:
International Commodities Clearing House Ltd. is basically a guaranteeing and clearing agency appointed by the Terminal Market Associations to guaranty and to clear contracts that are entered into between the members of their particular market.

The International Commodities Clearing House never takes the place of the principal who has traded the contract; its role is simply that of an agency standing between the first seller and the final buyer of a terminal market contract, having the necessary organization to accept delivery from the seller and to make delivery to the buyer; by the process of receiving a document of title to the goods from the seller, against payment of his sales contract value, and making delivery of the same document of title to the buyer or buyers in exchange for their payment calculated at their contract prices — whether higher or lower than that of the original seller.

However, the Company differs both in function and procedure from other clearings. For example, it provides its own guaranty supported by its own capital and reserves to the clearing members. It is able and willing to clear for any number of markets, either in the U.K. or overseas — such as Sydney and Paris, which it already serves. Moverover, it is prepared to accept as members (clearing members) any companies or firm able to satisfy the Board of Directors that they are responsible and are able to provide to International Commodities Clearing House, from banks acceptable to International Commodities Clearing House, a guaranty to cover their deposit and margin liabilities.

Intercom — a total computer service — was introduced in 1964 for Mincing Lane markets and later extended to include the New York, Chicago and Paris Futures Exchanges. It enables a member to examine his own and his client's positions, keep up to date on all trades which he has open on any markets in which he is active. In 1974 a real time facility was introduced and the system also allocates trades to clients within minutes after they occur, enables a member to have a contract printed by pressing a key on the terminal, and provides a wide variety of statistical information about margins and open positions, settlements, commissions, etc.

Memberships:
The initial fee is £5 and the annual fee is £1. However, the directors are very stringent in their examination of prospective as well as existing members. International Commodities Clearing House is not interested in members whose principal concern is trading in London commodity options. International Commodities Clearing House had 256 members, as of December 31, 1973.

Membership entitles a trader to have contracts registered in his own name on any of the markets cleared by International Commodities Clearing House and thus receive the Company's direct guaranty for the fulfillment of each contract.

Volume: Number of Lots Cleared and Guaranteed:
1. London Markets:

	Sugar	Cocoa	Coffee	Wool
1959	16,101	58,570	25,433	57,007
1960	22,978	51,578	22,896	54,035
1965	202,654	248,736	89,693	32,594
1969	579,479	990,045	48,537	8,392
1970	530,870	1,129,252	106,344	5,308
1971	676,146	1,028,948	78,240	2,874
1972	879,020	1,050,504	60,341	3,922
1973	854,045	1,322,946	155,335	3,640

2. Overseas Markets: Sydney

	Wool
1969	8,984
1970	65,074
1971	44,860
1972	103,284
1973	168,036

Commissions: Fees on commodity contracts are negotiated by International Commodities Clearing House with the various commodity market associations for whom it clears and guarantees futures contracts.

Historical Background:

1888 The present company was formed as the London Produce Clearing House, Ltd. by a group of merchant bankers and commodity merchants. The sugar and coffee trades were the first to use the Clearing House services after this year.

1928 London market in cocoa opened.

1950 The Company became part of the United Dominions Trust Group.

1953 London Produce Clearing House helped to found the London Wool Terminal Market.

1957 London Sugar Market reopened.

1958 London Coffee Market reopened.

1964 Computer clearing services introduced for Mincing Lane markets.

1967 Computer clearing services expanded to include New York, Chicago and Paris futures exchanges. London market for vegetable oils opened.

1968 Computer clearing services made available to London Metal Exchange members. Paid up capital of the company was raised by £ 500,000.

1969 A branch office was opened in Sydney, Australia.

1972 Paid up capital raised again by a further £ 1,250,000 in August. Capital and reserves then stood at £ 3 million. Clearing services for Paris sugar and cocoa markets opened in June.

1973 Name changed to International Commodities Clearing House Ltd. in May. Clearing services for Paris coffee market began in April. The full international off-setting of margins between London and Paris were also introduced. In September London Market for Mild Arabica Coffee opened. Capital raised to £ 5 million in November.

THE LONDON COCOA EXCHANGE TERMINAL MARKET ASSOCIATION

Title: The London Cocoa Exchange Terminal Market Association

Address: Corn Exchange Building
52/57 Mark Lane
London EC3, England

The Cocoa Association of London was established in 1926. A Terminal Market began operations in 1928. Trading was halted during World War II; the Terminal Market did not reopen until January, 1951.

There are four classes of members: Brokers and Home Members, who carry out the floor trading; U.K. Associate Members and Overseas Member firms, who cannot trade on the floor but receive concessions as to brokerage paid.

The contract calls for 10 tons of Ghana Good Fermented, ex-store London, Liverpool, Hull, Avonmouth, Teesside, Amsterdam, Antwerp, Rotterdam, or Hamburg, and sellers have the option to deliver other growth at a premium or discount.

LONDON COMMODITY EXCHANGE

Title: The London Commodity Exchange

Address: Corn Exchange Building, 52/57 Mark Lane, London EC3R 7NE, England

Telephone: 01-488 3736/9
Telex: 884370
Officers:
Chairman: R. E. Liddiard*
Vice Chairman: A. J. P. Woodhouse*
Executive Director: P. A. S. Rucker*
Directors:

D. J. Allen	C. C. B. Morris
W. Brighton	M. S. S. Stockdale
D. St. C. Harcourt	

*Also Director

Hours of Business: 10:00 A.M. - 5:00 P.M. (weekdays)

Regulatory Laws: The Board of Directors of the exchange exercises no control over the methods or conditions of trading in the various markets; this responsibility is vested in the respective trade associations.

Commodities Traded: Cocoa, coffee, general produce, rubber, sugar, vegetable oil, wool.

The Markets: Futures Call Markets (commodities are sold for delivery at some future date) have several features in common.
  a. Trading is done by "open outcry" on the trading floor, by exchange members authorized to do so.
  b. The markets open and close with a "Call," when all trading members assemble under a call chairman. At the call, prices are established and trading takes place for all the months quoted, transactions being dis-

played in the market. Calls usually last about fifteen minutes. Sellers are responsible for recording business done between calls.

Clearing House members' contracts are registered with the International Commodities Clearing House, which guarantees that they be fulfilled in accordance with the rules of the Terminal Market Associations concerned. The method of working is as follows:

a. Contracts. All contracts for future delivery are on the forms prescribed by the Clearing House and in accordance with the rules of the Terminal Market Association concerned.

b. In the case of every contract the buyer and seller lodge with the clearing house a deposit, which is held by the clearing house until the contract is liquidated.

c. Should the market price move against either buyer or seller, the clearing house calls for additional margin in order to maintain the deposit intact. Margins are reclaimable on demand when the position reverses itself.

Memberships: Shareholding membership consists of the Terminal Market Associations using the exchange which form the voting membership, while the non-voting associate membership comprises other commodity associations which are not shareholding members. Shareholding and associate members may nominate their member companies to be elected to exchange membership.

Historical Background:

10th Century The "Galley Men"—so called because they landed their merchandise at Galley Quay in Thames Street — began trading in commodities in Mincing Lane, where nuns of the order of Minchins occupied several houses. The Guild of Pepperers was established.

1570 Queen Elizabeth I opened the Royal Exchange. It was built by Sir Thomas Gresham and modeled on the Antwerp Bourse.

1666 Royal Exchange destroyed in the Fire of London. During the next four years, while it was being rebuilt, the various trades found accommodation in coffee houses.

1748 Most coffee houses destroyed by fire.

1811 London Commercial Sale Rooms opened June 1, on the east side of Mincing Lane, but it was unpopular compared with the coffee houses, especially Garraways.

1840 Auction sales averaged 20 a day; by 1880, the average was 60.

1920 Selling by auction was gradually replaced by sale by "private treaty."

1941 Most of Mincing Lane destroyed in an air raid.

1954 The London Commodity Exchange was formed.

LONDON JUTE ASSOCIATION

Title: The London Jute Association

Address: 69 Cannon Street, London, EC4, England

A large part of the world jute trade is handled by members of the London Jute Association under the terms of the appropriate contracts. The Association was established in 1875. The trade is carried out in the spot and ready positions and also in future shipments by the members, who operate as principals to the contract designed to safeguard the interests of both buyer and seller, and which includes comprehensive terms for prompt settlement of disputes by arbitration in London. Trade on the London Jute Association contract is world wide and the Association itself is extremely active.

The principal producing countries are Pakistan, Thailand and India. The Indian crop is consumed almost entirely by local Indian mills which then export the jute fabric. Pakistan exports 60% to 65% of her crop, whereas Thailand exports nearer 80%. Thailand, however, does not produce true jute but kenaf, a jute substitute. The three countries produce some 16 million bales annually, but the amount varies.

LONDON METAL EXCHANGE

Title: The London Metal Exchange

Address: Whittington Avenue, London EC3V 1LB, England

Telephone: 01 - 626 1011

Cable Address: METMA, LONDON, EC3

Officers: Executive Secretary: Robert Gibson-Jarvie

LONDON VEGETABLE OIL TERMINAL MARKET ASSOCIATION

Title: The London Vegetable Oil Terminal Market Association

Address: Corn Exchange Building, 52 Mark Lane, London EC3R 7NE, England

Telephone: 01 - 488 3736

Hours of Business:
1. Soya Bean Oil: 10:10 A.M. - 12:40 P.M.; 2:30 P.M. - 5:10 P.M.
2. Palm Oil: 10:25 A.M. - 12:50 P.M.; 2:40 P.M. - 5:20 P.M.

Contract Details Quality:
1. Crude degummed Soya Bean Oil with the following specifications:
   a. F.F.A. (As Oleic-Molec Weight 282)   Max. 0.75%
   b. Moisture and Volatile Matter   Max. 0.20%
   c. Impurities (insoluble in petrol ether)   Max. 0.10%
   d. Lecithin (expressed as phosphorous)   Max. 0.02%
   e. Sediment (Gardner Break Test)   Max. 0.10%
   f. Color (1" Lovibond cell) yellow + 5 red   Max. 50
   g. Oil with a flash point below 121°C (250°F) is not tenderable.

Profile Data

185

2. Crude unbleached Palm Oil with the following specifications:
   a. On arrival:
      i. Max. % F.F.A. (Palmitic-Molecular Weight 256) acceptable for storage   4%
      ii. Max. % Moisture and impurities acceptable for storage   0.5%
   b. On re-delivery:
      i. Max. % F.F.A. (Palmitic-Molecular Weight 256) Guaranteed by the Tank Installation   6%
      ii. Max. % Moisture and Impurities guaranteed by the Tank Installation   0.75%
      iii. The price is basis 5% F.F.A. and basis purity, with premiums and discounts based on outturn.

	Soya Bean Oil	Palm Oil
Trading Unit	50 metric tons	50 metric tons
Price Quotations	U. S. currency per metric ton	Sterling per metric ton
Contract Basis	Ex Tank, Rotterdam, Antwerp, Hamburg, or London	In Tank Rotterdam, Antwerp, Hamburg (all Origins). In Tank London, Liverpool (East and West Malaysia only).
Minimum Fluctuation	$0.25 per metric ton	£ 0.25 per metric ton
Trading Positions	Jan., Mar., May, July, Sept., Nov., Jan. (7 positions)	Apr., June, Aug., Oct., Dec., Feb., Apr., (7 positions)
Tenderable Origins	Canada, E.E.C. Countries, Austria, Norway, Portugal, Sweden, Switzerland, Israel, Spain, U.S.A.	Sumatra, East Malaysia, West Malaysia, Ivory Coast.
Tender Ports	Rotterdam, Antwerp, Hamburg, London	Rotterdam, Antwerp, Hamburg (all origins), London, and Liverpool (East and West Malaysia only).

Memberships: London Floor Member Firms: 28, as of November, 1973.

Commission or Fees: Buying or selling Soya Bean Oil or Palm Oil, per 50 ton lot.

	Normal	Day Trade	Straddle
Associate Members:	£ 4.00	£ 2.00	£ 2.00
Non-members:	£ 8.00	£ 4.00	£ 4.00

International Commodities Clearing House fees: I.C.C.H. Registration Fees are payable by each contracting party in addition.

Deposits and margins: Deposits and Margins at the rates fixed from time to time are required.

Historical Background:
1967 The London Vegetable Oil Terminal Market Association was instituted with 33 floor members. Trading took place in Soya Bean Oil, Coconut Oil, and Sunflower Seed Oil, but after a few years trading was suspended owing to lack of support.
1973 A new Soya Bean Oil contract, traded in dollars, was introduced in September.
1974 A new contract for Palm Oil, traded in sterling, was initiated in January. This is the world's first terminal market contract for Palm Oil.

THE RUBBER TRADE ASSOCIATION OF LONDON

Title: The Rubber Trade Association of London

Address: Cereal House, 58 Mark Lane, London, EC3R 7HP, England

Telephone: 01 - 480 5388/9

Branches and Affiliates:
1. The London Rubber Exchange Co. Ltd. Cereal House, 58 Mark Lane, London EC3R 7 HP, England
   Secretary: Mrs. M. V. Greene
2. Rubber Settlement House
   Temple Chambers, 3 Temple Avenue, London EC3M 3LR, England

Officers:
Chairman: J. M. Hobbs
Vice Chairmen: B. W. C. Marshall
                J. F. Worthington
Chief Executive: A. E. Davies
Committees:
  1. Classes "P" and "A"

J. K. Barlow	T. M. Davis
M. J. W. Belt	J. M. Hobbs
P. A. Cunningham	

  2. Class "B"

H. D. Carritt	N. A. Symons
D. S. J. Figgis	J. F. Worthington
T. S. E. Figgis	

  3. Class "C"

D. R. S. Huntley	D. A. Symington
B. W. C. Marshall	R. R. Windsor
R. G. Lanyi	

Secretary: Mrs. M. V. Greene

Hours of Business: Trading is conducted on the floor of the Commodity Exchange by "private treaty" between 9:30 A.M. and 5:00 P.M. on weekdays. Business is normally transacted through brokers who guaranty the solvency of their principals, their brokerage being paid by the seller.

Regulatory Laws: The Association maintains a Panel of Arbitrators consisting of some 45 individuals drawn from among its membership who adjudicate on disputes, either on questions of quality or of a technical nature arising out of contracts made by members of the Association. Machinery exists for the hearing of appeals against arbitration awards should any party be dissatisfied with an award.

Contracts:

1. The standard Settlement House contract is for 5 tons of No. 1 International Ribbed Smoked Sheet (R.S.S.). The usual positional trading is in equal monthly quantities over three monthly periods, but business can be done in single months. Thus, it is possible for manufacturers and producers, as well as traders, to hedge their commitments as far as three years ahead.
2. The Rubber Settlement House operates differently from a full clearing house, in that between the date of contract and maturity the Settlement House collects, or pays out, differences as the price fluctuates; these cash settlements are usually fixed at fortnightly intervals. Interest is paid on sums collected and charged on sums paid out by the Settlement House.
3. The Association plans to change from its present Rubber Settlement House system to a Call Market/Clearing House system, within the International Commodities Clearing House Ltd., sometime in 1974.

Memberships:

1. Class and number of brokers (1974):

Class "P" Producer Members	- 30
Class "A" Selling Agents and Importers	- 12
Class "B" Brokers	- 10
Class "C" Dealers	- 42

2. Membership in these classes is restricted to individuals, firms, or companies domiciled in the United Kingdom.
3. A class of Associate Members was introduced January 1, 1967. In 1973, there were 38 such members. This class is open to any firm or company domiciled anywhere in the world concerned with the rubber trade, which trades in its own name and not solely as an agent, and which is not eligible for full membership in the Association. This class is not designed to include firms or companies engaged in the manufacturing industry.
4. Entrance Fee

	Entrance Fee		Annual Subscription	
Class "P"	£ 2	10	£ 4	20
Class "A"	10	50	31	50
Class "B" & "C"	10	50	105	00
Associate Members	5	25	10	50

   Note: The above amounts are subject to Value Added Tax (with the exception of Associate Members).

Commissions or Fees: For Private Operators - £ 6 per 5 tons. For overseas dealers - £ 4 50 per 5 tons. In both cases, the brokerage covers purchases and sale.

Historical Background:

1899	The first export of plantation rubber was made from Ceylon. Prior to this, the only plantation rubber was grown in Brazil.
1910	A boon year for rubber. Production was about 85,000 tons, of which

7,500 came from the Far East. It brought a then record price of 12 shillings - 10½ pence per lb.

1913   The Rubber Trade Association was formed.

1918   A heavy demand after World War I pushed rubber to 4 shillings - 6 pence per lb.

1922   The Rubber Settlement House was established. Although the idea of futures or terminal commodity trading was not new, it was a comparative innovation in the world's rubber markets.

1932   The price of rubber dropped to a record low of 2 pence per lb.

THE STOCK EXCHANGE

Title: The Stock Exchange

Address: London, EC2N 1HP, England

Telephone: 01 - 588 - 2355

Teletype: SHARANLOAN LONDON

Telex: 886557

Cable Address: STOCKEX London EC2

Branches and Affiliates: Administrative Departments:

1. Belfast:
   General Manager: Frederick Stewart Mullan
   The Stock Exchange; Northern Bank House 10 High Street, Belfast, BT1 2BP
   Telephone: Belfast 21094
   Telex: 747050

2. Irish:
   General Manager: William Albert Edward Campbell
   The Stock Exchange, 28 Anglesea Street, Dublin, 2
   Telephone: 0001 - 778808
   Telex: 4537
   and at 12 Marlboro' Street, Cork
   Telephone: Cork 20875

3. Midlands & Western:
   General Manager: Peter Ricardo Davis
   The Stock Exchange, Margaret Street, Birmingham, B3 3JL
   Telephone: 021 - 236 9181
   Telex: 338397

4. Northern:
   General Manager: Colin Greenhough Smith
   The Stock Exchange, 4 Norfolk Street, Manchester M2 1BS
   Telephone: 061 - 833 0931
   Telex: 667708
   Assistant General Manager: Frederick Ronald Parry
   The Stock Exchange, Silkhouse Court, Tithebarn Street, Liverpool, L2 2LT
   Telephone: 051 - 236 0869

5. Provincial:
    General Manager: Walter Brydon Douglas
    The Stock Exchange, Melrose House 3 St. Sampson's Square, York, YO1 2RL
    Telephone: York 4982
6. Scottish:
    General Manager: William Alexander Stupart
    The Stock Exchange, Stock Exchange House PO Box 141, 69 St. George's
        Place, Glasgow, G2 1BU
    Telephone: 041 - 221 7060
    Telex: 77726
    And at 12 Dublin Street
    Edinburgh, EH1 3PP
    Telephone: 031 - 556 9761

Officers:
    Chairman: George Arthur Loveday
    Deputy Chairmen:
        David Henry LeRoy-Lewis
        James Dundas Hamilton
        Gordon Russell Simpson
    Secretary-General: George Walter Richard Brind
    Secretary to the Council: Giles Colston Wintle
    Head of Finance Department: Edward Brian Bakhurst
    Head of Membership Department: Norman Steward McMurtrie Kemp
    Head of Quotations Department: Jeffrey Russell Knight
    Head of Public Relations Department: John Denzil Hollis
    Information Systems & Settlement: Michael Bennett (Managing Director)

Hours of Business:
1. 9:30 A.M. - 3:30 P.M. (weekdays)
2. Dealings by telephone are permitted after market hours.

Regulatory Laws:
1. There is no legislation regulating the constitution or conduct of The Stock
   Exchange. Members are exempted from the need to obtain licenses as
   dealers in securities by virtue of their membership.
2. The Stock Exchange is governed by a council of 46, elected by the individual members from their own number. The Government Broker, who represents the Bank of England, is ex-officio a member of the council but has no
   vote. The council and its committees are assisted by an administrative staff
   numbering nearly 800 under the Secretary General.
3. The Stock Exchange is in no way controlled by government in its internal
   operations, nor are its powers of regulating the requirements for listing in
   any way controlled by any outside body. In fact, Stock Exchange requirements in this respect are more stringent than the Company Law. The council
   also exercises disciplinary powers over the members entirely on its own
   authority. There is, however, continuous liaison with the authorities on such
   matters as taxation and Company Law, where The Stock Exchange's advice
   is frequently sought. In addition, members of The Stock Exchange are
   automatically exempt from the need to be licensed under the Prevention of
   Fraud (Investments) Act.

Issues Traded and Volume:

1. Listed Securities*:

	No. of Securities	Nom. Val. (£ 000)	Mkt. Val. (£ 000)
Gilt-edged & Foreign Stocks:	1,488	33,688,139	23,221,893
Corporate Securities:	8,066	29,844,652	162,405,456

2. Unlisted Securities:
   There is virtually no over-the-counter market; the service provided by The Stock Exchange is adequate for nearly all circumstances. Exchange members may deal with each other in any security listed on any stock exchange in the world, even if it is not officially listed on The Stock Exchange.

3. Overseas Companies:
   Nearly 400 are also "officially listed," of which the largest group are South African mining and industrial companies. The market value of the equity capital of such companies currently exceeds that of domestic companies by some 40%.

4. Government Securities:
   These account for 30% of the nominal value of listed securities and over 50% of the total value of turnover. This arises because it is the practice in the United Kingdom for the Government debt to be managed, and new loans to be issued by the Bank of England operating through the Government Broker on the floor of The Stock Exchange. This leads to the existence of the uniquely flexible market in the full range of Government securities over the whole range of maturities.

5. Volume:
   a. Value — all securities traded (£ 000)

1965	20,486,418	1970	38,767,437
1966	21,590,532	1971	64,192,910
1967	35,956,264	1972	56,383,077
1968	31,976,269	1973*	55,769,000
1969	30,390,948		

   *April — December totals included here represent The (amalgamated) Stock Exchange.

   b. No. of Bargains**

1965	4,360,582	1970	5,311,974
1966	4,143,547	1971	6,623,349
1967	5,006,107	1972	7,986,599
1968	6,523,198	1973*	6,031,503
1969	5,787,359		

   *April — December totals included here represent The (amalgamated) Stock Exchange.

   **Transactions between or on behalf of members of the exchange.

Unit of Trading:

1. Shares: Prices are expressed in terms of pence per share.
2. Bonds and Loans: Prices are expressed as so many pounds per £ nominal value.
3. Odd-lots: The system of dealing through jobbers allows odd-lots to be treated the same as round-lots at no additional charge.

4. Under the British system of registered share holdings, it is possible to transfer any number of shares, and certificates can be issued for any quantity. The jobber, in turn, is prepared to trade in any quantity and it is not necessary to find a counter-party, who can match the sale in quantity as well as price, before arranging a bargain.

   This has two important consequences:

   a. It is possible in London to deal, to invest, to raise a precise sum of money, rather than to buy or sell a given number of shares. This is particularly important to trustees or administrators of estates.

   b. Companies can be more flexible in issuing more shares, whether as rights or as consideration for the take-over of other companies, and can tailor the terms of issue (say, 5 shares for every 11 held) precisely to their requirements.

Membership:

1. No. of members:

1878	2,000	1930	3,939
1904	5,482	1939	4,083
1914	4,855	1947	3,950
1920	4,000	1973	4,600*

   *representing about 400 firms, of whom 27 are jobbers.

2. Membership costs: an entry fee of £1,050 plus a nomination redemption fee of £1,000. This latter is in substitution for the old system of buying the nomination (seat) of a retiring member. The fund is used to pay off members who bought seats prior to the termination of that system. Annual subscription: £300.00

3. Until recently, all firms were partnerships, which meant that the partners in the firm (all of whom must be individually members) had unlimited personal liability for the firm's debts. Firms are now also permitted to organize themselves as companies with limited liability. In these cases they are permitted to introduce outside capital, but it is still required that the directors are full personal members and retain personal unlimited liability. This is considered to be a protection, both to their clients and to other member firms with whom they deal. No corporate members are permitted to trade who are controlled by directors, who are not personal members.

Commissions or Fees:

1. British Government Securities

   a. Bargains up to £50,000 consideration:

	Under 5 years to redemption	5-10 years	over 10 years
first £2,000	at discretion	0.5 %	0.5%
on the next £2,000	at discretion	0.1 %	0.2%
on the next £10,000	at discretion	0.05%	0.2%
on the next £36,000	at discretion	0.05%	0.1%

   b. Bargains over £50,000 consideration

on the first £250,000	at discretion	0.07 %	0.14 %
on the excess	at discretion	0.0625%	0.125%

2. Debentures, Bonds, etc.
   a. Registered*:

0.75%	on the first	£	5,000	consideration
0.375%	on the next	£	15,000	consideration
nil	on the next	£	5,000	consideration
0.375%	on the next	£	25,000	consideration
0.325%	on the next	£	50,000	consideration
0.3%	on the next	£	150,000	consideration
0.25%	on the next	£	500,000	consideration
0.2%	on the next	£	1,000,000	consideration
0.125%	on the excess.			

*Including new issues passing by delivery in scrip form or by letters of renunciation.

   b. bearer:

0.5%	on the first	£	5,000	consideration
0.25%	on the next	£	15,000	consideration
nil	on the next	£	5,000	consideration
0.25%	on the excess.			

3. Stocks and Shares: Registered or bearer, whether partly or fully paid.

1.25%	on the first	£	5,000	consideration
0.625%	on the next	£	15,000	consideration
nil	on the next	£	5,000	consideration
0.625%	on the next	£	25,000	consideration
0.5%	on the next	£	50,000	consideration
0.4%	on the next	£	150,000	consideration
0.3%	on the next	£	500,000	consideration
0.2%	on the next	£	1,000,000	consideration
0.125%	on the excess			

4. American and Canadian Shares: Shares of companies incorporated in the United States or Canada (whether dealt in in London on a dollar or sterling basis), with the exception of shares which are deliverable by transfer.

0.75%	on the first	£	5,000	consideration
0.375%	on the next	£	15,000	consideration
nil	on the next	£	5,000	consideration
0.375%	on the excess.			

Historical Background:

1600	Stock dealers met in the Royal Exchange.
1669	Second Royal Exchange opened.
1694	Bank of England established.
1697	The earliest List of the Stock Exchange was published (March 26). Parliament acted to curb speculation and provided a system for licensing brokers.
1700-1800	The coffee house era for stock dealers.
1720	South Sea Company collapsed.
1734	Sir John Barnard's Act was first serious attempt to regulate securities speculation by law.
1761	First book published about a stock exchange: *Every Man His Own Broker, or A Guide to Exchange Alley,* by J. Mortimer.

1773	London Stock Exchange founded at "New Jonathon's," a coffee house on 'Change Alley, Cornhill. 'The Stock Exchange' was wrote over the door." Daily admission: sixpence.
1793	Dublin Stock Exchange founded.
1801	The Stock Exchange moved to its present site. Foundation stone was laid May 18.
1802	The Exchange opened March 27, with 500 subscribers. The Deed of Settlement, which defined the authority that bestowed powers in the matter of stock exchange government was drawn up. Nine trustees and managers were appointed.
1812	First formal set of rules adopted.
1836	Manchester Stock Exchange founded.
1844	Glasgow Stock Exchange and Edinburgh Stock Exchange were founded.
1845	Birmingham Stock Exchange founded.
1860	Sir John Barnard's Act repealed after 146 years.
1875	The Deed of Settlement of 1802 was redrafted, December 31.
1877	A Royal Commission, appointed by the government, began investigating the constitution, customs and practices of the Stock Exchange on March 20.
1890	The Council of Associated Stock Exchanges was founded in May. In 1958, it embraced 22 exchanges, each with its own official list and its own rules and regulations.
1939	Prevention of Fraud (Investments) Act was passed. "Trans Lux" indicators first installed on January 16.
1945	Deed of Settlement was amended March 25, to establish one supreme legislative body, the Council of the Stock Exchange.
1953	Visitor's Gallery opened on November 16.
1971	The nationality qualification for exchange membership was removed. Candidates may now be of any nationality provided they meet other requirements.
1973	Stock exchanges in Great Britain and Ireland amalgamated with London to form The Stock Exchange in March.
1974	The Financial Times' Industrial Index declined a record 24 points to 313.8 at the close of trading, March 1.

THE TEA BROKERS' ASSOCIATION OF LONDON

Title: The Tea Brokers' Association of London

Address: Sir John Lyon House, (River Block), 5 High Timber Street, Upper Thames Street, London, EC4V 3LA, England

Telephone: 01 - 236 - 3368/9

Cable Address: TEABROKAS, London

Officers:

Secretary: Mrs. D. Mayne
The International Tea Committee:
    Chairman: A. D. McLeod
    Secretary: Mrs. E. E. E. Mooijen
    Statistician: Peter Abel

London is a world center as far as tea is concerned, with growths from all over the world freely bought and sold. Indeed, it has frequently been said that London is the barometer by which world prices are calculated.

A Tea Futures Association is expected to be formed sometime in the latter part of 1974, or early in 1975, which would operate similarly to the associations concerned with coffee, cocoa, and spices.

For further information about this, or matters connected with tea in general, the Tea Brokers' Association has suggested that contact be made directly with them at the above address.

Apparent Consumption of Tea
(Ten Largest Consumers)

	1970-1972 (per head*)	1964-1966 (per head*)
Ireland (Republic)	4.02	3.71
United Kingdom**	3.81	4.14
New Zealand	2.66	2.89
Australia	2.08	2.53
Hong Kong	1.59	1.30
Ceylon	1.51	1.38
Sudan	1.07	.81
Japan	1.02	.84
Canada	.94	1.00
Morocco	.86	.78

   * Per head of total population (in kg.)
  ** Includes Channel Islands

Source: Annual Bulletin (1973) International Tea Committee. Consumption of tea per head in the U.S.A. equaled .34 in 1970-1972 and .31 in 1964-1966.

THE UNITED TERMINAL SUGAR MARKET ASSOCIATION

Title: The United Terminal Sugar Market Association

Address: Corn Exchange Building 52/57 Mark Lane, London EC3, England

Hours of Business: Calls take place at 10:40 A.M.; 12:30 P.M.; 3:30 P.M.; 4:45 P.M.; — on weekdays.

Contracts: Each contract is for 50 tons, or any multiple thereof. Prices are quoted for various delivery months, up to about 15 months ahead.

Memberships:
1. Full Members (brokers) are limited in number to 35. Only they, or their market representatives, are permitted to deal, free of commission, on the trading floor.

2. British and Overseas firms — 251 in number — deal through full members at a reduced commission rate.
3. Associate Members are located all over the world.

Historical Background:

1921 The United Terminal Sugar Market Association, reformed in this year, is the membership organization which administers the London Sugar Futures Market. Members are engaged in marketing sugar internationally and domestically, either as principals or brokers. The market functions under a carefully planned system of rules and regulations, which ensure equitable treatment for all who trade in sugar futures.

1957 The market reopened after being closed during World War II. Since then, the basis has been Raw Cane Sugar basis 96% polarization c.i.f. London or Liverpool or Greenock limited in origin to members of the Commonwealth Sugar Agreement. Prior to 1914, the basis was 88% Raw Beet of European origin f.o.b. Hamburg.

URUGUAY

MONTEVIDEO

The following information was received from the Embassy of the United States of America in Montevideo, in response to our request for data relative to stock and commodity exchanges operating in Uruguay. Efforts to open contact with these organizations had been unproductive, as of the time when this directory went to press.

AGRICULTURAL COMMODITY EXCHANGE

Title: Agricultural Commodity Exchange (Camara Mercantil de Productos del Pais)

Address: Avenida Gral. Rondeau 1908, Montevideo, Uruguay

Telephone: 8 - 81 - 91; 8-76-61

Cable Address: CAMERTIL

Officers:
President: Antonio Otegui
Secretary: Carlos Romagnoli

The Exchange: Federation of producers and dealers handling agricultural commodities: Asociacion de Exportadores de Lanas del Uruguay; Asociacion de Vendedores & Consignatorios de Lanas; Gremial de Exportadores de Cuero; Centro de Exportadores de Cereales Oleaginosos; Gremial de Elaboradores de Raciones Balanceadas; etc. Maintains a national registry of wool, grain, and oil seed transactions. Publication: "Informacion Semanal," weekly.

Memberships:
1. Regular Members: 300
2. Member Organizations: 10

Historical Background:
1891 The exchange was founded

MONTEVIDEO STOCK EXCHANGE

Title: Bolsa de Valores de Montevideo

Address: Calle Misiones 1400, Montevideo, Uruguay

Telephone: 91 - 77 - 55

Cable Address: BOLSAMONT

Officers:
President: Pedro Perez Marexiano
Manager: Edison M. Fradiletti

The Exchange: Member of Camara Nacional de Comercio (National Chamber of Commerce). Private securities exchange for the purchase and sale of stocks and bonds of some 65 domestic and foreign companies, through member brokers located throughout Uruguay. Publication: "Bolsa de Valores," daily, quarterly, and annual.

Memberships: Regular Members: 75

Historical Background:
1867 The exchange was founded.

VENEZUELA

Venezuela has two stock exchanges: La Bolsa de Comercio de Caracas; La Bolsa de Comercio del Estado de Miranda (incorporated March, 1958). The exchanges are located only about four miles apart: membership requirements, commission rates and trading methods are generally identical. The majority of activity occurs in dually-listed securities. However, the exchanges transact only about half of Venezuela's total share business. Banks account for the other half, using prices established by the exchanges as the basis for their transactions with other banks.

CARACAS STOCK EXCHANGE

Title: Bolsa de Comercio de Caracas, C.A.

Address: Esquina de San Francisco, Edificio Banco Mercantil y Agricola (5 Piso), Caracas, Venezuela

Telephone: 41 - 81 - 51; 41 - 83 - 41

Officers:
Board of Directors:
President: Jose Manuel Sanchez
Vice-President: Jacinto Gutierrez
Secretary: Andres Franceschi Calvani
Members:
Alfredo Pardo
Felix Martinez Espino O.
Casimiro Vegas

Hours of Business: 10:30 A.M. - 12:00 noon

Regulatory Laws:
1. Rules and Regulations of the Caracas Chamber of Commerce, which supervises the stock exchange under Venezuelan law.
2. The exchange is managed by a Board of Directors, consisting of six members appointed by the Chamber of Commerce.

Issues Traded and Volume:
1. Listed Issues: a. fixed income securities: 122
                   b. stocks: 191
2. Volume:

	1972*	1973*
Value of all transactions	Bs. 318,811,660	Bs. 504,106,724
Number of Trades	3,859	4,134
Share Volume	1,350,453	1,688,812
Share Value	Bs. 47,510,852	Bs. 52,757,698
Bond Volume (nominal)	Bs. 274,701,800	Bs. 455,348,700
Bond Volume (Actual)	Bs. 271,300,808	Bs. 451,349,027

*Through November

Unit of Trading: There is no special trading unit: any amount of shares may be bought or sold. Most transactions are "for cash."

Membership:
1. Regular Members: 26
2. Only an individual, as opposed to a corporation, may acquire a "seat" on the exchange.

Historical Background:
1947 The Bolsa de Comercio de Caracas was formally established with 22 members. Trading commenced April 21 with 54 security lisings.

MIRANDA STOCK EXCHANGE

Title: Bolsa de Comercio del Estado de Miranda
Address: Chacao, Estado de Miranda, Venezuela

WEST GERMANY

THE STOCK EXCHANGES OF WEST GERMANY

The Federal Republic of Germany has eight stock exchanges, where about 410 companies representing a nominal capital approximately DM 31 billion are traded: Berlin, Bremen, Dusseldorf, Frankfurt, Hamburg, Hannover, Munich (Bavarian Stock Exchange), Stuttgart. More than 75% of the volume on all exchanges is traded by Dusseldorf and Frankfurt.

Regulatory Laws: The constitution and organization of these exchanges are based on special legislation — the "Borsengesetz," or Stock Exchange Law of June 22, 1896 — which stipulates that no exchange may open without the approval of the Government of the German Land in whose territory it is to operate. The Land Government must also approve all of its rules and regulations. The exchanges are supervised closely by "State Commissioners" of the Land Government involved and by their own governing bodies. Germany has no institutions comparable to the U. S. Securities and Exchange Commission.
In the U. S. and Great Britain, commercial banking and investment banking are separate industries. In Germany, they operated under one roof as diversified, but integrated, banks. New issues are managed by the banks. They purchase the entire issue and then offer the securities for subscription, or for direct sale, to the public without the mediation of a stock exchange. An application for quotation on an exchange is filed only after the placement has been made.

Listing Requirements: Securities must fulfill certain requirements to be granted listing privileges. These are set forth in the Borsengesetz and in the Notification Regarding the Admission of Securities for Official Quotation. They are basically identical to those of other countries and are virtually the same for foreign issues.
Normal deviations caused by different conditions in the country of issue, or from common usage in foreign exchange, are usually accepted. The sponsoring bank generally works out a solution that best reconciles the foreign use of registered shares with the German system. Most stocks listed on German exchanges are in bearer form.

Listing Expenses:
  1. Admission fee;
  2. Printing and publishing costs connected with the prospectus and the appli-

cation for admission;

3. The bank's commission for managing the listing.

Stock Exchange Fees:

1. Bonded Loans: DM 150 for each DM 1 million, or any part thereof;
2. Stocks:
   a. DM 300 for each DM 1 million or part thereof up to DM 20 million;
   b. DM 200 for each DM 1 million or part thereof for amounts between DM 20 million and DM 50 million;
   c. DM 100 for each DM 1 million, or part thereof for amounts exceeding DM 50 million.
3. Admission fees for foreign companies are arranged individually in each case.

Corporate balance sheets, profit and loss statements, announcements of dividends, meetings, etc., must be published in the "Bundesanzeiger" (Federal Gazette) and in at least one journal or newspaper approved by the stock exchange.

Settlements: Settlements connected with purchase prices and deliveries are channeled through the Security Depository; neither cash, nor the securities physically change hands. All banks maintain cash and security accounts with the Security Depository, which handles transfers.

Once a transaction has been effected, the cash account of the purchasing bank is debited with the purchase price. This then is credited to the cash account of the selling bank. An appropriate quantity of securities is then transferred from the portfolio of the selling bank to that of the purchasing bank. Both banks thereupon make the necessary entries and adjustments in the accounts and portfolios of their clients.

Who May Deal? The German Kreditwesengesetz (a specialized legislation with respect to the banks) determines, that every firm which buys or sells securities by order of a third party, or which deposits and assumes safe custody for a third party is a bank.

That is the reason why in Germany only banks may handle private clients orders.

Three groups are authorized to deal on an exchange:

1. The Banks, which deal as commission agents for private clients, or in their own name for their own account;
2. The Official Broker: ("Kursmakler"), or specialist, who has been appointed by the Land Government to fix prices for a certain number of stocks or bonds. He may not deal in his own name for his own account. Any client has the legal right to have his order executed, at a price which must at least be equal to the price which the Kursmakler has authorized for the day on which the order is entered. The quotations settled by the Kursmakler are announced on the floor by remotely-controlled quotation boards. Every quotation at which a deal was concluded is published in the Official List, edited by the Stock Exchange itself or by the Board of Brokers (Maklerkammer) of the various exchanges. They are available to the public each trading day.
3. The Unofficial Broker, or Floor Broker ("freier Makler"), who is appointed by the Stock Exchange Board. He may give business only to those who are

permitted to deal on the trading floor. He cannot fix prices and, therefore, can deal as an intermediary in his own name for his own account.

Trading Procedures: Trading on a stock exchange is not compulsory. The German banks, however, have undertaken to bring all private clients orders to the market for execution, unless they are instructed otherwise by their clients. Institutional business is normally carried on without the mediation of the stock exchange.

A private individual who wishes to buy or sell securities contacts his bank. The bank agent transmits the order to the exchange trading floor, where it is generally relayed to the official broker (Kursmakler), the only one who can fix a price and solely in those securities which have been entrusted to him by the Governing Body of the Brokers' Association. The Kursmakler keeps records of all orders to buy or sell and their price limits. Based on this information, he fixes a price at which most orders can be executed and he announces it. This price then becomes the official price or quotation for that day.

Unit of Trading: German stock exchanges have two pricing procedures: the continuous or consecutive and the once-a-day quotation (the standard price, as it is called). The regularly active shares of companies whose capital amounts to at least 10 million Deutschmark belong to the former category. Transactions in them may be effected at any time during regular trading hours, as long as the number of shares involved exceed a minimum quantity; for example, 50 shares, or a multiple thereof. Orders for less than that amount (odd-lots) and residual lots not divisible by 50 are traded at the standard price.

This once-a-day price is established about half-way through the regular trading session and all executions are made at that price. Shares are quoted "per unit"; fixed interest securities are traded and listed as a percentage of their nominal value. There is no extra fee or commission for buying or selling odd-lots.

Membership Prices: Stock exchange members do not pay for their "seat" (membership). They may be assessed for contributions toward the exchange's operating costs, but there are no standard fixed fees for this purpose.

BERLIN

BERLIN STOCK EXCHANGE

Title: Berliner Wertpapierborse

Address: Berlin 12 (Charlottenburg), Hardenbergstrabe 16-18, Federal Republic of Germany

Telephone: 31 - 07 - 21

Telex: 183 663

Officers:
President: Gernot Ernst
Vice-President: Gerhard Herbst
Vice-President: Ebehard Winkler

Hours of Business (trading):
1. Stock Exchange: 11:30 A.M. - 1:30 P.M.
2. Currency Exchange: 1:00 P.M. - 1:45 P.M.

Regulatory Laws:
1. The "Borsengesetz", a special law enacted June 22, 1896, on which the constitution and organization of all German stock exchanges are based.
2. Rules and regulations of the Berlin Stock Exchange.
3. See "The Stock Exchanges of West Germany."

Unit of Trading: The same for all German stock exchanges. See "The Stock Exchanges of West Germany."

Memberships (1972):
1. Bank representatives: 33
   Official Brokers ("Kursmakler"): 8
   Unofficial, or Floor, Brokers ("Freie Makler"): 11
2. Membership Costs: See "The Stock Exchanges of West Germany."

Commissions or Fees:
1. The commission received by the "Kursmakler" varies according to the volume of business transacted: ⅜ - ¾% of the nominal value for fixed-interest securities and usually 1% of the price for stocks.
2. Stock Exchange turnover tax, brokerage, bank commission amount to 1 - ¼% of the final amount on shares and to about ½ - ¾% on fixed-interest securities.

Historical Background:
1970 Option trading began on all German exchanges, July 1.
1974 Transactions on the stock exchange began to be processed by a computer, which supplies volume figures and other data covering the entire field of security trading. The same computer began to handle transactions of the Munich Stock Exchange in April 1973. The complex is based at and primarily serves the Dusseldorf Stock Exchange where it originated. It will eventually collaborate with all German stock exchanges.

BREMEN

BREMEN STOCK EXCHANGE

Title: Bremer Wertpapierborse

Address: 28 Bremen, Langenstr. 12, Postfach 1633, Federal Republic of Germany

Telephone: (0421) 32 30 37

Officers:
President: Werner Fischer
Vice-President: Georg Walter Martens

Hours of Business (trading): 11:30 A.M. - 1:30 P.M.

Regulatory Laws:
1. The "Borsengesetz," a special law enacted June 22, 1896.
2. Regulations of the Bremen Stock Exchange of July 11, 1947.
3. See "The Stock Exchanges of West Germany."

Issues Traded and Volume:
1. Listed:
   a. shares of 40 domestic companies with par value totaling DM 17,254 million;
   b. 446 fixed-interest securities, with issue price of DM 57,080.2 million.
2. Unlisted:
   a. shares of 13 companies with par value totaling DM 248.4 million;
   b. 16 fixed-interest securities with issue price of DM 383.3 million.
3. Volume: The Bremen Exchange does not release these figures.

Unit of Trading: The same for all German stock exchanges. See "The Stock Exchanges of West Germany."

Membership:
1. Regular Members: 17
2. Membership costs: See "The Stock Exchanges of West Germany."

Commissions and Fees:
1. The commission received by the "Kursmakler" (official broker) varies according to the volume transacted: ⅜ - ¾% of the nominal value for fixed-interest securities and usually 1% of the price for stocks.
2. Stock Exchange turnover tax, brokerage, bank commission amount to 1 - 1¼% of the final amount on shares and to about ½ - ¾% on fixed-interest securities.

Historical Background:
1864 The Borse was established, November 5.
1935 German stock exchanges reorganized; reduced to 9 from 25.
1948 The Association of Members of the Bremen Stock Exchange was founded, November 26.

DÜSSELDORF

DÜSSELDORF STOCK EXCHANGE

Title: Rheinisch-Westfalische Boise zu Düsseldorf
Address: 4 Düsseldorf, Berliner Allee 10, Federal Republic of Germany
Telephone: 10 21
Telex: 8 582 600
Cable Address: Borse Düsseldorf
Officers: Stock Exchange Council:
   President: Johannes C. D. Zahn

Vice-Presidents:

F. Wilhelm Christians   Alfred Freiherr von Oppenheim
Rolf Diel   Johannes Völling
Heinz Niederste-Ostholt

Hours of Business (trading):
Stock Exchange: 11:30 A.M. - 1:30 P.M.
Foreign Exchange: 1:00 P.M. - 2:00 P.M.

Regulatory Laws: The "Borsengesetz," as amended, a special law enacted June 22, 1896. See "The Stock Exchanges of West Germany."

Issues Traded and Volume:
1. Listed Issues:

   a. shares:

	No. of Companies			German	
	German*	Foreign		German	
1970	208	32	DM	24.3 bill.	DM 22.6 bill.
1971	204	34	DM	25.9 bill.	DM 23.2 bill.
1972	195	40	DM	26.6 bill.	DM 28.9 bill.
1973	185	50	DM	27.7 bill.	DM 35.5 bill.

   b. bonds:

	Issues		Issue Amount		
	German	Foreign	German		Foreign
1970	1,590	108	DM 89.7 bill.		DM 11.5 bill.
1971	1,682	138	DM 98.1 bill.		DM 14.2 bill.
1972	1,832	162	DM 111.0 bill.		DM 16.9 bill.
1973	1,976	176	DM 124.5 bill.		DM 19.6 bill.

   *Diminishing number of companies due to mergers, especially in steel, mining, and brewing industries.

2. Volume:

a. shares:		b. bonds:	
1971	DM 5,267,000	DM 2,574,000	
1972	DM 7,876,500	DM 5,178,900	
1973	DM 7,042,800	DM 6,161,600	

Unit of Trading: See "The Stock Exchanges of West Germany."

Options:

	Calls		Puts	
	No.	No.	No.	No.
	Transactions	Shares	Transactions	Shares
1971	2,501	213,400	547	59,850
1972	3,459	343,250	1,233	136,100
1973	3,787	325,750	1,877	203,200

Semi-Official Security Trading:
This represents regulated, but unofficial, dealings which are under the jurisdiction of the "Committee for Dealings in Securities Not Officially Quoted," rather than the Stock Exchange Council which supervises transactions in officially listed securities. At the close of 1973, the shares of 20 companies with a capital par value of DM 163.7 m. were traded. Apart from 1.74 m. non-voting dividend right certificates issued by Audi-NSU Auto-Union, pricing included 12 Foreign

Bonds. 11 Federal Treasury Bonds, 33 Short Term Bonds, 30 other fixed interest items.

Memberships (1973):
1. Banks: 120
   Official Brokers: 17
   Alternate Brokers: 12
   Private Brokers: 18
   Assisting Members: 15
2. Membership Costs: See "The Stock Exchanges of West Germany."

Commissions or Fees:
1. The commission received by the "Kursmakler" (official broker) varies according to the volume transacted: ⅜ - ¾% of the nominal value for fixed interest securities and usually 1% of the price for stocks.
2. Stock Exchange turnover tax, brokerage, bank commission amount to 1 - 1¼% of the final amount on shares and to about ½ - ¾% on fixed interest securities.

Historical Background:
1553 The Cologne Stock Exchange was created.
1865 The Essen Stock Exchange was created.
1875 The Düsseldorf Stock Exchange was created.
     The Düsseldorf Exchange and the Essen Exchange were known as the Mining Exchanges; the domain of the Cologne Stock Exchange was the trading in insurance stocks.
1880 "Negotiable securities" were dealt in on Düsseldorf Stock Exchange, also various commodities. In this year the exchange laid down its first "General Rules," as well as rules for brokers. Commodities then were the most important part of exchange dealings.
1884 The exchange received state recognition and thereby official status, June 18. Securities took over in importance from commodities. The mining sector of the trading list was most prominent, but for many years (until 1924) the exchange had no suitable headquarters.
1905 The exchanges of Düsseldorf and Essen began sharing trading days. Essen took Mondays and Thursdays; Düsseldorf took Tuesdays and Fridays. Each took alternate Wednesdays.
1921 Dealings were so active that quotations were divided into "official" and "unofficial" groups.
1924 The exchange provided quotations on 182 securities.
1935 January 1 — German stock exchanges were reorganized and reduced in number from 21 to 9. The Cologne and Essen Exchanges merged with the Düsseldorf Stock Exchange and Düsseldorf became the home of the united stock exchange. At year's end, the new exchange had 380 securities listed — excluding Reich and provincial loans.
1943 Quotations were discontinued and the number of meetings reduced to three a week, February 13. February 17 — it was decreed that closing prices for January 25, would be the ceiling for all transactions. June 12 — Stock Exchange headquarters in Wilhelm Marx House were destroyed by air raid. The Exchange resumed work in the Deutsche Bank in July.

1944 The exchange moved to the Commerzbank, May 2.
1945 Last Düsseldorf Stock Exchange meeting was held the day before Allied troops occupied Düsseldorf, April 16.
1946 First postwar stock exchange meeting held in canteen of the Commerzbank, April 15.
1948 New rules initiated, July 17; in October, the Borsenverein appointed a new council.
1950 Foreign exchange dealings resumed, May 15.
1951 The Düsseldorf Stock Exchange returned to the restored Wilhelm Marx House, April 17.
1957 Düsseldorf Stock Exchange moved into a modern building equipped with up-to-date facilities for transmitting market news and reports.
1962 Electric quotation board installed — the first built in the Federal Republic of Germany.
1970 Option trading began, July 1. Electronic data processor put in operation. (The 12,000 transactions a day are processed by this computer.)
1973 The transactions of the Munich Stock Exchange also handled by the computer.
1974 The Stock Exchange in Berlin and Stuttgart tied into the electronic data processor.

FRANKFURT

FRANKFURT STOCK EXCHANGE

Title: Frankfurter Wertpapierborse

Address: 6000 Frankfurt am Main, Postfach 2913, Federal Republic of Germany.

Telephone: (0611) 21971

Teletype: 411412 borse d

Telex: 04 11412

Officers: Stock Exchange Directors: Herbert Schlicht, Wolfgang Stoeck

Hours of Business: 11:30 A.M. - 1:30 P.M.

Regulatory Laws:
1. The Stock Exchange Act of 1896, as amended.
2. Rules and Regulations of the Frankfurt Stock Exchange, approved March 19, 1963, by decree of the Government of Hesse.
3. See "The Stock Exchanges of West Germany."

Issues Traded and Volume:
1. Securities officially quoted (12/31)

	a. stocks:		b. bonds:	
	German	Foreign	German	Foreign
1968	272	42	2,223	92
1969	263	49	2,363	148

1970	257	58	2,596	174
1971	257	64	2,792	209
1972	254	73	3,070	255
1973	253	103	3,275	286

   c. Generally, before securities may be admitted for official quotation, they must be licensed. Only certain public loans and bonds which the Stock Exchange Supervisory Board has released from the admission procedure are exempted.

2. Volume (all securities):

1970	DM 8,500,000	1972	DM 18,070,300
1971	DM 11,480,000	1973	DM 16,668,900*

*represents 44% of total turnover on all West German stock exchanges.

Unit of Trading (quotations):

1. Single Quotation. A price which is fixed once only — in each trading day from 12 noon onward — for every stock officially listed on the exchange. It is calculated by the "Kursmakler" (an official broker; a form of specialist), and is determined by balancing the buying and selling orders available until 12 o'clock. This establishes the price at which most orders may be executed.
2. Consecutive Quotation. Certain stocks with a large turnover may be traded not only at the single quotation, but also at a consecutive quotation; that is, during the full two-hour regular trading session. The Board of Governors will decide this upon application of the issuer;
3. The turnover in each case of the consecutive quotation must amount to a minimum, usually 50 shares for German securities, or a multiple thereof;
4. All dealings are on a cash basis. They are settled on the second full business day following the date of trade;
5. See "The Stock Exchanges of West Germany."

Option Trading: In general, options (puts and calls) are executed at a base price which corresponds more or less with the "single quotation" of the day in question. Option terms amount to 2 or 3 months, plus 5 calendar days each, or 6 months plus 10 calendar days from the date of trade.

Semi-Official Security Trading:

As distinguished from the official trade, which covers only officially listed securities, the semi-official trade is exclusively in the hands of the banks and the "freie Makler" (unofficial, or floor brokers).

As a rule, all securities including those officially listed may be traded in the semi-official market which is not confined to a certain place or time. In semi-official trade, however, distinction must be made between securities traded over-the-counter ("geregelter Freiverkehr") and those traded by telephone ("Telefonverkehr"). Over-the-counter business, which is transacted for practical reasons mainly during the regular trading session, concerns only those securities which have been introduced beforehand into the over-the-counter market, after the "Committee for Trade in Securities Not Officially Listed" at the Frankfurt Stock Exchange has examined a memorandum which must be submitted with an application. In trading by telephone, all securities may be handled including those which are neither officially quoted, nor included in the over-the-counter market.

It must be noted that in semi-official trade no quotations but only prices are fixed. In each case the price is settled by one transaction only, as in the variable quotation in official trade. All published prices in semi-official trade are so-called margin prices; that is, they indicate the range between a lower bid price and a higher offer price, between which the settled price lies.

Settlement prices for over-the-counter securities are published every trading day in a supplement to the Official List of the Frankfurt Stock Exchange. For securities traded by telephone, the settlement prices are published in the list "Offer and demand for unlisted securities in Frankfurt" edited by the Association of Frankfurt Security Dealers.

Memberships (1972):

1.

	Bank Representatives	Official Brokers	Unofficial or Floor Brokers	Total
1968	233	20	19	272
1969	215	21	24	260
1970	237	21	25	283
1971	238	21	25	284
1972	264	22	31	317
1973	287	23	29	339

2. Ordinary and extraordinary payments and fees are levied on every member of the exchange and are determined by the Board of Governors at the start of each year.

3. See "The Stock Exchanges of West Germany."

Commissions or Fees:

1. The commission received by "Kursmaklers" varies according to the volume transacted: ⅜ - ¾% of the nominal value for fixed interest securities and usually 1% of the price for stocks.

2. Stock Exchange turnover tax, brokerage, bank commission amount to 1 - 1¼% of the final amount on shares and to about ½ - ¾% on fixed interest.

Historical Background:

1585 The Frankfurt Stock Exchange was founded.

1727 The first exchange list of the Frankfurt Exchange was printed.

1820 The first dividend-yielding shares to be traded in Frankfurt were those of the Austrian National Bank issued in this year.

1829 Daily turnover reportedly totaled 1.5 million guilders.

1879 The present "New Stock Exchange" building was inaugurated. There were then 1,250 "admitted persons," or brokers.

1914 Prior to World War I, 388 foreign bonds and 51 foreign stocks were listed on the Frankfurt Exchange. In all, about 1,500 securities were traded.

1931 The exchange was closed temporarily during the worldwide depression.

1944 Trading floor was destroyed by an air raid.

1945 The exchange reopened in September, after having been closed temporarily at war's end.

1957 The rebuilt trading floor was inaugurated.

1966 A second trading floor was opened.

1968 Trading in gold was resumed.

1970 Option trading began, July 1.

HAMBURG STOCK EXCHANGE

Title: Hanseatische Wertpapierboerse Hamburg

Address: 2 Hamburg 11, Boerse, 1. Stock, Zimmer 151, Federal Republic of Germany

Telephone: 36 74 44-45

Teletype: hhwb d

Telex: 21 32 28

Officers: Director: Harald Degner; Assistant Director: Bernt-Dieter Koehler

Hours of Business (trading): 11:30 A.M. - 1:30 P.M.

Regulatory Laws: The "Boersengesetz" or Stock Exchange Law of June 22, 1896. See "The Stock Exchanges of West Germany."

Issues Traded and Volume:
1. About 200 share issues and 2,000 bond issues are traded.
2. Volume totals are known only by the Deutsche Bundesbank, Frankfurt.

Unit of Trading:
1. The accepted unit is 50 shares or a multiple thereof; for bonds, the unit is DM 5,000.
2. Odd-lots are settled by standard price. There is no extra fee or commission for buying or selling.

Memberships:
1. Regular Members: 112
2. Membership Prices: Members of a stock exchange in the Federal German Republic pay for their membership. On the Hamburg Stock Exchange, membership prices range from DM 200 to DM 13,000 yearly.

Commissions or Fees:
1. Commissions vary according to the volume transacted; they approximate ⅜% to ¾% of the nominal value for fixed interest securities and .1% of the price for stocks.
2. Stock exchange turnover tax, brokerage and bank commission amount to 1 - 2¼% of the final amount on shares and to about ½ - 1½% on fixed interest securities.

Historical Background:
1558 The Hamburg Stock Exchange was founded, originally as a general exchange for wholesale business. Colonial products — coffee, cotton, rubber, spices, drugs, etc. — became popular as overseas trade increased.
1815 Trading in stocks began at about this time.

HANNOVER

HANNOVER STOCK EXCHANGE

Title: Lower Saxony Stock Exchange at Hannover (Niedersachsische Borse zu Hannover)

Address: 3 Hannover, Rathenaustrasse 2, Federal Republic of Germany

Telephone: 0511 - 327661

Telex: 0922 158 (Deutsche Bank A G, Filiale Hannover)

Cable Address: BORSE HANNOVER

Officers: Director: Hans-Josef Hecking; Syndicate Director: Hans Litten

Hours of Business (trading): 11:30 A.M. - 1:30 P.M.

Regulatory Laws: See The Stock Exchanges of West Germany

Memberships: Regular Members — 19

Commissions or Fees: See The Stock Exchanges of West Germany

Historical Background: 1787 The Hannover Exchange was founded.

MUNICH

BAVARIAN STOCK EXCHANGE

Title: Bayerische Borse (Bavarian Stock Exchange)

Address: D-8 Munchen 2, Lenbachplatz 2 a/1, Federal Republic of Germany.

Telephone: 595 056, 593 849

Teletype: Boers D

Telex: 523515

Officers: Board of Governors
  Chairman: Rudolf Bayer
  Presiding Officers:
    Wilhelm Arendts
    Max Hackl
    Bernt W. Rohrer
  Governors:

Heinz Albrecht	Erich Huber
Paul Berwein	Christian Seidel
August von Finck jun.	Hans Dieter auf der Springe
Theodor J. Fischer	Franz Stern
Hans Hafner	Gerhard Tremer
Werner Hippler	

  Syndikus: Ernst Rohm
  State Commissioner: Fritz Janssen

Hours of Business: 11:30 A.M. - 1:30 P.M. (weekdays)

Regulatory Laws: Borsengesetz (June 22, 1896)

Issues Traded and Volume:
1. Listed Issues:
   a. bonds: 2236
   b. shares: 203
2. Unlisted or "other" issues: 37
3. Volume: not available.

Unit of Trading:
1. Shares: 50
2. Odd-lots: no difference in trading methods; no extra fee or commission is involved.

Membership:
1. Regular Members: 41
2. Membership prices: not available.

Commissions or Fees: Where the commission goes: from client to bank (the dealer); from bank to "Makler" (the middleman).

Dealers (banks)	Makler (middleman)
Shares: 1.0%	.1 %
Bonds: .5% (based on par value)	0 to DM 50,000 - .07 %
	DM 50,000 to DM 100,000 - .05 %
	over DM 100,000 - .038%

Historical Background: The Augsburg Exchange, the oldest German exchange was founded early in the 16th century. It merged in 1935 with the Munich Stock Exchange (founded 1830). The new name is Bayerische Borse (Bavarian Stock Exchange).

STUTTGART

STUTTGART STOCK EXCHANGE

Title: Wertpapierborse in Stuttgart

Address: 7000 Stuttgart 1, Hospitalstr. 12, Federal Republic of Germany

UNITED STATES OF AMERICA

The United States has three New York-based stock exchanges and nine regional exchanges. The latter range in size from the tiny, ten-member Honolulu Stock Exchange to the Midwest Stock Exchange, the largest outside New York. The nation's newest securities market — the Southeastern Stock Exchange (a division of the oldest exchange, Philadelphia's PBW Stock Exchange) — opened in Miami on March 4, 1974. All markets are supervised and regulated by the Securities & Exchange Commission, under legislation enacted during the early 1930's.

There are also some sixteen commodity exchanges in the United States. They operate under the Commodity Exchange Act, enforced by the Commodity Exchange Authority of the U. S. Department of Agriculture.

The feast or famine nature of the securities business has been typified in recent years. Leading market averages, such as the Dow Jones Industrials and Standard & Poor's 500-Stock Average have declined almost steadily on contracting volume, after reaching all-time highs early in 1973, and the public's interest in stocks has eroded commensurately. In 1973 the number of shareholders of American corporations dropped by 800,000.

Moreover, the banks have been making inroads in security market activities; more than 100 New York Stock Exchange firms have disappeared by merger or takeover since 1970; 87 firm-members of the National Association of Securities Dealers have vanished and 102 more are in liquidation. These and other adverse developments, coupled with a political crisis, a business recession, and hard-to-control inflation, have innudated the books and ledgers of the securities industry with red ink.

Nevertheless speculation is an inborn human desire that seldom is long suppressed. Many former stock traders have switched allegiance to the option market and, especially, to commodities, where horse race-like excitement may be experienced for only 10 percent of the purchase price of a contract. It has been estimated that more than 300,000 "outsiders" have entered the field. If a gold contract is introduced as seems possible, this number would greatly increase, at least for a time. In the year ended June 30, 1973, a record 47 million contracts of all commodities, worth $399 billion, were traded, compared with 20 million contracts worth $81 billion but five years earlier.

Broader federal regulation of all commodity futures trading appears imminent. On April 11, 1974, the House of Representatives passed a bill to create a new agency to oversee trading on American commodity markets. This agency, the Commodity Futures Trading Commission, would replace the Commodity Exchange Commission and take over the Commodity Exchange Authority of the U. S. Department of Agriculture. The new agency would have powers that the present authority does not possess; it would be able to regulate trading in all commodities, rather than only about half of them as at present.

Important changes are obviously in prospect for the commodity and security markets that may not please those who hark back continually to dear, old romantic yesterday. Yet change is always inevitable. As the hand of the century clock moves toward the final quarter, we should reflect upon changes effected over the past seventy-five years and consider that probably our fathers and grandfathers also objected initially to those that later became beneficial, just as we may fear or balk today at necessary changes that lie ahead.

COMMODITY EXCHANGES

CURRENCY FUTURES

Statistics that can be useful to the currency futures trader and the approximate times they are issued:

Weekly — UK bank rate and German reserves.

First Week of Month —
 US wholesale price index.
 US and German unemployment.
 UK, Canadian and Swiss reserves.
 German credit policy.
 German balance of payments.

Second Week of Month —
 US, UK, Canadian and Italian balance of payments.
 UK and Japanese wholesale price index.
 Canadian and Swiss consumer price index.
 UK real domestic product.
 UK and Japanese balance of trade.
 German cost of living.
 German industrial output.
 Canadian unemployment.
 Japanese exports.
 Italian reserves.

Third Week of Month —
 US and Japanese gross national product.
 US personal income, public sector deficit, overseas spending, overseas sales, real spendable earnings.
 UK unemployment, treasury bill rate, consumer expenditures, gross domestic product, money supply.
 German industrial turnover and wholesale price index.
 Canadian industrial index and exports.
 Swiss balance of trade.

Fourth Week of Month —
 US consumer price index, capital flows, reserves.
 US and Italian balance of trade.
 Canadian wholesale price index, real domestic product, treasury bill rate.
 Japanese reserves, balance of payments.
 Italian gross national product, cost of living, industrial index.

Source: Booklet of the International Monetary Market of the Chicago Mercantile Exchange.

COMMODITY FUTURES CONTRACTS TRADED
1969-1973

CHICAGO BOARD OF TRADE

	Per Contract	1973	1972	1971
*Wheat	5,000 bu	1,567,483	855,813	549,773
*Corn	5,000 bu	4,075,075	1,942,120	2,073,652
Oats	10,000 bu	182,963	36,282	45,006
*Rye	5,000 bu			3
*Soybeans	5,000 bu	2,742,513	4,043,474	3,113,038
*Soybean Oil	60,000 lbs	1,762,856	1,110,776	1,485,519
*Soybean Meal	100 tons	660,305	630,916	474,911
*Live Chce Steers	40,000 lbs	———	———	149
Iced Broilers	28,000 lbs	328,346	23,264	55,136
Silver	5,000 ozs	1,632,298	813,492	559,330
Plywood	69,120 sq ft	274,134	217,631	222,987
Stud Lumber	100,000 bd ft	8,059	411	———
		13,234,032	9,674,179	8,579,504

	Per Contract	1970	1969
*Wheat	5,000 bu	559,514	756,072
*Corn	5,000 bu	2,140,044	1,609,231
Oats	10,000 bu	91,816	133,730
*Rye	5,000 bu	3,957	19,549
*Soybeans	5,000 bu	2,031,272	1,002,972
*Soybean Oil	60,000 lbs	1,907,436	781,349
*Soybean Meal	100 tons	868,333	416,289
*Live Chce Steers	40,000 lbs	4,577	57,353
Iced Broilers	28,000 lbs	95,280	93,554
Silver	5,000 ozs	191,006	23,850
Plywood	69,120 sq ft	47,426	394
Stud Lumber	100,000 bd ft	———	———
		7,940,661	4,894,388

CHICAGO MERCANTILE EXCHANGE AND INTERNATIONAL MONEY MARKET

Butter	30,000 lbs	4	———	———
Frozen Eggs	36,000 lbs	6	86	———
*Fresh Eggs	22,500 doz	617,395	474,948	379,850
*Idaho Potatoes	50,000 lbs	9,532	6,137	23,916
*Pork Bellies, Fzn	36,000 lbs	1,154,873	2,057,064	1,695,386
*Live Hogs	30,000 lbs	1,061,770	543,257	261,001
*Live Cattle Mid-West	40,000 lbs	2,547,827	1,370,471	745,835
*Live Cattle-Western	40,000 lbs	———	———	———
*Hams, Fzn, Sknd	36,000 lbs	9	2	71
Turkeys, Tom	36,000 lbs	———	———	———
Lumber	100,000 bd ft	194,792	66,539	100,149

*The C.E.A. supplied the data regarding the number of contracts traded on the commodities designated by an asterisk. These commodities are regulated by the CEA.

*Frozen Beef	36,000 lbs	——	——	128
*Grain Sorghums	400,000 lbs	2,271	1,354	8,155
*Live Feeder Cattle	42,000 lbs	22,752	7,423	520
British Pound	50,000	31,412	14,790	——
Canadian Dollar	200,000	29,164	38,807	——
Deutschemark	500,000	77,272	19,320	——
Italian Lira	50,000,000	144	592	——
Japanese Yen	25,000,000	125,660	43,989	——
Mexican Peso	1,000,000	120,342	9,717	——
Swiss Franc	500,000	22,013	17,722	——
Dutch Guilder		11,327	——	——
U.S. Silver Coins		18,555	——	——
Canadian Silver Coins		509	——	——
		6,047,629	4,672,218	3,215,011

	Per Contract	1970		1969
Butter	30,000 lbs	——		13
Frozen Eggs	36,000 lbs	19		302
*Fresh Eggs	22,500 doz	678,627		447,457
*Idaho Potatoes	50,000 lbs	78,030		88,520
*Pork Bellies, Fzn	36,000 lbs	1,778,443		2,158,518
*Live Hogs	30,000 lbs	115,108		63,787
*Live Cattle Mid-West	40,000 lbs	578,525		999,224
*Live Cattle-Western	40,000 lbs	——		——
*Hams, Fzn, Sknd	36,000 lbs	216		431
Turkeys, Tom	36,000 lbs	——		23
Lumber	100,000 bd ft	85,513		744
*Frozen Beef	36,000 lbs	1,584		——
*Grain Sorghums	400,000 lbs	——		——
*Live Feeder Cattle	42,000 lbs	——		——
British Pound	50,000	——		——
Canadian Dollar	200,000	——		——
Deutschemark	500,000	——		——
Italian Lira	50,000,000	——		——
Japanese Yen	25,000,000	——		——
Mexican Peso	1,000,000	——		——
Swiss Franc	500,000	——		——
Dutch Guilder		——		——
U.S. Silver Coins		——		——
Canadian Silver Coins		——		——
		3,316,065		3,759,019

*The C.E.A. supplied the data regarding the number of contracts traded on the commodities designated by an asterisk. These commodities are regulated by the CEA.

	Per Contract	1973	1972	1971
COMMODITY EXCHANGE, INC.				
Copper	25,000 lbs	564,589	251,219	235,374
*Hides	40,000 lbs	——	——	——
Lead	60,000 lbs	——		——
Mercury	10 flasks	25	115	177
Propane	100,000 gal	——		347
Rubber	22,400 lbs	——	——	
Silver	10,000 ozs	1,237,860	815,168	616,244
Tin	11,200 lbs	——	——	10
Zinc	60,000 lbs	——	——	——
		1,802,474	1,066,502	852,152

	Per Contract	1970	1969
Copper	25,000 lbs	177,467	86,189
*Hides	40,000 lbs	7	267
Lead	60,000 lbs	35	146
Mercury	10 flasks	466	1,333
Propane	100,000 gal	674	569
Rubber	22,400 lbs	10	56
Silver	10,000 ozs	693,697	585,249
Tin	11,200 lbs	71	200
Zinc	60,000 lbs	3	108
		872,430	674,117

	Per Contract	1973	1972	1971
INTERNATIONAL COMMERCIAL EXCHANGE				
*Cottonseed Oii	60,000 lbs	2	4	25
Fishmeal	100 metric tons	5,361	5,700	235
Pepper	11,200 lbs	0	696	1,037
Foreign Currency		0	24,531	14,603
Pork Bellies, Fzn	18,000 lbs	0	2	52
British Pd. Sterling		0	——	——
Swiss Franc		0	——	——
French Franc		0	——	——
Deutschemark		101	——	——
Italian Lira		40	——	——
Japanese Yen		396	——	——
Canadian Dollar		0	——	——
Dutch Guilder		4,707	——	——
Belgian Franc		2,991	——	——
		13,598	30,933	15,952

	Per Contract	1970	1969
*Cottonseed Oil	60,000 lbs	25	13
Fishmeal	100 metric tons	406	1,018
Pepper	11,200 lbs	5	5
Foreign Currency		1,340	——

*The C.E.A. supplied the data regarding the number of contracts traded on the commodities designated by an asterisk. These commodities are regulated by the CEA.

	Per Contract		
Pork Bellies, Fzn	18,000 lbs	——	——
British Pd. Sterling		——	——
Swiss Franc		——	——
French Franc		——	——
Deutschemark		——	——
Italian Lira		——	——
Japanese Yen		——	——
Canadian Dollar		——	——
Dutch Guilder		——	——
Belgian Franc		——	——
		1,776	1,036

	Per Contract	1973	1972	1971
KANSAS CITY BOARD OF TRADE				
*Wheat	5,000 bu	346,118	292,921	150,452
*Corn	5,000 bu	354	——	——
*Grain Sorghums	280,000 lbs	1	2	100
		346,473	292,923	150,552

	Per Contract	1970	1969
*Wheat	5,000 bu	179,485	147,819
*Corn	5,000 bu	3	——
*Grain Sorghums	280,000 lbs	466	1,606
		179,954	149,425

	Per Contract	1973	1972	1971
MIDAMERICA COMMODITY EXCHANGE				
*Wheat	1,000 bu	74,662	15,544	7,601
*Corn	1,000 bu	102,572	12,579	10,443
*Oats	1,000 bu	9,323	2,132	724
*Rye	1,000 bu	——	——	2
*Soybeans	1,000 bu	56,546	81,205	46,076
Silver	1,000 ozs	400,048	80,800	49,805
U.S. Silver Coins	$5,000 value	141,712	43,092	——
		783,863	235,352	114,651

	Per Contract	1970	1969
*Wheat	1,000 bu	14,196	24,159
*Corn	1,000 bu	11,338	13,110
*Oats	1,000 bu	1,224	3,112
*Rye	1,000 bu	80	445
*Soybeans	1,000 bu	25,555	10,047
Silver	1,000 ozs	4,267	8,662
U.S. Silver Coins	$5,000 value	——	——
		56,660	59,535

*The C.E.A. supplied the data regarding the number of contracts traded on the commodities designated by an asterisk. These commodities are regulated by the CEA.

	Per Contract	1973	1972	1971
MINNEAPOLIS GRAIN EXCHANGE				
*Wheat	5,000 bu	171,660	116,874	54,229
*Corn	5,000 bu	———	———	58
*Oats	5,000 bu	———	———	
*Rye	5,000 bu	———	———	———
*Pork Bellies, Fzn	36,000 lbs	———	2,294	3,337
Durum Wheat	5,000 bu	417	———	———
		172,077	119,168	57,624

	Per Contract	1970	1969
*Wheat	5,000 bu	49,732	44,538
*Corn	5,000 bu	8	———
*Oats	5,000 bu	4	———
*Rye	5,000 bu	———	———
*Pork Bellies, Fzn	36,000 lbs	———	———
Durum Wheat	5,000 bu	———	———
		49,744	44,538

	Per Contract	1973	1972	1971
NEW YORK COCOA EXCHANGE				
Cocoa	30,000 lbs	430,836	278,416	212,802

	Per Contract	1970	1969
Cocoa	30,000 lbs	312,667	406,423

	Per Contract	1973	1972	1971
NEW YORK COFFEE & SUGAR EXCHANGE, INC.				
Coffee "C"	37,500 lbs	182,605	7,669	160
Coffee "U"	32,500 lbs	———	———	———
Molasses	40,000 gal	———	———	
Sugar-World (#8)	112,000 lbs	———	———	2,552
Sugar-Domest. (#10,#7)	112,000 lbs	21,797	19,644	7,658
Sugar #11	112,000 lbs	1,029,588	875,178	454,964
		1,233,990	902,482	465,334

	Per Contract	1970	1969
Coffee "C"	37,500 lbs	102	———
Coffee "U"	32,500 lbs	2	68
Molasses	40,000 gal	53	392
Sugar-World (#8)	112,000 lbs	266,667	536,077
Sugar-Domest. (#10,#7)	112,000 lbs	11,179	14,319
Sugar #11	112,000 lbs	75,944	———
		353,947	550,856

*The C.E.A. supplied the data regarding the number of contracts traded on the commodities designated by an asterisk. These commodities are regulated by the CEA.

	Per Contract	1973	1972	1971
NEW YORK COTTON EXCHANGE & ASSOCIATES				
*Cotton #1	50,000 lbs	———	———	———
*Cotton #2	50,000 lbs	450,272	365,372	358,847
*Orange Juice, FznCon	15,000 lbs	151,970	123,493	157,926
*Wool	6,000 lbs	4,677	3,778	3,559
*Wool Top	5,000 lbs	———	———	8
Propane	100,000 gal	7,013	925	1,544
Tomato Paste	26,500 lbs	———	100	222
		613,932	493,668	522,106

	Per Contract	1970		1969
*Cotton #1	50,000 lbs	———		47
*Cotton #2	50,000 lbs	33,657		64,366
*Orange Juice, FznCon	15,000 lbs	73,347		129,877
*Wool	6,000 lbs	3,741		6,347
*Wool Top	5,000 lbs	66		92
Propane	100,000 gal	———		———
Tomato Paste	26,500 lbs	———		———
		110,811		200,729

	Per Contract	1973	1972	1971
NEW YORK MERCANTILE EXCHANGE				
Aluminum	50,000 lbs	———	———	———
Apples	840 cartons	———	———	———
Palladium	100 ozs	1,888	489	106
Platinum	50 ozs	147,802	159,272	112,413
Plywood	70,000 sq ft	———	4,020	9,581
*Potatoes, Maine	50,000 lbs	673,672	246,603	151,369
*Idaho Russets	50,000 lbs	———	9	19
Nickel	2,000 lbs	———	———	1
Butter		4	———	———
*Shell Eggs	22,500 lbs	2	———	87
*Imported Fzn				
Boneless Beef	30,000 lbs	2,645	964	556
Silver Coins	$10,000 value	89,978	26,437	17,985
		915,991	437,794	292,117

*The C.E.A. supplied the data regarding the number of contracts traded on the commodities designated by an asterisk. These commodities are regulated by the CEA.

	Per Contract	1970	1969
Aluminum	50,000 lbs	2	———
Apples	840 cartons	124	331
Palladium	100 ozs	757	10,870
Platinum	50 ozs	98,867	84,009
Plywood	70,000 sq ft	792	5,299
*Potatoes, Maine	50,000 lbs	316,691	365,575
*Idaho Russets	50,000 lbs	119	535
Nickel	2,000 lbs	382	———
Butter		———	———
*Shell Eggs	22,500 lbs	26	———
*Imported Fzn, Boneless Beef	30,000 lbs	———	———
Silver Coins	$10,000 value	———	———
		417,760	466,619

	Per Contract	1973	1972	1971
PACIFIC COMMODITIES EXCHANGE				
*Coconut Oil	60,000 lbs	12,742	1,812	———
*Shell Eggs	22,500 lbs	3,498	———	———
W. Live Cattle	50,000 dzn	848	———	———
		17,088	1,812	

	Per Contract	1970	1969
*Coconut Oil	60,000 lbs	———	———
*Shell Eggs	22,500 lbs	———	———
W. Live Cattle	50,000 dzn	———	———

	Per Contract	1973	1972	1971
WEST COAST COMMODITY EXCHANGE				
Copper	25,000 lbs	11,374	3,191	5,009
Diamonds	20 carats	———	3,574	———
Gold	200 troy ozs	———	———	475
Silver	5,000 ozs	149,966	76,557	53,739
Cocoa	15,000 lbs	4,955	5,235	6,618
Sugar	56,000 lbs	45,975	38,033	10,929
Silver Coins	$5,000 value	———	18	756
Coffee		2,494	———	———
		214,764	126,608	77,526

	Per Contract	1970	1969
Copper	25,000 lbs	423	———
Diamonds	20 carats	———	———
Gold	200 troy ozs	———	———
Silver	5,000 ozs	6,379	———
Cocoa	15,000 lbs	2,510	———
Sugar	56,000 lbs	820	———
Silver Coins	$5,000 value	———	———
Coffee		———	———
		10,132	

*The C.E.A. supplied the data regarding the number of contracts traded on the commodities designated by an asterisk. These commodities are regulated by the CEA.

	1973	1972	1971
TOTAL ALL REGULATED CONTRACTS	18,285,377	14,345,711	11,810,383
TOTAL NON-REGULATED CONTRACTS	7,541,370	3,986,344	2,752,948
TOTAL ALL FUTURES CONTRACTS	25,826,747	18,332,055	14,563,331
CHANGE FROM PREVIOUS YEAR	40.90%	25.88%	6.91%

	1970	1969
TOTAL ALL REGULATED CONTRACTS	11,547,271	9,345,191
TOTAL NON-REGULATED CONTRACTS	2,075,336	1,861,494
TOTAL ALL FUTURES CONTRACTS	13,622,607	11,206,685
CHANGE FROM PREVIOUS YEAR	21.56%	20.09%

Source: Association of Commodity Exchange Firms, Inc.

CHICAGO

CHICAGO BOARD OF TRADE

Title: The Chicago Board of Trade

Address: 141 W. Jackson Blvd. (LaSalle & Jackson), Chicago, Illinois 60604

Telephone: (312) 435-3500

Officers:
Chairman of the Board: Frederick G. Uhlmann
Vice-Chairman: Thomas A. Geldermann
President: Warren W. Lebeck
Vice-President and Secretary: Thomas L. Triggs
Executive Vice-President and Treasurer: Robert E. Burmeister
Vice-President, Compliance: Herbert S. Sheidy
Vice-President, Economic Research and Planning: Richard L. Sandor

Hours of Business: (for most commodities): 9:30 A.M. - 1:15 P.M.

Regulatory Laws: The Commodity Exchange Act, enforced and supervised by the Commodity Exchange Authority of the United States Department of Agriculture.

Commodities Traded: Eleven (11)—Newest commodity—Gulf Hard Red Winter Wheat—added April 8, 1974.

1973 Contract Volume and Estimated Dollar Value

Commodity	No. Contracts	Estimated $ Value (000,000)
Wheat	1,563,764	$ 30,279.1
Corn	4,067,225	$ 53,105.7
Oats	193,857	$ 1,195.9
Soybeans	2,738,155	$111,941.2
Soybean Meal	661,103	$ 18,453.3
Soybean Oil	1,758,554	$ 25,064.6
Iced Broilers	328,346	$ 5,079.5

(Continued)

Commodity	No. Contracts	Estimated $ Value (000,000)
Silver	1,631,298	$ 21,916.4
Plywood	274,134	$ 2,598.7
Stud Lumber	8,059	$ 101.5
Total	13,224,495	$269,735.9

Unit of Trading:

	Contract Size	Daily Trading Limit	Initial Margin
Wheat	5,000 bushels	$0.20/bushel	$0.50/bushel
Corn	5,000 bushels	$0.10/bushel	$0.30/bushel
Oats	5,000 bushels	$0.06/bushel	$0.18/bushel
Soybeans	5,000 bushels	$0.20/bushel	$0.50/bushel
Soybean Oil	60,000 pounds	$0.01/pound	$1000/contract
Soybean Meal	100 tons/2000# ea.	$10.00/ton	$1000/contract
Iced Broilers	28,000 pounds	$2.00/100 pounds	$700/contract
Silver	5,000 troy ounces	$0.20/ounce	$2,500/contract
Plywood	69,120 sq. ft.	$7.00/1000 sq. ft.	$700/contract
Stud Lumber	100,000 board ft.	$5.00/1000 bd. ft.	$700/contract

Daily trading limits and initial margins are subject to change depending on market volatility. These limits and margins are now effective (April 8, 1974).

Delivery Months: Vary according to commodity

Memberships:
Regular Members: 1,402
Membership Prices: $73,000 (last sale)
Membership Dues: (Exchange Service Fee—approved March 14, 1973)—$100 per quarter for members; $0.25 per contract transaction ($0.50 per liquidation of a position) for non-members.
Clearing Corporation Members: 123

Commissions: Consult your broker

Historical Background:
1848 Chicago Board of Trade founded by 82 merchants. Seats sold for $5. Chicago Board of Trade is the world's oldest and largest commodities exchange.
1850 Annual dues raised from $2 to $3; Chicago Board of Trade became a corporation by special Illinois legislation.
1854 Chicago discarded the unreliable method of buying and selling grain by measured bushel, adopted the standard weight for a bushel of wheat as 60 pounds, oats 32 pounds.
1856 Chicago Board of Trade abandoned practice of furnishing free lunch to members at daily meetings. 122 new members admitted this year, versus total membership of 38 in 1851.
1861 All commercial transactions of Chicago Board of Trade were based on gold coin as the standard of value.
1864 New grain elevators gave Chicago a grain capacity of more than 10 million bushels.
1865 Chicago Board of Trade moved into first permanent home on southwest corner of LaSalle and Washington Streets. Margins introduced as a guaranty of performance in commodity trading.

1866 Chicago Board of Trade membership dropped from 1,462 to 1,401 when annual assessments were raised from $10 to $25.
1868 Board of Directors stated that any member engaged in "cornering" operations would be expelled.
1871 Chicago Board of Trade's first building and all records destroyed by Chicago Fire. A 90' x 90' wigwam, on Washington and Market Streets, became temporary home. Permanent headquarters rebuilt and occupied by December. New trading hours posted: 9:00 A.M. - 5:00 P.M.
1872 Dues reduced for nine months from $20 to $10 to compensate members for fire losses.
1874 Panic of 1873 had little effect on Chicago Board of Trade business, except to reduce speculative trading. "Corners" again prevalent despite fines, threats, etc.
1876 Rumble & Co., first "bucketshop" in Chicago.
1885 Chicago Board of Trade erected $500,000 building on Jackson and LaSalle Streets.
1893 Exchange galleries are opened to public. A maniac fired revolver into trading crowd, wounding three.
1895 A campaign began to compel all Chicago dealers to use official weights of the Chicago Board of Trade.
1896 Joseph Leiter cornered wheat, but subsequently lost $10 million.
1901 War on bucketshops continued by Chicago Board of Trade, with government assistance.
1907 James A. Patten cornered wheat, largest corner in Chicago Board of Trade history.
1916 World War I caused highest corn price since Civil War—$1.05 per bushel.
1917 Wheat at $3.25 per bushel—highest ever paid in an open market for future delivery.
1922 Government began regulating grain trading; established the Grain Futures Administration.
1925 Chicago Board of Trade directors given authority to declare emergency and establish daily price limitations. 26.9 billion bushels of grain traded—one of biggest years on Chicago Board of Trade.
1929 Chicago Board of Trade seat sold for then record of $62,500.
1930 Chicago Board of Trade moved into current home at LaSalle and Jackson Streets.
1931 Cotton, thought to be large trading item when added to Chicago Board of Trade commodities in 1924, proved inactive due to limited consumption.
1940 Open wheat futures shrank 37 million bushels in six days of liquidation and price decline when Paris fell in World War II.
1942 Seat prices fell to $25.
1966 Chicago Board of Trade introduced first examination in industry for commission house representatives.
1967 New, extremely fast automatic electronic wall displays installed. Choice Steer futures trading began (no longer an open contract).
1968 Chicago Board of Trade named first public directors. Trading began in iced broilers. First woman became a member. Chicago Board of Trade

planned to establish first central marketplace in U.S. for trading securities options.

1969 Trading began in silver and plywood.

1972 Stud lumber futures contract introduced. Peak volume recorded: 9.6 million contracts, worth about $123 billion. U.S.S.R. purchased 10.7 million metric tons of wheat; 6.8 million metric tons of corn; 107,239 metric tons of soybeans—total value $1.2 billion.

1973 Chicago Board Options Exchange (CBOE) opened in quarters adjacent to Chicago Board of Trade trading floor. All Chicago Board of Trade members given rights to assume Chicago Board Options Exchange membership. Chicago Board of Trade seat sold at all-time high in April—$65,000.

CHICAGO MERCANTILE EXCHANGE
INTERNATIONAL MONETARY MARKET

Title:
1. The Chicago Mercantile Exchange, Inc.
2. International Monetary Market of the Chicago Mercantile Exchange, Inc.

Address: 444 West Jackson Boulevard, Chicago Illinois 60606

Telephone: (312) 648 - 1000

Officers: Chicago Mercantile Exchange and International Monetary Market
President: Everette B. Harris
Administrator: Leonard S. Shaw
Executive Vice-President: Kenneth B. Mackay
Vice-President, Chicago Mercantile Exchange (Research and Education): Mark J. Powers
Senior Vice-President, International Monetary Market: Mark J. Powers
Vice-President (Audits and Investigations): William M. Phelan
Vice-President (Public Relations): Ronald J. Frost

Governors of the Chicago Mercantile Exchange:
Chairman: John T. Geldermann
First Vice-Chairman: Carl E. Anderson
Second Vice-Chairman: Laurence M. Rosenberg
Secretary: Leo Melamed
Treasurer: Donald L. Minucciani
Lloyd F. Arnold   Leslie Rosenthal
William S. Katz   Michael Weinberg, Jr.
Daniel E. O'Neil III   Alvin C. Winograd
Gerald Ordman

Directors of the International Monetary Market:
Chairman: Leo Melamed
First Vice-Chairman: Barry J. Lind
Second Vice-Chairman: William E. Goldstandt
Secretary: Carl E. Anderson
Treasurer: Alvin C. Winograd

All other governors of the Chicago Mercantile Exchange, plus:

Richard E. Boerke   William J. McDonough
Joseph F. Fox   Beryl W. Sprinkel
Henry G. Jarecki   Jerry D. Wetterling
Daniel R. Jesser

Hours of Business:

1. Commodities:

Frozen Pork Bellies	9:30 A.M. - 1:00 P.M.
Live Cattle	9:05 A.M. - 12:40 P.M.
Eggs (shell)	9:15 A.M. - 12:45 P.M.
Live Hogs	9:20 A.M. - 12:50 P.M.
Lumber	9:00 A.M. - 1:15 P.M.
Potatoes	9:00 A.M. - 12:50 P.M.
Milo	9:30 A.M. - 1:15 P.M.
Feeder Cattle	9:05 A.M. - 12:40 P.M.
Frozen Beef	9:15 A.M. - 12:45 P.M.
Hams	9:40 A.M. - 1:10 P.M.
Eggs (frozen)	9:15 A.M. - 12:45 P.M.
Turkeys	9:10 A.M. - 12:45 P.M.
Butter	9:35 A.M. - 12:30 P.M.

2. All currencies   8:55 A.M. - 1:10 P.M.

Regulatory Laws:

1. The Commodity Exchange Act, enforced and supervised by the Commodity Exchange Authority of the United States Department of Agriculture.
2. No governmental agency supervises the International Monetary Market; a 21-man directorate, including three public members, oversees its activities.

Contracts Traded:

1. Commodity Futures: 13.
   a. Frozen Pork Bellies: calls for frozen, uncured, unsliced slabs of bacon in the prime weight range of 12-14 lbs. in carlot quantities of 36,000 lbs.
   b. Live Cattle: calls for USDA "choice" or better steers meeting certain weight and yield requirements. One contract calls for 40,000 lbs. of live animals, or about 37 head.
   c. Shell Eggs: calls for high quality eggs, 85% to be U.S. Extras graded "A" quality or better. A single contract calls for 750 cases of 30 dozen each, which translates into 22,500 dozen or 270,000 fresh, large, white eggs.
   d. Live Hogs: calls for delivery of 30,000 lbs. of live hogs weighing an average of 200 to 230 lbs.
   e. Lumber: calls for 100,000 board feet of random length (8' to 20') 2x4s of kiln-dried or air-dried hem-fir.
   f. Potatoes: covers only potatoes grown in and shipped from Idaho. These potatoes must also meet the standards for Idaho Russet Potatoes set by the USDA, (U.S. No. 1's, size A). Potatoes are traded in units of 50,000 lbs.
   g. Milo: calls for 400,000 lbs. (7,273 bushels) of Number 2 Yellow Sorghum as described by the "Official Grain Standards of the United States."
   h. Feeder Cattle: calls for 42,000 lbs. of feeder steers (at least 80% USDA

"choice or better") averaging 650 lbs. This contract completes a three-sided complex along with live cattle and yellow sorghum (milo).

   i. Frozen Boneless Beef: calls for 36,000 lbs. of frozen boneless beef consisting of graded or ungraded boneless beef from beef cattle of any sex produced in domestic establishments.

   j. Frozen Hams: calls for frozen (uncured) skinned hams. The hams must be in the 14-17 lb. weight range and must be shipped from one federally-inspected packing plant. Each contract is for 36,000 lbs.

   k. Frozen Eggs: one contract calls for 36,000 lbs. of frozen eggs, the equivalent of 1,200 30-lb. cans.

   l. Turkeys: calls for 36,000 lbs. of frozen eviscerated U.S. Grade A Young Tom Turkeys, FFP (for further processing) with a minimum of 70% 20-26 lb. sizes.

   m. Butter: calls for fresh or storage butter of a high quality (92 score or better). This butter must meet federal regulations and is inspected before delivery. A trading unit calls for 40,000 lbs.

2. Currency Futures: 7.
British Pound; Canadian Dollar; Deutschemark; Dutch Guilder; Italian Lira; Japanese Yen; Mexican Peso; Swiss Franc.

3. Silver Coin Futures: 2.
U.S. and Canadian silver coins with a face value of $1,000 a bag. Contracts call for 5 bags (total face value of $5,000).

Trading Units:

1. Commodities:

	Contract Size	Maximum Daily Price Fluctuations* (Value of Price Fluctuation)	Speculative Minimum Initial Margins (in delivery Months)
Pork Bellies	36,000 lbs.	1½c/lb. (1c = $360)	$1,000 ($1,500)
Live Cattle	40,000 lbs.	1c/lb. (1c = $400)	$900 ($1,200) ($1,000)**
Eggs (shell)	22,500 doz.	2c/doz. (1c = $225)	$900 ($1,200)
Live Hogs	30,000 lbs.	1½c/lb. (1c = $300)	$900 ($1,200) ($1,000)**
Lumber	100,000 bd. ft.	$5/1,000 bd. ft. ($1 = $100)	$700 ($1,000) $500**
Potatoes	50,000 lbs.	35c/cwt. (35c = $175) Last 2 days 50c/cwt. (50c = $250)	$700
Milo	400,000 lbs.	15c/cwt. (1c = $40	$400 $300**

Feeder Cattle	42,000 lbs.	1c/lb. (1c = $420)	$900 $600
Frozen Beef	36,000 lbs.	1½c/lb. (1c = $360)	$600 ($800)
Hams	36,000 lbs.	1½c/lb. (1c = $360)	$500
Eggs (frozen)	36,000 lbs.	1½c/lb. (1c = $360)	$600 ($900)
Turkeys	36,000 lbs.	1½c/lb. (1c = $360)	$500
Butter	40,000 lbs.	1½c/lb. (1c = $400)	$750

*up or down from previous closing price.
**margin is lower for a "hedger"—one who takes a position in the futures market, opposite the position he holds in the cash or actual market.
Above information correct, as of April 5, 1974; but subject to change without notice.

2. Currencies:

	Contract Size	Max. Daily Price Fluctuations (Value of Price Fluctuations)
British Pound	25,000	$ .0500 ($1,250)
Canadian Dollar	100,000	$ .00750 ($750)
Deutschemark	250,000	$ .00500 ($1,250)
Dutch Guilder	125,000	$ .00600 ($750)
Japanese Yen	12,500,000	$.0000600 ($1,250)
Mexican Peso	1,000,000	$ .00075 ($750)
Swiss Franc	250,000	$ .00500 ($1,250)

3. Silver Coins:

	Contract Size	Max. Daily Price Fluctuations (Value of Price Fluctuations)
United States	5 bags with face value of $1,000 each	$120/bag ($600/contract)
Canadian	5 bags with face value of $1,000 each	$120/bag ($600/contract)

Delivery Months:
  Commodities:
    Pork Bellies: February, March, May, July, August.
    Live Cattle: February, April, June, August, October, December.
    Eggs (shell): All months.
    Live Hogs: February, April, June, July, August, October, December.
    Lumber: January, March, May, July, September, November.
    Potatoes: January, March, April, May, November.
    Milo: March, May, July, September, October, December.
    Feeder Cattle: March, April, May, August, September, October, November.
    Frozen Beef: February, April, June, July, December.
    Hams: March, July, November.
    Eggs (frozen): October, November, December.
    Turkeys: January, March, May, July, November, December.
    Butter: October, November, December.
  2. Currencies: March, June, September, December.
  3. Coins: March, June, September, December.

Volume:
  1. Commodities:

	Number of Contracts (one side only)		
	1973	1972	1971
Live Cattle	2,557,598	1,372,025	746,211
Pork Bellies	1,155,168	2,056,720	1,695,992
Live Hogs	1,061,440	542,599	262,358
Eggs (shell)	619,576	475,620	381,215
Lumber	194,792	66,539	100,148
Feeder Cattle	22,846	7,457	520
Potatoes	9,586	6,151	23,960
Milo	2,276	1,346	8,511
Eggs (frozen)	4	75	—
Hams	9	2	76
Frozen Beef	2	—	130
Turkeys	—	—	—
Butter	4	—	—
Totals*:	5,623,292	4,528,534	3,219,121

	1970	1969
Live Cattle	578,817	1,013,671
Pork Bellies	1,779,139	2,175,775
Live Hogs	115,141	63,869
Eggs (shell)	678,801	448,919
Lumber	85,513	744
Feeder Cattle	—	—
Potatoes	78,154	88,661
Milo	—	—
Eggs (frozen)	21	306
Hams	216	432
Frozen Beef	1,584	—
Turkeys	—	23
Butter	—	13
Totals*:	3,317,386	3,792,413

*May not add correctly due to exclusion of delisted commodities.

2. Currencies and coins:
   1973: 436,374 contracts; approximate value: $37.04 billion.
   1972: 7½ months — 144,928 contracts; approximate value: $20.96 billion.

Memberships:
1. Chicago Mercantile Exchange: limited to 500.
2. International Monetary Market: charter memberships were sold to 500 members of the Chicago Mercantile Exchange for $100 each. An additional 250 memberships were offered for sale to qualified applicants at $10,000 each. This offer expired March 15, 1973, at which time 150 such memberships had been sold. Memberships currently number 650, of which 500 are also members of the Chicago Mercantile Exchange.
3. Clearing House Members (Chicago Mercantile Exchange and International Monetary Market): 80

Commissions:
1. Commodities: Between $30 and $45 for a "round-turn" of buying and selling.
2. Currencies and coins: Consult a broker.
3. Both exchanges have announced plans to adopt a system of negotiated commission rates for non-member transactions over a 3-year period. The transition follows a pattern adopted by major security exchanges, as well as the general recommendations made by the Commodity Exchange Authority of the United States Department of Agriculture.

Historical Background:
1898 Chicago Butter and Egg Board formed with headquarters at LaSalle and Lake Streets, January 5.
1919 Butter and Egg Board reorganized, name changed to Chicago Mercantile Exchange, September 26. First day of organized trading on Chicago Mercantile Exchange. Three carloads of eggs traded during 45-minute session. Memberships sold for about $100, December 1.
1927 Exchange moved into new building at 110 North Franklin Street, November 11.
1961 Chicago Mercantile Exchange initiated frozen pork belly trading—its first entry into meat futures, September 18.
1964 Live cattle contract was listed—first successful futures contract for live animals, November 30.
1966 Agreement signed for expansion of facilities at 110 North Franklin Street, May 25.
1968 Congress greatly expanded control of Commodity Exchange Authority over commodity exchanges and gave them increased responsibility for self-regulation, June 18.
1969 Poultry and Egg building donated by Chicago Mercantile Exchange on its 50th anniversary was dedicated September 30. Trading started in lumber futures, October 1. Exchange established the Chicago Mercantile Trust of $1.5 million (since doubled) to provide further financial security to the public dealing through Chicago Mercantile Exchange members, a first for commodity exchanges, December 29.
1970 Plans for new building to be located at 444 West Jackson Boulevard were

announced, May 18. Work began November 1; building topped out May 4, 1971.

1971 Yellow sorghum (milo) listed for trading, March 2. Advisory Council to the Board of Governors held first meeting, July 21.

1972 Trading began in seven foreign currency futures contracts on new International Monetary Market of the Chicago Mercantile Exchange, May 16. New headquarters and trading complex opened November 27.

1973 All-time Chicago Mercantile Exchange single-day record of 42,134 contracts traded, March 8. Dutch Guilder was listed for trading on the International Monetary Market, May 16. Chicago Mercantile Exchange membership purchased for $125,000, highest in history of any commodity exchange, March 21. Trading in U.S. and Canadian silver coin contracts opened October 1, on the International Monetary Market. Business year ended with all-time Chicago Mercantile Exchange record of 5.6 million contracts traded. Estimated value of contracts was $96.8 billion. Combined Chicago Mercantile Exchange and International Monetary Market contracts for year totaled 6,059,666.

MIDAMERICA COMMODITY EXCHANGE

Title: MidAmerica Commodity Exchange (formerly The Chicago Open Board of Trade)

Address: 343 South Dearborn Street, Chicago, Illinois 60604

Telephone: (312) 939-0606

Officers:
President: J. Robert Collins
Vice-President: G. L. Findling
Secretary: Robert Martin
Directors:
Lawrence Carroll
Robert Dennis
Charles J. Fanaro, Jr.
Domenic Fratinardo
Frank DiMaria
Charles Noel
Robert Tallian
Ronald Wallauer
Officers are elected by the members. The Board of Directors is the governing body.

Regulatory Laws: The Commodity Exchange Act, enforced and supervised by the Commodity Exchange Authority of the United States Department of Agriculture.

Commodities Traded: wheat, corn, oats, soybeans, silver, U.S. silver coins.

Volume:

	Contracts traded (1973):	
	Wheat	373,311
	Corn	499,098
	Oats	9,323
	Soybeans	282,709
	Silver	400,021
	U.S. silver coins	141,762
		1,716,224

Memberships:
1. 400 members.
2. Membership prices: $5,000 (last sale).

Commissions: Rates are negotiated.

Historical Background:
1868 MidAmerica Commodity Exchange was founded. One of its main original features was to enable members and clients to deal in smaller amounts of grain (contracts of 1,000 bushels each). The clearing house method of settlement of futures contracts was originated and first used on this exchange.
1880 The Exchange was incorporated.
1972 The Exchange's present title was adopted late in this year.

KANSAS CITY

BOARD OF TRADE (KANSAS CITY, MISSOURI)

Title: The Board of Trade of Kansas City, Missouri, Inc.

Address: 4800 Main Street, Kansas City, Missouri 64112

Telephone: 816 - 753 - 7363 (Exec. Offices); 816 - 753 - 7800 (Trading Floor)

Officers:
President: Carlos Bradley
First Vice-President: J. B. Gregg
Second Vice-President: C. W. Polson
Executive Vice-President & Secretary: Walter N. Vernon III
Assistant Secretary: F. L. Burnham
Treasurer: H. C. Edwards
Assistant Treasurer: E. D. Romain
Director of Public Affairs: Roderick Turnbull
Transportation Commissioner: J. C. Hansen
Registrar: A. E. Davidson
Chief Inspector of Weights: W. D. Glick
Chief, Office of Audits & Investigations: J. H. Johnson
Editor, Grain Market Review: Ron Johnson

Hours of Business: Office: 8:30 A.M. - 4:30 P.M.; Trading Hours: 9:30 A.M. - 1:15 P.M.

Regulatory Laws: The Commodity Exchange Act, enforced and supervised by the Commodity Exchange Authority of the United States Department of Agriculture.

Profile Data
231

Futures Traded: Virtually all activity on the Board of Trade takes place in wheat, with a lesser interest in grain sorghums and corn.

Volume (bushels 000):

	Wheat	Corn	Soybeans	Sorghum	Total
1960	262,771	95	——	9,048	271,914
1961	360,825	——	——	575	361,400
1962	552,321	340	——	25	552,686
1963	560,544	360	60	855	561,819
1964	490,397	70	——	5	490,472
1965	531,065	——	820	——	531,885
1966	1,929,292	30,900	——	34,475	994,667
1967	1,194,915	9,245	——	35,410	1,239,570
1968	1,093,345	470	——	10,185	1,104,000
1969	739,095	——	——	8,635	747,730
1970	898,145	15	——	2,330	900,490
1971	792,260	——	——	500	792,760
1972	1,464,630	——	——	10	1,464,640
1973	1,730,590	1,770	——	280	1,732,640

Receipts of Grain at Kansas City (bushels 000):

	Wheat	Corn	Oats	Soybeans
1968	93,561.9	52,685.3	862.4	18,006.9
1969	74,403.3	38,596.3	1,741.0	21,002.0
1970	96,962.5	65,152.6	2,029.0	26,033.9
1971	90,382.7	48,554.3	795.5	22,584.5
1972	100,446.3	59,137.5	1,819.8	18,740.5
1973	117,320.2	108,184.9	1,682.5	22,988.9

	Sorghum	Rye	Barley	Total
1968	26,936.4	77.0	192.8	192,322.7
1969	29,378.4	119.2	664.5	165,904.8
1970	30,508.1	197.7	719.4	221,603.2
1971	46,844.6	238.2	724.5	210,124.3
1972	18,477.5	61.8	739.8	199,423.1
1973	44,620.4	372.3	8.4	295,177.6

Since 1933:	Wheat	Corn	Oats	Soybeans
High:	188,258.4	71,236.0	9,576.0	26,033.9
	(1947)	(1966)	(1946)	(1970)
Low:	44,057.0	10,696.4	778.4	4,027.3
	(1934)	(1941)	(1961)	(1953)

	Sorghum	Rye	Barley	Total
High:	46,844.6	2,253.0	7,372.8	295,177.6
	(1971)	(1943)	(1944)	(1973)
Low:	635.6	61.8	8.4	72,760.8
	(1935)	(1972)	(1973)	(1933)

Shipments of Grain at Kansas City (bushels 000):

	Wheat	Corn	Oats	Soybeans
1968	61,450.1	16,880.0	840.4	2,520.8
1969	38,040.7	21,320.6	1,039.8	4,449.5
1970	52,796.1	33,204.9	1,340.6	12,842.9
1971	62,474.8	23,122.0	1,053.6	8,091.4
1972	55,142.4	23,083.6	456.4	4,700.9
1973	97,562.8	68,099.3	1,703.5	10,735.9

	Sorghum	Rye	Barley	Total
1968	21,136.2	114.6	328.1	103,270.1
1969	21,384.7	43.9	322.3	86,601.4
1970	23,584.0	84.5	635.6	124,488.6
1971	29,352.7	281.7	552.5	124,928.7
1972	20,530.0	16.9	586.2	104,516.4
1973	35,212.7	317.3	430.5	214,062.0

Since 1933:	Wheat	Corn	Oats	Soybeans
High:	109,372.9	43,692.0	8,288.0	12,842.9
	(1947)	(1966)	(1946)	(1970)
Low	26,556.5	3,733.5	324.1	639.2
	(1935)	(1937)	(1961)	(1959)
	Sorghum	Rye	Barley	Total
High:	35,212.7	1,579.3	7,187.2	214,062.0
	(1973)	(1962)	(1945)	(1973)
Low:	471.6	16.9	65.6	37,757.6
	(1935)	(1972)	(1940)	(1933)

U. S. Grain Crop Production (bushels 000):

	Wheat	Corn	Oats	Soybeans
1968	1,576,251	4,393,273	939,228	1,103,129
1969	1,460,187	4,582,534	950,023	1,126,314
1970	1,351,558	4,151,938	917,159	1,127,100
1971	1,617,789	5,641,112	881,277	1,175,989
1972	1,544,936	5,573,320	691,973	1,270,630
1973	1,711,400	5,643,256	663,860	1,566,518

	Sorghum	Rye	Barley
1968	739,695	23,365	422,959
1969	747,280	31,583	423,547
1970	683,571	36,840	416,139
1971	875,752	49,288	463,601
1972	809,264	29,183	423,461
1973	936,587	26,398	424,483

Since 1900:	Wheat	Corn	Oats	Soybeans
High:	1,617,789	5,641,112	1,523,851	1,276,290
	(1971)	(1971)	(1945)	(1972)
Low:	526,052	1,146,734	544,247	4,875
	(1934)	(1934)	(1934)	(1925)
	Sorghum	Rye	Barley	
High:	875,752	103,362	477,368	
	(1971)	(1922)	(1958)	
Low:	19,209	16,146	96,588	
	(1934)	(1952)	(1900)	

Memberships: 211 individuals, representing 99 firms.

Commissions:

(5,000 bu. Contract)

	Members	Non-Members
Wheat	$11	$22
Corn	11	22
Sorghum	11	22
Soybeans	12	24

2414. Exempt Transactions. — From the effective date of this rule, the provisions of these rules and regulations respecting non-member rates of commission shall be superseded as follows:

(Note. The effective date of this rule is September 6, 1973).

2414.1 Futures Trading

2414.11 The provisions of the rules and regulations respecting non-member rates of commission for futures trading shall not apply:

i. in the first year after the effective day, to that part of a non-member transaction exceeding twenty-four (24) contracts;
    (Note. This provision is effective September 6, 1973).

ii. in the second year after the effective date, to that part of a non-member transaction exceeding nineteen (19) contracts;
    (Note. This provision is effective September 6, 1974).

iii. in the third year after the effective date, to that part of a non-member transaction exceeding fourteen (14) contracts;
    (Note. This provision is effective September 6, 1975).

iv. in the fourth year after the effective date, to that part of a non-member transaction exceeding nine (9) contracts;
    (Note. This provision is effective September 6, 1976).

v. in the first six months of the fifth year after the effective date, to that part of a non-member transaction exceeding four (4) contracts;
    (Note. This provision is effective September 6, 1977).

vi. in the last six months of the fifth year and thereafter, to any non-member transaction irrespective of size.
    (Note. This provision is effective March 6, 1978).

2414.12 The term "non-member transaction" means the total of all purchase contracts or the total of all sale contracts (both new positions and liquidations) in the same commodity executed on the same day pursuant to a single non-member order and within the same section of Rule 2414. For purposes of this paragraph, 2414.12, spreads in the same commodity shall be treated as two orders (one for the purchase and one for the sale).

2414.13 Commissions on futures trading shall be calculated, and may be billed, on each purchase and each sale. The minimum commission on each purchase or sale contract in that portion of a non-member transaction remaining subject to minimum rates shall be one-half the round-turn rate specified in Rule 2414. '

2414.2 Cash Trading. — The provisions of paragraph 2414.11 shall apply to cash transactions. An amount of cash commodity equal to that of a single futures contract in the same commodity shall constitute one "contract"; and the total of all purchases or the total of all sales executed on the same day pursuant to a single non-member order in the same commodity shall constitute one "non-member transaction."

2414.3 Interpretation. — All rules, regulations, rulings, and official actions of the Board of Trade shall be interpreted to conform to this rule, and any requirement or action in conflict with this rule shall be superseded hereby. No member, registered partnership or registered corporation shall conduct business with a non-member at a rate less than the minimum rate of commission, except as provided in this rule.

2414.4 Effective Date. — Rule 2414 shall be and become effective from and after September 6, 1973, being the date sixty (60) days following the effective date of the Master Settlement Agreement in the commodity exchange cases (Savett v. Board of Trade of the City of Chicago, et al., No. 72-C-1633) which was July 8, 1973.

Effective November 1, 1973 the trading variation, or minimum price fluctuation, in wheat and corn was changed from one-eighth of a cent to one-quarter of a cent.

Effective October 5, 1973 trading was prohibited during any day in contracts for future delivery at a price higher or lower than the closing price on the previous day plus or minus, as the case may be, the following sums with respect to the commodities named:

Wheat	25 cents per bushel
Corn	10 cents per bushel
Grain Sorghums	20 cents per cwt.

Margins: Minimum customer margins on grain futures contracts:

1. Initial margins on transactions for future delivery are not less than the following:

Type of Transaction	Cents per bushel			Cents per bushel
	Wheat	Corn	Soybeans	Sorghum
Hedging	30	10	10	12
Inter-Market spreads	15*	15*	—	—
Intra-Market spreads	15	5	3	5
All other trades	40	15	15	15

*on Kansas City side of the spread

2. Customer's margins on all commitments are maintained at the following minimum levels, or the Clearing House requirements, whichever is higher:

Type of Transaction	Cents per bushel			Cents per Bushel
	Wheat	Corn	Soybeans	Sorghum
Hedging	30	10	10	12
Inter-Market spreads	15*	15*	—	—
Intra-Market spreads	15	5	2	5
All other trades or				
1,000,000 bushels/less	30	10	12	12
1,000,000 to 2,000,000	30	10	12	12
2,000,000 to 3,000,000	30	10	14	12
3,000,000 to 4,000,000	30	10	16	12
over 4,000,000	30	10	18	12

*on Kansas City side of the spread
Stop loss orders are not acceptable in place of the minimum maintenance margins set forth above.

Historical Background:

1856 Grain merchants organized what they called a Board of Trade. It was located in the West Bottoms, but trading was eclipsed by the Civil War.
1869 Kansas City Board of Trade was reactivated.
1876 A "grain call" was held 2 or 3 times daily, where grain was sold at auction; from this developed the futures market.
1888 Business expanded; the grain trade moved into a new building.
1925 The Board of Trade moved further downtown.

1966 The Board of Trade occupied a new building in the Country Club Plaza District.

1973 The Board of Trade, an Association, became incorporated July 1 under the laws of the State of Delaware with a change of name to The Board of Trade of Kansas City, Missouri, Inc.

1974 Kansas City (Missouri . Kansas) now has 17 elevators with a total storage capacity of 83,458,429 bushels, which have been approved regular for delivery on futures contracts.

Trading began April 1 in a new Gulf Hard Red Winter Wheat Futures Contract, with the 17 Kansas City (Missouri . Kansas) elevators, plus 17 other elevators in St. Joseph, Mo.; Wichita, Hutchinson, Salina, Kansas; Enid, Oklahoma; Ft. Worth, Texas; and Omaha, Hastings, and Lincoln, Nebraska, with 177 million bushel storage capacity made regular for delivery.

MINNEAPOLIS

MINNEAPOLIS GRAIN EXCHANGE

Title: Minneapolis Grain Exchange

Address: 400 South 4th Street, Minneapolis, Minnesota 55415

Telephone: (612) 336 - 6361

Officers:
Executive Vice-President & Secretary: Alvin W. Donahoo
Treasurer & Assistant Secretary: Robert L. Johnson

Hours of Business: 9:30 A.M. to 1:15 P.M., Central Time.

Regulatory Laws: The Commodity Exchange Act, enforced and supervised by the Commodity Exchange Authority of the United States Department of Agriculture.

Any person holding 200,000 bushels or more in one grain future must report this position to the Exchange Authority. The Exchange Act further limits daily trading and positions in one wheat futures month, or in all futures months combined, to 2 million bushels in one market.

Commodities Traded:
1. Northern Spring Wheat of U.S. origin. Because of its high quality baking characteristics, spring wheat typically sells at substantial premiums. Therefore, owning and processing this commodity carry an inherent price risk not present in other classes of wheat.
   a. Contract grade: No. 2, as described by the Official Grain Standards of the U.S., with a protein content of 13.5% or higher. While No. 2NS is the contract grade, No. 1 is deliverable (at a premium). Also, wheat with 13% protein is likewise deliverable (at a discount).
   b. Trading unit: Futures contracts are traded in round-lots of 5,000 bushel multiples, or "job" lots of 1,000 bushel multiples.
   c. Fluctuations: Prices in a single day may not advance or decline more

than 10 cents from the previous day's close; the maximum trading range for any given day is 20 cents.

2. Hard Amber Durum Wheat of U.S. origin. Because of its use primarily for pasta products, this class of wheat sells at substantial premiums. Price range: 1971 - $1.50 to $1.85 a bushel; 1972 - $1.63 to $2.47 a bushel. The high in 1973 was $8.97. Therefore, owning and processing this commodity carry an inherent price risk.

   a. Contract grade: U.S. No. 3 Hard Amber Durum as described by the Official Grain Standards of the U.S. The following grades are deliverable at premiums: U.S. No. 3 Heavy Hard Amber Durum; U.S. No. 2 or U.S. No. 1 Hard Amber Durum; U.S. No. 2 or U.S. No. 1 Heavy Hard Amber Durum.

   b. Trading unit: Futures contracts are traded in round-lots of 5,000 bushel multiples.

   c. Fluctuations: Prices in a single day's trading may not advance or decline more than 20 cents from the previous day's close; the maximum trading range for any given day is 40 cents.

3. The following apply to both commodities:

   a. They are traded throughout the year. The five contracts used for each provide for delivery in September, December, March, May, July.

   b. Maturing futures contracts may not be traded during the last seven business days of the delivery month.

   c. Prices are quoted in dollars and cents, with fractions of eighths of a cent per bushel. A price change of ⅛ cent is $6.25 for a round-lot of 5,000 bushels.

Contract Settlements:

1. Off-Setting Contracts:
   Most futures contracts are settled by off-setting purchases or sales of the same futures.

   a. The trader who sells (assuming a long position) may settle his contract by selling an equal amount before the maturing contract month.

   b. The trader who sells (assuming a short position) may liquidate his contract with a purchase of an equal number of bushels at any time before the contract matures.

2. Delivery:
   Futures contracts may be settled by delivery. During a trading session in the maturing month the seller may serve notice to the Minneapolis Grain Clearing Corporation of intention to deliver. The Clearing Corporation notifies the buyer (long) holding the longest standing contract in the maturing month that a delivery has been tendered. The long must take the delivery intentions to the office of the seller (short) by 1:00 P.M. the next day. Here payment is made with a certified check and the buyer (long) receives warehouse receipts. Delivery may be made, at the option of the seller, any business day in the maturing month.
   The buyer may retender the delivery notice. If the buyer receives a notice during a session, on or before the final day of trading of the contract, he may sell the future and retender the same notice to the Clearing House before 12:00 noon the same business day. In other instances the notice is not

retenderable. A buyer who holds a warehouse receipt assumes the responsibility of ownership and attendant charges for storage and insurance.

Volume: The daily turnover in futures on the Minneapolis Grain Exchange approximates 5 million bushels.

Memberships:
1. Regular Members: 420.
2. The price of a "seat" is about $1,500.

Commissions and Margins: The only major cost of buying and selling (called a "round turn") a 5,000 bushel grain futures contract is the brokerage commission. Minimum margins, usually about 10% of the value of the grain, are set by the Exchange. Margins are deposited by both the buyer and the seller to insure the integrity of the contract. Details about margin requirements and the commission schedule are best obtainable from a broker.

Historical Background:
1881 The grain trade of Minneapolis really began through an organization, called the Minneapolis Chamber of Commerce, that was founded this year.
1885 Receipts of wheat were 32 million bushels, versus 16.3 million in 1881. The first Grain Exchange was built in this year.
1928 Wheat receipts totaled 126 million bushels.
1934 Depression and drought caused a drop by wheat receipts to 42 million bushels, the lowest since 1886.
1943 Record 208 million bushel wheat crop sold on the Minneapolis market.
1947 The organization known as the Chamber of Commerce, from 1881 through 1946, became the Minneapolis Grain Exchange.

NEW YORK

CITRUS ASSOCIATES OF THE NEW YORK COTTON EXCHANGE, INC.

Title: Citrus Associates of the New York Cotton Exchange, Inc.

Address: 37 Wall Street, New York, New York 10005

Telephone: (212) 269 - 7880

Officers:
President: Joe Marshburn
First Vice President: Frank Knell
Second Vice President: John St. John
Treasurer: Lawrence M. Arre
Executive Director and Secretary: J. William Donaghy
Assistant Secretary: Joseph J. O'Neill

Delivery Months: January, March, May, July, September and November
Trading Units: 15,000 pounds

Fluctuations:
a. Minimum .05 cents per pound ($7.50 per contract)
b. Maximum 3 cents above or below previous close, 3 cents range in one day except on and after the eighth day of the current month, when there is no limit.

Standards: "U.S. Grade A" with a Brix value of not less than 51° having a Brix value to acid ration of not less than 13 to 1 nor more than 19.0 to 1 and a minimum score of 94, with the minimums for the component factors fixed at 37 for color, 37 for flavor and 19 for defects.

Delivery Points: Exchange licensed Warehouses in the State of Florida

Trading Hours: 10:15 A.M. to 2:45 P.M.

Volume of Trading:

1967	22,500 contracts	1971	153,634 contracts
1968	140,531 contracts	1972	119,271 contracts
1969	127,986 contracts	1973	149,929 contracts
1970	71,284 contracts		

Memberships: The number of memberships on the Exchange is 650.450 Class A memberships (New York Cotton Exchange Members) and 200 Associate Members. The value of the Associate Memberships is about $1,100.00.

Commission Rates:

Sec. 75. The following rates of commission are the lowest that may be charged on transactions for futures delivery:

a. For each contract of frozen concentrated orange juice bought and sold for any person residing in the United States or Canada, who is not a member of the Exchange, $45.00.
b. Rates for members shall be $22.50 except for a member who has conferred upon a corporation of which he is an executive officer, the privilege of membership rates. In this latter event, and so long as such corporation has such privilege, such member shall not be entitled to member rates; shall not exercise floor brokerage rights as provided in subdivision (e) hereof; and shall not offer contracts for clearance as provided in subdivision (f) hereof.
c. (Straddles) On non-member business $27.00 for each contract of frozen concentrated orange juice bought and sold and on member business $15.00 for each contract of frozen concentrated orange juice bought and sold; provided, that such transactions shall be executed during the same trading session and carried in a separate account designated "Straddle Account", consisting of a like number of contracts or an equivalent weight in pounds of frozen concentrated orange juice on each side carried by any one commission house; that contracts in a straddle account may be liquidated at straddle rates by the transfer of one side from one month to another; that straddle rates shall not apply to transfers of contracts from one month to another in any accounts other than straddle accounts; and further provided that when any part of a straddle is broken by a subsequent transaction liquidating one side only, or by delivery or receipt of frozen concentrated orange juice on one side, the straddle rate shall apply to such side and the non-straddle rate shall then automatically apply to an equal number of

contracts on the opposite side, which must be transferred from "Straddle Account" to a "non-straddle account".

d. For each contract of frozen concentrated orange juice bought and sold for any person residing outside of the United States and Canada, the foregoing rates plus $3.00.

e. (Floor Brokerage) For each contract of frozen concentrated orange juice bought or sold by one member for another, giving up his principal on the day of the transaction, $2.25.

f. (Day Clearances) $3.00 for each contract of frozen concentrated orange juice bought and sold where one member clears for another member transactions made or initiated during the day by him personally or for his account while present on the floor of the Exchange. No member shall be entitled to the privilege of clearance of contracts for his account, unless the purchase and sale were personally made by him, or the transactions were initated and orders both of purchase and sale were given by him while actually present on the floor of the Exchange.

g. (15 Day Trades) The commission rate on contracts entered into by members, executing the orders themselves for their own personal account, shall be $12.50 for each contract bought and sold, provided such contracts entered into shall be closed out within fifteen (15) calendar days. On these contracts no floor brokerage may be charged. The above rate does not apply to a member who has conferred his membership rate privileges upon a corporation.

h. (Day Trades) For each contract of frozen concentrated orange juice bought and sold on the same day for a single account: for non-members $25.00 for each purchase and sale; for members $15.00 for each purchase and sale.

The above mentioned rates shall be in each case the minimum commission that may be charged by any member of the Exchange, and shall be absolutely net and free of all and any rebate, in any way, shape, or manner; nor shall any bonus or pro rata percentage of commission be given or allowed to any clerk or individual for business procured or sought for any member of the Exchange.

The penalty for violating or evading, or seeking, offering, proposing, promising, or agreeing to violate or evade the provisions of this section in any way, shape, or manner whatsoever, whether by an agreement, arrangement, or understanding, expressed or implied, either directly or indirectly, in person or through any firm or co-partnership of which a member may be or may appear to be a partner, or through any agent or agents, or otherwise, shall be, upon conviction for the first offense, suspension for a period not exceeding twelve months; the term of suspension to be fixed at the discretion of a majority of the Board of Directors present at a meeting therof; and for the second offense, expulsion.

RESTRICTIONS ON MINIMUM COMMISSION RATES

Sec. 75 A. From the effective date of this Section, the provisions of any By-Law or Rule respecting nonmember rates of commission shall be superseded as follows:

I. Futures Trading
  a. the provisions of the By-Laws respecting nonmember rates of commission for futures trading shall not apply:

     i. in the first year after the effective date, to that part of a nonmember transaction exceeding twenty-four (24) contracts;

     ii. in the second year after the effective date, to that part of a non-member transaction exceeding nineteen (19) contracts;

     iii. in the third year after the effective date, to that part of a nonmember transaction exceeding fourteen (14) contracts;

     iv. in the fourth year after the effective date, to that part of a nonmember transaction exceeding nine (9) contracts;

     v. in the first six months of the fifth year after the effective date, to that part of a nonmember transaction exceeding four (4) contracts; and

     vi. in the last six months of the fifth year and thereafter, to any non-member transaction irrespective of size.

  b. The term "nonmember transaction" means the total of all purchase contracts or the total of all sale contracts (both new positions and liquidations) executed on the Exchange on the same day pursuant to a single nonmember order for one account. For purposes of this subparagraph (b), straddles shall be treated as two orders (one for the purchase and one for the sale).

  c. Commissions on futures trading shall be calculated, and may be billed, on each purchase and each sale. The minimum commission on each purchase or sale contract in that portion of a nonmember transaction remaining subject to minimum rates shall be one-half the round-turn rate specified in the By-Laws.

II. Spot Transactions. The provision of subparagraph (a) of paragraph 1 shall apply to spot transactions on the Exchange.

III. Interpretation. All By-Laws, Rules, Regulations, rulings and official actions of the Exchange shall be interpreted to conform to this Section, and any requirement or action in conflict with this Section shall be superseded hereby. No member or member firm shall conduct business on the Exchange with a nonmember at a rate less than the minimum rate of commission, except as provided in this section.

IV. Effective Date. This section has been adopted to carry out the provisions of a settlement agreement with respect to class actions instituted against various commodity exchanges and their members, which settlement agreement is to become effective when certain conditions have been met. This Section shall become effective 60 days after the effective day of the settlement agreement, which date shall be announced by the Exchange. (Effective date is 9/7/73)

COMMISSIONS FOR SPOT FROZEN
CONCENTRATED ORANGE JUICE TRANSACTIONS

Sec. 76. Commissions for spot frozen concentrated orange juice transactions made across the ring during the period established for trading in spot frozen concentrated orange juice shall be as follows:

  $9.00 for each contract of frozen concentrated orange juice when executed for the account of a member.

  $15.00 for each contract of frozen concentrated orange juice when executed for the account of a non-member.

Floor brokerage and Exchange fees to remain the same as are charged in futures transactions. All other provisions of Sec. 75 shall apply to this section.

FROZEN CONCENTRATED ORANGE JUICE CONTRACT
Contract for Future Delivery
of Frozen Concentrated Orange Juice

Sec. 77. No contract for the future delivery of frozen concentrated orange juice shall be recognized, acknowledged or enforced by the Exchange or any Committee or officer thereof, unless both parties thereto shall be members of the Exchange. Members shall offer their contracts for clearance to the Commodity Clearing Corporation, which, upon acceptance thereof, shall become by substitution a party thereto in place of the member and thereupon such Corporation shall become subject to the obligations thereof and entitled to all of the rights thereunder, assuming to the buyer the position of the seller and to the seller the position of the buyer, provided, however, that said Corporation shall have no liability to the buyer or the seller on any such contract after a notice of delivery thereunder has been issued and stopped.

COMMODITY EXCHANGE, INC.

Title: Commodity Exchange, Inc.

Address: 81 Broad Street, New York, New York 10004

Telephone: (212) 943-5282

Cable Address: COMEXINC

Officers:
President: Charles Mattey
Vice-Presidents:
    H. Fred Baerwald   James S. Rothschild
    Stephen H. Fields   Arthur P. Silverberg
    Edward G. Newman
Treasurer: Irving Redel

Hours of Business:
1. Mercury—9:50 A.M. - 2:30 P.M.
2. Copper—9:45 A.M. - 2:10 P.M.
3. Silver—10:00 A.M. - 2:15 P.M.

Regulatory Laws: The Commodity Exchange Act, enforced and supervised by the Commodity Exchange Authority of the United States Department of Agriculture. However, some futures contracts are not "regulated." Many are traded internationally; hence, they are not under the regulations of the United States Department of Agriculture.

Commodities Actively Traded: 3.
1. Mercury: contract calls for delivery of ten (10) sealed iron or steel flasks of standard weight and size, each containing seventy-six (76) pounds minimum of mercury, not less than 99.9% pure, which shall be prime virgin, redistilled or triple-distilled mercury, but not scrap mercury.
   Delivery to be at seller's option at any time during the month specified in the contract from one of the exchange's licensed warehouses.

Mercury tendered in fulfillment of an exchange contract must be accompanied by an assay certificate issued by an assayer licensed by the exchange, covering the ten flasks in the lot. Each flask shall bear the unbroken seal of the assayer and shall carry a tag showing its lot number, its individual identification number or letter, and its gross, tare, and net weight as furnished by the assayer. Assay certificates and weight lists shall be in such form as prescribed by the exchange.

2. Copper: contract calls for delivery of 25,000 lbs. (2% more or less) of copper. The basis grade is electrolytic copper. Each contract must be made up exclusively of:
   a. one of the deliverable grades;
   b. one of the deliverable shapes of the grade;
   c. one of the brands officially listed by the exchange. Cathodes must bear a distinguishing mark and be the product of a refiner on the exchange-approved list.
   d. Other tenderable grades (and shape):
      i. The following at the option of the seller, may also be tendered against the contract at the contract price.
         Fire Refined High Conductivity Copper (in ingots, or ingot bars, or wire bars, or cakes, or slabs, or billets of standard weights and sizes); conforming to the specifications of A.S.T.M.* designation for electrolytic copper (B5-43) (except that it is not produced by electrolytic process).
         Lake Copper, assaying 99.90%, (in ingots, or ingot bars, or wire bars, or cakes, or slabs, or billets, of standard weights and sizes); conforming to the specifications of A.S.T.M. designation (B4-42).
      ii. The following, at the option of the seller, may also be tendered against the contract at the respective discount set forth below:
         Electrolytic Copper Cathodes (full plate or cut); conforming to the specifications of A.S.T.M. designation (B115-43), at ⅛c per pound discount. Fire Refined Copper (other than Lake and Fire Refined High Conductivity Copper) assaying 99.88% copper, (plus silver) (in ingots, or ingot bars, or cakes, or slabs, or billets, of standard weights and sizes); conforming to the specifications of A.S.T.M. designation (B216-49), at ¼c per pound discount.
         *American Society for Testing Materials.

Delivery is at the seller's option at any time during the month specified in the contract from one of the warehouses licensed by the exchange located at various delivery points in the U.S.A.

Daily price fluctuations are limited to 5c per lb. above or below the lowest price of the closing range for any traded month established at the close of the preceding business day.

3. Silver: contract calls for delivery of 10,000 troy ounces (5% more or less) of refined silver, assaying not less than 999 fineness, in bars cast in basic weights of 1,000 or 1,100 troy ounces with customary trade tolerances above and below said basic weights.

Delivery is at the seller's option at any time during the month specified in the contract from one of the warehouses or vaults licensed by the exchange in the City of New York.

Daily price fluctuations are limited to 20c per oz. above or below the settlement price for any traded months established at the close of the preceding business day.

Contract Details:

	Trading Unit	Price Multiples	Trading Months
Mercury	10 sealed flasks each holding 76 lbs. minimum of mercury.	$1 per flask	Mar., May, July, Sept., Dec. within 18 months period
Copper	25,000 lbs.	10/100 of 1c per lb.	Jan., Mar., May, July, Sept., Oct., Dec. within 14 months period.
Silver	10,000 troy ozs.	10/100 of 1c per lb.	Jan., Mar., May, July, Sept., Dec. within 17 months period. Trading conducted also for delivery in every current calendar month and the immediately following 2 calendar months.

Memberships:
1. The "Comex" has 386 members; multiple memberships are available.
2. The highest price paid for a "seat" was $22,000 on May 2, 1973; on May 14, 1974 a membership sold for $19,500.

Commissions or Fees:
1. Mercury:
   For residents (members and non-members) of the U.S. and Canada
   Regular Rates: Round Turn

	Buying or Selling per contract		Contract Bought & Sold
Members	$10.00	Members	$20.00
Non-Members	20.00	Non-Members	40.00

   Day Trades: Straddle Rates

	Round Turn		Per Straddle	Round Turn
Members	$10.00	Members	$14.00	$28.00
Non-Members	20.00	Non-Members	28.00	56.00

   For residents (members and non-members) outside the U.S. and Canada:
   A commission of $1.25 for each contract bought or sold will be charged in addition to the above rates.

2. Copper:

Regular Rates:	Commission for Buying or Selling; per contract	Commission for Round Turn
Members residing in the U.S. and Canada	$ 9.00	$18.00
Non-Members residing in the U.S. and Canada	18.00	36.00

Day Trades: (on a minimum of two contracts per transaction) (Contract bought and sold, both entered into and liquidated same day for single account)

For Members and Non-Members residing in the U.S. or Canada

	Round Turn
Members	$ 9.00
Non-Members	18.00

Straddle Rates:

(For straddle transactions conforming to the provisions of Copper By-Laws Section 924 (h).

Members ... 70% of the Member's Regular Rate for Round Turn

Non-Members ... 70% of the Non-Member's Regular Rate for Round Turn

For members and non-members residing outside the United States and Canada a commission of $1.00 per contract will be charged in addition to the above Regular and Day Trade and Straddle rates.

3. Silver:

For residents (members and non-members) of U.S. or Canada

Regular Rates:	Buying or Selling per contract	Round Turn (contract Bought & Sold)
Members	$11.25	$22.50
Non-Members	22.50	45.00

Day Trades:

	Round Turn
Members	$11.25
Non-Members	22.50

Straddle Rates:

	Per Straddle	Round Turn
Members	$15.75	$31.50
Non-Members	31.50	63.00

(for straddle transactions conforming to the provisions of Silver By-Law Section 933 (i)).

For residents (members and non-members) outside of U.S. or Canada:
A commission of $1.25 for each contract bought or sold will be charged in addition to the above Regular and Day Trade and Straddle Rates.

Historical Background:

1933 The "Comex" was formed by a merger of four exchanges.

1970 Trading in rubber and hides was suspended.

1973 Volume totaled 1,802,475 contracts. Eleven billion troy ounces of silver and more than 7 million tons of copper were traded.

1974 "Comex" is one of the two most active copper futures trading markets and the most active silver futures market in the world. Purchases and sales of futures contracts are made according to standard contract terms. Actual transactions result from the meeting of bids and offers by open outcry at trading rings.

NEW YORK COCOA EXCHANGE

Title: New York Cocoa Exchange, Inc.

Address: 127 John Street, New York, New York 10038

Telephone: (212) 825 - 9531 and 9532

Cable Address: "COCOCHANGE"

Branches and Affiliates: New York Cocoa Clearing Association (affiliate)

Officers:
President: Bernhard S. Blumenthal
Vice-President: Thomas P. H. Aitken
Treasurer: Warren Heilbron
Secretary: Felix J. Brennan

Hours of Business: 10:00 A.M. - 3:00 P.M.

Regulatory Laws: The market is not regulated by any government body; cocoa is an international commodity.

Contract Size: Each futures contract requires delivery of 30,000 lbs. (net) of cocoa beans in original shipping bags, 1% more or less, and in a specified delivery month. Under exchange rules this may be the current month, or any one of the following seventeen months. But most trading is confined to March, May, July, September, December.
This trading unit (30,000 lbs.) is usually referred to as a "lot" or "contract." There is no provision for trading in "job lots" or split contracts, comparable to an odd-lot with stocks. Thus, the contract unit is the minimum quantity that may be bought or sold on the exchange. All contracts are guaranteed by the New York Cocoa Clearing Association.

Quotations and Fluctuations:
Prices are quoted in cents and 1/100c per lb. This minimum fluctuation, of one-hundredths of a cent per lb. permitted by the exchange, is known as a "point." Each point change is equal to $3.00 for a contract unit. Thus, if you are "long" or own one contract and the market advances 10 points, this is the same as ten one-hundredths of a cent per lb., and the cash value of the 10 point advance is $30. A fluctuation of 100 points, or a full cent, consequently represents a change of $300 in the value of the contract.
The maximum fluctuation permitted on any one day is presently fixed at 200 points, or two cents per lb., above or below the previous day's close, with the exception of the spot month in which there is no limit after the first transferable notice day.

Volume:

Fisc. Yr.*	No. Contracts
1967-68	345,993
1968-69	476,782
1969-70	334,011
1970-71	228,245
1971-72	233,714
1972-73	435,979

*Fiscal year ending September 30.

Price Range: (fiscal year ending September 30):

High	Month	Date
85.98 (record)	September 1973	July 25, 1973
Low	Month	Date
30.24	July 1973	January 22, 1973

Memberships:
1. 183, nearly one-third of which also belong to the New York Cocoa Clearing Association.
2. Membership Prices (1973): High — $23,500; Low — $19,000.

Commissions: Minimum commissions are being phased out over an approximate 4½ year period from September 7, 1973.

Minimum commissions for domestic non-members, as of April 1, 1974:
1. $60 for buying and selling combined.
2. "Day Trades" — for buying and selling the same contract during the same day, the rates are one-half the above rates for buying and selling combined.
3. Customers who are not residents of the United States, the Commonwealth of Puerto Rico, the Virgin Islands, or Canada, pay a surcharge of $5.00 per contract of 30,000 pounds for buying and selling combined, or $2.50 per contract for buying and selling.
4. The trader is invoiced for commissions when the futures transaction is closed. For example, when a purchase has been liquidated, the trade is considered closed. Similarly, when a sale has been repurchased, or "covered" as with a short sale, that transaction is also called closed.

Historical Background:
1925 New York Cocoa Exchange became the world's first established cocoa futures market.

NEW YORK COFFEE AND SUGAR EXCHANGE

Title: New York Coffee and Sugar Exchange, Inc.

Address: 79 Pine Street, New York, New York 10005

Telephone: (212) 269 - 8637

Officers:

Chairman: George D. F. Lamborn
Vice-Chairman: Joseph L. Fraites
President: Earle T. MacHardy

Treasurer: Lawrence H. Dixon
Secretary: William P. Cleaver

Hours of Business (trading):
1. Green Coffee Futures Contracts*:
   "B" - 10:30 A.M. - 2:50 P.M.
   "C" - 10:30 A.M. - 2:45 P.M.
   "U" - 10:30 A.M. - 2:40 P.M.
   *The Exchange has established differences in value as follows:
   "B" For grade, port and quality.
   "C" Between grades, growths and kinds.
   "U" Between growth, grade, description and treatment.
2. Raw Sugar Futures Contracts:
   World No. 11 - 10:00 A.M. - 3:00 P.M.
   Domestic No. 10 - 10:00 A.M. - 2:50 P.M.

Regulatory Laws:
1. The exchange is not presently subject to federal regulation.
2. Administration of the Exchange is vested in a Board of Managers working primarily through some twenty committees.

Memberships: The Exchange now has 344 memberships; the membership limit is 350.

Trading Units:
1. Coffee:
   a. "B" and "U": 32,500 lbs. in approx. 250 bags.
   b. "C" and "U"; 37,500 lbs. in approx. 250 bags.
2. Sugar (lot): 50 long tons (112,000 lbs.).

Trading Months:
1. Coffee: trading is conducted for delivery during the current month and twelve succeeding months.
   Delivery points: a licensed warehouse in the port of New York. However, the "C" contract also permits delivery at the customary commercial coffee dock in the port of New York where the coffee was originally discharged.
2. Sugar:
   a. World No. 11 — trading permitted for delivery during 18 months. Trading months are January, March, May, July, September, October. Delivery must be to a port in the country of origin or in the case of landlocked countries, at a berth or anchorage in the customary port of export, f.o.b. and stowed in bulk.
   b. Domestic No. 10 — trading permitted for any delivery month except December during an 18-month period.
   Delivery Points: New York and Philadelphia.

Price Quotations — Minimum Fluctuations:
1. Coffee:
   a. quoted on a pound price, i.e. 54.75 or 54 and 75/100 cents per pound.
   b. fluctuation unit is 1/100th or .01 cents per pound which is equal to $3.25 per lot for contracts "B" and "U" and $375 for contract "C".
2. Raw Sugar:
   a. quoted on a pound price, i.e. 6.75 or 6 and 75/100 cents per pound.

b. fluctuation unit is 1/100 or .01 cents per pound which is equivalent to $11.20 per lot.

Daily Trading Limits:
1. Coffee: Prices may move no more than (2 cents) 200 points per contract above or below the previous day's settlement price. The maximum range is (4 cents) 400 points per contract. These limits, however, do not apply on or after the first notice day of the spot month.
2. Sugar: No limit to price fluctuations for the nearest Contract #11 delivery month during the preceding month's trading or for Contract #10 on the last day of trading for the delivery month. Otherwise, prices may move no more than 1 cent or $1,120 per lot above or below the previous day's settlement price. Maximum range is 2 cents or $2,240 per lot.

Basic Grade:
1. Coffee:
   a. "B" Santos Coffee type number 4 strictly soft in the cup, fair to good roast, solid bean. Delivery consists of coffee shipped through one Brazilian port only. Soft or softish coffee in the cup are deliverable at discounts.
   b. "C" Coffee sweet in the cup, good roasting quality and as per types established by the exchange. The delivery is to consist of one growth and in the case of Colombian, one kind only.
   c. "U" Coffee must be (1) Commercially sound in the cup for the growth and grade, (2) Free from rioy flavor and (3) Free from outside foreign contamination. The delivery must consist of coffee of one growth, description, treatment and, in the case of Brazils, one port of shipment only.
2. Sugar: Raw centrifugal cane sugar based on 96% average polarization.

Growths Deliverable:
1. Coffee:
   a. "B" Brazilian coffee shipped through the ports of Santos, Paranagua, Angra dos Reis, Rio de Janeiro, Niteroi or Antonina.
   b. "C" Mexico, Salvador, or Guatemala and Colombia of the kinds known as Medellin, Armenia, Manizales, Bogota, Sevilla, Girardot, Libano, or Tolima.
   c. "U" Robusta Coffees of any growth and treatment and arabica coffees of any growth, washed, mild, and unwashed, including Robusta and Arabica Coffees of growths and treatments new or yet unknown.
2. Sugar:
   a. World No. 11: Growths of Argentina, Australia, Brazil, British Honduras, Colombia, Costa Rica, Dominican Republic, El Salvador, Ecuador, Fiji Islands, French Antilles, Guatemala, Haiti, Honduras, India, Jamaica, Mauritius, Mexico, Nicaragua, Peru, Republic of Congo (Brazzaville), Republic of the Philippines, Reunion, South Africa, Swaziland, Taiwan, Thailand, Trinidad and Venezuela, delivered f.o.b. and stowed in bulk.
   b. Domestic No. 10: Cane sugars of continental U.S. and foreign origin, duty paid or duty free, eligible under U.S. Government quota or allotment regulations, delivered in bulk.

Basic Grades Deliverable:

Coffee:

a. "B" Brazilian types grading from numbers 2 to 6. The contract shall not be below a grade averaging number 5.

b. "C" Mexican, Salvador, Guatemalans, or Colombian according to respective types, ten points deducted for each imperfection below type. No delivery permitted of coffee containing more than 10 imperfections below type. There is no premium for coffee grading better than type.

c. "U" Coffee grading under type No. 8 is not deliverable. Coffee must average 14 screen or better but in no event shall contain 12 screen in excess of 10%.

Commissions (minimum, in and out per lot) —subject to negotiation on the portion of any transaction exceeding 24 contracts at present, 19 contracts beginning September 7, 1974. After March 7, 1978 all commissions will be negotiable.

Coffee:

(50c to 74.99c)	Regular	Day Trade	Straddle
Member	$35	$27.63	$42
Non-Member	$70	$37.75	$84
(75c and over)			
Member	$40	$31.38	$48
Non-Member	$80	$42.75	$96

Sugar:

	Member		Non-Member	
	#10	#11	#10	#11
Regular	$21.00	$31.00	$42.00	$62.00
Day Trade	10.50	15.50	21.00	31.00
Straddle	21.00	31.00	42.00	62.00

Margins: Requirements for coffee are about 5% of the value of the contract; for sugar, about 10% of the value. Minimum requirements can be raised or lowered by the New York Coffee and Sugar Clearing Association, or the clearing broker, based on price volatility and speculative risks.

Historical Background:

1881 New York Coffee Exchange incorporated December 7.

1882 The Exchange formally opened on March 7. The first transaction involved 250 bags of "Rio strict good ordinary" at eight and one-quarter cents for May delivery.

1914 Coffee Exchange expanded its facilities to include futures trading in sugar. December 16.

1916 Name changed to New York Coffee & Sugar Exchange, Inc., October 1.

1972 902,482 contracts, valued in excess of $7.6 billion, were traded.

1973 1,233,990 contracts, valued in excess of $14 billion, were traded.

NEW YORK COTTON EXCHANGE

Title: New York Cotton Exchange

Address: 37 Wall Street, New York, New York 10005

Telephone: (212) 269 - 7880

Officers:

Chairman of the Board: Eugene M. Grummer

Vice-Chairman: Stephen Greenberg

Treasurer: Lawrence M. Arre

Managers:

Gedney H. Baldwin	Frank Knell
Charles W. Bassett	William C. Layton, Jr.
J. D. Butler	W. Gordon McCabe, Jr.
Donald B. Conlin	Robert D. McCallum
Preston H. Davis	Joseph P. McMahon
Frederick J. Dickson	Philip M. O'Cone
W. B. Dunavant, Jr.	Ben F. Tipton
Hubert F. Fisher, Jr.	Charles B. Vose
Joseph J. Gollatz	Dudley S. Weaver II

Secretary: J. William Donaghy

Assistant Secretary: Joseph J. O'Neill

Hours of Business: Contract No. 1: 10:30 A.M. - 2:50 P.M.; Contract No. 2: 10:30 A.M. - 3:00 P.M.

Trading begins each day with a "call" or auction in which each month in succession is opened by call for bids and offers and trades are made which establish the initial prices. The trading ring is then opened to bids and offers in all months simultaneously. However, the highest bid and lowest offer in each month rule at all times in the ring.

Regulatory Laws: The Internal Revenue Code (cotton futures) and the Commodity Exchange Act, enforced and supervised by the Commodity Exchange Authority of the United States Department of Agriculture.

Cotton Futures Contracts: Contract No. 1; Contract No. 2.

1. Basis grades: Contract No. 1 — "Middling 15/16 inch" cotton, largely produced in Oklahoma and Texas.
   Contract No. 2 "Middling 1-1/16 inch" cotton until the expiration of the July 1974 contract. Beginning with the October 1974 delivery the basis of the contract is "Strict Low Middling 1-1/16 inch" cotton.
   Price premiums are awarded for better qualities and discounts assessed for inferior qualities.

2. Trading unit: Exchange rules specify that each separate futures contract shall be for 50,000 pounds (about 100 bales) of cotton, tare included.

3. Delivery months: The seller is bound to deliver the quality specified in the contract, or at his option, certain other allowable grades and staples.
   a. Contract No. 1 trading is conducted in and confined to contracts providing for delivery in the months of January, April, June, August, November. No trading is permitted beyond the 18th month following the current

month, except by order of the Board of Managers and then not beyond the 24th month.

   b. Contract No. 2 trading can be made for the current month and one or more of the 17 succeeding months, or if so ordered by the Board of Managers for one or more of the six months, next succeeding the 17 months.

4. Quotations and Fluctuations: Prices are those at which buyer and seller agree at open outcry in open trading in the trading ring or "pit" of the exchange floor. Price changes are sometimes called "points," one point (the minimum fluctuation) being one/one-hundredth of a cent a pound, or $5 per contract of 50,000 pounds. No trades may be made at more than two cents per pound above or below a previous day's close. However, this does not apply to the current delivery month, on or after the first notice day thereof.

Volume: Trading volume in Cotton for future delivery (in bales*)

Season			
1949-50	40,309,500	1965-66	53,500a
1950-51	57,367,000	1965-66	200b
1951-52	68,403,400	1966-67	43,700a
1952-53	64,270,400	1966-67	127,200c
1953-54	32,311,400	1967-68	3,700a
1954-55	36,793,900	1967-68	22,349,400c
1955-56	28,713,900	1967-68	18,000d
1956-57	17,928,600	1968-69	12,847,400c
1957-58	20,905,800	1968-69	20,800d
1958-59	14,787,200	1969-70	3,264,100c
1959-60	3,873,800	1969-70	0d
1960-61	2,874,100	1970-71	20,827,100c
1961-62	3,377,800	1970-71	0d
1962-63	2,868,800	1971-72	39,241,200c
1963-64	874,500	1971-72	Od
1964-65	167,000a	1972-73	43,972,400c
1964-65	16,100b	1972-73	0d

*Changed from 500-lb. gross weight to 500-lb. net weight commencing with the October, 1971, delivery.

   a. No. 1 contract.
   b. No. 2 (world price) contract.
   c. No. 2 (Basis Mid. 1-1/16") contract.
   d. New No. 1 (Basis Mid. 15/16") contract.

Memberships:

1. Number of members: 450
2. Membership prices: In area of $8,000 (1974)

Commissions: A "one way" commission only is charged for each future against which a contract is received or delivered. For each 100 bales bought or sold (non-member, in U. S., Mexico or Canada) when the price of the transaction is not over 50 cents per pound, the rate of commission is $25.00, plus the exchange fee. When the price is above 50 cents per pound, the rate of commission is $30.00 plus exchange fee. Member rates when the price of the transaction is not over 50 cents per pound, the rate of commission is $15.00 per side, plus exchange fee. When the price is above 50 cents per pound, the rate of commission is $17.50, plus exchange fee. The foregoing rates, plus an additional charge of $1.50 per contract, applies to a purchase or sale for those residing outside the U. S., Mexico or Canada. Special rates are provided for Day Trades and Straddle orders.

Historical Background:

1870   On July 20, 106 merchants and brokers agreed to support plans for organizing a cotton exchange. Officers and a Board of Managers were elected, August 15; a constitution and by-laws were adopted, September 7; New York Cotton Exchange opened for business September 10, in rented quarters at 142 Pearl Street. Memberships were bought at $200; annual dues fixed at $25.00.

1872   Exchange moved into larger quarters in what is now the India House, Hanover Square. Unit of trading was in cents and fractions thereof; pricing got down to hundredths of a cent in 1877. Year's volume was 5 million bales.

1885   Exchange moved into new building at William, Beaver and Pearl Streets on April 30.

1887   Certificate System created, which permitted cotton to be classed by the Classification Committee, which issued a certificate certifying the grades that could be exchanged like a stock certificate.

1915   Clearing House was created.

1923   New home of exchange completed May 1, on same site, after old building was torn down. Membership expanded to 450 seats valued at $35,000.

1930   Exchange diversified by founding the Wool Associates of the New York Cotton Exchange, Inc.

1931   Trading began in Wool Top futures contracts, May 18.

1941   A new contract providing for delivery of wool in the grease inaugurated, March 17.

1966   The Citrus Associates of the New York Cotton Exchange was founded. Trading in frozen concentrated orange juice futures contracts began, October 26.

1966-67 Trading volume in cotton futures approximated 50,000 bales — less than one day's trading in normal times — due to Commercial Credit Corp's. activities in buying and selling cotton.

1968   Domestic cotton consumption at lowest level since 1957.

NEW YORK MERCANTILE EXCHANGE

Title: New York Mercantile Exchange

Address: 6 Harrison Street, New York, New York 10013

Telephone: (212) 966 - 2600

Branches and Affiliates: New York Mercantile Exchange, Maine Information Office, 440 Main Street, Presque Isle, Maine

Officers:
Chairman of the Board: Jacob Stern
First Vice-Chairman: Benjamin Pressner
Second Vice-Chairman: Frederick Lowenfels
Secretary: David Meierfeld
Treasurer: Charles Cohen
President: Richard B. Levine
Executive Vice-President: Howard A. Gabler
Vice-President, Research & Education: Allen E. Abrahams

Hours of Business (trading):

Maine Potatoes	10:00 A.M. - 1:30 P.M.	
Idaho Potatoes	10:00 A.M. - 2:00 P.M.	
Long Island Potatoes	10:00 A.M. - 2:00 P.M.	
Butter (spot)	11:00 A.M. - 11:15 A.M.	(Fri. only)
Butter (future)	10:30 A.M. - 12:00 noon	
Imported Boneless Beef	10:15 A.M. - 1:45 P.M.	
Platinum	9:45 A.M. - 1:40 P.M.	
Palladium	10:20 A.M. - 12:55 P.M.	
U. S. Silver Coins	9:35 A.M. - 2:15 P.M.	
Nickel	11:15 A.M. - 2:15 P.M.	
Aluminum	10:30 A.M. - 1:30 P.M.	
Silver Dollars (spot)	12:00 noon - 1:00 P.M.	
Plywood	11:00 A.M. - 2:05 P.M.	
Apples	10:45 A.M. - 1:45 P.M.	

1. The majority of trading on the New York Mercantile Exchange is in Maine Potatoes, Platinum, U. S. Silver Coins, Palladium, Imported Boneless beef. Other futures contracts are less active.
2. The exchange will soon introduce trading in petroleum and charter tanker futures contracts. If they attract interest, other futures contracts will be made available to those interested in hedging or insuring against volatile price movements.
3. At press time for this Directory (May, 1974), the International Commodity Exchange was actively studying the following contracts with the objective, depending upon feasibility, of reintroducing in improved form: currencies, fishmeal, and cottonseed oil.

Regulatory Laws: The Commodity Exchange Act, enforced and supervised by the Commodity Exchange Authority of the United States Department of Agriculture. However, some futures contracts are not "regulated." Many are traded internationally; hence, they are not under the regulations of the United States Department of Agriculture.

Commodity Summary

Commodity	Contract	Min. Fluct.
Maine Pot.*	Car = 50,000 lb.	1c per 100 lb.
Idaho Pot.*	Car = 50,000 lb.	1c per 100 lb.
Long Is. Pot.*	Car = 50,000 lb.	1c per 100 lb.
Butter*	Pounds = 30,000	.0002½c per lb.
Imported Boneless Beef*	Pounds = 30,000	2c per 100 lb.

Platinum	Ounces = 50 Troy	10c per oz.	
Palladium	Ounces = 100 Troy	5c per oz.	
U. S. Silver	10 bags of	$1 per bag	
Coins	$1000 each		
Nickel	Pounds = 2000	¼c per lb.	
Aluminum	Pounds = 50,000	1/100c per lb.	
Spot Silver	$1000 face val.	$5 per contract	
Dollars			
Plywood	Square Feet = 70,000	10c per 1000 sq. Ft.	
Apples	Cartons = 840	1c per ctn.	

	Minimum Value Change		Max.
Commodity	Per Cont.	Per Sp Increment	Fluct.
Maine Pot.*	$5.00	$25.00	$250 a
Idaho Pot.*	$5.00	$25.00	$175 ab
Long Is. Pot.*	$5.00	$25.00	$175 ab
Butter*	$7.50	$30.00	$600
Imported Boneless Beef*	$6.00	$30.00	$450 c
Platinum	$5.00	$25.00	$500 a
Palladium	$5.00	$25.00	$400 ad
U.S. Silver Coins	$10.00	$50.00	$1500 a
Nickel	$5.00	$50.00	$500 ae
Aluminum	$5.00	$25.00	$500 af
Spot Silver Dollars	$5.00	——	None
Plywood	$7.00	$35.00	$420 a
Apples	$8.40	$42.00	$294 ag

*Regulated commodities
(a) no limit on last trading day
(b) $250 during delivery month
(c) $600 during delivery month
(d) $500 during delivery month
(e) $650 during delivery month
(f) $750 during delivery month
(g) $420 during delivery month

Delivery Dates

Commodity	Trading Terminates	Delivery Months
Maine Potatoes	5th bus. day of Month*	Jan., Nov., Mar., Apr., May
Idaho Potatoes	10th day of Month*	Jan., Mar., Apr., May, Nov.
Long Island Potatoes	14th day of month*	Sept., Oct., Nov., Dec.,

(Continued)

Profile Data

Commodity	Trading Terminates	Delivery Months
Butter (future)	14th day of month*	Mar., Oct., Dec.**
Imported Boneless Beef	15th day of month*	Jan., Mar., May, Jul., Sept., Nov.
Platinum	14th day of month*	Jan., Apr., Jul., Oct.
Palladium	14th day of month*	Mar., June, Sept., Dec.
U.S. Silver Coins	14th day of month*	Jan., Apr., Jul., Oct.
Nickel	10th day of month*	Feb., Apr., June, Aug., Oct., Dec.
Aluminum	3rd. bus. day prior to last bus. day of prev. month	Jan., Mar., May, Jul., Sept., Oct., Dec.
Plywood	last bus. day preceding spot month	Feb., Apr., June Aug., Oct., Dec.,
Apples	5th day of month*	Jan., Mar., May, Nov., Dec.

*on the first exchange business day immediately prior thereto
**or any other months decided by the Clearing House Committee

Volume: (no. of contracts traded):

Commodity	1973	1972	1971
Maine Potatoes*	695,678	244,277	151,369
Idaho Potatoes*	—	8	19
Eggs (shell)*	—	—	87
Imported Boneless Beef*	2,645	962	556
Platinum	147,802	159,272	112,413
Palladium	1,888	487	106
Silver Coins	89,978	26,429	17,985
Nickel	—	—	1
Aluminum	—	—	—
Plywood	—	4,020	9,581
Apples	—	—	—
	937,995	435,455	292,117

Commodity	1970	1969	1968
Maine Potatoes*	316,691	365,757	454,848
Idaho Potatoes*	119	535	—
Eggs (shell)*	26	—	—
Imported Boneless Beef*	—	—	—
Platinum	98,867	84,009	96,906

Palladium	757	10,870	42,636
Silver Coins	—	—	—
Nickel	382	—	—
Aluminum	2	—	—
Plywood	792	5,299	—
Apples	124	331	—
	417,760	466,619	594,390

*Regulated Commodities:

When volume is heavy, trading is done auction fashion, by open outcry, in a pit, or ring; when volume is light to moderate, blackboard trading is employed. Each trading method has its own rules.

Memberships:

1. No. of members: membership is authorized at 500.
   a. clearing members are permitted to deal directly with the exchange in settling trades.
   b. non-clearing members must settle their own trades through a clearing member.
   c. membership assessments and clearing fees are used for employees' salaries, maintenance and operating necessities.

2. Membership Prices:

Year	High .	Low	Year	High	Low
1968	$40,000	$18,500	1971	12,000	4,150
1969	46,000	25,000	1972	10,000	7,000
1970	35,000	7,100	1973	14,000	7,000

As of January 1, 1974, seats were quoted $10,000 bid, offered at $11,300. The last sale was $11,300 on January 22, 1974.

Margins and Commissions:

1.		Maine Potatoes :x 74 only	Platinum	Palladium
Margins				
Customer	$800	:$400	$1500	$800
Clearing Member	$500	:$250	$1000	$600
Extra Margins	$125		$500	$600
Straddle		K74, x 74,H,J,K 75 and Two Crop Yr		
Customer		:$400	$300	$150
Clearing Member		:$250	$200	$150
Floor Brokerage Fees	$2.00 $1/buy & sell on spread		$3.00	$2.50

(Continued)

Margins	Maine Potatoes	Platinum		Palladium
Clearing Fees				
Cust. Day				$ .50
Cust. Ovrnt	**	Included	**	$1.00
House Day		in		$ .12½
House Ovrnt		Commission		$ .50
Commission (Mem./Non-Mem.)				
Round Turn	$15/30	$22.50/ 45		to $59.95 $20/40 $60.00/ & over $25/50
Day Trade	$10/15+	$11.25/ 22.50		to $59.95 $10/20+ $60.00 & over $12.50/25+
Day Clear.	$2.00	$2.75		$2.50
Pass Outs	$1.25	$1.25		$1.00
Spreads	$15/30	$22.50/45		to $59.95 $20/40 $60.00 & over $25/50
Roll Over	$7.50/15.00	$11.25/ 22.50		to $59.95 $10/20 $60.00 & over $12.50/25

Margins	Spot Silver Dollar	Coins	Beef
Customer	——	$3000	$1200
Clearing Member	——	$2500	$1000
Extra Margins	——	750 Cust 600 House	$200
Straddle			
Customer	——	$150	$600
Clearing Member	——	$100	$500
Floor Brokerage Fees	$2.00	$2.00	$2.50
			Beef

		**	Only
Clearing Fees			
Cust. Day	——	Included	$ .75
Cust. Ovrnt	$2.00	in	$1.50
House Day		Comm.	$ .12½
House Ovrnt			$ .75
Commission (Mem./Non-Mem.)			
Round Turn	$25/50	$17.50/35	$20*/40
Day Trade	——	$8.75/17.50+	$10/20+
Day Clear	——	$2.75	$2.00
Pass Outs	——	$1.25	$1.25
Spreads	——	$17.50/35	$20*/40
Roll Over	——	$8.75/17.50	$10/20

Ten Day Brokerage Rate = one-half (½) rate for qualified floor traders within ten (10) days.

* Ten Day Brokerage Rate = one-quarter (¼) rate for qualified floor traders within ten (10) days.

\+ Applies when two or more contracts are bought and sold on the same day.

** Clearing Fees (included in comm.) Cust. Day $.50, Custo. Ovrnt $1.00, House Day $.12½, House Ovrnt $.50.

2.

	Idaho Pot.	L. I. Pot.	Rice	Nickel
Margins				
Customer	$300	$3.00 or less $200 $3.01-3.50 $250 $3.51-4.00 $300	$8.00 or less $600 $8.01-9.00 $700 $9.01-10.00 $800	$300
Member	$200	$200	$600	$300
Extra			Double	
Margins	$150	$125	existing margin	$300
Straddle				
Customer	$150	$100	$300	$100
Member	$100	$100	$300	$100
Floor	$2.00			If comm.
Brokerage	$1/buy & sell on spread	$1.25	$2.00	$40- $2
Fees				If comm. $50 - $3

(Continued)

Margins	Idaho Pot.	L. I. Pt.	Rice	Nickel
Clearing Fees				
Cust. Day	Included	$.50	$.50	$.50
Cust. Ovrnt	in	$1.00	$1.00	$1.00
House Day	Commission	$.12½	$.12½	$.12½
House Ovrnt		$.50	$.50	$.50
Commission (Mem./ Non-Mem.)				
Round Turn	$15/30	$10.50/21	$25/50	to $3.99 $20/40 $4.00+ $25/50
Day Trade	$10/15	$6/10/50	$12.50/25	$12.50/25
Day Clear.	$2.00	$1.75	$3.75	$2.50
Pass Outs	$1.25	$1.00	$1.00	$1.00
Spreads	$12.50/25	$10.50/21	$25/50	$20/40
Roll Over	$6.25/12.50	——	——	$10/20

	Aluminum	Apples	Spot Silver Dollar
Margins			
Customer	$500	$400	——
Member	$500	$300	——
Extra Margins Straddle		$150	
Customer	——	$200	——
Member	——	$200	——
Floor Brokerage Fees	$2.00	$2.00	$2.00
Clearing Fees			
Cust. Day	$.50	$.50	.——
Cust. Ovrnt	$1.00	$1.00	$2.00
House Day	$.12½	$.12½	——
House Ovrnt	$.50	$.50	$2.00
Commission (Mem./ Non-Mem.)			
Round Turn	$25/50	$12.50/25	$25/50
Day Trade	$12.50/25	$7/11.50	——
Day Clear.	$2.00	$1.75	——
Pass Outs	$1.00	$1.00	——
Spreads	$35/70	$12.50/25	——
Roll Over	——	$6.25/12.50	——

Historical Background:

1872 New York butter and cheese merchants met and agreed upon the necessity to establish an organization of the trade that would "guard and protect the interests of all . . ."

1873 The merchants formally organized the Butter and Cheese Exchange of New York (June 5), with headquarters in the Stuart Building, corner of Greenwich and Reade Streets. It was resolved to provide a fund of $1 million to erect an exchange. All trading at that time was for "spot" delivery.

1875 Butter and Cheese Exchange changed name to American Exchange of New York.

1880 Exchange changed name to Butter, Cheese and Egg Exchange.

1882 The exchange adopted its present title — New York Mercantile Exchange.

1886 Mercantile Exchange moved into its present headquarters, corner of Harrison and Hudson Streets.

1941 Trading began in Maine potato futures in December. Prior to this most of the activity was in eggs.

1961 New York Mercantile Exchange created the National Stock Exchange, located in the New York Mercantile Exchange building on Harrison Street. Mercantile Exchange membership permits members to join the National Stock Exchange additionally for a nominal sum.

1971 Trading began in U. S. silver coins and imported beef futures.

1974 In April, the Mercantile Exchange announced plans to initiate futures dealings in international petroleum products and tanker freight contracts. The new contracts will involve four basic items: heavy industrial fuel oil; the lighter heating or "gas oil" used in large buildings and factories and two charter tanker rates — from the Persian Gulf to Rotterdam and from the Persian Gulf to Aruba in the Caribbean.

WOOL ASSOCIATES OF THE NEW YORK COTTON EXCHANGE, INC.

Title: Wool Associates of the New York Cotton Exchange, Inc.

Address: 37 Wall Street, New York, New York 10005

Telephone: (212) 269 - 7880

Officers:
President: Gedney H. Baldwin
First Vice President: Clayton B. Jones, Jr.
Second Vice President: Malcolm A. Fellman
Treasurer: Lawrence M. Arre
Secretary: Horace D. Wood
Assistant Secretary: J. William Donaghy

Delivery Months: March, May, July, October and December

Trading Units: 6,000 pounds

Fluctuation:
  a. Minimum .10 cents per pound ($6.00 per contract)
  b. Maximum 10 cents per pound in advance or decline except on and after the eighth day of the current month when there is no limit

Standards: Standard 64's quality 2-¾ inches in length, with deviations and allowances as established by the Exchange.

Delivery Points: From Exchange licensed warehouses in the following areas: Greater Boston, Mass.; Charleston, S. C.; Columbus, Ohio; Minneapolis, Minn.; Kansas City, Mo.; San Angelo, Texas; Salt Lake City, Utah; Craig, Colorado; Rawlings, Wyoming; San Francisco-Stockton, California

Trading Hours: 10:00 A.M. to 2:30 P.M. (New York Time)

Volume of Trading:

1965	35,250 contracts	1970	4,016 contracts
1966	32,370 contracts	1971	3,458 contracts
1967	17,750 contracts	1972	3,735 contracts
1968	11,362 contracts	1973	4,693 contracts
1969	6,225 contracts		

Memberships: 450 Class A members (Members of the New York Cotton Exchange). 100 Class B Members. The value of Associate Memberships is about $200.00.

Commissions: Please see Citrus Associates of the New York Cotton Exchange, Inc.

SAN FRANCISCO

PACIFIC COMMODITIES EXCHANGE

Title: Pacific Commodities Exchange, Inc.

Address: 315 Montgomery Street, San Francisco, California 94104

Telephone: (415) 398 - 1000

Officers:
  President and Chief Executive Officer: Nathan Most
  Chief Operating Officer and Treasurer: Raymond F. Abeling
  Director of Marketing and Public Relations and Assistant Secretary: Larissa Nicolayev

Hours of Business:
  1. 7:00 A.M. - 4:00 P.M.
  2. See Trading Hours.

Regulatory Laws: Regulated by the Commodity Exchange Authority, U.S. Department of Agriculture.

Commodities Traded: Western Live Cattle, Western Shell Eggs, Crude Coconut Oil, Silver.

Contract Details:
1. Western Live Cattle
   a. Quantity: The par delivery quantity shall be 50,000 pounds after a shrink-age allowance of 4% and, if necessary, an appropriate allowance for caked on mud as determined by the Official Grader (s). The weight after allowances for shrinkage and mud must be between 47,000 and 53,000 pounds.
   b. Average Weight: The average weight of the steers comprising the delivery unit must be between 925 and 1,075 pounds. No individual steer may deviate from the average weight per head of the delivery unit by more than 100 pounds. Individual steers weighing less than 875 pounds or more than 1,125 pounds shall not be deliverable.
   c. Quality Grade: Delivery units containing steers below the top half of the USDA Good grade shall not be acceptable. Units containing less than 50% USDA Choice or better steers shall not be accepted. Steers in the top half of the USDA Good grade in excess of 40% of the animals in the delivery unit, but not exceeding 50% of the animals in the delivery unit, shall be acceptable at a discount of 2 cents per pound. A premium of 1 cent per pound shall be paid for USDA Choice or better steers in excess of 75% of the animals in the delivery unit. The cattle shall be graded in accordance with the official USDA standards prevailing at the time of delivery. Steers must be healthy and merchantable.
   d. Yield Grade: Steers with estimated USDA yield grade numbers of 4 and 5 shall be discounted 3 cents per pound.
2. Western Shell Eggs
   a. Quantity: Deviation in quantity of a delivery unit not in excess of 5% over or under 750 - 30 dozen cases shall be permitted with appropriate adjustment of the settlement amount to reflect the delivered quantity but with no penalty. Determination of adjustments because of any such deviations shall be based on the settlement price on the last trading day preceding the day of delivery of the eggs. No partial cases shall be allowed.
   b. Lot Size: The delivery unit shall consist of from 1 to 3 lots, each of which shall contain no less than 200 cases.
   c. Average Weight: The weight requirements and allowances specified herein shall be applied individually to each lot in the delivery unit, and if any lot fails to meet such requirement, the entire unit shall fail inspection. The average net weight required for par delivery shall be a minimum of 48 pounds per case. Lots having average weights per case of 46 to 48 pounds shall be discounted ½c/dozen (15c/case) for each ½ pound or fraction thereof by which the average weight falls below 48 pounds per case.
   Lots having average weights per case of less than 46 pounds or more than 52 pounds per case shall not be acceptable. No individual sample case test weighed shall deviate from the average weight of the sample cases in the lot by more than 2 pounds.
   d. Grade: The eggs shall be U.S. Nest Run 20% AA Quality or better and

must be at least 90% A and AA Quality. These requirements must be met individually by each lot in the delivery unit.

    e. Oil Treatment: The eggs shall be oil treated.

3. Crude Coconut Oil (grades deliverable) Crude Coconut Oil produced either in the United States or abroad and conforming to the following specifications:

    a. Maximum 6% free fatty acid as oleic.

    b. Maximum ¼% moisture and impurities.

    c. Guaranteed to be unadulterated and free from any substance unnatural to crude coconut oil.

4. Silver: The contract grades for delivery on futures contracts shall be refined silver in bars cast in basic weights of 1,000 or 1,100 Troy ounces (each bar may vary no more than 10% more or less); assaying not less than 999 fineness; and made up of one or more brands and markings officially listed and approved by the exchange. Only whole bars may be delivered. A Notice of Intention to Deliver must be tendered to the exchange not later than 10:00 A.M. Pacific Time one business day prior to the day of actual delivery. Delivery may be made on any business day of the contract month, except the last eight.

	Live Cattle	Shell Eggs
Trading Hours*	7:05 A.M. - 11:30 A.M.	7:15 A.M. - 11:05 A.M.
Delivery Months	Feb., Apr., June, Aug., Oct., Dec.	All Months
Trading Units	50,000 lbs. of live steers	750 cases of 30 dozen eggs each
Price Quotations	Cents per lb.	Cents per doz.
Minimum Fluctuations	2/100th of one cent per lb.	5/100th of one cent per doz.

	Coconut Oil	Silver
Trading Hours*	7:30 A.M. - 11:15 A.M.	7:00 A.M. - 11:45 A.M.
Delivery Months	Jan., Mar., May, July, Sept., Nov., Dec.	Any month as determined by P.C.E.
Trading Units	60,000 lbs, equivalent of a standard size tank car.	1,000 Troy ozs.
Price Quotations	Cents per pound	10/100 of one cent per Troy oz.
Minimum Fluctuations	1/100th of one cent per lb.	10/100 of one cent per Troy oz.

    * Pacific Time

Position and Trading Limits:

1. Western Live Cattle: No person shall hold or control more than 300 contracts in any delivery month, or more than 300 contracts net long or net short in all delivery months combined, and no person shall buy or sell during a single business day more than 450 contracts in all delivery months combined.

2. Western Shell Eggs: No person shall hold or control more than 150 contracts in any delivery month or more than 150 contracts net long or net short in all delivery months combined, and no person shall buy or sell on one business day more than 150 contracts in any one delivery month or in all delivery months combined.

3. Crude Coconut Oil: 125 contracts of 60,000 lbs. in any one futures, and 320 contracts in total in all futures combined, with certain exceptions. A position of 25 contracts is a reportable position. Prices may not fluctuate more than 100 points or 1 cent above or below the previous day's settlement price. However, there are no limits within the current delivery month after the first notice day.

4. Silver

    a. No person shall hold or control more than 500 contracts in any delivery month, or more than 500 contracts net long or short in all delivery months combined, and no person shall buy or sell on one business day more than 500 contracts net in any one delivery month, or in all delivery months combined, unless authorized by the exchange. These limits shall not be construed to apply to bonafide hedging transactions or positions, nor to spreads against silver contracts on the Chicago Board of Trade or the New York Commodity Exchange, Inc.

    b. Daily limits on price movements shall be as set by the Board of Directors. Limits in this contract shall be 25 cents per Troy ounce above or below the settlement price on the previous business day, until changed under Rule 632. These provisions shall not apply to trading in the current month on or after the first notice day thereof.

    c. Exchange of cash silver for futures shall be permitted as prescribed in Rule 620.

Last Trading Day: No trading shall be conducted in the current delivery month during the last seven business days of that month for Live Cattle and Coconut Oil. For Shell Eggs the time period is the last ten business days; for Silver the last eight business days.

Memberships: Since the P.C.E. is a publicly held corporation, membership is by ownership of shares rather than by ownership of a "seat." The exchange presently has about 82 Trading Members and 7 Clearing Members. Membership requirements are as follows:

Class of Membership	Regular	Trading	Clearing
Ownership in P.C.E. shares	2	2	8
Working Capital	-	$50,000	$200,000 - Clear own trade only $500,000 - Clear trades for others

(Continued)

Class of Membership	Regular	Trading	Clearing
Initiation Fee	$100	$ 500	$2,200
Annual Membership Fee	$ 50	$ 150	$ 300

P.C.E. shares are traded on the over-the-counter market. They are known to have traded recently at $3,000 per share.

Clearing Fees, Commissions, Margins:

1. The exchange charges $2.50 per contract bought or sold for a floor trader trading for his own account and $5.00 per contract bought or sold for all others. The P.C.E. does not set commissions; thus, they are negotiated.
2. Margin requirements shall be as determined by regulations issued by the exchange. Consultation with a broker is admissable.

Historical Background:

1970 The Pacific Commodities Exchange was incorporated October 26. It is the only publicly-held commodities exchange in the world.

1972 Trading in crude coconut oil began October 31.

1973 Trading in western shell eggs began February 21. Trading in western live cattle began October 31.

1974 Trading in silver began in July.

STOCK EXCHANGES

LISTING REQUIREMENTS OF
MAJOR AMERICAN STOCK EXCHANGES

The requirements of the Securities and Exchange Commission are basically the same for all U. S. exchanges. Those of the individual exchanges differ widely —usually according to the size of the exchange. However, all exchanges stipulate that prompt and full disclosure be made of any changes in the general character of the company's business, the form and nature of its listed securities, accounting policies, amendments to its charter or by-laws, etc.

Listed companies must agree also to abide by the rules and regulations of the exchange involved and to keep it informed and up-to-date respecting all notices and reports sent to the holders of its securities.

Since the following are only brief "guidelines" to a stock exchange listing, it is suggested that contact be made directly with the exchange itself for more complete and detailed information. It should be emphasized too that the exchanges may at any time suspend or delist a security, which fails to meet certain standards set by the exchange or adhere to the listing agreement.

American Stock Exchange

1. Shares publicly held: 400,000, of which 150,000 must be in 100 to 500-share lots.
2. Market value publicly held shares: $3 million.
3. Number of stockholders: 1,200 including 800 holders of round-lots, of which 500 must be holders of 100 to 500-share lots.

4. Net income last fiscal year (pre-tax): $750,000
5. Net income last fiscal year (after all charges): $400,000
6. Net tangible assets: $4 million

Boston Stock Exchange
(guidelines only)

1. Shares publicly held: 250,000 outstanding; 100,000 floating;
2. Market value publicly held shares: $300,000;
3. Number of stockholders: 500;
4. Reported net income in 2 or 3 prior years;
5. Total assets: $1 million.

Cincinnati Stock Exchange

"The Cincinnati Stock Exchange has no set requirements for the listing of companies. Each company is judged individually by the Board of Trustees. Therefore, we can only state that companies desiring to list on the Exchange must make application in such form as prescribed by the Board of Trustees and shall be approved only upon recommendation or opinion of the Stock Listing Committee. Final decision rests with the discretion of the Board of Trustees."

Detroit Stock Exchange

According to the Exchange: "In the early days of the Exchange transactions were in securities regional in nature. Today the Exchange presents to investors a list of 300 nationally-known companies representing every important line of industry.

"Companies desiring to have their shares listed must make application to the Committee on Stock List. The applicant company must meet the high standards established by the Committee and furnish financial statements and information of its operation and management. These documents can then be made available to the public through the medium of the Exchange."

Honolulu Stock Exchange

The requirements of this exchange for listing are fairly simple. All applications must be made on the Listing Application, which requests information about the amount of each class of securities covered by the application and formal titles or designations of the securities plus the name of any other stock exchange upon which the securities covered by the application are listed.

The applicant must forward to the exchange a copy of its annual report to stockholders and a copy of all notices sent to stockholders. The company must agree also to comply with all applicable rules and regulations of the exchange covering issues of listed securities.

When the requirements of the exchange and those of the Securities and

Exchange Commission have been met, the application is referred to the Listing Committee for their recommendation. A majority vote of the members is necessary for final approval of listing.

The rules of the exchange provide that no fee will be charged for listing of a security, but do provide for an annual "carrying charge." The carrying charge is currently $200 for a single issue and $100 for each additional issue of preferred stock or bonds. The carrying charge is payable in advance the first of each year and shall be pro-rated quarterly if the security is listed after the first quarter.

Intermountain Stock Exchange

1. Market value of the outstanding stock of each company must be at least $100,000;
2. Market value of the stock held by other than "control" persons must be at least $50,000;
3. Minimum number of stockholders: 200 holders of round-lots.

Midwest Stock Exchange

1. Net tangible assets: $2 million, minimum;
2. 250,000 shares or more outstanding of the common or preferred stock to be listed, including "control" holdings;
3. Dually listed stocks (general guide): 3 million shares publicly held, and about 10,000 stockholders to gain all the benefits of a dual listing;
4. If the stock sells below $15 per share, outstanding shares should be owned by about 1,000 stockholders. In the price range of $15 to $50, it is advisable to have 1,500 holders; from $50 to $100, 2,500; and above $100, in excess of 3,000 stockholders.
   These amounts should be weighed in the light of type of issue, current activity over-the-counter, and in consideration of near future secondary distributions, stock splits and/or new under-writings;
5. The company must be actively engaged in business and have been so operating for at least three consecutive years;
6. The exchange must be satisfied a) that the company's working capital is adequate; b) that the management is competent and reputable; c) that net earnings will total at least $100,000 annually; and d) that the company will publish periodic reports.

National Stock Exchange

Latest information on listing requirements of this exchange were not received by press time and readers are therefore advised to contact the National Stock Exchange directly.

New York Stock Exchange
(Initial Requirements*)

1. Demonstrated earning power under competitive conditions of $2.5 million before Federal income taxes for the most recent year and $2 million pre-tax for each of the preceding two years;
2. Net tangible assets of $16 million, but greater emphasis will be placed on the aggregate market value of the common stock;
3. A total of $16 million in market value of publicly held common stock;
4. A total of 1,000,000 common shares publicly held;
5. 2,000 holders of 100 shares or more.

   *Effective since July 13, 1971

Note: On July 11, 1974 the New York Stock Exchange announced that it was proposing to boost its listing-fees.

Pacific Stock Exchange

Common Stock:
1 . At least 250,000 shares issued and outstanding and a minimum market value of issued and outstanding shares of $1 million, excluding "control" holdings; and a minimum price per share of $2 for at least six months prior to the date of application;
2 . 750 stockholders, minimum;
3*. Demonstrated earning power of $200,000 annually before taxes for two prior years, excluding non-recurring income;
4*. Total net tangible assets of $1 million;
5*. Stockholder approval be obtained for:
   a. Options or remuneration plans substantially affecting rights of share-holders;
   b. Change in control of company; and
   c. Acquisitions:
      1. Direct or indirect, from a director, officer or substantial security holder;
      2. Potential issuance of a security resulting in a 20% increase of the outstanding common stock; or
      3. Consideration paid has fair value of 20% market value of outstanding common stock.
* These requirements are applicable when listing warrants, preferred stock and similar issues, and bonds.

PBW Stock Exchange

Securities on the PBW Stock Exchange are listed or unlisted.
A listed security indicates that the corporation it represents has taken the initiative in requesting the exchange to permit its securities to be traded. The corporation makes a formal application to the exchange and promises to abide by certain rules; filing annual financial statements and others.

In the case of unlisted securities, the exchange itself takes the initiative. If there is sufficient interest in a security that is listed on another exchange the PBW may request the Securities and Exchange Commission and the corporation involved to allow the security to be traded on the exchange. If they comply the security is then traded in the same way as a listed security.

CANADIAN - UNITED STATES STOCK EXCHANGES
(Volume - Value, 1972)

EXCHANGE	SHARE VOLUME	DOLLAR VALUE
New York Stock Exchange	4,593,898,615	$160,177,579,947
American Stock Exchange	1,188,062,120	21,379,252,734
Vancouver Stock Exchange	906,053,892	784,102,576
Toronto Stock Exchange	635,885,589	6,258,151,656
Montreal Stock Exchange	330,125,289	2,057,293,935
Pacific Stock Exchange	269,201,659	8,126,060,118
Midwest Stock Exchange	230,641,870	8,434,018,760
PBW Stock Exchange	144,496,426	5,282,478,456
Boston Stock Exchange	38,604,763	1,562,881,575
National Stock Exchange	15,911,808	112,447,878
Calgary Stock Exchange	12,208,365	6,492,516
Detroit Stock Exchange	9,843,967	362,790,491
Spokane Stock Exchange	9,257,970	4,498,135
Intermountain Stock Exchange	3,841,433	2,325,808
Cincinnati Stock Exchange	2,353,776	103,445,483
Honolulu Stock Exchange	565,490	3,989,676
Winnipeg Stock Exchange	521,025	840,634
TOTAL	**8,391,474,057**	**$214,658,650,378**

BOSTON

BOSTON STOCK EXCHANGE

Title: Boston Stock Exchange

Address: 53 State Street, Boston, Massachusetts 02109, U.S.A.

Telephone: 617 - 723 - 9500

Branches and Affiliates:

Boston Stock Exchange Clearing Corporation
53 State Street, Boston, Massachusetts 02109
Boston Stock Exchange Service Corporation
53 State Street, Boston, Massachusetts 02109

Officers:
Chairman of the Board: Vincent M. Cantella
Vice-Chairman of the Board: Theodor Schmidt-Scheuber
President: James E. Dowd
Executive Vice-President and Treasurer: Robert E. Hallagan
Secretary: Walter E. Cummings
Assistant Secretary: Connie L. Murphy
Assistant Treasurer: Thomas E. Roberts

Hours of Business: 10:00 A.M. - 3:30 P.M. (weekdays)

Regulatory Laws: Supervised and enforced by the Securities and Exchange Commission.

Issues Traded and Volume:

1. Issues Traded:

Year	No. Issues	Year	No. Issues
1963	421	1969	523
1964	418	1970	610
1965	413	1971	656
1966	462	1972	788
1967	505	1973*	830
1968	530		

   * As of June 30

2. Volume:

Year	No. Shares	Year	No. Shares
1963	5,504,418	1969	23,872,722
1964	5,835,576	1970	20,990,395
1965	7,032,273	1971	26,493,334
1966	13,381,796	1972	38,471,536
1967	21,263,566	1973*	40,800,000
1968	42,406,072		

   * As of December 31

Unit of Trading:

1. Number of shares: 100
2. a. Odd-lots are executed on the basis of the next completed round-lot transaction that occurs on the exchange where the primary market for the stock exists.

   b. Every odd-lot order is time stamped immediately upon its receipt on the floor of the exchange and transmitted directly to the odd-lot dealer. The dealer waits two minutes from the recorded time of receipt and, if the ticker tape which records the primary market transactions is on time, the next regular-way sale of the stock to appear on the tape is regarded as the next round-lot transaction. Two minutes is determined as the average normal time elapsing between the entering of an order in Boston, its transmittal to the exchange where the primary market exists and the printing of that transaction by the ticker.

   c. If the ticker tape happens to be late in recording transactions, such lateness is added to the normal two minutes in determining the next completed round-lot transaction.

   d. The differential, or fee, charged by the odd-lot dealer for executing an odd-lot order is ⅛ point. It is added to the execution price on orders to buy and subtracted from it on orders to sell.

Membership:

Year	Regular Members	Associate Members	Pref. Rate Non-Member Access and "Other" Members	Membership Prices
1963	95	242	——	$ 1,200
1964	95	245	——	2,000
1965	93	253	——	3,800
1966	100	230	——	11,500
1967	100	231	——	12,500
1968	101	216	——	24,500
1969	163	256	——	14,000
1970	180	275	——	14,000
1971	189	278	15	10,000
1972	193	305	110	5,000
1973	197	288	145	3,900

Commissions or Fees:

1. Stocks, rights, warrants (rates to Non-Members and Associate Members):
   a. on each 100 share order:

Amount involved in order	Minimum Commission
Above $2,000-but under $2,500	1.3% of money involved + $12
$2,500-but above	0.9% of money involved + $22

   Notwithstanding the foregoing:
   - i. When the amount involved in an order is $2,000 or less, the minimum commission is as mutually agreed.
   - ii. The minimum commission on an order for 100 shares shall not exceed $65.00.

   b. On each multiple round-lot order for 200 shares or more:

Amount involved in order	Minimum Commission
Above $2,000-but under $2,500	1.3% of money involved + $ 12
$2,500-but under $20,000	0.9% of money involved + $ 22
$20,000-but under $30,000	0.6% of money involved + $ 82
$30,000-to and including $300,000	0.4% of money involved + $142

   Plus a charge for each round-lot of 100 shares within the order as follows:
   First to tenth round-lot . . . . $6.00 per round-lot
   Eleventh round-lot and above . . . . $4.00 per round-lot
   Notwithstanding the foregoing:
   - i. When the amount involved in an order is $2,000 or less, the minimum commission shall be as mutually agreed.
   - ii. The minimum commission per round-lot shall not exceed the single round-lot commission computed in accordance with the provisions of paragraph 1a.

   c. On any odd-lot order, commissions are based on the amount involved in the order and shall not be less than the rates specified in paragraph 1a., less $2.00.

Notwithstanding the foregoing:
   i. When the commission involved in an odd-lot order is $2,000 or less, the minimum commission shall be as mutually agreed.
   ii. The minimum commission on an odd-lot order shall not exceed $65.00.
   iii. When one or more odd-lot orders plus one or more round-lot orders are executed in the same security, on the same day, for the same account, on the same side of the market, the commission(s) on such odd-lot order(s) shall not exceed the commission which would be chargeable with respect to the nearest round-lot in excess of such odd-lot order(s).
   d. Stocks below $1 per share: on that portion of an order involving an amount of $300,000 or less, on stocks selling below $1.00 per share, commissions shall be based upon the amount involved in the order and shall not be less than the rates hereinafter specified:

Amount involved in order	Minimum Commission
Above $2,000-but under $10,000	5.0% of money involved + $ 34.00
$10,000-and above	4.0% of money involved + $134.00

Notwithstanding the foregoing, when the amount involved in an order is $2,000 or less, the commission shall be as mutually agreed.
   2. Corporate Bonds (rates to non-members):

Price per $1,000 of Principal	Rates per $1,000 of Principal
Selling at less than $10	$ .75
Selling at $10 and above but under $100	1.25
Selling at $100 and above	2.50

Historical Background:

1834 Thirteen men organized a voluntary association for the orderly trading of securities.

1885 The Boston Stock Exchange became the first exchange to initiate a continuous auction market, replacing the "call system."

1888 Boston Stock Exchange was the first exchange to give publicity to its transactions at a time when financial statements and financial services were non-existent.

1892 The exchange provided a clearing house as part of its operation to help reduce money requirements for daily settlements and to minimize the loss of securities delivered between offices.

1911 The exchange moved into its present location in the Exchange Building at 53 State Street.

1942 The Boston Stock Exchange Clearing Corporation as a separate entity was incorporated in 1942, as a wholly-owned subsidiary of the exchange.

1965 A full-time non-member president was hired to improve floor operations and attract new members to the exchange.

1968 German-American Securities Corporation joined the exchange and thus became the first foreign member admitted to any United States stock exchange.

1969 First and only exchange to provide securities custodial services for its members.
1971 Boston Stock Exchange became first U.S. exchange to give representation on its board of Governors to listed companies.

CHICAGO

CHICAGO BOARD OPTIONS EXCHANGE

Title: Chicago Board Options Exchange, Inc.

Address: 141 W. Jackson Boulevard, Chicago, Illinois 60604

Telephone: (312) 939 - 4020

Subsidiary: Chicago Board Options Exchange Clearing Corporation, 141 W. Jackson Boulevard, Chicago, Illinois 60604
Telephone: (312) 939 - 4020
Officers:
  President: Wayne P. Luthringshausen
  Executive Vice-President: Fred D. Casey
  Vice-President: Jack L. Pecot

Officers:
  President: Joseph W. Sullivan
  Executive Vice-President, Secretary & Counsel: Jerry W. Markham
  Vice-President: Richard R. Cowles
  Vice-President: Douglas K. Traynor
  Treasurer: Robert E. Burmeister

Hours of Business (trading): 9:00 A.M. - 2:30 P.M.

Regulatory Laws: Securities Exchange Act of 1933; Securities Exchange Act of 1934.

Classes of Options: 32 on December 31, 1973, versus 16 on April 26, 1973 when the exchange opened. Options expire on the last Monday of January, April, July, October. Exercise ("striking") prices are set at the round dollar figure approximating the price of the underlying stock at the time the option is introduced for trading.

Volume: Number of contracts traded, April 26 through December 31, 1973: 1,119,488. One contract covers 100 shares of the underlying stock. Contracts are not written on odd-lots. Highest single-day volume in 1973 was 17,188 contracts covering 1.7 million shares on October 29.

Memberships:
  1. Regular Members: 526
  2. Membership Prices: $10,000 prior to April 26, 1973. As of December 31, 1973: bid $25,000; asked $27,500.

Commissions: The following minimum commissions are charged by members to their non-member customers on the purchase or writing of an option and on the exercise of an option with respect to that portion of an order involving not more than $30,000. (On that portion of an order involving an amount over $30,000, and with respect to orders aggregating under $100, the commission shall be as agreed between the customer and his broker).

1. Orders for the purchase, sale or exercise of a single option.

Money involved in the order	Minimum Commission
$ 100 - 2,499	1.3% plus $12
2,500 - 4,777	0.9% plus 22
4,778 - 29,999	65

2. Orders for the purchase, sale or exercise of multiple options:

Money involved in the order	Minimum Commission
$ 100 - 2,499	1.3% plus $12
2,500 - 19,999	0.9% plus 22
20,000 - 29,999	0.6% plus 82

Plus:

First to tenth option covered by the order: $6 per option.

Eleventh option and over covered by the order: $4 per option.

Notwithstanding the foregoing, the minimum commissions on a single option order involving over $100 and under $30,000 shall not be less than $25 nor more than $65, and the minimum commission per single option within a multiple option order shall not be more than the commission applicable to that option if it were in a single option order.

The following example illustrates the minimum commission charges imposed by exchange members upon their non-member customers. In a transaction where an option covering 100 shares of XYZ stock at an exercise price of $100 per share is purchased by A and written by B at a premium of $1,200 (which A pays to B), A and B must each pay their respective brokers a minimum commission of $27.60 (1.3% of $1,200 plus $12). Should either A or B subsequently liquidate his position in a closing transaction, another commission will have to be paid by him based upon the dollar amount of the premium involved in the closing transaction. Should A exercise the option, paying $10,000 for the 100 shares of XYZ, both A and the writer who is assigned the exercise notice will be required to pay their respective brokers a minimum commission of $65.

The non-member commissions discussed above are minimum commissions, and exchange members may charge their non-member customers commissions which are higher than these minimums. Customers are advised to determine from their brokers the actual commissions which will be charged in connection with options transactions. In addition to these non-member commissions, the rules of the exchange also provide minimum commissions which are charged for floor brokerage clearing services in transactions between members.

Historical Background:

1973 The first exchange in the United States for trading options on securities opened, April 26—the Chicago Board Options Exchange. Volume for May (first full month of operation) averaged 1,600 contracts daily covering 160,000 shares. December daily volume averaged 10,000 contracts covering 1 million shares. Chicago Board options are registered securities under the Securities Act of 1933. The Chicago Board Options Exchange Clearing Corporation, a subsidiary, is the issuer and obligor of every Chicago Board option.

MIDWEST STOCK EXCHANGE

Title: Midwest Stock Exchange, Incorporated.

Address: 120 South LaSalle Street, Chicago, Illinois, 60603.

Telephone: (312) 368-2222

Teletype: TWX 312 - 222 - 9512 and 312 - 222 - 9513

Branches and Affiliates:
1. Midwest Stock Exchange, Incorporated: New York Center, 160 Water Street, New York, N.Y. 10038
2. Midwest Stock Exchange, Incorporated: Mercantile Building, 1802 Main Street, Dallas, Texas 75201

Officers:
President: Michael E. Tobin
Executive Vice-Presidents:
    Laurence J. Barr (Marketing and Planning)
    David R. Rubin (Member Services)
    John G. Weithers (Governmental and Member Affairs)
Senior Vice-President & Secretary: Ralph H. Yount, (Floor Department)
Senior Vice-President & Treasurer: R. Thomas Rehwald, (Administration and Finance)
Senior Vice-Presidents:
    Albert M. Anderson, Jr. (Clearing)
    James E. Rushing (Computer Operations)
Vice-President & Controller: George V. Jonscher
Vice-President & Counsel: Kenneth L. Rosenblum
Vice-Presidents:
    A. Jerald Boehm (Marketing)
    Allan A. Bretzer (Floor Operations)
    Lawrence V. Conway (Training)
    Bryan P. Coughlin, Jr. (Regulatory Planning & Development)
    Lloyd W. Gravengaard (Marketing)
    Richard F. Kearns (N.Y. City Operations)
    James P. O'Donnell (Marketing)
    Donald L. Quinn (National Systems)
    Henry S. Roberts (Brokerage Systems)
    George A. Roper (Programming)
    Barry R. Rundle (Clearing Operations)
    Patrick E. Ryan (Signet 80 Communications)
    Richard D. Sbarbaro (Communications Administration)
    Theodore W. Seweloh (Marketing)
    Claude A. Thomas (Marketing)

Robert W. Thompson (Back Office Accounting Training)
Raymond F. Travaglio (Personnel Services)
Assistant Secretary: Loretta Kemp
Public Relations Counsel: E. Gene Lewis
Hours of Business: 9:00 A.M. - 2:30 P.M.
Regulatory Laws: Stock Exchange Act of 1933; Securities and Exchange Act of 1934.
Issues Traded and Volume:

	1. No. of Issues	2. No. of Shares Traded
1960	456	31,290,000
1965	520	68,701,000
1966	482	85,447,000
1967	478	110,751,000
1968	487	145,076,000
1969	595	148,590,000
1970	665	147,480,000
1971	672	206,630,000
1972	742	235,823,000
1973	711	238,140,000

Unit of Trading:
1. 100 shares.
2. Odd-lots: Specialists in dual system issues also act as odd-lot dealers. Odd-lots are executed on the basis of round-lot sales in the primary market and with the same odd-lot differential. In order to effect Midwest odd-lot executions on the proper New York round-lot transaction, a time differential of two minutes has been established. A market order, for example, is executed on the basis of the first New York round-lot sale occurring two minutes after receipt of the order by the Midwest odd-lot dealer. Lateness of the New York tape, if any, is added to the two minute period.
3. a. Midwest issues dually traded with the New York Stock Exchange have the same differential as that used on the latter exchange, ⅛ of one point.
   b. Midwest issues dually traded with the American Stock Exchange have the same differential as that used on the latter exchange.
   c. Midwest exclusive issues (not traded on the New York Stock Exchange or American Stock Exchange) shall have a differential of ⅛ of one point.
   d. For orders executed on the Midwest Stock Exchange, there is no odd-lot differential on that portion of an order in excess of a full round-lot, but less than the next multiple of a full round-lot.

Memberships:
1. Regular Members: 435
2. Membership Prices:

1960	$10,240	1969	50,890
1965	11,070	1970	32,950
1966	18,960	1971	38,970
1967	20,975	1972	12,535
1968	40,000	1973	15,580

Commissions or Fees:
Stocks, Rights and Warrants.
Rule 2 (a) On that portion of an order involving an amount of $300,000 or less,

on business for non-members, including joint account transactions in which any such person is interested:

1. Commissions on 100 share orders. On each order for 100 shares, commissions shall be based upon the amount involved in the order and shall not be less than the rates hereinafter specified:

Amount involved in the order	Minimum Commission
Above $2,000-	
but under $2,500	1.3% of money involved + $12.00
$2,500-and above	0.9% of money involved + $22.00

Notwithstanding the foregoing:
   i. When the amount involved in an order is $2,000 or less the commission shall be as mutually agreed.
   ii. The minimum commission on an order for 100 shares shall not exceed $65.00.

2. Commissions on Multiple Round-Lot Orders. On each multiple round-lot order for 200 shares or more, commissions shall be based upon the amount involved in the order and shall not be less than the rates hereinafter specified:

Amount involved in the order	Minimum Commission
Above $2,000-	
but under $2,500	1.3% of money involved + $ 12.00
$2,500-but under $20,000	0.9% of money involved + $ 22.00
$20,000-but under $30,000	0.6% of money involved + $ 82.00
$30,000-to and	
including $300,000	0.4% of money involved + $142.00

Plus a charge for each round-lot of 100 shares within the order as follows:

First to tenth round-lot .... $6.00 per round-lot
Eleventh round-lot and above .... $4.00 per round-lot

Notwithstanding the foregoing:
   i. When the amount involved in an order is $2,000 or less the commission shall be as mutually agreed.
   ii. The minimum commission per round-lot shall not exceed the single round-lot commission computed in accordance with the provisions of subparagraph (1) of this paragraph.

3. Commission on Odd-Lot Orders. On any odd-lot order, commissions shall be based upon the amount involved in the order and shall not be less than the rates so specified in subparagraph (1) of this paragraph, less $2.00. Notwithstanding the foregoing:
   i. When the amount involved in an odd-lot order is $2,000 or less, the commission shall be as mutually agreed.
   ii. The minimum commission on an odd-lot order shall not exceed $65.00.
   iii. When one or more odd-lot orders plus one or more round-lot orders are executed in the same security on the same day, for the same account, on the same side of the market, the commission(s) on such odd-lot order(s) shall not exceed the commission which shall be chargeable with respect to the nearest round-lot in excess of such odd-lot order(s).

4. Commissions on Stocks selling below $1 per share.
   i. Notwithstanding the foregoing subparagraphs (1), (2) and (3) of this

paragraph, on that portion of an order involving an amount of $300,000 or less, on stocks selling below $1.00 per share, commissions shall be based upon the amount involved in the order and shall not be less than the rates hereinafter specified:

Amount involved in the order	Minimum Commission
Above $2,000-	
but under $10,000	5.0% of money involved + $ 34.00
$10,000-and above	4.0% of money involved + $134.00

    ii. Notwithstanding the foregoing, when the amount involved in an order is $2,000 or less the commission shall be as mutually agreed.

    iii. Notwithstanding the foregoing, on business for non-members involving rights and warrants selling below 50 cents, the commission shall be as mutually agreed.

5. Notwithstanding the rates prescribed in subparagraphs (1) and (2) of this paragraph, when the amount involved in an order exceeds $300,000, the minimum commission to be charged pursuant to those subparagraphs shall apply to the maximum number of round-lot transactions involving an aggregate amount not in excess of $300,000.

6. Notwithstanding any other provision of this Rule, on an order for a non-member which is handled in part on this Exchange and in part on another market or markets, the commission shall be allocated between or among the markets involved on a pro rata basis according to the number of shares traded in each such market in the same manner as commissions are allocated between or among different executions in the same market.

7. On any order involving an amount not in excess of $5,000 the commission computed in accordance with the foregoing provisions of this Rule 2 (a) shall be increased by 10%, and on any order involving an amount in excess of $5,000, the commission computed in accordance with such provisions shall be increased by 15%; (b) On that portion of an order involving an amount over $300,000, commissions shall be as mutually agreed.

8. From April 1, 1974, to April 30, 1975, the Securities & Exchange Commission has required that brokers experiment with a partial unbundling of their services. This might result in an eventual schedule of commission rates that would vary according to the services rendered. The services most likely to be targeted for change are those involving research; the holding of a stock in a "street name," rather than transferring it into a client's name and shipping to his address, etc. This "meaningful experimental period" that began April 1, seems to have great significance for the future commission rate structure.

Historical Background:

1882 Founded as the Chicago Stock Exchange.

1949 Consolidated with the St. Louis, Cleveland and Minneapolis-St. Paul Stock Exchanges as the Midwest Stock Exchange.

1960 Added the New Orleans Mart to the Midwest Stock Exchange, thus becoming the third largest stock exchange in the United States; a national exchange with over 500 member firms, with more than 2,800 branch offices in 757 cities in 49 states and 27 foreign countries. Some 200 members belong to no other exchange.

1961 The first stock exchange to offer a comprehensive automated common back office accounting system to help member firms keep ahead of the back office logjam by formation of the Midwest Stock Exchange Service Corporation.

1965 Began a coast-to-coast hook-up of a high speed data communications system to service member firms faster.

1969 The first major stock exchange to permit member firms to offer a comprehensive life insurance program for their customers.

1971 The Midwest Stock Exchange Clearing Corporation, a subsidiary, implemented a continuous net settlement system, which enables sales and purchases in a given issue to be continuously and automatically offset against each other and against a firm's opening position, with settlement made on the net balance.

1972 Introduced SIGNET 80—a dynamic high speed communications system which, for the first time, offered the "locked-in" trade concept of the future, with automated order processing designed to interface with a firm's back office accounting system. Also, in this year, began operation as a corporation—the Midwest Stock Exchange, Incorporated.

1973 Announced formation of the Midwest Securities Trust Company, an integrated clearing/depository system. Working with the midwest banking community, the Midwest Securities Trust Company will be the comprehensive depository to serve the midwest financial community and will interface with other autonomous depositories, eventually forming a nationwide depository system.

1974 Introduced Quote 'N Trade, a service network which enables firms, via high speed transmission, to have instantaneous access to the best market and at the best price, besides providing communications with clearing facilities in all major locations. The benefits of this service will prove most advantageous in the developing central market system.

CINCINNATI

CINCINNATI STOCK EXCHANGE

Title: The Cincinnati Stock Exchange

Address: 205 Dixie Terminal Building, Cincinnati, Ohio 45202.

Telephone: 513 - 621 - 1410

Officers:
Chairman of the Board: Richard M. Pauly
President: Donald E. Weston
Vice-President: Jack W. Levi, Jr.
Treasurer: Gerald L. Oaks
Executive Secretary: D. Rosemary Goodrich

Hours of Business: 10:00 A.M. - 3:30 P.M. (Weekdays)

Regulatory Laws: Supervised and enforced by the Securities and Exchange Commission.

Issues Traded and Volume:
1. Listed Issues — Unlisted Issues:

Year	Listed	Unlisted
1964	37	124
1965	34	135
1966	34	138
1967	33	130
1968	30	141
1969	27	104
1970	15	124
1971	17	192
1972	16	214
1973	15	238

A few bonds are also traded, but the market is small. The maximum listing fee is $1,000, plus an annual service charge of $100.
2. Volume:

Year	Total Shares	Year	Total Shares
1964	831,257	1969	335,708
1965	1,299,635	1970	1,056,667
1966	1,777,814	1971	2,346,469
1967	1,129,641	1972	2,417,722
1968	614,176	1973	2,875,337

Record high volume day: 57,708 shares (9/13/66)

Unit of Trading:
1. 100 shares; the trading unit for several preferred issues is 10 shares.
2. Odd-lots are handled by special dealers. There is no extra fee or commission involved.

Membership:

1. Regular Members: 29
2. Limited Members: 4
3. Access Members: 4
4. Membership costs:

Year	High	Low	Year	High	Low
1969	$9,000	$7,500	1971*	4,175	4,000
1970	8,750	8,500	1972	4,000	
1971	8,400	8,000	1973	2,500	

* After two-for-one split
Record High: $38,500 (1929); Low: $50 (1885)

Commissions or Fees: Non-member commission rates are the same as those of the New York Stock Exchange.

Historical Background:

1858	Original meetings held Wednesday and Saturday at 83-85 Walnut Street.
1885 (March 11)	Cincinnati Stock Exchange formally organized by 12 brokers at 29 West Third Street.
1886 (Feb. 16)	Permanent constitution adopted.
1887 (March 31)	Cincinnati Stock Exchange incorporated as a non-profit corporation.

1916 (March 14)	Quotations were changed from a percent of par value to a dollar per share basis.
1940	The exchange applied to the SEC for its first trading privileges in unlisted stocks.
1946	The sale of limited memberships was authorized for $1,000 each. They are no longer available today.
1948	The "Call" system of trading was terminated.
1952	Saturday sessions eliminated; weekday trading was extended one-half hour.
1965	Membership certificates were split three-for-one.
1971	Membership certificates were split two-for-one. There are presently 60 certificates outstanding, representing 28 members and 20 registered firms (4 of which are limited).
1972	"Access memberships" were initiated. For a $100 filing fee, an accepted individual with a minimum net capital of $25,000 may trade on the Cincinnati Stock Exchange for one year. At the end of this period, the access member must become a full member, or the trading privilege is terminated.

DETROIT

DETROIT STOCK EXCHANGE

Title: Detroit Stock Exchange

Address: 2314 Penobscot Building, Detroit, Michigan 48226

Telephone: (313) 963-1600

Branches and Affiliates: Detroit Stock Clearing Corp.

Officers: Governing Committee -
President: Hal H. Smith III
Vice President: Julius Pochelon
Treasurer: Michael J. O'Donnell
Other Members:

Robert A. Benton	Ernest J. Olde
Paul P. Chester	Robert A. Reid
Peter M. Macpherson	Donald E. Weeden
David T. Marantette III	Herman F. Zerweck

Executive Vice President & Secretary: M. Edward Denny
Assistant Secretary: George E. White

Hours of Business (trading): 10:00 A.M. - 3:45 P.M. (weekdays)

Regulatory Laws: Securities Act of 1933: Securities Exchange Act of 1934.

Issues Traded and Volume:
1. Listed issues: 1960 - 243; 1973 - 405.

2. Volume:

	a. No. Shares Traded	b. Dollar Value
1964	11,538,975	$481,319,571.00
1965	14,223,709	630,472,341.32
1966	15,133,192	706,054,117.73
1967	15,319,250	709,628,613.00
1968	17,070,664	696,554,561.46
1969	6,443,336	216,582,932.88
1970	5,250,744	145,107,993.48
1971	8,622,589	350,759,657.01
1972	9,843,967	362,790,489.78
1973	10,688,329	380,594,829.00

Unit of Trading:

1. Round-lots: 100 shares or any multiple thereof.
2. Odd-lots are executed automatically. The price of execution depends upon the price of the next completed round-lot transaction that takes place in the primary market for the stock involved.
3. The differential, or extra fee, charged for executing an odd-lot order—that is not part of a round-lot order—is ⅛ point. It is added to the execution price on buy orders and deducted from it on sell orders. When an odd-lot order is coupled with a round-lot order to buy or sell in the same stock, the execution price of the odd-lot will be the same as the round-lot price. No ⅛ point differential is involved.

Memberships:

1. Regular Members: 55. The constitutional limit is 60.
2. Membership prices: a seat may be bought or sold in the same manner as a security. Bid and asked prices are available from the exchange.

	High	Low		High	Low
1964	$15,000	$3,800	1969	$6,100	$5,500
1965	19,000	5,000	1970	6,300	5,500
1966	5,200	4,100	1971	5,000	2,750
1967	4,250	4,250	1972	1,600	1,500
1968	11,000	8,000	1973	3,000	1,500

Commissions or Fees: Stocks, Rights and Warrants.

1. On that portion of any order involving an amount of $300,000 or less, non-member commissions shall be based on the following:
   On 100 share orders
   a. On each order for 100 shares, commissions shall be based upon the amount involved in the order and shall not be less than the rates hereinafter specified:

Amount Involved in the Order	Minimum Commission
Above $2,000 - but under $2,500	1.3% of money involved plus $12.00
$2,500 - and above	0.9% of money involved plus $22.00

   Notwithstanding the foregoing:
   i. When the amount involved in an order is $2,000 or less, the minimum commission shall be as mutually agreed.
   ii. The minimum commission on an order for 100 shares shall not exceed $65.

Multiple Round-Lot Orders

2. On each multiple round-lot order for 200 shares or more, commissions shall be based upon the amount involved in the order and shall not be less than the rates hereinafter specified:

Amount Involved in the Order	Minimum Commission
Above $2,000 - but under $2,500	1.3% of money involved plus $ 12.00
$2,500 - but under $20,000	0.9% of money involved plus $ 22.00
$20,000 - but under $30,000	0.6% of money involved plus $ 82.00
$30,000 - to and including $300,000	0.4% of money involved plus $142.00

Plus a charge for each round-lot of 100 shares within the order as follows:

First to tenth round-lot	$6 per round-lot
Eleventh round-lot and above	$4 per round-lot

Notwithstanding the foregoing:

    i. When the amount involved in an order is $2,000 or less, the minimum commission shall be as mutually agreed.

    ii. The minimum commission per round-lot shall not exceed the single round-lot commission computed in accordance with the provisions of Section 1a.

Historical Background:

1707 Pierre Mouet rented the lot which approximates the present site of the Detroit Stock Exchange for less than five silver dollars annually.

1907 The Detroit Stock Exchange was founded by seven citizens, as an outgrowth of a broker's association dealing in securities by door-to-door methods. First president was Louis H. Case, one of the founders.

1921 Annual volume: 1,812,740 shares.

1925 Volume topped 3 million shares.

1929 Turnover crossed 11 million mark.

1931 More than 170 securities comprised the trading list. Moved into own building on lower Griswold Street.

1950 Instituted a unique rule permitting 40% Commission Discount to non-members (adopted by certain other exchanges in mid-1960's and by the New York Stock Exchange in 1972).

1961 Established the Detroit Stock Clearing Corporation as a wholly owned subsidiary of the Exchange. Also, automated the Stock Clearing operation via IBM Service Bureau Corp.

1968 Established own computer operation utilizing IBM System 3 equipment. Share volume exceeded 17 million shares.

HONOLULU

HONOLULU STOCK EXCHANGE

Title: Honolulu Stock Exchange

Address: 843 Fort Street, Honolulu, Hawaii, 96813

Telephone: 538 - 6244

Cable Address: EXCHANGE Honolulu

Officers:
President: Richard F. Guard
Vice-President: Hideo Kawano
Executive Secretary: Rollin W. Walker
Assistant Secretary and Treasurer: Oliver M. S. Ching

Hours of Business: 8:30 A.M. - 8:45 A.M. (approx.) 1:45 P.M. - 2:00 P.M. (approx.)

Regulatory Laws: Securities and Exchange Commission

Issues Traded and Volume:
1. Listed: 45 stocks and 5 bonds, 19 of which are also listed on other U. S. exchanges. Listing requirements are not spelled out, but S.E.C. forms must be filed and official approval given before listing can be accomplished on the exchange.
2. Volume: Dollar volume in the past thirteen years has declined from $25,377,864 to approximately $2,000,000, due to a decline in the number of listings occasioned by mergers, dissolution, etc. Also, where dual listings are concerned, orders may have already been executed on other exchanges, since the morning session begins at 8:30 Honolulu time (2:30 P.M. New York time).

Unit of Trading: Trading is limited to common and preferred stocks, bonds, and rights or warrants. There are no specialists and no odd-lot differential.

Membership: Memberships are in the names of member firms, who may be corporations, partnerships, or individual proprietorships. Each member appoints a principal to represent it on the exchange at trading sessions and other meetings. There are ten member firms, although the constitution of the exchange allows for fifteen. Members clear their own transactions. The original cost of an exchange seat was $500.00; the last recorded sale was $4,000.

Commissions or Fees: None; this is essentially "an accommodation exchange."

Historical Background: The Honolulu Stock Exchange was organized in 1898, shortly after Hawaii became a Territory of the United States.

NEW YORK

AMERICAN STOCK EXCHANGE

Title: American Stock Exchange, Inc.

Address: 86 Trinity Place, New York, New York 10006

Telephone: 212-938-6000

Telex: TWX — 710-581-2308 Telex 12-9297

Cable Address: None

Branches and Affiliates: American Stock Exchange Stock Clearing Corp. American Stock Exchange Realty Associates, Inc.

Officers:
Chairman: Paul Kolton
President: Richard M. Burdge
Executive Vice Presidents:
James W. Walker, Jr.
Winsor H. Watson, Jr.
Senior Vice Presidents:
Robert J. Birnbaum   Norman S. Poser
Joseph J. Gulick   Henry G. Riter, IV
Edwin B. Peterson
Vice·President and Treasurer: Frank M. Casey
Vice Presidents:
Robert A. Coplin   Steven L. Gerard
J. Hamilton Crawford, Jr.   John M. Griswold
Joseph A. Derose   Bernard H. Maas
Robert T. Eckenrode   John J. Sheehan
Vice President and Secretary: H. Vernon Lee, Jr.
Assistant Vice Presidents:
Thomas F. Concannon   Benjamin D. Krause
William F. Jaenike   John T. McLoughlin
Robert M. Keane   James B. Neal
Donald A. Kepler   Frank J. Savarese
Assistant Secretary: Peter J. Armstrong
Assistant Treasurer: Alvin W. McGee
Controller: Thomas P. Loughlin

Hours of Business (trading): 10:00 A.M. - 3:30 P.M. (weekdays)

Regulatory Laws: Securities Act of 1933; Securities Exchange Act of 1934.

Issues Traded and Volume:
1. Listed: No. issues   2. Unlisted: No. issues

	Stocks	Bonds		Stocks	Bonds
1964	883	70	1964	139	21
1965	910	79	1965	118	19
1966	929	81	1966	109	17
1967	960	124	1967	101	13

1968	995	156	1968	89	11
1969	1,088	164	1969	64	11
1970	1,160	164	1970	62	5
1971	1,249	178	1971	59	4
1972	1,337	191	1972	57	2
1973	1,309	188	1973	51	2

3. All Stock Issues (including warrants):

	No. Issues	No. Shs. Outstanding	Market Value
1964	1,022	1,761,562,222	$28,219,995,088
1965	1,028	1,726,201,246	30,986,708,582
1966	1,038	1,828,119,000	27,858,504,091
1967	1,061	1,864,062,321	42,965,024,505
1968	1,084	2,191,991,185	61,213,429,994
1969	1,152	2,630,807,387	47,715,650,395
1970	1,222	2,857,275,369	39,535,679,374
1971	1,308	3,173,178,000	49,049,702,210
1972	1,394	3,360,820,685	55,648,369,691
1973	1,360	3,387,047,905	38,721,575,138

4. Volume:

a. Listed and Unlisted Issues

	Stocks (shs.)	Bonds (par val.)
1964	374,183,842	$103,886,000
1965	534,221,999	146,927,000
1966	690,762,585	159,724,000
1967	1,145,090,300	554,824,000
1968	1,435,765,734	970,403,000
1969	1,240,742,012	913,940,000
1970	843,116,260	641,270,000
1971	1,070,924,002	932,000,000
1972	1,117,989,153	728,524,000
1973	759,840,245	457,940,000

b. Public odd-lot purchases - sales:

	Purchases	Sales		Purchases	Sales
1964	13,311,798	15,368,267	1969	47,747,885	44,775,431
1965	19,183,187	18,628,938	1970	21,453,678	22,830,362
1966	27,019,040	24,282,696	1971	17,888,485	26,926,603
1967	44,822,314	42,996,757	1972	16,049,518	24,007,910
1968	58,782,733	54,947,082	1973	9,225,834	13,496,100

c. Foreign stocks:

	Issues	Shares	% Total A.S.E. Vol.
1964	102	69,306,521	18.52
1965	99	80,539,250	15.08
1966	99	118,153,994	17.10
1967	91	132,699,750	11.59
1968	83	143,890,798	10.02
1969	73	132,790,020	10.70
1970	67	76,822,710	9.11
1971	67	71,020,810	6.63
1972	68	69,621,170	6.23
1973	69	62,598,660	8.23

Unit of Trading:
1. Round-lots: 100 shares, or a multiple thereof.
2. Odd-lots: 1-99 shares. An extra fee or commission—a so-called odd-lot charge—is charged for executing an odd-lot order. Amounting to 12½ cents a share on trades when round-lot sells below $40 per share, 25c when round-lot sells at $40 per share or over it is added to the effective round-lot price on orders to buy and subtracted from it on orders to sell.
3. Unit stocks: As of December 31, 1973, 7 stocks traded in 50-share units; 7 in 25-share units; 17 in 10-share units.

Memberships:
1. Regular Members: Limited in number to 650. "Seat" holders have direct access to the trading floor.
2. Associate Members: 186, as of December 31, 1973. They are entitled to do business on the trading floor only through a regular member and at an average cost of not less than 40% of non-member commissions.
3. Allied Members: 6,850, as of December 31, 1970 (latest available figure). They are general partners or voting stockholders of regular member organizations.
4. Membership dues: $750 per year for regular and associate members.
5. Regular membership prices:

	High	Low		High	Low
1921*	$ 6,800	$ 3,750	1969	$350,000	$150,000
1929	254,000	150,000	1970	185,000	70,000
1935	33,000	12,000	1971	150,000	65,000
1940	7,250	6,900	1972	145,000	70,000
1950	11,000	6,500	1973	100,000	27,000
1960	60,000	51,000			

*from June 27, when the New York Curb Market moved indoors.

Commissions or Fees: (Subject to change; at present same as New York Stock Exchange)
1. Commissions are presently charged at fixed rates on orders involving $300,000 or less; above that level large customers have negotiated commissions with their brokers.
   a. on 100 share orders the rates are:

Money Involved	Percent of Money Involved	Plus Stated Amount
Under $ 100	as mutually agreed	—
$ 100-but under $ 800	2.0%	$ 6.40
$ 800-but under $2,500	1.3%	$12.00
$2,500-and above	0.9%	$22.00

   Notwithstanding the foregoing, the commission on any order for 100 shares shall not exceed $65.
   b. on multiple round-lot orders the rates are:

Money Involved	Percent of Money Involved	Plus Stated Amount
Under $ 100	as mutually agreed	—
$ 100-but under $ 2,500	1.3%	$ 12.00
$ 2,500-but under $20,000	0.9%	$ 22.00

$20,000-but under $30,000	0.6%	$ 82.00
$30,000 to and including		
$300,000	0.4%	$142.00

Plus a charge for each round-lot order of 100 shares within the order as follows:

| First to tenth round-lot | $6.00 per round-lot |
| Eleventh round-lot and above | $4.00 per round-lot |

Notwithstanding the foregoing, the commission on each round-lot order within a multiple round-lot order cannot exceed the commission for a 100 share order computed as in (a) above. The price to be used in calculating the single round-lot commission referred to above is the lowest price at which any round-lot order within the order is executed.

c. On odd-lot orders the rates are the same as for orders of 100 shares except that the added stated amount is $2.00 less. Further, the commission on any odd-lot order cannot exceed $65.

2. From April 1, 1974, to April 30, 1975, the Securities & Exchange Commission has required that brokers experiment with a partial unbundling of their services. This might result in an eventual schedule of commission rates that would vary according to the services rendered. The services most likely to be targeted for change are those involving research; the holding of a stock in a "street name," rather than transferring it into a client's name and shipping to his address, etc. This "meaningful experimental period" that began April 1, seems to have great significance for the future commission rate structure.

Historical Background:

1840's Unlisted securities were traded in the Outdoor Curb Market at Wall and Hanover Streets. Market later moved to Wall and Broad Streets, gradually shifting south along Broad.

1908   The New York Curb Agency was founded.

1911   New York Curb Market, or Market Association, was organized with established trading rules.

1921   The Association moved indoors to 86 Trinity Place, changed name to New York Curb Market. Ticker service was inaugurated.

1929   New York Curb Market became New York Curb Exchange.

1931   Telephone Quotation Department formed to disseminate stock quotes directly to member firm offices.

1934   Electrically operated quotation board developed.

1939   First paid president elected.

1946   Listed stocks outnumbered unlisted stocks for first time.

1953   Name changed to American Stock Exchange, June 5.

1958   First woman governor elected.

1964   Computerized telephone-quotation service offered for first time through Am-Quote.

1965   First woman elected to regular membership.

1966   Computer complex installed. The Amex introduced its own market averages.

1967   Major capital improvement program undertaken to increase trading floor capacity.

1968   Maximum ticker speed increased to 900 characters a minute. Last sale data of American Stock Exchange stocks made available abroad, with first transmissions to European countries.

1969   American Stock Exchange approved long range automation program to report and clear transactions faster and more accurately.

1970   American Stock Exchange joined industry groups to form Banking and Securities Industry Committee and Securities Investor Protection Corp. Computer-driven mechanisms installed at trading posts to display last sale, bid and asked prices and plus-minus "ticks" on all securities traded at post.

1971   All eligible Amex-listed securities entered into New York Stock Exchange's electronic Central Certificate Service; part of a joint-exchange effort to combine key computer, service and planning facilities.

1973   American Stock Exchange's Price Change Index replaced by Market Value Index on September 4.

NATIONAL STOCK EXCHANGE

Title: National Stock Exchange, Inc.

Address: 91 Hudson Street, New York, N.Y. 10013

Telephone: 212 - 966 - 6508

Branches and Affiliates: New York Mercantile Exchange (affiliate), 6 Harrison Street, New York, N.Y. 10013

Officers:
President: John D. Girard
Vice-President and Secretary: Michael J. Geoghan
Vice-President: Warren M. Knight
Treasurer: Frederick C. Lowenfels

Hours of Business: 10:00 A.M. - 3:30 P.M. (weekdays)

Regulatory Laws: Securities Acts of 1933 and 1934.

Issues Traded and Volume:

1. Issues Traded*:

1963	12	1969	107
1964	10	1970	146
1965	11	1971	154
1966	14	1972	161
1967	22	1973	125
1968	53		

*All National Stock Exchange issues are primary issues; no issues are traded on an unlisted basis.

2. Volume:

	Shares	Dollars		Shares	Dollars
1963	388,712	$408,221	1969	25,217,211	$179,718,693
1964	633,325	644,918	1970	12,430,727	44,621,042
1965	237,641	290,492	1971	14,366,040	57,334,293
1966	408,068	1,148,631	1972	15,805,073	115,000,000
1967	3,082,812	22,213,684	1973	7,761,637	23,973,319
1968	16,099,043	115,690,324			

Unit of Trading:
1. 100 shares
2. Odd-lots are traded the same as round-lots, except that an odd-lot differential of ⅛ point is added to the execution price on buy orders and subtracted from the price on sell orders.

Membership:
1. Regular Members: 135
2. Associate Members: 3
3. A membership on the National Stock Exchange is available for $500 only to members of the Mercantile Exchange.

Commissions or Fees: The National Stock Exchange presently fixes minimum commission rates for orders involving $500,000 or less; above that limit, commissions are subject to negotiation. For more complete information, contact the National Stock Exchange directly.

Historical Background:
1961 National Stock Exchange was founded; the first new exchange cleared by the Securities and Exchange Commission.
1965 Exchange quotations began to be transmitted by various electronics systems, with instruments in brokers' offices.
1969 The 100th company added to the trading list.
1970 Extensive financial reporting requirements and disciplinary examinations were initiated.
1972 The National Stock Exchange appointed its first public governor; opened its own high-speed ticker service.

NEW YORK STOCK EXCHANGE

Title: The New York Stock Exchange, Inc.

Address: 11 Wall Street, New York, New York 10005

Telephone: (212) 623-3000

Teletype: 710-5815464

Branches and Affiliates: Subsidiary Corporations: Depository Trust Company; Security Industry Automation Corporation; Stock Clearing Corporation.

Officers: Chairman: James J. Needham

Hours of Business: 10:00 A.M. - 3:30 P.M. (weekdays)

Regulatory Laws: Securities Act of 1933; Securities Exchange Act of 1934.

Issues Traded and Volume:

1. All securities traded on the New York Stock Exchange are listed.

   (a) Stocks:

Year	No. of Companies	No. of Issues	No. of Shares (000,000)	Market Value (000,000)
1964	1,247	1,606	9,229	$474,322
1965	1,273	1,627	10,058	537,481
1966	1,286	1,665	10,939	482,541
1967	1,274	1,700	11,623	605,817
1968	1,273	1,767	13,196	692,337
1969	1,311	1,789	15,082	629,453
1970	1,351	1,840	16,065	636,380
1971	1,426	1,927	17,500	741,827
1972	1,505	2,003	19,159	871,540
1973	1,560	2,058	20,967	721,012

   (b) Bonds:

Year	No. of Issuers	No. of Issues	Market Value (000,000)
1964	485	1,186	$127,725
1965	496	1,210	132,373
1966	538	1,272	128,142
1967	608	1,388	125,159
1968	664	1,455	120,407
1969	741	1,574	100,618
1970	843	1,729	112,622
1971	959	1,988	129,445
1972	999	2,105	128,302
1973	1,006	2,188	120,536

   (c) Foreign Security Listings*:

   i. Number: 186

   ii. Market Value (000):

stocks:	$17,692,647
corporate bonds:	$ 689,165
government bonds:	$ 1,778,372
total:	$20,160,184

   iii. Europe had the most listings - 90; followed by North America - 39; Australasia - 20; Asia - 17; Central & South America - 18; Africa - 2.
   *as of 12/31/73

2. Volume:

   (a) Stocks: (shs.)

1900	138,981,000	1960	766,693,818
1910*	163,705,000	1965	1,556,300,000
1920	227,636,000	1970	2,937,400,000
1930	810,632,546	1971	3,891,300,000
1940	207,599,749	1972	4,138,188,000
1950	524,799,621	1973	4,053,201,306

   *Includes unlisted trading up to and including March 10, 1910.

   Record Highs:
   Year: 4,138,188,000 (1972) shs.   Day: 31,731,000 (8/16/71)
   Month: 405,634,000 (11/72)   Month: 422,900,466 (10/73)

(b) Bonds (par value):

1900	$ 579,293,000	1960	$1,346,400,000
1910*	634,863,000	1965	2,975,200,000
1920	3,868,422,000	1970	4,494,900,000
1930	2,720,301,800	1971	6,563,800,000
1940	1,669,438,000	1972	5,444,100,000
1950	1,112,425,170	1973	4,424,671,800

    *Includes unlisted trading up to and including March 10, 1910.

Record highs:
  Year: $6,563,800,000 (1971)
  Day: $83,100,000 (9/6/39)

(c) Odd-lots:

	Purchases (000,000)	Customer's Sales (000,000)	Short Sales (000)
1964	99.6	101.6	1,064
1965	112.3	115.2	972
1966	135.0	122.0	2,719
1967	143.2	158.7	1,823
1968	137.5	163.5	2,082
1969	115.9	126.9	1,341
1970	86.5	99.6	1,985
1971	71.8	132.1	973
1972	68.8	121.9	893
1973	73.0	101.8	1,578

(d) International transactions (000,000):

	Dealings in U.S. Stocks*		Dealings in Foreign Stocks**	
	Foreign Purchases from Americans	Foreign Sales to Americans	Foreign Purchases from Americans	Foreign Sales to Americans
1964	$ 3,076	$ 3,425	$ 748	$ 548
1965	3,720	4,133	906	617
1966	4,740	5,074	960	731
1967	8,033	7,276	880	1,037
1968	13,118	10,848	1,252	1,566
1969	12,429	10,942	1,519	2,037
1970	8,927	8,031	1,033	998
1971	11,626	10,894	1,385	1,434
1972	14,361	12,173	2,532	2,123
1973	12,757	9,955	1,729	1,554

  *Excludes transactions between foreigners, but includes transactions between Americans on foreign markets.

  **Excludes transactions between Americans, but includes transactions between Americans with other foreigners on American markets.

Unit of Trading:
1. Round-lots: 100 shares, or a multiple thereof.
2. Odd-lots: 1-99 shares. An extra fee or commission - a so-called differential - is charged for executing an odd-lot order. Amounting to 12½ cents a share on all such trades, it is added to the effective round-lot price on orders to buy and subtracted from it on orders to sell.
3. Unit stocks: The full and accepted trading unit on some preferred and common stocks (usually relatively inactive issues) is 10 shares. Orders in

these stocks are executed the same way as a round-lot order; no extra commission or fee is involved.

Memberships (seats):

1. Regular Members: 1,366. As members, they pay no commission in buying or selling for their own account.
2. Membership dues: $1,500 per year.
3. Membership prices: Seats were first made salable on October 23, 1868. The highest price ever paid was $625,000 in February, 1929. The lowest price since 1900 was $17,000 in 1962. The only way to acquire a seat is through purchase from a member or his estate. A new member must prove his solvency and his intention of devoting full time to securities and convince the Committee on Admissions of his good character and knowledge of the business. The first woman was admitted to N.Y.S.E. membership December 28, 1967.

Commissions or Fees:

1. Commissions are presently charged at fixed rates on orders involving $300,000 or less; above that level large customers have negotiated commissions with their brokers.

   (a) on 100 share orders the rates shall be based upon the amount involved in the order and shall not be less than the rates hereinafter specified:

Amount Involved in the Order	Minimum Commission
Above $2,000 but under $2,500	1.3% of money involved + $12.00
$2,500 - and above	0.9% of money involved + $22.00

   NOTWITHSTANDING THE FOREGOING:

   i. When the amount involved in an order is $2,000 or less, the minimum commission shall be as mutually agreed.
   ii. The minimum commission on an order for 100 shares shall not exceed $65.00.

   (b) on multiple round-lot orders for 200 shares or more, commissions shall be based upon the amount involved in the order and shall not be less than the rates hereinafter specified:

Amount Involved in the Order	Minimum Commission	
Above $2,000 but under $2,500	1.3% of money involved	$ 12.00
$2,500 - but under $20,000	0.9% of money involved	$ 22.00
$20,000 - but under $30,000	0.6% of money involved	$ 82.00
$30,000 - to and including $300,000	0.4% of money involved	$142.00

   Plus a charge for each round-lot of 100 shares within the order as follows:

First to tenth round-lot	$6.00 per round-lot
Eleventh round-lot and above	$4.00 per round-lot

   Notwithstanding the foregoing:

   i. When the amount involved in an order is $2,000 or less, the minimum commission shall be as mutually agreed.
   ii. The minimum commission per round-lot shall not exceed the single round-lot commission computed in accordance with the provisions of 1 (a) above.

   (c) on any odd-lot order, commissions shall be based upon the amount involved in the order and shall not be less than rates specified in 1 (a) above, less $2.00.

NOTWITHSTANDING THE FOREGOING:

    i. When the amount involved in an order is $2,000 or less, the minimum commission shall be as mutually agreed.

    ii. The minimum commission on an odd-lot order shall not exceed $65.00.

    iii. When one or more odd-lot orders plus one or more round-lot orders are executed in the same security, on the same day, for the same account, on the same side of the market, the commission(s) on such odd-lot order(s) shall not exceed the commission which would be chargeable with respect to the nearest round-lot in excess of such odd-lot order(s).

(d) on that portion of an order involving an amount of $300,000 or less, on stocks selling below $1.00 per share, commissions shall be based upon the amount involved in the order and shall not be less than the rates hereinafter specified:

Amount Involved in the Order	Minimum Commission
Above $2,000 but under $10,000	5.0% of money involved + $ 34.00
$10,000 - and above	4.0% of money involved + $134.00

Notwithstanding the foregoing, when the amount involved in an order is $2,000 or less, the commission shall be as mutually agreed.

(e) on any order involving an amount not in excess of $5,000, the commission computed in accordance with sections (b) - (e) shall be increased by 10%. On any order involving an amount in excess of $5,000, the commission computed in accordance with sections (b) - (e) shall be increased by 15%.

Note: From April 1, 1974, to April 30, 1975, the Securities & Exchange Commission has required that brokers experiment with a partial unbundling of their services. This might result in an eventual schedule of commission rates that would vary according to the services rendered. The services most likely to be targeted for change are those involving research; the holding of a stock in a "street name," rather than transferring it into a client's name and shipping to his address, etc. This "meaningful experimental period" that began April 1, seems to have great significance for the future commission rate structure.

Historical Background:

1792 (May 17)	Twenty-four brokers formed an organization that was the forerunner of the New York Stock Exchange.
1817 (March 18)	New York Stock & Exchange Board formed with 8 firms and 19 brokers trading as individuals.
1830 (March 16)	Only 31 shares traded - the dullest day in Exchange history.
1853-1854	Exchange memberships cost $400. There were 209 "regular brokers."
1857 (August 24)	Volume hit new daily peak of 70,000 shares in so-called Banking Panic.

1863 (January 29)	New York Stock & Exchange Board changed name to New York Stock Exchange.
1867 (November 15)	Stock tickers introduced.
1868 (October 23)	Memberships first made salable.
1869 (May 8)	Government Bond Board, Open Board of Brokers and New York Stock Exchange joined under one management.
1870 (February 7)	First all-female brokerage firm opened.
1871 (September)	Continuous market in stocks established.
1873 (September 20-30)	Exchange closed to allay panic.
1878 (November 13)	Telegraph and telephone lines installed at New York Stock Exchange.
1879 (November 12)	Forty new Exchange seats authorized, bringing membership to 1,100.
1881 (January 29)	Annunciator boards for paging members installed.
1885 (March 25)	An "Unlisted Department" was established.
1886 (December 15)	First million-share day (1,200,000).
1888 (March 11-14)	Only 32 brokers on trading floor due to blizzard.
1892	"Post" system of trading adopted.
1901 (January 7)	First 2 million-share day.
(May 9)	Volume at record 3,336,695 shares during Northern Pacific panic.
1909 (January 1)	Trading in bonds "and interest" inaugurated.
1910 (March 31)	Unlisted Securities Department abolished.
1914 (July 31-Dec. 12)	Exchange was closed for World War I.
1919 (January 2)	Separate tickers for bonds installed.
1920 (April 26)	Stock Clearing Corp. established.
1922 (April 26)	Questionnaire for regular examination of the financial condition of member firms inaugurated.
1922 (October 2)	New 24-story office building at 11 Wall Street formally opened.
1925 (February 5)	Special code of listing requirements for foreign government bonds announced.
1926	The Exchange stopped listing nonvoting stock.
1927 (January 3)	Trading inaugurated in inactive stocks on the basis of a 10-share unit of trading.
(October 7)	Special requirements for listing of foreign internal shares announced.
1928 (May 14)	New Bond Room opened.
(June 12)	First 5 million-share day - (5,252,425).
(November 23)	Seven million shares traded.
1929 (February 11)	Central quotation system for reporting bid and asked prices inaugurated at all trading posts.
(February 18)	Exchange membership increased to 1,375.
(June 7)	Special, tentative requirements for listing investment trust shares announced.
(October 29)	Day's volume at record 16,410,030 shares as stock market crashed.
1930 (September 2)	New high speed ticker service started.

1934 (June 6)	Enactment of Securities Exchange Act.
1938 (February)	"One-Eighth Rule" governing short selling in round-lots became effective.
(June 30)	William McC. Martin, Jr. became first salaried president.
1939 (April 1)	Capital requirements of member firms doing general business with the public were increased about 25%.
1942 (January)	Board of Governors adopted "special offerings" plan to handle large block sales on trading floor.
(March 16)	Higher commission rates became effective.
1943	"Quote Girls" introduced on trading floor.
1952 (September 29)	Saturday trading discontinued; weekday sessions extended to 3:30 p.m.
1953 (June 4)	First member corporation - Woodcock, Hess & Co.
1961 (January 16)	Fidelity insurance compulsory for member firms.
1963 (August 20)	First transaction made under proposed Interest Equalization Tax.
1964 (January 4)	New capital requirements for New York Stock Exchange's 33 registered traders.
(February)	First ticker service to Puerto Rico, Hawaii, Switzerland.
(August 3)	New member classification - registered trader.
(December 1)	900 - characters-per-minute tickers introduced.
1965 (March 8)	Fully automated quote service inaugurated.
(April 23)	Listing requirements updated for common stocks.
(October 5)	Electronic Systems Center created.
(November 1)	Tighter credit rules announced for unusually active stocks.
1966 (April 21)	Minimum equity required to open a brokerage account was raised.
(April 24)	Day Trader rules tightened.
(July 14)	Exchange introduced its own market averages.
(December 20)	Transmission of trade and quote data from trading floor became fully automated.
1967 (March 10)	Busiest opening hour on record (5.1 million shares).
(December 21)	Exchange memberships made available to qualified Canadian firms.
(December 28)	First woman admitted to membership.
1968 (April 10)	First twenty million share-day (20,410,000).
(October 29)	Seat sold for $500,000
(December)	Nation's stock markets banned customer-directed give-ups.
1969 (February 24)	CEDE & Co.—an automated method of transferring stock ownership—began operations.
(December 5)	Volume discounts on commissions initiated.
1970 (April 24)	First public offering of a member firm.
(December 30)	Securities Investor Protection Act signed into law.

1971	(January 29)	Weekly volume topped 100 million shares for first time.
	(February 18)	New York Stock Exchange added "Incorporated" after its name.
	(April 5)	Negotiated brokerage rates on portion of orders over $500,000 permitted for first time.
	(June 24)	First black-owned member firm — Daniels & Bell.
	(July 27)	First member organization became listed — Merrill Lynch.
1972	(August 28)	First salaried Chairman — James J. Needham.
	(December 21)	Short interest for past month at record high—22.3 million shares.
	(December 31)	Stock margin debt at new peak—$7.9 billion.
1973	(March 20)	Price of New York Stock Exchange seat dropped below that of another U.S. market place for first time. New York Stock Exchange—$105,000 versus $115,000 for Chicago Mercantile Exchange membership.
	(September 14)	Higher commission rates became effective.
	(December 31)	New York Stock Exchange ended Block Automation System as an economy move.

PHILADELPHIA

PBW STOCK EXCHANGE, INCORPORATED

Title: PBW Stock Exchange, Inc.

Address: 17th Street and Stock Exchange Place, Philadelphia, Pa., 19103

Telephone: (215) 563 - 4700

Teletype: 215 - 569 - 9616

Telex: 083 - 385

Branches and Affiliates:
1. Associated Stock Exchanges:
   Boston Stock Exchange, 53 State Street, Boston, Mass. 02109
   Montreal Stock Exchange, Place d'Armes, Montreal, P.Q., Canada
2. Stock Clearing Corporation Branch Offices:
   Keyser Building, Baltimore, Maryland 21202
   Southern Building, Washington, D.C. 20005
   333 Fourth Avenue, Pittsburgh, Pa. 15222

Trading Facilities:
   Philadelphia Trading Floor, 17th & Stock Exchange Place, Philadelphia, Pa. 19103
   Pittsburgh Trading Floor, 333 Fourth Avenue, Pittsburgh, Pa. 15222
   Miami Trading Floor, One Biscayne Tower, Miami, Fla. 33131

Officers:
 Chairman of the Board: Barry E. Tague
 Vice-Chairman: Henry L. McKay
 Vice-Chairman: Art Judson
 President: Elkins Wetherill
 Vice-President & Chief Examiner: Michael A. Finnegan
 Vice-President & Controller: Nicholas A. Giordano
 Vice-President: George S. Hender
 Vice-President: Arnold F. Staloff
 Vice-President & General Counsel: J. G. G. Yocum
 Vice-President S. E. Division: John L. Tiernan
 Assistant Vice-Presidents: Roy Carr, Alix Tuten
 Secretary: William E. Hewlett

Hours of Business (trading): 10:00 A.M. - 4:00 P.M. (weekdays)

Regulatory Laws:
 1. Securities Act of 1933; Securities Exchange Act of 1934.
 2. The exchange is administered by a governing board, composed of the president, chairman, the vice-chairman and twenty-three others, who may be members of the exchange, or general partners of a member firm, or officers of a member corporation, and are elected by the membership at large. All other officers of the exchange are appointed by the board of governors.
 Policy matters of the exchange are administered by eight standing committees and ten special committees, whose members are nominated by the president, subject to approval of the board of governors.

Issues Traded and Volume:
 1. No. of issues:

	Listed*	Unlisted**	Total
1963	179	477	656
1964	176	495	671
1965	174	514	688
1966	181	535	716
1967	181	575	756
1968	183	613	796
1969	220	684	904
1970	235	726	961
1971	253	784	1,037
1972	266	915	1,181
1973	274	935	1,209

 *Securities traded on the PBW Stock Exchange are either listed or unlisted. A listed security is one which the corporation it represents has taken the initiative in requesting the exchange to allow its security to be traded. The corporation makes a formal application to the exchange and promises to abide by certain rules of financial reports, stock outstanding in the hands of the public, etc.

 **An unlisted security is one where the exchange takes the initiative. If there is sufficient interest in a security listed on another exchange, the PBW Stock Exchange may request the Securities and Exchange Commission and the corporation involved to allow the security to be traded on it. If they comply, the security is then traded in the same manner as a listed security.

2. Volume:

	No. of Shares	Dollar Value (000,000)
1929	35,500,000	
1930	27,234,000	
1931	10,598,000	
1936	5,363,000	
1940	3,285,000	
1945	4,837,000	
1948	4,025,000	$107.5
1953	4,826,000	174.0
1955	7,825,000	341.4
1961	15,645,000	663.3
1964	18,619,000	827.9
1965	20,857,000	1,009.0
1966	28,591,000	1,365.3
1967	38,454,038	1,867.9
1968	48,095,969	2,361.9
1969	62,457,561	2,572.2
1970	80,106,622	2,510.0
1971	117,797,520	4,309.7
1972	145,624,311	5,490.1
1973	123,363,035	4,551.4

3. Odd-lots: Trades made in dually listed securities are based on New York prices. The price obtained on a buy or sell order depends on the price that appears on the New York ticker tape, two minutes after the PBW Stock Exchange dealer receives the order. The dealer's commission, or "odd-lot differential," is 1/8 point. It is added to the execution price on buy orders and subtracted from the price on sell orders. The "differential" is eliminated when the odd-lot order is combined with a round-lot order. Odd-lot transactions are paid for on settlement day. Round-lot transactions are paid for on receipt of the stock, or transfer instructions.

Membership:

1. No. of Members: Member Organizations

	Regular	Associated	Regular	Associate	Clearing
1948	187	0	87		67
1949	200	0	104		87
1953	200	0	117		118
1955	198	34	150		143
1957	197	94	193		155
1961	202	131	248		173
1964	200	119	243		177
1965	201	146	257		180
1966	212	129	261		194
1967	217	128	154	108	197
1968	233	129	170	109	216

1969*	370	130	237	157	297
1970	409	162	283	147	304
1971	440	157	304	143	308
1972	452	157	329	144	334
1973	444	138	297	127	305

*Denotes year of merger with Pittsburgh Stock Exchange.

2. Seats:

	Number Transferred	Closing Price
1946	11	$2,000
1949	31	500
1952	5	325
1955	11	1,500
1958	14	3,250
1961	18	7,500
1964	16	7,500
1967	26	27,500
1968	40	16,500
1969*	114	16,500
1970	85	16,500
1971	95	9,500
1972	109	9,500
1973	85	3,500

*Denotes year of merger with the Pittsburgh Stock Exchange.

3. Dues:

Annual membership dues are currently established at $600, versus $120 in the early 1920's.

There have been no changes since 1963, when dues were increased to their present level.

Commissions or Fees:

A. Stocks, Rights and Warrants, $1 per share and above.

1. 100 share orders: On each order for 100 shares, commissions shall be based upon the amount involved in the order and shall not be less than the rates hereinafter specified:

Amount Involved	Minimum Commission
$ 100 - but under $ 800	2.0% of money involved plus $ 6.40
$ 800 - but under $2,500	1.3% of money involved plus $12.00
$2,500 - and above	0.9% of money involved plus $22.00

Notwithstanding the foregoing:

  i. when the amount involved in an order is less than $100, the minimum commission shall be as mutually agreed.

  ii. the minimum commission on an order for 100 shares shall not exceed $65.00.

2. Multiple round-lot orders: On each multiple round-lot order for 200 shares or more, commissions shall be based upon the amount involved in the order and shall not be less than the rates hereinafter specified:

Amount Involved	Minimum Commission
$ 100 - but under $ 2,500	1.3% of money involved plus $ 12.00
$ 2,500 - but under $20,000	0.9% of money involved plus $ 22.00
$20,000 - but under $30,000	0.6% of money involved plus $ 82.00
$30,000 - to and including $300,000	0.4% of money involved plus $142.00

Plus a charge for each round-lot of 100 shares within the order as follows:

First to tenth round-lot $6.00 per round-lot
Eleventh round-lot and above $4.00 per round-lot

Note: The following tables do do reflect increases that became effective September 25, 1973. In using the tables please apply the following: "On any order involving an amount of $5,000 or less, the commission shall be increased by 10%; on any order involving an amount in excess of $5,000, the commission shall be increased by 15%."

Notwithstanding the foregoing:

    i. when the amount involved in an order is less than $100, the minimum commission shall be as mutually agreed.

    ii. the minimum commission per round-lot shall not exceed the single round-lot commission computed in accordance with the provisions of paragraph 1 above.

3. On any odd-lot order, commissions shall be based upon the amount involved in the order and shall not be less than the rates specified in paragraph 1 above, less $2.00.

Notwithstanding the foregoing:

    i. when the amount involved in an odd-lot order is less than $100, the minimum commission shall be as mutually agreed.

    ii. the minimum commission on an odd-lot order shall not exceed $65.00.

    iii. when one or more odd-lot orders plus one or more round-lot orders are executed in the same security, on the same day, for the same account, on the same side of the market, the commission (s) on such odd-lot order (s) shall not exceed the commission which would be chargeable with respect to the nearest round-lot order in excess of such odd-lot order (s).

B. Stocks, Rights and Warrants, below $1 per share

On that portion of an order involving an amount of $300,000 or less on stocks selling below $1.00 per share, commissions shall be based upon the amount involved in the order and shall not be less than the rates hereinafter specified:

Amount Involved	Minimum Commission
0 - but under $1,000	8.4% of money involved
$1,000 - but under $10,000	5.0% of money involved
$10,000 - and above	4.0% of money involved

Notwithstanding the foregoing, when the amount involved in an order is less than $100, the commission shall be as mutually agreed.

Historical Background:

1746   Philadelphia Mayor, James Hamilton, appropriated 150 pounds to establish common marketplace.

1754   Marketplace, known as "Broker's Exchange," opened in London Coffee House.

1790   Philadelphia Board of Brokers formed. Matthew McConnell, first president.

1792   Dealings conducted in U.S. Government bonds and securities of Bank of North America and United States Bank.

1798-
1801   Brokers occupied a specific corner in Merchant's Coffee House — renamed Exchange Coffee House; Admission fee: $30.

1831   Philadelphia Merchant's Exchange voted to erect new exchange building.

1832   Cornerstone laid; new building opened for business in 1834.

1846   Telegraphic equipment installed.

1861   Elections to Board's presidency placed on annual basis.

1868   Formal rules governing admissions were adopted; provided for the sale of "seats" (memberships).

1875   Board of Brokers name changed to Philadelphia Stock Exchange. Gratuity Fund system adopted.

1876   Exchange moved to a building on Third Street. Advertising sales of securities by brokers without permission became subject to $100 fine for first offense; suspension for further infraction.

1881   Mining Annex of Philadelphia Stock Exchange formed to deal in stocks not traded on exchange floor.

1883   Listing Committee arranged for members to put "wanted" and "for sale" advertisements on nonactive stocks in Philadelphia newspapers. Mining Annex formed in 1881, dissolved.

1884   Stock tickers introduced.

1885   Governing Committee voted to confer with New York Stock Exchange and Chicago Board of Trade about cutting off ticker service to bucketshops.

1886   Special room designated for members trading in unlisted securities.

1888   Philadelphia Stock Exchange moved to Drexel Building. Fireproof-burglarproof vaults installed at Clearing House.

1892   Exchange members permitted to have telephone connection with their office for $100 paid in advance.

1898   Amendment to bylaws prohibited circulars and newspaper advertising to buy or sell without governing committee's permission. (Amendment cancelled in 1900.)

1899   Memberships limited to 230. Seats obtainable only by transfer.

1900   Philadelphia Stock Exchange accepted offer to use old Merchant's Exchange Building.

1902   Philadelphia Stock Exchange moved into old Merchant's Exchange Building after $200,000 remodeling job.

1907   Pennsylvania Legislature passed bill outlawing bucketshops.

1913   Exchange moved to 1411 Walnut Street.

1914   Philadelphia Stock Exchange reopened, after having been closed four months for World War I. Minimum prices were established and posted in board room each morning.

1915   All trading restrictions removed (August 15).

1918   Exchange closed to celebrate Armistice (November 11).

1921   Certain officers of exchange empowered to buy up to ten memberships at $2,500 each.

1922   Constitution amended to permit Philadelphia Stock Exchange members to trade in New York Curb Market Association stocks, and in Boston and Pittsburgh Stock Exchange stocks at prices prevailing on such exchanges. Resolution adopted (April 5) that corporations filing applications for listing securities shall agree to file statement of earnings and expenses, as well as assets and liabilities, within four months of the expiration of their fiscal year. One Exchange-owned membership cancelled; five purchased — bringing total membership to 220, as of October 18. Dues increased $50 to $180.

1924   Night clearing operations of odd-lots began. Also, an experiment in executing odd-lot orders under so-called Three Minute Rule, which the Securities and Exchange Commission subsequently approved for regional exchanges.
Rules committee recommended the "clearing of odd-lots of stock through the Clearing House" (became effective June 16).
Dues set at $100 for 1925.

1925   Pennsylvania Railroad added to list of stocks of which odd-lots were to be cleared through clearing house. Dues fixed at $80 for 1926.

1926   Constitution amended to provide that orders executed by one floor broker for another floor broker may be executed with no commission charge.

1927   State of Pennsylvania granted corporate charter to Stock Clearing Corp.; all its capital stock was subscribed by Philadelphia Stock Exchange.

1928   Stock Clearing Corp. took over functions previously performed by Philadelphia Clearing House. Night clearing of odd-lots continued; a central delivery service was provided.

1929   A record 501,703 shares traded (October 29).

1930   Dues set at $175, unchanged from 1928-1929.

1931   Short selling banned (September 21); rescinded two days later. All securities listed on New York Stock Exchange. New York Curb Exchange, Chicago Stock Exchange, Boston Stock Exchange and Pittsburgh Stock Exchange admitted to trading in Unlisted Department of Philadelphia Stock Exchange.

1933   Second-day delivery rule effective September 8.

1934   Exchange officers authorized to apply for registration as a National Securities Exchange under SEC Act of 1934.

1942   Secretary of exchange empowered to buy seats for $100 if any were offered.

1943   Stock Clearing Corp. discontinued night clearing, initiated present plan of operations; admitted to Philadelphia Stock Exchange membership.

1945   Stock Clearing Corp. charter amended to permit it to act for banks, trust companies, nonmembers of Philadelphia Stock Exchange.

1946   Third-day delivery rule effective.

1949   Merged with Baltimore Stock Exchange; became first regional exchange to cross state boundaries. New Title: Philadelphia-Baltimore Stock Exchange.

1950   Stock Clearing Corp. inaugurated clearance of securities by mail.

1951   Philadelphia-Baltimore Exchange and Clearing House moved to 1401 Walnut Street. Branches of Philadelphia-Baltimore Exchange and Stock Clearing Corp. of Philadelphia established in Washington.

1953   Merged with Washington Stock Exchange; became third largest in U. S.

1955   Philadelphia-Baltimore Exchange entered into mutual trading agreements with Pittsburgh Stock Exchange. Stock Clearing Corp. absorbed facilities of Pittsburgh Stock Exchange Clearing House. Auditing Department of Philadelphia-Baltimore Exchange established.

1956   Stock Clearing Corp. of Philadelphia established branch in Pittsburgh

Stock Exchange. Philadelphia-Baltimore Exchange undertook to audit 14 Pittsburgh Stock Exchange member firms periodically. Governing Boards of Philadelphia-Baltimore Exchange and Boston Stock Exchange agreed to install direct telephone wire between their trading floors.

1957 Philadelphia-Baltimore Exchange entered into mutual trading agreements with Boston Stock Exchange. Stock Clearing Corp. inaugurated clearing by mail for firms outside Philadelphia. Pennsylvania Stock Transfer Tax repealed.

1959 Data processing machines installed by Stock Clearing Corp. Private wire systems established for southern member firms.

1961 Philadelphia-Baltimore Exchange entered into mutual trading agreements with Montreal Stock Exchange. Constitution amended to permit governing board to issue 10 additional memberships. This raised authorized membership to 210 (July 10).

1962 Telex — a direct dial printer — installed for southern member firms. Trading floor of Washington branch of Philadelphia-Baltimore Exchange discontinued; name changed to Philadelphia-Baltimore-Washington Stock Exchange. Questionnaires forwarded to member organizations requesting their capital positions, as of May 31.

1963 Contributory pension plan established for full-time employees of both the Philadelphia-Baltimore-Washington Exchange and the Stock Clearing Corp. Pittsburgh National Bank became member of Stock Clearing Corp. of Philadelphia, for purpose of clearing transactions through the Pittsburgh branch of the Stock Clearing Corp. Dues 1963-1973: $600.

1964 First woman admitted to Philadelphia-Baltimore-Washington membership.

1965 Philadelphia-Baltimore-Washington business crossed $1 billion in dollar volume for first time. Mutual funds permitted to direct 25% of the commission generated by their orders on Philadelphia-Baltimore-Washington to National Association of Securities Dealers members. Amendment passed opening membership to non-U.S. citizens.

1966 Members equity in Philadelphia-Baltimore-Washington totaled $402,507 as of January 1, versus $268,468 on 1/1/50. Philadelphia-Baltimore-Washington moved into present headquarters in Stock Exchange Building, 17th Street and Exchange Place. 20.3 million shares traded in first nine months, against 20.9 million for all of 1965. Constitution amended to increase authorized membership to 225 from 210. As of December 31, 212 memberships were issued and outstanding. The amount of commission that mutual funds could direct to National Association of Securities Dealers members, from orders executed on Philadelphia-Baltimore-Washington Exchange was raised to 40% from 25%.

1969 Philadelphia-Baltimore-Washington Exchange and Pittsburgh Stock Exchange merged.

1972 Philadelphia-Baltimore-Washington Exchange considered forming a Satellite trading floor in Atlanta.
Robert I. Burden, Treasurer of State of Connecticut, became exchange member. Connecticut Nutmeg Sales, Inc. registered as a member or-

ganization; first state, or other governmental body to own seat on a registered national securities exchange. Name officially changed to PBW Stock Exchange, Inc.

1974 Southeastern Stock Exchange, a division of the PBW Exchange, opened in Miami, Florida on March 4.

SALT LAKE CITY

INTERMOUNTAIN STOCK EXCHANGE

Title: Intermountain Stock Exchange

Address: 39 Exchange Place, Salt Lake City, Utah 84111
:01) 363 - 231

Officers:
President: Ernest Muth
Vice-President: G. Richard Condie
Secretary-Treasurer: Clyde Summerhays

Hours of Business:
1. 9:00 A.M. - 12:00 noon
2. The Intermountain Stock Exchange is the only registered stock exchange in the nation to use the auction or "call" system of trading. The daily call is at 9:00 A.M.; the second call is at 10:30 A.M.

Regulatory Laws: Securities Act of 1933; Securities Exchange Act of 1934

Issues Traded and Volume:
1. Listed issues: 50
2. Unlisted or "other" issues: 1
3. Volume and Value: 1972 — 3,841,433 shares; $2,325,808
   1973 — 2,262,473 shares;   996,461

Unit of Trading: Round-lots.
Stocks selling under 5c .... 5,000 shares
Stocks selling at 5c and under 25c .... 1,000 shares
Stocks selling at 25c and under 75c .... 500 shares
Stocks selling at 75c and above .... 100 shares

Memberships:
1. Regular Members: 45
2. Membership Prices (1960-1973): High — $1,750
                                   Low — $700

Commissions or Fees:
1. Commissions are identical with those of the New York Stock Exchange, except that no quantity discounts are given;
2. The exchange allows a 40% commission rebate to registered broker dealers.

Historical Background:
1899 The Salt Lake Stock and Mining Exchange was incorporated, March 16.
1934 Became a registered stock exchange under Securities & Exchange Acts of 1933 and 1934.
1968 Total shares traded — 23,501,808.
1972 Name changed to Intermountain Stock Exchange in May.

SAN FRANCISCO

PACIFIC STOCK EXCHANGE

Title: Pacific Stock Exchange, Incorporated

Address: 1. 301 Pine Street, San Francisco, California 94106
2. 618 S. Spring Street, Los Angeles, California 90014

Telephone: 1. San Francisco: (415) 392-6533
2. Los Angeles: (213) 627-8741

Branches and Affiliates:
Subsidiaries—Pacific Clearing Corporation; PC Service Corp.

Officers:
Chairman of the Board: J. P. Guerin
Vice Chairman of the Board: Ross L. Cobb
President: G. Robert Ackerman
Senior Vice-President: Kenneth S. Uston
Vice-Presidents:
Jeremiah J. Brady   Carlton K. Lowen
Charles J. Henry   Herbert F. Neubig
Philip J. Lo Bue
Secretary-Treasurer: Howard R. Helwig
Assistant Secretary: Charles E. Rickerhauser, Jr.

Hours of Business: 7:00 A.M. - 2:30 P.M.

Regulatory Laws: Securities Act of 1933; Securities Exchange Act of 1934.

Issues Traded and Volume:
1. Nearly all the most active stocks (more than 1,000) traded on the New York and American Stock Exchanges are listed on the Pacific Stock Exchange (dually listed). There are also approximately 100 local listings, that is, companies listed solely with the Pacific Stock Exchange.

		Volume		Value
2.	1960	44,853,085	3.	$ 883,355,671
	1961	73,198,461		1,279,815,968
	1962	50,565,911		1,097,208,446
	1963	53,136,243		1,542,442,811
	1964	56,216,672		1,800,041,760
	1965	62,440,906		2,179,923,578
	1966	88,931,688		3,524,017,989

(Continued)

	Volume	Value
1967	114,323,089	4,538,551,441
1968	143,276,875	5,242,049,849
1969	171,884,085	5,513,669,262
1970	172,459,807	5,019,252,489
1971	223,181,128	7,064,184,099
1972	260,728,393	8,122,255,031
1973	214,783,572	6,359,459,610

Unit of Trading:

1. 100 shares.
2. Odd-lots are handled by specialists, or odd-lot dealers and are processed through COMEX — a computerized system which automatically executes several common types of securities trades.
3. Odd-lot orders are executed off the next round-lot transaction which appears on the New York or American exchange tapes. The fee, or "differential," charged for executing an odd-lot is ⅛ point, or 12½ cents per share. On the Pacific Stock Exchange, however, no such extra fee is charged for executing an odd-lot when coupled with a round-lot; for example, 190 shares. This type of order is known as a PRL (Part Round-Lot).

Memberships:

1. Authorized; 220
2. There is also a type of membership which allows a "preferred rate," or commission discount of 25%.
3. Membership ("seat") prices:

	High	Low	Last Sale
1960	$12,000	$10,500	$12,000
1961	15,000	9,000	15,000
1962	15,000	10,000	10,000
1963	7,000	6,000	7,000
1964	10,000	7,000	10,000
1965	37,500	7,500	36,500
1966	40,000	35,000	37,500
1967	50,000	35,000	50,000
1968	65,000	50,000	55,000
1969	70,000	55,500	70,000
1970	70,000	24,000	52,500
1971	52,500	48,000	35,000
1972	37,500	26,000	26,000
1973	23,000	5,000	9,600

Commissions or Fees:

1. Commissions are presently charged at fixed rates on orders involving $300,000 or less; above that level large customers have negotiated commissions with their brokers.
   a. on 100 share orders the rates are:

Money Involved	Percent of Money Involved	Plus Stated Amount
Under $ 100	as mutually agreed	—
$ 100-but under $ 800	2.0%	$ 6.40
$ 800-but under $2,500	1.3%	$12.00
$2,500-and above	0.9%	$22.00

Notwithstanding the foregoing, the commission on any order for 100 shares shall not exceed $65.

b. on multiple round-lot orders the rates are:

Money Involved	Percent of Money Involved	Plus Stated Amount
Under $ 100	as mutually agreed	—
$ 100-but under $ 2,500	1.3%	$ 12.00
$ 2,500-but under $20,000	0.9%	$ 22.00
$20,000-but under $30,000	0.6%	$ 82.00
$30,000 to and including $300,000	0.4%	$142.00

Plus a charge for each round-lot of 100 shares within the order as follows:

First to tenth round-lot	$6.00 per round-lot.
Eleventh round-lot and above	$4.00 per round-lot.

Notwithstanding the foregoing, the commission on each round-lot within a multiple round-lot order cannot exceed the commission for a hundred share order computed as in (a) above. The price to be used in calculating the single round-lot commission referred to above is the lowest price at which any round-lot within the order is executed.

c. On odd-lot orders the rates are the same as for orders of 100 shares except that the added, stated amount is $2.00 less. Further, the commission on any odd-lot order cannot exceed $65.

2. From April 1, 1974, to April 30, 1975, the Securities & Exchange Commission has required that brokers experiment with a partial unbundling of their services. This might result in an eventual schedule of commission rates that would vary according to the services rendered. The services most likely to be targeted for change are those involving research; the holding of a stock in a "street name," rather than transferring it into a client's name and shipping to his address, etc. This "meaningful experimental period" that began April 1, seems to have great significance for the future commission rate structure.

Historical Background:

1957 The Pacific Stock Exchange was founded January 2 through a merger of the Los Angeles (founded 1887) and the San Francisco (founded 1882) Stock Exchanges. The trading floors maintained in both cities operate as one and are linked to members through a highly computerized electronics system. There is a composite tape and trading continues for two hours after the eastern markets are closed.

1959 Net-by-net clearing system introduced.

1964 Clearing and accounting for specialists.

1965 Over-the-counter clearing. Clearing for non-members.

1968 Bank clearing.

1969 Automated odd-lot executions—COMEX.

1970 Transcontinental OTC clearing. Standard Cusip (Committee on Uniform Security Identification Procedures) numbering.

1971 Securities depository with segregation. Automated round-lot executions—COMEX.

1972 Round-lot orders coupled with an odd-lot order executed at one price (PRL).

SPOKANE STOCK EXCHANGE

Title: Spokane Stock Exchange

Address: 225 Peyton Building, Spokane, Washington 99201

Telephone: (509) 624 - 4632

Officers and Trustees:
> President: G. C. George
> Vice-President: R. E. Nelson
> Secretary-Treasurer: Ben Redfield
> Other Trustees:
> > C. O. McCartney
> > W. C. Lasswell, Jr.

Hours of Business: Daily calls: 9:30 A.M. - 11:00 A.M.

Regulatory Laws: Securities Act of 1933; Securities Exchange Act of 1934.

Issues Traded and Volume:
1. Listed issues: 36. The Spokane Stock Exchange is the only exchange in the U. S. dealing almost exclusively in mining stocks; only two non-mining stocks are traded.
2. Over-the-counter: 90, approximately.
3. Volume: 12,945,919 shares valued at $6,625,600 (1973); 9,257,970 and $4,498,135, respectively, (1972).

Unit of Trading:
1. Mining stocks:
> 1,000 shares on stocks selling under 25c.
> > 500 shares on stocks selling at 25c and under $1.00
> > 100 shares on stocks selling at $1.00 and under $50.00.
> > 10 shares on stocks selling at $50.00 and over.
2. The Spokane Exchange is the only one in the U. S. which allows open trading. Spectators can give orders to brokers across a counter on the trading floor. A separate over-the-counter market for unregistered mining stocks is conducted daily by exchange members.

Membership:
1. Regular Members: 13.
2. Membership prices: The last seat sold for $3,500.

Commisssions or Fees:
1. Minimum commission is $6.

Stocks Selling - Under 5c per share		Comm. per share ¼c
5c and under	10c per share	½c
10c and under	15c per share	¾c
15c and under	20c per share	1c
20c and under	30c per share	1½c

30c and under	50c per share	2c
50c and under	75c per share	3c
75c and under	$1.00 per share	4c
$1.00 and under	$2.00 per share	7c
$2.00 and under	$3.00 per share	10c
$3.00 and under	$5.00 per share	12c
$5.00 and under	$10.00 per share	20c
$10.00 and under	$20.00 per share	25c
$20.00 and under	$50.00 per share	35c
$50.00 and above	per share	40c

Historical Background:

1897 The Spokane Stock Exchange opened for business January 18, with 32 members and 37 stocks. The initial listings were almost entirely of mining companies in British Columbia.

ADDENDUM AT PRESS TIME

In addition to trading in propane futures, the Petroleum Associates of the New York Cotton Exchange will buy and sell crude oil in lots of 5,000 bbl. starting September 10, 1974. Prices will be quoted for Rotterdam deliveries four times a year with a maximum time limit of three years in advance. President of the Petroleum Associates is Donald B. Conlin. (See also New York Cotton Exchange, page 251.)

STOCK & INTERNATIONAL COMMODITY EXCHANGE DIRECTORY

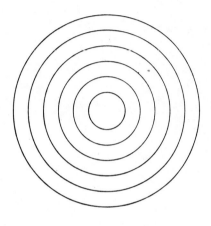

SECTION 2

RELATED
INFORMATION

TIME ZONE DESIGNATIONS

Unfortunately all stock and commodity exchanges are not open for trading at the same time due to the various time zones under which the nations of the world live. Those who do business with exchanges outside their own country must know when, in terms of their own local time, exchanges in foreign lands are open.

The following tables of cities and countries (each entry followed by a time zone designation) will enable every user of this Directory to figure out easily and quickly the time difference between any two of the cities or countries listed. The earth's surface has been divided into twenty-four theoretical time zones, each of which is the distance which the sun moves east to west within the span of an hour. The starting point or "zero zone" is Greenwich Mean Time (GMT). Other zones east or west of the zero zone or GMT are marked by numbers which tell the time difference in hours between GMT and that time zone. Minus denotes the hours which are earlier or slower than GMT, pluses the hours which are later or faster.

The easiest and quickest way to determine the time difference between two time zones is to subtract like numbers and add dissimilar numbers. Thus the time difference between Boston (-5) and Honolulu (-10) is 5 hours; between Calcutta ($+5+30$ minutes) and Rio de Janeiro (-3) is 8 hours $+30$ minutes. Cities lying to the west will be earlier or slower, those to the east later or faster.

Locations of all stock and commodity exchanges included in this Directory are listed below by city, together with the time zone designation for each. In addition, a list of countries follow for those Directory users who may not live in any of the cities mentioned.

TIME ZONE DESIGNATIONS FOR PRINCIPAL COUNTRIES

Afghanistan, $+4+30$ minutes
Algeria, 0
American Samoa, -11
Angola, $+1$
Arab Republic of Egypt, $+2$
Argentina, -3
Ascension, 0
Australia, $+10$ (Darwin, Adelaide and central area, $+9+30$ minutes)
Austria, $+1$
Azores, -2

Bahamas, -5
Bangladesh, $+6$
Barbados, -4
Belgium, $+1$
Bermuda, -4
Bolivia, -4
Borneo, $+8$
Botswana, $+2$
Brazil, -3 (Interior is -4)

British Honduras, -6
British Solomon Islands, $+11$
Bulgaria, $+2$
Burma, $+6+30$ minutes
Burundi, $+2$

Cambodia, $+7$
Cameroon, $+1$
Canada, -4 to -8
Canary Islands, 0
Cape Verde Islands, -2
Cayman Islands, -5
Central African Republic, $+1$
Ceylon, $+5+30$ minutes
Chad, $+1$
Chile, -4
China, $+8$
Cocos Islands, $+6+30$ minutes
Colombia, -5
Comoro Islands, $+3$
Congo Republic, $+2$

Costa Rica, −6
Cuba, −5
Cyprus, +2
Czechoslovakia, +1

Dahomey, +1
Denmark, +1
Dominican Republic, −5

Ecuador, −5
Egypt, +2
Equatorial Guinea, 0
Ethiopia, +3

Falkland Islands, −4
Faroes, +1
Fiji, +12
Finland, +2
France, +1
French Guiana, −3

Gabon, +1
Gambia, 0
Germany (East), +2
Germany (West), +2
Ghana, 0
Gibraltar, 0
Great Britain, 0
Greece, +2
Greenland, −3
Guadeloupe, −4
Guam, +10
Guatemala, −6
Guinea, 0
Guyana, −4

Haiti, −5
Honduras, −6
Hong Kong, +8
Hungary, +1

Iceland, −1
India, +5+30 minutes
Indonesia, +7
Iran, +3+30 minutes
Iraq, +3
Ireland, 0
Israel, +2
Italy, +1
Ivory Coast, 0

Jamaica, −5
Japan, +9
Jordon, +2

Kenya, +3
Kuwait, No standard time

Laos, +7
Lebanon, +2
Liberia, 0+44 minutes
Libya, +2
Liechtenstein, +1
Luxembourg, +1

Madagascar, +3
Malawi, +2
Malaysia, +7+30 minutes
Mali, 0
Malta, +1
Martinique, −4
Mauritania, 0
Mauritius, +4
Mexico, −6
Midway Island, −11
Monaco, +1
Morocco, 0
Mozambique, +2

Nepal, +5+30 minutes
Netherlands, +1
Netherlands Antilles, −4
New Zealand, +12
Nicaragua, −6
Niger, +1
Nigeria, +1
North Korea, +9
North Vietnam, +7
Norway, +1

Oman, No standard time

Pakistan, +5
Panama, −5
Paraguay, −4
Peru, −5
Philippines, +8
Poland, +1
Portugal, 0
Puerto Rico, −4

Reunion, +4
Rhodesia, +2
Rumania, +2
Rwanda, +2

Salvador, El, −6
Samoa, −11
Saudi Arabia, No standard time
Senegal, 0
Sierra Leone, 0
Singapore, +7+30 minutes
Somalia, +3
South Africa, +2
South Korea, +9
South Vietnam, +8
South West Africa, +2
South Yemen, +3
Spain, +1
Sri Lanka, +5+30 minutes
Sudan, +2
Sweden, +1
Switzerland, +1
Syria, +2

Taiwan, +8

Tanzania, +3
Thailand, +7
Togo, 0
Trinidad and Tobago, −4
Tunisia, +1
Turkey, +3

Uganda, +3
Union of Soviet Socialist Republics
   (Moscow, Leningrad, +2 to +8)
United States of America, −5 to −8
Uruguay, −3

Vatican City, +1
Venezuela, −4
Virgin Islands, −4
Voltaic Republic, 0

Wake Island, +11

Yemen, No standard time
Yugoslavia, +1

Zaire, +2
Zambia, +2

Time Zone Designations For All Cities Named In The Profile Data Section

Adelaide, Australia, +9+30 minutes
Amsterdam, Netherlands, +1
Antwerp, Belgium, +1
Athens, Greece, +2
Auckland, New Zealand, +12

Bahia, Brazil, −3
Barcelona, Spain, +1
Bari, Italy, +1
Basle, Switzerland, +1
Bergen, Norway, +1
Berlin, West Germany, +1
Berne, Switzerland, +1
Bilboa, Spain, +1
Bologna, Italy, +1
Bombay, India, +5+30 minutes
Boston, United States, −5
Bremen, West Germany, +1
Brisbane, Australia, +10

Brussels, Belgium, +1
Buenos Aires, Argentina, −3

Cairo, Arab Republic of Egypt, +2
Calcutta, India, +5+30 minutes
Calgary, Canada, −7
Caracas, Venezuela, −4
Chicago, United States, −6
Christchurch, New Zealand, +12
Cincinnati, United States, −5
Columbo, Sri Lanka, +5+30 minutes
Copenhaven, Denmark, +1
Cordoba, Argentina, −3

Delhi, India, +5+30 minutes
Detroit, United States, −5
Dominican Republic, −5
Dublin, Ireland, 0

Dunedin, New Zealand, +12
Dusseldorf, West Germany, +1

Espirito Santo, Brazil, −3
Estado do Rio de Janeiro, Brazil, −3

Firenze, Italy, +1
Florianopolis, Brazil, −3
Frankfurt, West Germany, +1
Fukuoka, Japan, +9

Geneva, Switzerland, +1
Ghent, Belgium, +1
Goias, Brazil, −3
Guadalajara, Mexico, −6

Hamburg, West Germany, +1
Hannover, West Germany, +1
Le Havre, France, +1
Helsinki, Finland, +2
Hiroshima, Japan, +9
Hobart, Australia, +10
Hong Kong, +8
Honolulu, United States, −10

Invercargill, New Zealand, +12
Istanbul, Turkey, +2

Johannesburg, South Africa, +2

Kansas City, United States, −6
Karachi, Pakistan, +5
Kingston, Jamaica, −5
Kuala Lumpur, Malaysia, +7+30
    minutes
Kyoto, Japan, +9

Lagos, Nigeria, +1
Lahore, Pakistan, +5
Lausanne, Switzerland, +1
Liege, Belgium, +1
Lima, Peru, −5
Lisbon, Portugal, 0
London, England, 0
Luxembourg, Grand Duchy of Luxem-
    bourg, +1

Madras, India, +5+30 minutes
Madrid, Spain, +1

Makati, Philippines, +8
Malaysia, Malaysia, +7+30 minutes
Managua, Nicaragua, −6
Manila, Philippines, +8
Mauritius, Mauritius, +4
Melbourne, Australia, +10
Mendoza, Argentina, −3
Mexico City, Mexico, −6
Milan, Italy, +1
Minas, Brazil, −3
Minneapolis, United States, −6
Miranda, Venezuela, −4
Monterrey, Mexico, −6
Montevideo, Uruguay, −3
Montreal, Canada, −5
Munich, West Germany, +1

Nagoya, Japan, +9
Nairobi, Kenya, +3
Napoli, Italy, +1
Neuchatel, Switzerland, +1
New York, United States, −5
Niigato, Japan, +9

Osaka, Japan, +9
Oslo, Norway, +1

Padova, Italy, +1
Panama, −5
Paris, France, +1
Parma, Italy, +1
Perth, Australia, +8
Philadelphia, United States, −5
Porto, Portugal, 0
Puerto Rico, −4

Recife, Brazil, −3
Reykjavik, Iceland, −1
Rio de Janeiro, Brazil, −3
Rio Grande do Norte, Brazil, −3
Rio Grande do Sul, Brazil, −3
Rome, Italy, +1
Rosario, Argentina, −3
Rotterdam, Netherlands, +1

St. Gall, Switzerland, +1
Salt Lake City, United States, −7
San Francisco, United States, −8
Santiago, Chile, −4

Santos, Brazil, −3
Sao Paulo, Brazil, −3
Sapporo, Japan, +9
Seoul, Korea, +9
Singapore, +7+30 minutes
South Vietnam, +8
Spokane, United States, −8
Stockholm, Sweden, +1
Stuttgart, West Germany, +1
Sydney, Australia, +10

Taipei, Taiwan, Republic of China, +8
Teheran, Iran, +3+30 minutes
Tel-Aviv, Israel, +2

Torino, Italy, +1
Tokyo, Japan, +9
Toronto, Canada, −5
Trondheim, Norway, +1

Valencia, Spain, +1
Valparaiso, Chile, −4
Vancouver, Canada, −8
Vienna, Austria, +1

Wellington, New Zealand, +12
Winnipeg, Canada, −6

Zurich, Switzerland, +1

GLOSSARY OF COMMODITY MARKET TERMS

ACTUALS:
Commodities readily available; i.e. "on hand." The commodity itself, as opposed to a futures contract.

AFLOATS:
Commodities on board vessels; already underway, or ready to sail.

ARBITRAGE:
An operation which consists of selling or buying contracts in one market, simultaneously making the opposite transactions in a different market.

BACKWARDATION:
A market situation where prices are progressively lower in the future delivery months, than in the nearest delivery month. The opposite of contango.
In London, a securities market term meaning that a "bull" receives a rate for contango facilities, rather than paying one; and a "bear", instead of receiving a rate, has to give one.

BASIC CROPS:
Certain agricultural commodities (corn, wheat, rice, tobacco, peanuts, cotton), which are subject to price supports under the Agricultural Act of 1954 and the Soil Bank Act of 1956.

BASIS:
The difference between the cash price and a futures price.

BASIS GRADE:
The specific grade, or grades, referred to in a futures contract.

BASIS QUOTE:
The offer or sale of a cash commodity expressed as a difference over or under a futures price.

BOARD TRADING
Futures trading where verbal bids and offers are recorded on blackboards. Not conducted in the pit or ring.

BOM SPREAD:
Term referring to a beans, oil and meal spread that is the difference between the value of the products derived from a bushel of soybeans and the price of a bushel of beans.

BUYING BASIS:
The difference between the cost of a cash commodity and a future sold to hedge it. See Selling Basis.

CALL:
A period designated for buying and selling. It resembles an auction, whereby trading on many exchanges is conducted to establish a price or price range for a particular time. During a call, trading is confined to one delivery month at a time.

C.&.F.:
Cost and freight (paid to destination).

CARRYING CHARGES:
The costs connected with warehouse storage, insurance, etc.; sometimes includes interest and estimated changes in weight.

CASH COMMODITY:
See Spot.

CERTIFIED STOCKS:
Supplies which have been rated as deliverable.

C.I.F.:
The price, including the cost, insurance and freight, to deliver a commodity to a specified location.

CLEARANCES:
Aggregate shipments of a commodity made by sea, as of a specified date.

CLEARING HOUSE:
An organization whose primary function is to "clear" or verify and record all trades (both purchases and sales) submitted by various clearing members. The C.H., in clearing trades, is substituted as the "opposite side" of each trade; in this way it assumes all the rights and responsibilities of the two floor brokers who originally made the contract.

COMMERCIAL STOCKS:
Stocks of grain at all prominent grain centers, east and west, issued by the U. S. Department of Agriculture.

COMMISSION MERCHANT:
The member or member firm (N.Y. Cotton Exchange, for example), which carries the futures contract for the customer. He need not be a clearing member.

COMMODITY:
A transportable article of commerce or trade, such as corn, wheat, cotton, sugar, coffee, oats; also, a natural resource or industrial product, such as silver, lumber, plywood.

COMMODITY CLEARING CORP.:
The organization which acts as a medium for clearing transactions in commodities for futures delivery, or for effecting settlements of contracts for futures delivery.

COMMODITY CREDIT CORP.:
A division of the Agricultural Stabilization and Conservation Service, an agency of the U.S. Department of Agriculture, under which U.S. Government loan programs are operated.

COMMODITY EXCHANGE ACT:
The act which established the Commodity Exchange Commission.

COMMODITY EXCHANGE AUTHORITY:
An agency of the U.S. Department of Agriculture, which regulates various commodity exchanges under the Commodity Exchange Act. The enforcement agency of the Commodity Exchange Commission.

COMMODITY EXCHANGE COMMISSION:
A Federal commission consisting of the Secretaries of Agriculture and Commerce and the Attorney General. It regulates the commodity exchanges and dealers in futures contracts. See Commodity Futures Trading Commission.

COMMODITY EXCHANGES:
Organized exchanges where commodities are traded; usually located near adequate transportation facilities and generally in cities through which a substantial portion of the actual commodity passes each year.
Commodity exchanges are member organizations. They have their own governing board, which sees to it that business is carried out fairly and efficiently under the rules. The exchanges do not buy or sell or set prices. All prices are established through open trading around the trading rings, or pits, provided by the exchange.

COMMODITY FUTURES TRADING COMMISSION:
A new Federal agency that would replace the present Commodity Exchange Commission and absorb the Agriculture Department's Commodity Exchange Authority, under a bill passed by the House of Representatives.

COMMODITY PRICE INDEX:
An index, or average, of commodity price movements, such as the Commodity Research Bureau Daily Commodity Futures Index, the Dow Jones Commodity Futures Index. Other indexes are compiled from daily quotations in the spot markets, i.e. the daily spot index of the U.S. Bureau of Labor Statistics. Commodity price changes in European and other markets are reflected by Reuters Daily Index.

CONTANGO:
A market situation in which prices are progressively higher in the future delivery months, than in the nearest delivery month. The opposite of backwardation.
In London, a securities market term meaning the continuation of an open position for a consideration. Contangoed securities are said to be "carried over"; the consideration agreed upon for this operation is called a "rate."

CONTRACT:
An agreement to buy or sell a given amount of a certain commodity on a certain commodity Futures Exchange. It specifies the amount and grade of the product and the date on which the contract will mature and become deliverable, if not previously liquidated.

CONTRACT GRADES:
Those that are deliverable on a futures contract. The basic contract grade is the one deliverable at par. There may be more than one basic grade.

CONTRACT MARKET:
Any board of trade or commodity exchange, which has been designated by the U.S. Secretary of Agriculture to conduct a futures market, such as The Chicago Board of Trade, The Chicago Mercantile Exchange, The New York Cotton Exchange.

CONTRACT MONTH:
The month in which a given contract becomes deliverable, if not liquidated or traded out before a specified date.

CONTRACT WEIGHTS:
The deliverable weights of a contract, as shown on warehouse receipts.

COST OF TENDER:
The total of various charges incurred in having a commodity certificated and delivered. See Tenders.

CROP YEAR:
Term indicating the period from the harvest of a crop to the corresponding period of the following year, as used statistically. The U.S. wheat crop year begins July 1 and ends June 30; cotton begins August 1 and ends July 31; other commodities have varying dates.

CULL:
A coin which has been mutilated or disfigured by physical tampering, including but not limited to denting, nicking, clipping, soldering, corroding, holing, out-of-round or worn excessively smooth so that the design is no longer discernible.

DAY TRADING:
Buying and selling one or more futures contracts on the same day. See Scalper.

DELIVERABLE GRADE:
See Contract Grades.

DELIVERY:
In commodities, there are three types of delivery: current — delivery during the present month; nearby — delivery during the nearest active month; distant — delivery in a month further off.

DELIVERY BASIS:
Specified locations at which the commodity named in a futures contract may be physically delivered to terminate the contract.

DELIVERY MONTH:
A calendar month stipulated as the month of delivery in a futures contract.

DELIVERY NOTICE:
Notification of intention to deliver a specified amount of a commodity to settle a futures contract.

DELIVERY PRICE:
The price fixed by the clearing house at which futures deliveries are invoiced. Also, the price at which a commodities futures contract is settled when deliveries are made.

DIFFERENTIALS:
The premiums paid for grades better than the basic grade, or the discounts allowed for grades below the basic grade. Differentials are generally fixed by contract terms; in cotton, however, commercial forces apply.

E.F.P. (Exchange for Physical):
  A trade between two parties wherein one of the parties is the buyer of the Physicals and the seller of the futures contracts, and the other party is the seller of the Physicals and a buyer of futures contracts. Such an E.F.P. is made up of four parts: the purchase and sale of futures contracts, coupled with the simultaneous sale and purchase by the same two parties of an equal quantity of the physical commodity. Such transactions may be made at such prices as are mutually agreed upon by the two parties to the transaction.

EXCHANGE OF SPOT OR CASH COMMODITY FOR FUTURES:
  The simultaneous exchange of a specific amount of a cash commodity for the equivalent in futures. Usually done when both parties carry opposite hedges in the same delivery month. Also known as "against actuals." See Hedge.

FIRST NOTICE DAY:
  The first day when notices indicating delivery in a specific delivery month may be issued.

FIXATION:
  The fixing of a price in the future, as used in commodity call purchase and call sale trades.

F.O.B.:
  Free On Board.

FORWARD SHIPMENT:
  A contract covering actual commodity shipments at a specified future date.

FREE SUPPLY:
  Term meaning total stocks less what is owned or controlled by the government. Applicable to commodities' surpluses where the government owns large portions of the surplus.

FUTURES:
  Contracts traded for future delivery on a hedge or futures market. The majority of all commodity trades are in futures.

FUTURES CONTRACT:
  A contract which calls for delivery of a commodity in a stated future month, if not liquidated before the contract matures.

FUTURES EXCHANGE:
  An association where commodity futures are traded.

FUTURES MARKET:
  Same as a hedge market — a market trading in future deliveries. Also known as a commodity exchange, or terminal market.

GRADES:
  Standards set up for judging the quality of a given commodity.

GRADING CERTIFICATES:
  Certificates which verify the quality of a commodity.

GROWTH:
  The country of origin; the locale in which a particular commodity is grown or produced.

HAND SIGNALS:
  A means by which vocal activity (open outcry) across a trading ring or pit is

supplemented by use of a highly efficient set of hand and finger signals, which indicate prices and amount and whether the trader wishes to buy or sell.

HEDGE:

A temporary futures market sale made against a spot purchase, or a temporary futures market purchase made against a spot sale. Its purpose is to reduce the risk from possible price fluctuations on the physical transaction, until the reverse futures market operation cancels the hedge, or liquidates the original operation.
See Liquidation; Short Hedges.

HEDGE MARKET:

Same as futures market.

HEDGING:

A practice consisting of 1. the sale of futures against the purchase of a physical commodity, or its equivalent, with the objective of obtaining protection against a price decline, or 2. the purchase of futures against anticipated inventory needs, or forward sales of the physical commodity as protection against a price rise.

IN SIGHT:

Term denoting the amount of a product being delivered to a specified location.

IN TRANSIT:

The amount of a commodity en route to specific destinations.

INVERTED MARKET:

A futures market in which distant-month contracts are selling below near-month contracts.

INVISIBLE SUPPLY:

Uncounted stocks held by manufacturers, wholesalers and eventual consumers.

JOB LOT:

A unit of trading smaller than the regular contract unit; equivalent to an "odd-lot" in the securities markets. See Lot.

LIFE OF DELIVERY:

The interval between the first and last transaction in a futures contract.

LIMIT PRICE:

The largest fluctuation in price of a futures contract permitted during a trading session, as fixed by the contract market's rules.

LIQUIDATION:

The sale of a long contract to offset a previously made purchase, or a purchase made against a short contract. The term is loosely used for any operation which cancels a previously existing position.

LOAN PRICES:

Prices at which the U.S. Government will loan producers money for their crops.

LONG HEDGE:

The purchase of futures made as a hedge against the sale of a cash commodity.

LONG OF THE BASIS:

The position of a commodity trader who has bought cash or spot goods and hedged them with sales of futures. See Hedge.

LOT:
  The standard contract unit in a hedge or futures market. In practice, the term is synonymous with option and contract. See Job Lot.

MARGIN:
  The amount deposited as a guarantee of performance on a futures purchase or sale. On hedge markets, such deposit is called the original margin. If the contract later fluctuates against the holder of the contract, he is required to provide for the difference between his contract price and the current market price, by paying "variation margin" differences. In this manner, the original margin continues to fully guarantee the performance of the contract at any market price level.

MARGIN CALL:
  A commodity broker's request for "variation margin." See Margin.

MAXIMUM PRICE FLUCTUATION:
  The limit, as set by the rules of a commodity exchange, of the fluctuation in the price of a futures contract during any one trading session.

MINIMUM PRICE FLUCTUATION:
  The minimum unit by which the price of a commodity can fluctuate per trade on a commodity exchange.

NEARBY DELIVERY:
  The nearest active month of delivery as specified in a futures contract.

NET POSITION:
  The difference between the number of open commodity contracts held long and short in an account.

OFFSET:
  The elimination of a current long or short position by the opposite transaction: a sale offsets a long position; a purchase offsets a short position.

OPEN CONTRACTS:
  Contracts bought or sold and not yet offset by an opposite trade.

OPEN INTEREST:
  The total number of contracts, bought or sold, which are not offset by the opposite transactions, or by physical delivery of the goods involved.

OPEN OUTCRY:
  A method by which trading is conducted; that is, by calling out bids and offers across a ring or pit and having them accepted orally. See Hand Signals.

OPTION:
  A term basically interchangeable with contract. However, "option" stresses the month of due delivery of a contract, while "contract" stresses the tonnage unit.

ORIGINAL MARGIN:
  The initial margin deposit made with respect to a given commitment.

PEGGED PRICE:
  The price at which any commodity has been fixed (pegged) by agreement, custom, or law.

PIT:
  An octagonal structure where futures are traded on the floor of a commodity exchange. One commodity is dealt in at each pit, which corresponds to a "post" on a stock exchange. Also known as ring.

POINT:
The minimum price unit in which a commodity price is quoted. Each cent, for example, is usually a point for contracts quoted in dollars, although minimum price changes may be 10 cents, or 10 points.

POSITION:
The overall status of the purchases and sales of an individual or firm; i.e. "he has a large short position in XYZ." See Open Interest.

POSITION LIMIT:
The maximum non-hedge position that may be held or controlled by one person. Set by a commodity exchange authority, it applies to either a single commodity future or to all futures in one commodity.

POSITION TRADER:
An individual who takes long (buy) or short (sell) positions in futures markets, because he has formed an opinion that prices are about to advance or decline.

PREMIUM:
The amount by which a cash commodity price sells over a futures price, another cash commodity price, or the excess of one futures contract price over another.

PRIMARY MARKETS:
With foreign markets — the producing nation; with domestic markets — centers where country producers deliver their goods.

REGULAR WAREHOUSE:
An officially approved warehouse for commodity deliveries under futures contracts.

REPORTING LIMIT:
The position limit set on various commodities by the U. S. Secretary of Agriculture. The Commodity Exchange Authority considers all accounts with positions at or above these limits. Example: 200,000 bushels of grain, 25 contracts in frozen pork bellies, 25 carlots of potatoes are reporting limits.

RING:
Space on a trading floor where futures are traded. Also known as pit.

SCALPER:
A trader whose primary interest is in the immediate supply and demand situation in the pit where he is trading. He operates on the thinnest of profit margins (eighths or quarters of a cent); he seldom carries a position overnight. See Day Trading.

SELLER'S CALL:
The purchase of a commodity of a specified quality under a contract that fixes the price in the future.

SELLING BASIS:
The buying basis increased to include costs and the expected or desired profit.

SHORT HEDGES:
Sales of futures made as hedges against holdings of the spot commodity, or products thereof. See Hedge.

SPLIT CLOSE:
Term referring to price discrepancies and to the range of trading in prices of commodities at the close of any market session.

SPOT:
Term meaning immediate delivery for cash, as distinguished from future delivery. An actual, or cash, market as opposed to a futures market.

SPOT COMMODITY:
The actual or physical commodity, as opposed to a futures contract.

SPOT PRICE:
The cash price at which a commodity is selling, as opposed to a futures price.

SPREAD:
An order to buy one contract month and sell another contract month in the same commodity, usually on the same exchange.

SPREADER:
An arbitrageur who hopes to profit by taking advantage of abnormal price differences between commodities, or between delivery months, or between commodity markets. He must watch and assess prices in several markets, instead of just one. See Arbitrage.

STRADDLE:
The simultaneous purchase and sale of the same commodity on the same market. Designed to take advantage of unusual differences between two different options. Example: the sale of a September option and the simultaneous purchase of a January option made in the expectation that a later simultaneous purchase of the September and sale of the January options will produce a profit. See Arbitrage; Spreader.

SWITCH:
To change an existing position by advancing or postponing the original contract into a different month. This is done by liquidating the original contract and reestablishing the same position by a new purchase or sale, as the case may be.

TARE:
The actual weight of the bagging and bands covering a bale of cotton.

TENDERABLE GRADES AND STAPLES:
Grades and staples designated as deliverable in settlement of a futures contract.

TENDERS:
Transferable announcements of intent to deliver a physical commodity. See Cost of Tender.

TERMINAL ELEVATOR:
An elevator located at a point of accumulation and distribution in the movement of agricultural products, especially grains.

TERMINAL MARKET:
Term generally synonymous with commodity exchange or futures market, especially in the United Kingdom.

TRADING LIMIT:
See Maximum — Minimum Price Fluctuation.

TRADING UNIT:
See Job Lot; Lot; Point.

TRANSFERABLE NOTICE:
A notice of intent to make actual delivery, given by the seller of a futures contract; usually designating a day about one week hence.

VARIATION MARGIN:
See Margin.

VISIBLE SUPPLY:
The supply of a commodity at certain locales; varies according to the commodity.

WAREHOUSE RECEIPT:
A document acknowledging receipt of a commodity by a licensed or authorized warehouseman, and issued as tender on futures contracts.

WARRANT OR WAREHOUSE RECEIPT:
A certificate of physical deposit, which gives title to the physical commodity and which is recognized as good delivery against a short position. Title to the commodity passes when the warrant is endorsed by the current owner to the new owner.

MONETARY CONVERSION RATES

COUNTRY	MONETARY UNIT	As quoted July 1, 1974 (in U.S. dollars)
Arab Republic of Egypt	Egyptian pound	N.A.
Argentina	Peso	.1020
Australia	Australian dollar	1.4925
Austria	Schilling	.0548
Belgium	Franc	.026270
Brazil	Cruzeiro	.1540
Canada	Canadian dollar	1.0280
Chile	Escudo	N.A.
Denmark	Krone	.1669
Finland	Markka	.2770
France	Franc	.2074
Greece	Drachma	.0338
Hong Kong	Dollar	.1983
Iceland	Krona	N.A.
India	Rupee	.1290
Iran	Rial	.01502
Ireland	Pound	2.3900
Israel	Israeli pound	.2385
Italy	Lira	.001547
Jamaica	Jamaican dollar	N.A.
Japan	Yen	.003506
Kenya	Kenya shilling	N.A.
Korea	Won	N.A.
Luxembourg	Luxembourg franc	N.A.
Malaysia	Malaysian dollar	N.A.
Mauritius	Rupee	N.A.

Mexico	Peso	.08006
Netherlands	Guilder	.3760
New Zealand	New Zealand dollar	1.4650
Nicaragua	Cordoba	N.A.
Nigeria	Naira	N.A.
Norway	Krone	.1834
Pakistan	Rupee	.1020
Peru	Sol	.0234
Philippines	Peso	.1490
Portugal	Escudo	.0401
Puerto Rico	U.S. Dollar	
Republic of China - (Taiwan)	Taiwan dollar	.0264
Singapore	Singapore dollar	.4059
South Africa	Rand	1.5025
Spain	Peseta	.01748
Sri Lanka	Rupee	N.A.
Sweden	Krona	.2275
Switzerland	Franc	.3330
Turkey	Lira	N.A.
United Kingdom	Pound	2.3900
Uruguay	Peso	.00097
Venezuela	Bolivar	.2335
West Germany	Deutsche Mark	.3910
United States of America	Dollar	

Founding Dates of Stock & Commodity Exchanges

Adelaide Stock Exchange	1887	Chicago Board of Trade	1848
Agricultural Commodity		Chicago Board	
Exchange	1891	Options Exchange	1973
American Stock Exchange	1908	Chicago Mercantile Exchange	1919
Amsterdam Stock Exchange	1876	Coffee Association	
Barcelona Stock Exchange	1251	of London	1926
Basle Stock Exchange	1503	Coffee Terminal	
Bavarian Stock Exchange	1935	Market Association	1958
Berlin Stock Exchange	1685	Commodity Exchange, Inc.	1933
Board of Trade (Kansas		Copenhagen Stock Exchange	1870
City, Missouri)	1856	Delhi Stock Exchange	1947
Bombay Stock Exchange	1875	Detroit Stock Exchange	1907
Boston Stock Exchange	1834	Dublin Stock Exchange	1799
Bremen Stock Exchange	1864	Dusseldorf Stock Exchange	1875
Brussels Stock Exchange	1901	Frankfurt Stock Exchange	1585
Buenos Aires Stock		General Produce Brokers'	
Exchange	1929	Association of London	1876
Calcutta Stock Exchange	1908	Geneva Stock Exchange	1850
Calgary Stock Exchange	1913	Grain and Produce	
Caracas Stock Exchange	1947	Exchange of Bern	1913
Cincinnati Stock Exchange	1885	Hamburg Stock Exchange	1558

Hannover Stock Exchange	1787	Nairobi Stock Exchange	1954
Le Havre Commodity Exchange	1786	National Stock Exchange	1961
Helsinki Stock Exchange	1912	New York Cocoa Exchange	1925
Hobart Stock Exchange	1891	New York Coffee	
Hong Kong Stock Exchange	1891	and Sugar Exchange	1881
Honolulu Stock Exchange	1898	New York Cotton Exchange	1870
Intermountain Stock Exchange	1899	New York Mercantile	
International Commodities		Exchange	1873
Clearing House Ltd.	1888	New York Stock Exchange	1792
International Federation		Osaka Stock Exchange	1878
of Stock Exchanges	1961	Oslo Stock Exchange	1818
International Monetary Market	1972	Pacific Commodities Exchange	1970
Jamaica Stock Exchange	1968	Pacific Stock Exchange	1957
Johannesburg Stock Exchange	1887	Paris Commodity Exchange	1961
Karachi Stock Exchange	1949	Paris Stock Exchange	1141
Korea Stock Exchange	1956	Parma Board of Trade	1970
Lagos Stock Exchange	1960	PBW Stock Exchange, Inc.	1754
Lahore Stock Exchange	1970	Perth Stock Exchange	1889
Lausanne Stock Exchange	1873	Rio de Janeiro	
Lima Stock Exchange	1860	Stock Exchange	1850
London Cocoa Exchange		Rubber Association	
Terminal Market Association	1928	of Singapore	1910
London Commodity Exchange	1954	Rubber Trade	
London Grain		Association of London	1913
Futures Market	1929	St. Gall Stock Exchange	1932
London Jute Association	1875	Santiago Stock Exchange	1893
London Stock Exchange	1773	Sao Paulo Stock Exchange	1890
London Vegetable Oil		Singapore Stock Exchange	1930
Terminal Market Association	1967	Spokane Stock Exchange	1897
London Wool Terminal		Stock Exchange Association	
Market Association	1953	of New Zealand	1915
Luxembourg Stock Exchange	1927	Stockholm Stock Exchange	1901
Madras Stock Exchange	1920	Sydney Futures	
Madrid Stock Exchange	1831	Exchange Limited	1960
Makati Stock Exchange	1963	Sydney Stock Exchange	1871
Managua Stock Exchange	1973	Taiwan Stock Exchange	1961
Manila Stock Exchange	1927	Tehran Stock Exchange	1967
Mauritius Stock Exchange	1804	Tel-Aviv Stock Exchange	1935
Melbourne Stock Exchange	1861	Tokyo Stock Exchange	1878
Mexico City Stock Exchange	1895	Toronto Stock Exchange	1852
Mid America		United Terminal Sugar	
Commodity Exchange	1868	Market Association	1921
Midwest Stock Exchange	1882	Vancouver Stock Exchange	1907
Milan Stock Exchange	1808	Vienna Commodities Exchange	1873
Minneapolis Grain Exchange	1947	Vienna Stock Exchange	1771
Monterrey Stock Exchange	1949	Winnipeg Commodity Exchange	1887
Montevideo Stock Exchange	1867	Winnipeg Stock Exchange	1903
Montreal Stock Exchange	1874	Zurich Stock Exchange	1877
Nagoya Stock Exchange	1866		

INDICES

INDEX OF DIRECTORS AND OFFICERS OF
STOCK AND COMMODITY EXCHANGES

Cantella, Vincent, M., 271
Carr, Roy, 299
Carritt, H. D., 187
Carroll, Lawrence, 230
Carvalho, Fernando Souza Ribeiro de, 28
Casal, Adolfo, 4
Casey, Frank M., 286
Casey, Fred D., 274
Cassi, Giancarlo, 98
Castilho, Althemar Dutra de, 28
Castro, Alejandro T. de 145
Caulton, Christopher C., 45
Cerezo, Miguel, 158
Champaklal, Vasantlal, 79
Chao, K. P., 149
Charpentier, Yves, 122
Chaudhry, M. I., 140
Chester, Paul P., 282
Chhotalal, Jasvantlal, 79
Chien, S. C., 149
Chin, Joseph, 154
Ching, Oliver M. S., 285
Chiong, Anthony Dee K., Jr., 147
Christians, F. Wilhelm, 204
Clarke, R., 156
Clay, C. J. J., 181
Cleather, E. G., 36
Cleaver, William P., 247
Cobb, Ross L., 307
Cohen, Charles, 254
Collins, J. Robert, 230
Collison, Richard Lloyd, 10
Concannon, Thomas F., 286
Condie, G. Richard, 306
Conlin, Donald B., 251, 311
Conway, Laurence V., 276
Coplin, Robert A., 286
Coughlin, Bryan P., Jr., 276
Coulet, Mme., 62
Coussement, Andre, 122
Cowles, Richard R., 274
Cowley, L. A., 177
Cowley, N. G., 172
Crawford, J. Hamilton, Jr., 286
Cummings, Walter E., 271
Cunningham, P. A., 187
Curran, C. P., 18
Currie, Ailsa M., 40
Cuthill, R. J., 133

Davidson, A. E., 231
Davidson, I. N., 13
Davies, A. E., 187
Davies, W. G., 17
Davis, Peter Ricardo, 189
Davis, Preston H., 251
Davis, T. M., 187
De, P. K., 81
Dee, Martin Q., 147

Degner, Harald, 209
Delanney, M. Louis, 88
Delcourt, Patrick, 122
Dellepiane, Jorge H. B., 4
Dennis, Robert, 230
Denny, M. Edward, 282
Derose, Joseph A., 286
Deslauriers, Paul J., 36
Després, Robert, 37
Devchand, Chhotalal, 79
Dickson, Frederick J., 251
Diel, Rolf, 204
Dillon, Michael F., 91
DiMaria, Frank, 230
Dixon, Lawrence H., 247
Dineur, Marcel, 23
Dlouhy, Dominik, 36
Dobe, R. P., 86
Donaghy, J. William, 238, 251, 261
Donahoo, Alvin W., 236
Douglas, Walter Brydon, 190
Dowd, James E., 271
Drake, Ernest C., 45
Drugmand, Pierre, 23
Dumont, J., 59
Dunavant, W. B., Jr., 251
Dyckerhoff, Octavio, 28

Eckenrode, Robert T., 286
Edwards, H. C., 231
Ehinger, M., 165
Eichler, Harald, 21
Elliott, D. W., 47
Englebright, W. J., 178
Ennis, R. S., 47
Ernst, Gernot, 201
Espino, Felix Martinez, 198

Fai, Yau Meng, 154
Fanaro, Charles J., Jr., 230
Fanfani, Giovanni, 98
Faraoni, Franco, 98
Farias, Juan S., 129
Fava, Rolando, 102
Fellman, Malcolm A., 261
Fernandez, Juan Jesus Roldan, 160
Fernandez, R. J., 4
Fields, Stephen H., 242
Figgis, D. S. J., 187
Figgis, T. S. E., 187
Findling, G. L., 230
Finnegan, Michael A., 299
Fischer, Theodore J., 210
Fischer, Werner, 202
Fisher, Hubert F., Jr., 251
Flament, Leon, 23
Fleming, K. Maxwell, 45
Flores, Jose T., Jr., 145
Fonade, Pierre, 58
Formoso, Nilda M. E., 4

Iturraspe, Eduardo C. Perez, 4
Iwamiya, Shigeo, 111
Jae Chol, Chang, 120
Jaenike, William F., 286
Jamnadas, Laldas, 79
Janssen, Fritz, 210
Jarecki, Henry G., 225
Jeanmonod, Pierre, 167
Jeejeebhoy, P. J., 79
Jeker, R., 165
Jesser, Daniel R., 225
Jivatlal, Vasantlal, 79
Johnson, J. H., 231
Johnson, Robert L., 236
Johnson, Ron, 231
Johnston, J. C., 13
Jones, Clayton B., Jr., 261
Jones, H. A., 36
Jong Seung, Pai, 120
Jonscher, George V., 276
Joo, Tan Eng, 151
Judson, Art, 299
Kampani, N. C., 79
Kantilal, Vasantlal, 79
Karpen, Francois, 122
Katz, William S., 224
Kawano, Hideo, 285
Keane, Robert M., 286
Kearns, Richard F., 276
Kemp, Loretta, 277
Kemp, Norman Steward McMurtrie, 190
Kempf, Roger, 61
Kepler, Donald A., 286
Kessler, H. C., 169
Khandelwal, B. N., 79
Kheradjou, A., 90
Kimber, J. R., 40
Knell, Frank, 238, 251
Knight, Jeffrey Russell, 190
Knight, P. J., 177
Knight, Warren M., 290
Kobayashi, Shizuo, 113
Kobbernagel, J., 54
Koehler, Bernt-Dieter, 209
Kokorinos, D., 71
Kolton, Paul, 286
Komatsu, Yasuhiro, 113
Komninos, E., 71
Komninos, K., 71
Koster, Fernand, 122
Kotitsas, G., 71
Krause, Benjamin D., 286
Kremer, Remy, 122
Krishnamoorthy, K., 85
Krishnamurti, E. R., 86
Krogh, Torben, 54
Krucker, Andre, 61
Kryger, G. T., 18

Lamb, L. J., 133
Lamboray, Camille, 122
Lamboray, Marcel, 122
Lamborn, George D. F., 247
Lanyi, R. G., 187
Larijani, N. F., 90
La Roche, H. B., 165
Larrain, Alfredo, 52
Larrea, Osv Ido, 4
Lasswell, W. C., Jr., 310
Lauchli, M., 165
Layton, William C., Jr., 251
Lebeck, Warren, W., 221
Leclercq, Emile, 23
Leclezio, Pierre, 125
Lee, H. Vernon, Jr., 286
Lee, R. B., 13
Leeson, J. S., 91
Le Fur, R., 59
Lehmann, E., 93
Leleux, Jacques, 23
Lenzi, Renzo, 98
LeRoy-Lewis, David Henry, 190
Lesieur, M., 62
Levi, Jack W., Jr., 280
Levine, Richard B., 254
Levy, Paulo Roberto Ferreira, 31
Lewis, E. Gene, 277
Leydenbach, Joseph, 122
Liberal, Carlos de Almeida, 28
Liddiard, R. E., 183
Lim, Eduardo, 145
Lind, Barry J., 224
Lis, Manual Richi Bertran de, 160
Litten, Hans, 210
Llovera, Humberto, 129
Lloyd, Ian Howard, 10
Lo Bue, Philip J., 307
Lockyer, E., 174
Longden, Maurice Edmund, 10
Lopez-Isla, Manuel de la Concha y, 160
Loughlin, Thomas P., 286
Loveday, George Arthur, 190
Lowe, Lester, 40
Lowen, Carlton K., 307
Lowenfels, Frederick C., 254, 290
Lozano, Don Cesar, 129
Luire, R., 156
Luthringshausen, Wayne P., 274

Maas, Bernard H., 286
Macchi, Julio A., 4
MacHardy, Earle T., 247
Mackay, Kenneth B., 224
Mackie, J. C. S., 178
MacMillan, K. B., 47
Macpherson, Peter M., 282
Magalhaes, Mauricio Figueiredo, 31
Maggiotti, Domingo G., 4

Perier, Michel, 68
Peterson, Edwin B., 286
Petit, Daniel, 68
Petroni, Italo, 98
Phelan, William M., 224
Phillips, K. C., 18
Phillips, Thomas Nash, 10
Piazza, Maurizio, 102
Pinat, Jacques, 68
Pinto, Roberto, Vianna, 28
Pirla, Jose Maria Fernandez, 160
Pochelon, Julius, 282
Polson, C. W., 231
Ponga, M. Pedro Rodriguez, 88
Porzio, Carlos A., 4
Poser, Norman S., 286
Powers, Mark J., 224
Powis, G. H., 34
Pressner, Benjamin, 254
Puggina, Evandro Oliveira, 31
Pullen, L., 178

Quinlan, K. J., 13
Quinn, Donald L., 276
Quintana, M. V., 145

Rahn, R., 169
Raman, C. R. Pattabhi, 86
Ramaswami, S., 85
Ramburn, L., 125
Ramet, G., 125
Ramirez, Fernando Vidal, 143
Rampelbergs, Paul, 23
Ravn, Børschef Erik, 54
Ray, P. K., 81
Rebhuhn, Joseph, 122
Recanati, D., 93
Recio, Roberto L., 147
Reckinger, Robert, 122
Redel, Irving, 242
Redfield, Ben, 310
Regnard, C., 125
Rehwald, R. Thomas, 276
Reid, I. T. S., 18
Reid, Robert A., 282
Reiff, Aloyse, 122
Reyers, Jean, 23
Reyes, H. B., 145
Reyter, Victor, 122
Richards, R. W., 51
Rickerhauser, Charles E., Jr., 307
Riley, R. J., 134
Riter, Henry G., IV, 286
Rizkallh, Alfredo Nagib, 31
Roberts, Henry S., 276
Roberts, Thomas E., 271
Robertson, W. A., 47
Robson, A. C., 17
Rodriguez, Enrique Jose de Benito y, 160

Roesle, E., 169
Roguin, Jean de, 168
Rohm, Ernst, 210
Rohrer, Bernt W., 210
Romagnoli, Carlos, 196
Romain, E. D., 231
Roper, George A., 276
Rosenberg, Laurence M., 224
Rosenblum, Kenneth L., 276
Rosenthal, Leslie, 224
Rossi, A., 169
Rothschild, James S., 242
Rouleau, Charles, 36
Roxas, Simplicio J., 147
Roy, I. N., 125
Rozas, Jaime Vial, 52
Rubin, David R., 276
Rucker, P. A. S., 183
Ruia, P. G., 79
Ruiz, Eugenio Blanco, 52
Ruffino, Luigi, 102
Rundle, Barry R., 276
Rushing, James E., 276
Rutherford, B. McC., 178
Ryan, Patrick E., 276

Sá, Geraldo Tosta de, 28
Sada, Adrian, Jr., 129
St. John, John, 238
Saiz, Guillermo Lecuona, 127
Salazar, Pedro Rodriguez-Ponga y Ruiz de,
  160
Salgado, Francisco Xavier Sandee Castro,
  29
Samaldas, Mathradas, 79
Samis, Robert B. E., 45
Sánchez, Fernando A., 129
Sanchez, Jose Manuel, 198
Sandor, Richard L., 221
Sankaran, M., 85
Santamaria, Enrique, 147
Santos, Don Cayetano, 129
Sarasin, A. E., 165
Savarese, Frank J., 286
Savi, Antonio, 102
Savi, Umberto, 102
Sawada, Haruo, 113
Sbarbaro, Richard D., 276
Schait, R., 169
Scheffer, J. G. N. de Hoop, 131
Schlicht, Herbert, 206
Schmidt-Scheuber, Theodor, 271
Schmit, Alphonse, 122
Schoeller-Szuts, Friedrich, 21
Schwall, George S., 122
Segota, Enrique, 4
Seidel, Christian, 210
Sellar, K., 133
Servais, Henri, 122

Seung Man, Cho, 120
Seweloh, Theodore W., 276
Shadforth, T. K., 12
Shah, A. J., 79
Shaw, Leonard S., 224
Sheehan, John J., 286
Sheidy, Herbert S., 221
Sherwood, George D., 45
Shoraka, J., 90
Shun, Mok Chiu, 73
Silva, Eduardo Duarte Leopoldo e, 31
Silverberg, Arthur P., 242
Simpson, Gordon Russell, 190
Sivasubramanian, M. S., 85
Smith, Colin Greenhough, 189
Smith, Hal H., III, 282
Smith, J. V., 177
Smitten, C. F., 13
Somayajulu, J. V., 85
Somerville, W. L., 40
Sosa, Carlos J. R., 4
Soteras, Fernando Ximenez, 160
Soucarros, J. J. Rodolfo, 4
Springe, Hans Dieter auf der, 210
Sprinkel, Beryl W., 225
Sprod, Harold Nevill, 10
Stagg, Carlos Carvallo, 52
Staloff, Arnold F., 299
Sterckx, Roger, 23
Stern, Franz, 210
Stern, Jacob, 254
Stern, P., 164
Stevenson, Richard H., 36
Stockdale, M., 181
Stockdale, M. S. S., 183
Stoeck, Wolfgang, 206
Studer, E., 169
Stupart, William Alexander, 190
Sullivan, Joseph W., 274
Summerhays, Clyde, 306
Sung Kuk, Kang, 120
Swee, Yeo Eng, 154
Symington, D. A., 187
Symons, N. A., 187

Tague, Barry E., 299
Takahashi, Kenzo, 116
Tallian, Robert, 230
Tanimura, Hireshi, 116
Tapias, Luis, 29
Tavares, Arnaldo Borges, 28
Taylor, Derek W., 36
Theodorides, Chr, 71
Thiem, Maurice, 10
Thomas, Claude A., 276
Thompson, Robert W., 277
Thomson, J. R., 34
Thuo, Francis M., 118
Tiernan, John L., 299

Tilley, C. J., 178
Tilley, W. J., 18
Timmermans, Charles, 23
Tipton, Ben F., 251
Tobin, Michael E., 276
Tolonen, Matti, 56
Tomita, Minoru, 113
Tosato, Guido, 98
Travaglio, Raymond F., 277
Traynor, Douglas K., 274
Treichl, Heinrich, 20, 21
Treliving, N. E., 177
Tremer, Gerhard, 210
Trevino, Don Arturo Garza, 129
Treyvaud, J-B1, 165
Triggs, Thomas L., 221
Trigos, Augusto, 129
Trigos, Don Augusto, 129
Tsai, T. Y., 149
Turmel, Antoine, 37
Turnbull, Roderick, 231
Tuten, Alix, 299

Uehara, Yukio, 116
Uhlmann, Frederick G., 221
Unsworth, P. J., 15
Urdapilleta, Wenceslao, 4
Ureta, Manuel Jose, 52
Uston, Kenneth S., 307
Utz, R. G., 18

Valder, J. H., 18
Valdes, Alamiro, 52
Valle, Adolfo Ruiz de Velasco y del, 160
Valle, Don Bernabe A. del, 129
Van Den Bosch, Henri, 23
Vegas, Casimiro, 198
Velarde, Francisco Javier de Oyarzabal y,
    160
Velazco, Don Federico, 129
Verma, H. C., 84
Vernon, Walter N., III, 231
Vial, Leonidas Larrain, 52
Vieira, Luiz Carlos Azevedo, 31
Vieites, Andres Moar, 4
Völling, Johannes, 204
von Finckjum, August, 210
von Oppenheim, Alfred Freiherr, 204
Vose, Charles B., 251

Walker, James, W., Jr., 286
Walker, Rollin W., 285
Wallauer, Ronald, 230
Watson, Winsor H., Jr., 286
Weaver, Dudley S., II, 251
Weber, Paul, 122
Weeden, Donald E., 282
Weinand, Marc., 122
Weinberg, Michael, Jr., 224
Weithers, John G., 276

INDEX OF COMMODITIES

Spices, 59
Sugar, 62, 64, 66, 182-183, 195-196, 247-250
Sunflower seed oil, 187
Tea, 194, 195
Textiles, 21
Tomato extract, 103
Turkey, 225-228

Vegetable oil, 98, 183, 185, 187
Vegetables, 103
Wax, 177
Wheat, 50, 98, 178, 179, 221-223, 230-233, 235-237
Wine, 98
Wool, 17-18, 63, 172-174, 182-183, 196, 253, 261

INDEX OF STOCK AND COMMODITY EXCHANGES

Adelaide Stock Exchange, 10
Agricultural Commodity Exchange, 196
American Stock Exchange, 286
Amsterdam Stock Exchange, 130
Antwerp Stock Exchange, 23
Athens Stock Exchange, 71
Auckland Stock Exchange, 132
Australian Associated Stock Exchanges, 7

Bahia Stock Exchange, 30
Barcelona Stock Exchange, 158
Bari Commodity Exchange, 97
Basle Stock Exchange, 164
Bavarian Stock Exchange, 210
Bergen Stock Exchange, 137
Berlin Stock Exchange, 201
Bern Stock Exchange, 166
Bilboa Stock Exchange, 160
Board of Trade (Kansas City, Missouri), 231
Bologna Commodity Exchange, 98
Bologna Stock Exchange, 98
Bombay Stock Exchange, 78
Bordeaux Stock Exchange, 58, 66
Boston Stock Exchange, 270
Bremen Stock Exchange, 202
Brisbane Stock Exchange, 12
British Fur Trade Association
Brussels Stock Exchange, 23
Buenos Aires Stock Exchange, 4

Cairo Stock Exchange, 3
Calcutta Stock Exchange, 81
Calgary Stock Exchange, 34
Caracas Stock Exchange, 198
Cincinnati Stock Exchange, 280
Chicago Board of Trade, 221
Chicago Board Options Exchange, 274
Chicago Mercantile Exchange, 224
Christchurch Stock Exchange, 132
Citrus Associates of the New York Cotton Exchange, 238
Coffee Importers and Exporters Association of London, 174
Coffee Terminal Market Association of London, 175
Colombo Brokers' Association, 163
Commodity Exchange, Inc., 242
Copenhagen Stock Exchange, 54
Cordoba Stock Exchange, 6

Delhi Stock Exchange, 84
Detroit Stock Exchange, 282
Dublin Stock Exchange, 91
Dunedin Stock Exchange, 133
Dusseldorf Stock Exchange, 203

Espirito Santo Stock Exchange, 33
Estado do Rio de Janeiro Stock Exchange (Niteroi), 27

Firenze Commodity Exchange, 98
Firenze Stock Exchange, 99
Florianopolis Stock Exchange, 27
Frankfurt Stock Exchange, 206
Fukuoka Stock Exchange, 110

General Produce Brokers' Association of London, 177
Geneva Stock Exchange, 167
Genova Stock Exchange, 99
Ghent Stock Exchange, 25
Goias Stock Exchange, 27
Grain and Feed Trade Association, 177
Grain and Produce Exchange of Bern, 166
Guadalajara Stock Exchange, 126

Hamburg Stock Exchange, 209
Hannover Stock Exchange, 210
Le Havre Commodity Exchange, 59
Helsinki Stock Exchange, 56
Hiroshima Stock Exchange, 110
Hobart Stock Exchange, 12
Hong Kong Stock Exchange, 73
Honolulu Stock Exchange, 285

Instanbul Stock Exchange, 171
Intermountain Stock Exchange, 306
International Commodities Clearing House Ltd., 180
International Federation of Stock Exchanges, 88
International Monetary Market, 224
Invercargill Stock Exchange, 133

Jamaica Stock Exchange, 104
Johannesburg Stock Exchange, 156

Karachi Cotton Association, 140
Karachi Stock Exchange, 140
Korea Stock Exchange, 119
Kyoto Stock Exchange, 111

Lagos Stock Exchange, 135
Lahore Stock Exchange, 142